V&Runipress

Representations & Reflections
Studies in Anglophone Literatures and Cultures

Volume 8

Edited by
Uwe Baumann, Marion Gymnich
and Barbara Schmidt-Haberkamp

Marion Gymnich (ed.)

Who's afraid of...?

Facets of Fear in Anglophone Literature and Film

With 2 figures

V&R unipress

Bonn University Press

Bibliographic information published by the Deutsche Nationalbibliothek

The Deutsche Nationalbibliothek lists this publication in the Deutsche Nationalbibliografie;
detailed bibliographic data are available in the Internet at http://dnb.d-nb.de.

ISBN 978-3-8471-0050-8
ISBN 978-3-8470-0050-1 (E-Book)

Publications of Bonn University Press
are published by V&R unipress GmbH.

Cover image: Schönwiesner, Jan (www.12frames.de). Title: "Psycho", source: photocase.com
Printing and binding: CPI Buch Bücher.de GmbH, Birkach

Printed in Germany

Contents

Marion Gymnich

Fictions of Fear – Representations of Fear in Anglophone Literature and Audiovisual Media

I.   Introduction

Fear in its different facets appears to constitute an intriguing and compelling subject matter for writers and screenwriters alike. After all, many literary texts, movies and TV productions address fear more or less extensively. Moreover, there are a number of (literary and audiovisual) genres where the depiction of fear is virtually a necessary element; Gothic fiction and the horror movie are among the most obvious cases in point. To a certain extent, the omnipresence of references to and representations of fear in works of fiction may certainly be accounted for by the fact that the depiction of fear often turns out to be a crucial ingredient in the process of creating suspense. Yet the almost overwhelming interest in fear one encounters in works of fiction is also encouraged by the fact that fear is a truly universal phenomenon.

In the course of one's life everyone is presumably bound to experience situations that trigger fear (in a more or less intense way). This is due to the fact that fear can be classified as a basic human emotion – an emotion that is closely linked to the survival instinct, which is in and of itself one of the essential forces governing human as well as animal life. What distinguishes fear from other, related emotional states is that fear is always associated with a particular object or situation, or, as Julian Hanich puts it, "[w]hile anxiety is free-floating, in fear we are afraid *of* something, whether real or imagined".[1] Fear is a perfectly normal reaction to situations where the individual is confronted with some kind of danger; yet there are also people who suffer from fears that are either excessive or that do not seem justified by the circumstances in which they occur at all. Phobias, which may be triggered by a wide range of objects and situations that are subjectively perceived to be threatening, are a case in point. Both fear as a natural reaction to danger and fear as a pathological state are referred to and

---

1 HANICH, Julian. *Cinematic Emotion in Horror Films and Thrillers: The Aesthetic Paradox of Pleasurable Fear.* New York/London: Routledge, 2010. 19.

explored in countless works of fiction. Of course fictional texts may vary considerably in terms of how prominent, how detailed and how psychologically sound the depiction of fear is. In addition, the representation of fear in a particular work of fiction is inevitably shaped by historically and culturally variable notions of human psychology.

The study of the phenomenon of fear from the point of view of psychology can be traced to the very beginnings of psychology as a discipline.[2] Sigmund Freud already established the basic distinction between fear as a temporary state, i. e. as a reaction to a specific situation, on the one hand, and fear as a person's disposition or character trait on the other hand.[3] According to psychological studies, fear is among the most basic and universal human emotions.[4] Thus, one may safely assume that fear is known in all cultures and all historical periods, even if one has to admit that emotions tend to be culture-specific to a certain extent.[5] Fear may be triggered by the perception of physical danger as well as by situations which threaten an individual's self-esteem, such as exams and public performances.[6]

Fear as a temporary affective phenomenon is defined by psychologists as a state that is characterised by an increased activity of the nervous system, combined with the awareness of being excited, a feeling of suspense and the subjective impression of being threatened.[7] Like any other emotional state, fear can be described in terms of physiological and behavioural-expressive parameters as well as the subjective cognitive assessment of the emotional state.[8] The physiological parameters of fear include multiple processes in the central nervous system as well as muscular reactions, for instance ocular movements.[9] The behavioural-expressive parameters include facial expressions, vocalization and movements.[10]

In psychological experiments, fear is measured by means of different methods. Reports of a test person grant access to the subjective parameters, i. e. the way an individual experiences fear on the cognitive level, whereas the

---

2 Cf. STÖBER, Joachim and Ralf SCHWARZER. "Angst." In: Jürgen H. Otto, Harald A. Euler and Heinz Mandl (eds.). *Emotionspsychologie: Ein Handbuch.* Weinheim: Beltz, 2000. 189–98, 196.
3 Cf. KROHNE, Heinz Walter. *Psychologie der Angst.* Stuttgart: Kohlhammer, 2010. 14.
4 Cf. for instance HOCK, Michael and Carl-Walter KOHLMANN. "Angst und Furcht." In: Veronika Brandstätter and Jürgen H. Otto (eds.). *Handbuch der Allgemeinen Psychologie – Motivation und Emotion.* Göttingen et al.: Hogrefe, 2009. 623–32, 623.
5 Cf. for instance HEELAS, Paul. "Emotion Talk across Cultures." In: Rom Harré (ed.). *The Social Construction of Emotions.* Oxford: Blackwell, 1986. 234–66.
6 Cf. HOCK and KOHLMANN. "Angst und Furcht." 624 as well as STÖBER and SCHWARZER. "Angst." 192.
7 Cf. KROHNE. *Psychologie der Angst.* 17.
8 Cf. KROHNE. *Psychologie der Angst.* 15.
9 Cf. KROHNE. *Psychologie der Angst.* 49–63.
10 Cf. KROHNE. *Psychologie der Angst.* 43.

method of recording a person's heartbeat falls back on physiological parameters of fear, for example. Neither of these methods is regarded as an ideal way of measuring fear, however.[11] One of the reasons for this is that the different systems that are involved in the experience of fear do not necessarily react simultaneously. In other words, the reactions on the different levels do not always set in at the same time; nor do they invariably stop simultaneously: If a person is suddenly faced with a dangerous situation, the behavioural reaction (for instance: running away) is typically activated more quickly than physiological reactions such as an accelerated beating of the heart or an increased frequency of breathing.[12] The different physiological reactions may also be differentiated quite clearly in terms of how fast the respective reaction sets in. A person's heartbeat is typically accelerated before the frequency of breathing increases, for instance.[13] Although people without expertise in psychology in all likelihood are largely unaware of the interaction between the different parameters of the experience of fear, the symptoms mentioned above tend to play an important role in fictional representations of fear as well. Fictional depictions of fear do not just fall back on a representation of subjective assessments of a situation or behavioural-expressive parameters of fear; very often they allude to physiological parameters such as the heart beginning to beat faster or an increased frequency of breathing as well.

II.   Fear on the Plot Level – Thrills for the Reader and Viewer

Given the fact that the experience of fear is a universal phenomenon, it seems hardly surprising that one encounters more or less extensive descriptions of fear in a wide range of literary texts and audiovisual productions. In many works of fiction moments of fear experienced by a character are just mentioned in passing, but fear may also be presented as an experience that has a lasting impact on a character's life. Right at the beginning of Charles Dickens' well-known novel of development *Great Expectations* (1860/61), the grown-up narrator looks back upon an incident in which he experienced fear during his childhood. According to the grown-up narrator, this incident has made him aware of his identity:

> My first most vivid and broad impression of the identity of things, seems to me to have been gained on a memorable raw afternoon towards evening. At such a time I found out for certain, that this bleak place overgrown with nettles was the churchyard, and that Philip Pirrip, late of this parish, and also Georgiana wife of the above, were dead and

---

11 Cf. KROHNE. *Psychologie der Angst.* 15.
12 Cf. KROHNE. *Psychologie der Angst.* 15.
13 Cf. KROHNE, *Psychologie der Angst.* 16.

buried; and that Alexander, Bartholomew, Abraham, Tobias, and Roger, infant children of the aforesaid, were also dead and buried; and that the dark flat wilderness beyond the churchyard, intersected with dykes and mounds and gates, with scattered cattle feeding on it, was the marshes; and that the low leaden line beyond was the river; and that the distant savage lair from which the wind was rushing, was the sea; and that the small bundle of shivers growing afraid of it all and beginning to cry, was Pip. (*Great Expectations* 5–6)

Becoming aware of one's mortality certainly is an experience that is likely to evoke fear, in particular for children.[14] Likewise, a feeling of being lonely or left behind (in this case by the protagonist's deceased parents and brothers) is apt to trigger fear. Finally, the gloomy atmosphere evoked by the description of the bleak landscape contributes to the feeling of fear that appears to overwhelm the boy.[15] All of this reduces the protagonist Pip to a "small bundle of shivers growing afraid of it all", as the narrator puts it. But worse is to come. Soon Pip's crying is roughly cut short by an escaped convict, who threatens Pip in "a terrible voice" (*Great Expectations* 6): "'Keep still, you little devil, or I'll cut your throat!'" (*Great Expectations* 6) Now there is a new reason for fear on Pip's part; the fear caused by feeling alone in a desolate landscape and by pondering the fact that he is bound to die eventually is replaced by a reaction to a tangible danger he is suddenly faced with – the encounter with the convict who threatens him and causes the boy to feel "mortal terror" (*Great Expectations* 16). The scene thus illustrates very well that fear may be caused by a range of different triggers – in reality as well as in fiction. Moreover, as was pointed out above, the complex experience of fear in this scene is clearly a defining moment for the protagonist Pip and thus reminds the reader that moments of intense fear may have a lasting impact on a person's life.

The ways in which fear is depicted in works of fiction may of course differ substantially in terms of how plausible they seem and with respect to the literary strategies that are used. Fear is often presented by providing a verbal description of a character's emotions and/or of physiological symptoms of fear, such as the character's heart beginning to race. Alternatively, a character's fear can be portrayed by focusing on the character's facial expression and/or his/her body language (including utterances). In films and TV productions various camera techniques may be employed very effectively to express a character's fear, for instance point-of-view shots or frequent cuts which visualise a character's sense

---

14 Cf. the article by Sara Strauß in this volume for the perspective of children in this context. Imke Lichterfeld explores the presentation of the fear of death – *timor mortis* – in Frank McGuinness' historical play *Speaking Like Magpies* (2005).

15 The strategy of presenting a gloomy and desolate landscape in order to create a threatening atmosphere is of course familiar from genres such as the Gothic novel, but also from audiovisual depictions of ominous situations.

of disorientation and panic. Moreover, the visual track may create an impression of danger and gloom by means of showing a surrounding that appears to be threatening in some way or other. In audiovisual media the soundtrack likewise tends to play a very important role for evoking suspense and portraying the characters' fear. Sound effects and musical themes (such as drums alluding to the accelerated beating of a character's heart) may alert viewers to the presence of danger or create an uncanny atmosphere.[16] Fictional depictions of fear are shaped by different cultural and historical parameters: Firstly, the depiction of fear is likely to be influenced by the knowledge of psychology that exists in the cultural and historical context in which a work of fiction is produced. Secondly, emotions in general, including fear, are to a certain extent shaped by attitudes that are prevalent in a particular cultural and historical context. The depiction of fear in works of fiction may thus also respond to the way fear or emotions in general are judged in a particular cultural context.[17] Likewise the emergence and popularity of specific 'genres of fear' may be seen as a reaction to a particular cultural and historical constellation. A striking lack of fear displayed by characters in a work of fiction or the suppression of fear in a text or a genre may also turn out to be highly interesting. In her contribution to this volume Barbara Puschmann-Nalenz explores the implications of the surprising lack of fear displayed by the clones in Kazuo Ishiguro's dystopian novel *Never Let Me Go* (2005). Another contribution that addresses in particular a suppression of fear is Antonio Wojahn's reading of J.G. Ballard's *Crash* (2008).

The popularity of genres such as the Gothic novel and the horror film can hardly be explained by the fact that they actually frighten readers or viewers. Instead, for most readers and viewers at least, these genres tend to instill merely a pleasurable thrill, a mixture of excitement and unease. This type of reaction is also displayed by one of the most famous fictional readers of Gothic fiction, the protagonist Catherine Morland in Jane Austen's novel *Northanger Abbey* (1818).[18] Catherine is an avid reader of Gothic novels, which presumably provide her with the thrills her own life seems to lack. Catherine's reaction to Ann Radcliffe's *The Mysteries of Udolpho* (1794) certainly does not suggest that she feels truly frightened by the threatening scenarios she reads about in one of the

---

16 On the function of music in horror movies, cf. HENTSCHEL, Frank. *Töne der Angst: Die Musik im Horrorfilm.* Berlin: Bertz + Fischer, 2011. As HENTSCHEL points out, the use of sound effects and music to evoke a sense of danger tends to be highly conventionalised.

17 Cf. for instance Andrea Rummel's exploration of the staging of fear in Romantic drama and Stella Butter's contrastive analysis of constructions of fear and empathy in a nineteenth-century novel and a contemporary bestseller in this volume.

18 On the relationship between *Northanger Abbey* and the Gothic tradition see in particular the article by Angela WRIGHT. "Disturbing the Female Gothic: An Excavation of the *Northanger Novels.*" In: Diana Wallace and Andrew Smith (eds.). *The Female Gothic: New Directions.* Houndmills, Basingstoke: Palgrave Macmillan, 2009. 60–75.

classics of Gothic fiction. Instead, she excitedly anticipates the revelation of new terrors, which might be waiting, for instance, behind the famous 'black veil', as Catherine tells her friend Isabella Thorpe:

> '[…] what can it be? – But do not tell me – I would not be told upon any account. I know it must be a skeleton, I am sure it is Laurentina's skeleton. Oh! I am delighted with the book! I should spend my whole life in reading it. I assure you, if it had not been to meet you, I would not have come away from it for all the world.' (*Northanger Abbey* 60 – 61)

In the same conversation Catherine eagerly asks Isabella, who has just read out a list of further Gothic novels the young women might read in the future: "'[…] but are they all horrid, are you sure they are all horrid?'" (*Northanger Abbey* 61) Thus, Austen's protagonist is looking for new, possibly more intense thrills in her reading, enjoying in the safety of her ordinary environment the vicarious pleasure of reading about threatening situations faced by various damsels-in-distress. In the context of "[t]he mixed mocking and defence of fiction in *Northanger Abbey*",[19] reading offers Catherine excitement and thrills in her otherwise quite uneventful life. In this respect, Catherine is certainly a prede-cessor of today's fans of horror movies, who might also be looking for thrills everyday life tends to be devoid of.

In addition to entertaining readers/viewers, fiction that depicts fear may arguably also fulfil a 'therapeutic' function by allowing individuals to ponder danger from a safe distance. Reading about or watching characters faced with situations that would frighten the readers/viewers in real life may make it pos-sible to confront one's own (latent) fears. In this respect it is quite interesting that horror films in recent years increasingly invite viewers to feel empathy with the characters' fear, as Jason Davis points out:

> Of course, elements like surprise, scares, and imagery are essential to crafting a compelling nightmare, but the modern horror film is foremost a study of character and emotion. While bygone eras carved up their characters like a monster's smorgasbord, the current variety wants to insure that the viewer feels the character's fear.[20]

Psychologically convincing fictional studies of fear may make readers/viewers aware of the mechanisms governing the experience of fear and may even point out possibilities of coping with it. This hypothesis of course applies less to horror films and Gothic fiction than to the depiction of fears that are closer to the readers'/viewers' life, such as the fear of death, of illnesses or of making a fool of oneself in a public performance.

---

19 BROWNSTEIN, Rachel M. "*Northanger Abbey, Sense and Sensibility, Pride and Prejudice.*" In: Edward Copeland and Juliet McMaster (eds.). *The Cambridge Companion to Jane Austen.* Cambridge: Cambridge University Press, 1997. 32 – 57, 36.
20 DAVIS, Jason. "The Character of Fear: Writing the Horror Film." In: *Creative Screenwriting* 13,5 (2006): 66 – 70, 66.

Although the depiction of fear in literary works and audiovisual media certainly does not have the primary function of frightening readers/viewers, fiction still has the potential of making readers and viewers feel uncomfortable or even causing nightmares, as Julian Hanich points out in his discussion of horror films and thrillers:

> The most powerful movies manage to leave us afraid (or at least uneasy) after we have turned off the TV or entered our car to drive back from the theater. By denying full narrative closure and leaving the end open many contemporary filmmakers reveal that this is a goal they *deliberately* aim at. Think of the surviving monster or psychopath in films like *Halloween* (1978), *The Texas Chainsaw Massacre, Henry - Portrait of a Serial Killer* or *The Silence of the Lambs:* Michael Myers, Leatherface, Henry and Hannibal Lecter are not dead or behind safe prison bars, but still haunt the imaginary streets – and possibly our imagination.[21]

In a similar vein, Davis argues that "the best horror films tend to stay with their audience",[22] making the viewers see certain things or situations in a different light. Presumably the thin line between a pleasant shiver on the one hand and being haunted by nightmares after having watched a horror movie on the other hand adds much to the fascination 'fictions of fear' have exerted throughout the centuries, occasionally bringing the vicarious pleasure of being thrilled by what one reads about or watches a bit closer to the actual experience of fear than one might have anticipated. Curiosity plays a crucial role in making readers and viewers wish to be exposed to narratives and images that may frighten them. This attitude is illustrated quite well by the reaction displayed by one of the characters in Ann Radcliffe's Gothic novel *The Romance of the Forest* (1791) when this character discovers a human skeleton in a deserted abbey:

> Upon the ground [...] stood a large chest, which he went forward to examine, and, lifting the lid, he saw the remains of a human skeleton. Horror struck upon his heart, and he involuntarily stepped back. During a pause of some moments, his first emotions subsided. That thrilling curiosity, which objects of terror often excite in the human mind, impelled him to take a second view of this dismal spectacle. (*The Romance of the Forest* 53 – 54)

What Radcliffe describes here as the "thrilling curiosity, which objects of terror often excite in the human mind" makes the character look again; this impulse is also what makes readers and viewers interested in fiction depicting situations that are associated with fear. In other words, curiosity is certainly one of the main reasons for the enormous success of genres in which fear plays a prominent role.

---

21 HANICH. *Cinematic Emotion in Horror Films and Thrillers.* 11.
22 DAVIS. "The Character of Fear." 70. DAVIS (ibid.) quotes one of the scriptwriters of the horror film *Saw III,* James Wan, who pointed out: " 'I saw *Poltergeist* at the age of seven and it's made me terrified of anything that is clown- or doll-related. It pretty much scarred me for life.' "

III.   Genres of Fear

References to fear and descriptions of characters experiencing fear as well as of
settings and situations which are likely to trigger suspense can be found in a wide
range of different genres. Still there are some genres for which the depiction of
fear appears to be a necessary feature. Typically, these genres are also meant to
offer the readers or viewers a pleasant shiver. The Victorian sensation novel,
which reached its climax in the 1860s with classics such as Wilkie Collins' *The
Woman in White* (1860) and Mary Elizabeth Braddon's *Lady Audley's Secret*
(1862), is a case in point. The sensation novel was described by contemporary
critics as "prey[ing] on the 'sensations' of the body, giving goose-bumps – what
Punch in 1863 called 'Making the Flesh Creep' – as well as producing sweats,
sudden frights, heightened blood pressure, and worse still, sexual stimulation".[23]
Novels like the ones mentioned above tend to show characters in all sorts of
dangerous and uncanny situations. In this respect, the sensation novel is very
similar to the older genre of the Gothic novel, which has been referred to as
'literature of terror' by David Punter in his influential study[24] and as "a genre of
darkness".[25] Traditional Gothic novels such as Horace Walpole's *The Castle of
Otranto* (1764), Ann Radcliffe's *The Mysteries of Udolpho* (1794), Matthew
Lewis's *The Monk* (1796), Mary Shelley's *Frankenstein* (1818) and Bram Stoker's
Dracula (1897) have provided a rich inventory of settings, character constellations, situations and, last but not least, strategies apt to make the reader
anticipate further terrors that are still drawn upon today when writers or producers seek to evoke a threatening atmosphere. In her article in the present
volume Elena Baeva explores the modification of Gothic devices in Shirley
Jackson's novel *We Have Always Lived in the Castle* (1962) and Quentin Tarantino's movie *Inglourious Basterds* (2009), showing that the motif of fear may
be used in extremely flexible ways.

As far as audiovisual media are concerned, the horror film is certainly the
foremost 'genre of fear'. According to Georg Seeßlen and Fernand Jung, this
genre tends to draw upon fears that are situated on three different levels: firstly,
the horror film exploits fears which are part of cultural mythology, i.e. fears
which were already drawn upon in fairy tales for instance (such as the fear of
wolves); secondly, horror films make use of fears which tend to accompany
people from their childhood onwards (e.g. the fear of darkness); thirdly, the

23 PURCHASE, Sean. *Key Concepts in Victorian Literature.* Houndmills, Basingstoke: Palgrave
   Macmillan, 2006. 189.
24 PUNTER, David. *The Literature of Terror: A History of Gothic Fictions from 1765 to the Present
   Day.* London: Longman, 1980.
25 KAYE, Heidi. "Gothic Film." In: David Punter (ed.). *A Companion to the Gothic.* Oxford:
   Blackwell, 2000. 180–92, 180.

horror film often addresses fears which are informed by sexual (phallic or vaginal) symbolism.[26] Typically, horror films rely on visual shock effects to create thrills for the viewer. The strategies used in horror films for this purpose include specific sequences of shots and what Hanich refers to as the strategy of "disrupted relief", where "the film lures us into a position of *non*-expectation. We relax and forget the offscreen threat. Precisely at this moment, the un-expected sting of shock penetrates."[27] Similar to other genres of fear, horror films are informed by changing cultural contexts with respect to the threats they present. In his article in this volume Christian Knöppler addresses specifically the cultural functions of horror film remakes.

Genres may also change in terms of how much fear they allow their characters to display. A genre that has changed considerably in terms of its depiction of the characters' fear is the war film. Traditionally, war movies often sought to present a heroic attitude on the part of the soldiers, and heroes were not supposed to betray any obvious signs of fear. Yet war films have changed considerably in this respect, as Klaus Scheunemann shows in his contribution to the present volume; he argues that the concept of heroism has changed in recent war films along with the representation of fear.

While the genres mentioned so far are quite obvious examples of works of fiction that are closely associated with fear, other fictional genres may also react to fears that are particularly prominent in a certain historical and cultural context.[28] Given the fact that genres may be regarded as responding to social and cultural problems and concerns,[29] it is hardly surprising that they often address anxieties that shape a society at a particular point in time.[30] The industrial novel, for instance, which reached the peak of its popularity in the middle of the nineteenth century with works including Elizabeth Gaskell's *Mary Barton: A Tale of Manchester Life* (1848), *North and South* (1854/55) and Charles Dickens's *Hard Times* (1854), can be seen as a response to widespread fears regarding the possibility of violent class conflicts in Victorian England. In a particularly memorable scene in Gaskell's *North and South* the middle-class protagonist

---

26 Cf. SEEßLEN, Georg and Fernand JUNG. *Horror: Geschichte und Mythologie des Horrorfilms.* Marburg: Schüren, 2006. 31.

27 HANICH. *Cinematic Emotion in Horror Films and Thrillers.* 139. For an overview of filmic techniques used in horror films, cf. ibid. *passim.*

28 James Eli ADAMS, for instance, refers to the British novels of the 1830s as "lightning rods for political anxiety" (ADAMS, James Eli. *A History of Victorian Literature.* Malden, MA/Oxford: Wiley-Blackwell, 2009. 82). Cf. also Marcel Inhoff's discussion of literary reactions to per-sonal and political fears in the years dominated by Richard Nixon.

29 Cf. VOßKAMP, Wilhelm. "Gattungen als literarisch-soziale Institutionen." In: Walter Hinck (ed.). *Textsortenlehre – Gattungsgeschichte.* Heidelberg: Quelle & Meyer, 1977. 27–42.

30 Jason DAVIS, for instance, argues that "horror is essentially defined by what scares a given society at a specific time" (DAVIS. "The Character of Fear." 66–67).

Margaret Hale and the factory owner John Thornton face a threatening group of workers. When the angry workers have gathered in front of Thornton's factory, they are shown to be dangerous, being referred to, for instance, as an "angry sea of men" (*North and South* 178) by the heterodiegetic narrator. Margaret Hale is eventually injured quite seriously by a stone that was meant to hit the factory owner. The way the working-class characters are described in Gaskell's novel makes it clear that it is the collective that is seen as dangerous, whereas individuals can be talked to, reasoned and negotiated with. After all, there are many scenes in *North and South* where individual workers, most of all Nicholas Higgins and his daughter Bessie, are presented in an extremely positive manner. The novel thus clearly reflects the widespread Victorian fear of workers uniting in trade unions or, worse, in angry mobs threatening the middle class and the upper class. The industrial novel thus is one of several genres that reflect and renegotiate collective fears of the Victorian period. In her contribution to this volume Gislind Rohwer-Happe discusses the ways in which another genre that is typical of the Victorian period, the dramatic monologue, explores a range of themes associated with collective fears in Victorian England.

In recent years, terrorism and in particular the terrorist attacks in New York City on September 11, 2001 have played a prominent role in the context of the exploration of collective and individual fears in literature as well as in audio-visual media. Many poems, plays, novels (including novels written for children), movies and television series address the fear of terrorist attacks in the aftermath of 9/11.[31] Fiction may explore the fear experienced by people after 9/11, but it may also show possible ways of coping with fear and trauma. Novels addressing 9/11 often present characters that feel the impact of 9/11 and seek to overcome their fears in various ways. In Jonathan Safran Foer's novel *Extremely Loud and Incredibly Close* (2005), for instance, nine-year-old Oskar Schell, who has lost his father in the attacks on the World Trade Center, talks about suffering from fears that are clearly related to the terrorist acts:

> There was a lot of stuff that made me panicky, like suspension bridges, germs, airplanes, fireworks, Arab people on the subway (even though I'm not racist), Arab people in restaurants and coffee shops and other public places, scaffolding, sewers and subway grates, bags without owners, shoes, people with mustaches, smoke, knots, tall buildings, turbans. (*Extremely Loud and Incredibly Close* 36)

Most of what Oskar claims to be afraid of is directly associated with the fear of an (Islamist) terrorist attack. In the course of the novel the protagonist's attempts at

---

31 Cf. for example Hoth, Stefanie. *Medium und Ereignis. 9/11 im amerikanischen Film, Fernsehen und Roman.* Heidelberg: Winter, 2011.

overcoming his fears are shown. He, for instance, manages to visit the top of the Empire State Building despite his fear of high buildings.

Fictional texts addressing 9/11 and its aftermath may fulfil a range of different functions with respect to the representation of fear: Firstly, they explore different manifestations and effects of individual and collective fears, thus arguably making the mechanisms governing fear specifically in the aftermath of 9/11 more transparent. Secondly, fictional works addressing 9/11 may potentially have a 'therapeutic' effect in so far as they show possible ways of coping with fear. Thirdly, they may try to render the supposedly dangerous 'other' more accessible and thus arguably less threatening. Instead of presenting the terrorist acts as the work of a faceless terrorist network, Don DeLillo's *Falling Man* (2007) includes the perspective of a terrorist in his novel, seeking to formulate hypotheses concerning the motivations and the personal background of the men behind the 9/11 terrorist acts. A novel such as Mohsin Hamid's *The Reluctant Fundamentalist* (2007), which is discussed by Nina Liewald in her contribution to this volume, likewise invites the readers to explore the perspective of the 'other' in the aftermath of 9/11, thus rendering the 'other' more understandable.

IV.   Case Study: *The Village*

As was pointed out above, literary texts and audiovisual media make use of a wide range of different strategies in order to depict characters' fear and to make the readers or viewers shiver. The following brief analysis of a film that exemplifies a considerable range of possibilities of addressing fear is meant to round off this introduction to the representation of different facets of fear in literature and audiovisual media. The movie that was chosen for this purpose is *The Village* (2004), which was produced, written and directed by M. Night Shyamalan, who is well-known for exploring fear in his films. In his début *The Sixth Sense* (1999), for instance, Shyamalan addresses the basic human fear of death and specifically the fear of ghosts. *The Village*, which "was the top-grossing film in the U.S. market for the first several weeks after its release on July 30, 2004",[32] arguably explores fear on even more levels than *The Sixth Sense*. Moreover, the depiction of fear in *The Village* is particularly interesting because it provides insights into the psychological and social mechanisms that generate fear in individuals as well as in a community.

---

32 COLLIER, Patrick C. "'Our Silly Lies': Ideological Fictions in M. Night Shyamalan's *The Village.*" In: *Journal of Narrative Theory* 38,2 (2008): 269–92, 269.

The Village, which has been referred to as "the darkest and most cynical of Shyamalan's films",[33] features Covington Woods, a small settlement in a valley surrounded by woods that is completely cut off from other settlements. Due to the way the characters are dressed and are shown to live, the viewers are first led to believe that the story is not set in the present, but in the late nineteenth century. This impression is reinforced by a gravestone the viewers see in one of the first scenes of the movie, which suggests that a child who has just been buried died in the year 1897. Much later, the viewers find out that the story is set in the present and that the quaint way of life portrayed in *The Village* is in fact the result of a social experiment triggered by the wish to escape from the dangers people are exposed to in contemporary society. The viewers learn that Covington Woods was founded by a group of people who wanted to leave modern civilization behind. As Jeffrey Andrew Weinstock puts is,

> each of the elders in the village of Covington Woods [...] has suffered a loss so profound that, in the language of the film, he or she 'questioned the merit of living at all' and made the decision to drop out of the world. Edward Walker's (William Hurt) father was murdered by a business partner, Alice Hunt's (Sigourney Weaver) husband was robbed and murdered, Mrs. Clack's (Cherry Jones) sister was raped and murdered, and so on.[34]

Being disillusioned by modern American society, the founders of the village, who are referred to as 'the Elders', have established a utopian community which propagates the idea of "a simplified existence and pastoral values exemplified in communal meals and collective governance".[35] The nostalgia felt for a supposedly better past has led the inhabitants of the village to make their children, who were born in the village and who do not even know what exists beyond the woods, believe that they actually live in the late nineteenth century. In other words, life in Covington Woods is based on constant lies: "[...] in order to maintain this community, the elders resort to deception and hypocrisy, thereby inviting into their community the same evils from which they fled".[36]

In order to ensure that their way of life is not endangered by contact with the modern world beyond the woods, the Elders face a twofold task: keeping intruders out and preventing their children from leaving the village. The first of these tasks does not seem to constitute a major challenge. In order to prevent outsiders from finding the village, the area is surrounded by a high fence which is constantly controlled by guards, as the viewer finds out near the end of the

---

33 WEINSTOCK, Jeffrey Andrew. "Introduction: Telling Stories about Telling Stories – The Films of M. Night Shyamalan." In: Jeffrey Andrew Weinstock (ed.). *Critical Approaches to the Films of M. Night Shyamalan: Spoiler Warnings*. Houndmills, Basingstoke: Palgrave Macmillan, 2010. ix-xxix, xx.
34 WEINSTOCK. "Introduction." xx.
35 WEINSTOCK. "Introduction." xx.
36 WEINSTOCK. "Introduction." xx.

movie. The latter task, which turns out to be significantly more difficult, is accomplished by instilling fear in the younger inhabitants of the settlement. The founders of the village teach their children that the 'towns' beyond the forest are "wicked places where wicked people live" (9:35mins.). Since it is a well-known fact that warnings do not necessarily keep people from doing what is forbidden, the Elders have devised additional measures to keep the younger inhabitants of the village from straying away from the settlement. They tell their children that the woods surrounding the village are inhabited by dangerous creatures which will not harm the villagers as long as they do not enter the forest. In order to make this lie more convincing, the Elders take turns at creating eerie noises in the woods and donning fanciful, bright-red costumes to impersonate the creatures. These efforts stress that "like all ideological narratives, [...] the story of the creatures is subject to discursive contestation, and must be periodically re-iterated, defended, and adapted in response", as Collier puts it.[37] As a consequence of these efforts on the part of the Elders, "the children of the village are as fearful of 'Those We Do Not Speak Of' as the elders are of the ambient violence of modern existence in 'The Towns'".[38] Thus, for the younger inhabitants of Covington Woods fear is an ingredient of everyday life in the supposedly idyllic, utopian community. The fact that the younger inhabitants take turns at keeping watch near the edge of the forest each night further emphasises that fear is their constant companion.

For the younger inhabitants of Covington Woods life in the village is strongly linked with taboos, which illustrate very well how fear operates. Firstly, there is a taboo concerning references to the mysterious creatures that are supposedly haunting the woods. Instead of giving the creatures a name, the inhabitants of Covington Woods consistently refer to them as 'Those We Do Not Speak of'. Thus, the creatures remain part of the unknown, which is likely to increase their potential of evoking fear; after all, we tend to be more easily frightened of what we do not understand. Taboos concerning names are a feature that exists in many different cultures. Such taboos tend to be an expression of a feeling of fear and awe; they establish a distance and maintain a lack of knowledge, which is apt to induce fear. Breaking the taboo by using a name thus may turn out to be empowering and may contribute to defeating fear. In the fairy tale of "Rumpelstiltskin", for instance, finding out the name of the supernatural creature that threatens the protagonist means that the spell can be broken; knowing the name of the threatening creature deprives the latter of its power and restores the freedom of the human protagonist.

---

37 COLLIER. "'Our Silly Lies': Ideological Fictions in M. Night Shyamalan's *The Village*." 277.
38 WEINSTOCK. "Introduction." xxi.

Secondly, the younger inhabitants of the village have been taught that the colour red (i.e. the colour linked with the creatures) is the 'bad colour'.[39] In several scenes the characters are shown to bury red flowers or shun red berries in a way that suggests that they feel uncomfortable or even frightened in the presence of red objects. The colour symbolism used in *The Village* is reinforced by the idea that yellow appears to be regarded as a protective colour. The re- actions triggered by encounters with the 'bad colour' are indicative of a neurotic fear rather than the kind of fear that can be accounted for as a natural reaction to danger. Yet the way the camera singles out the red flowers and berries suggests that there is indeed a reason for being afraid of the 'bad colour'. The fact that the younger inhabitants of the village have been taught that red is the 'bad colour', which must be avoided, reinforces the impression that they have grown up in an atmosphere saturated with fear. Moreover, the red flowers growing all of a sudden in the middle of the village may be read as a reminder of the fact that one cannot avoid danger, no matter how hard one may try to do so. Red objects turning up in Covington Woods seem to foreshadow what is going to happen. After all, Noah Percy, who has grown up in the supposedly idyllic and safe community, will soon attack two of the inhabitants of the village. The real danger comes from inside the community and not from the outside.

Thirdly, the woods are presented as a place that is taboo because it is asso- ciated with danger. The fact that the forest is seen as a threatening place har- bouring unknown dangers is clearly an archetypical notion. Fairy tales and folk ballads are among the genres that have traditionally shown the forest as a place where one may encounter dangerous and supernatural creatures. The film *The Blair Witch Project* (1998) is a more recent case in point, which proves that forests are still regarded as places where dangerous things may happen to more or less unsuspecting victims. Forests have also tended to play an important role in the tradition of the American Gothic, often replacing the aristocratic castles and abbeys that loom large in the British Gothic tradition.[40] When the title character of one of the classics of American Gothic literature, Nathaniel Haw-

---

39 As SEEßLEN and JUNG point out, in Gothic and horror fiction the colour red tends to be associated with blood, with the body and sexuality, but red is also linked with power, since red robes have traditionally been worn by monarchs. Cf. SEEßLEN and JUNG. *Horror: Ge- schichte und Mythologie des Horrorfilms.* 62. This complex symbolism has certainly also informed the choice of red as the 'bad colour' in *The Village*. The association with blood may serve as a reminder of the Elders' reasons for leaving the ordinary world behind, i.e. their experience with extreme violence.

40 Cf. Allan LLOYD-SMITH's comment on nineteenth-century American Gothic writers "using the resources of the wilderness and the primitive emotions of the rough settlers for its effect" (LLOYD-SMITH, Allan. "Nineteenth-Century American Gothic." In: David Punter (ed.). *A Companion to the Gothic.* Oxford: Blackwell, 109–21, 113), which suggests that *The Village* is indeed a variation on traditional examples of the American Gothic.

thorne's short story "Young Goodman Brown" (1835), ventures into the forest he meets the devil himself and faces a Witches' Sabbath in which most of his neighbours seem to participate. Similar to Hawthorne, the Elders in *The Village* have established a dichotomy between the supposedly safe village and the dangerous forest, thus creating a boundary which must not be breached, but which turns out to be deceptive, because evil resides in the very midst of the community.

The boundary in *The Village* is visually introduced quite early in the movie by "an overhead, night-time establishing shot [that] reveals a watchtower, lit by a line of torches and manned by villagers, from which the line between the village and the woods is surveilled and maintained".[41] The way the boundary is guarded is reminiscent of further archetypical fears, namely the fear of the dark and the fear of wild animals, which are kept away by fire. Moreover, the visual demarcation suggests that "[t]he threshold to the forest must not be crossed by any means: beyond it you are immediately inside the forest, enwrapped, as it were, by its frightening spell".[42] Both the visual track and the soundtrack support the idea that the forest is dangerous right from the beginning of the movie. Already during the opening credits the viewers see bare, black branches of trees in front of a leaden sky and are exposed to a musical theme that introduces the eerie and threatening atmosphere that is going to shape much of the movie.[43] Ultimately, of course, the viewers find out that "[t]he woods are forbidden in order to protect

---

41 COLLIER. "'Our Silly Lies': Ideological Fictions in M. Night Shyamalan's *The Village*." 278.
42 HANICH. *Cinematic Emotion in Horror Films and Thrillers.* 176.
43 COLLIER provides a thorough description of the opening sequence which shows why the beginning of the movie already makes the viewers expect frightening things to happen: "The sequence begins with a slow upwards tilt through some tree branches, framed medium-close and in dim light, over which the names of the lead actors are one-by-one superimposed in titles, while ominous music slowly gathers on the soundtrack. With the startling beat of a bass drum, an abrupt blackout clears the screen, and the film's title appears. Then the light slowly comes up on a diagonal, slightly right-to-left pan through tree branches (and thus a change in the direction of the camera movement). A second blackout provides a background for the names of supporting actors, and again the light comes up on tree branches, again with the camera direction having shifted. This pattern of alternation between blackness and images of the forest – between not seeing and seeing, as it were – continues until the credits conclude with a more distant, more formally composed shot of the woods in which individual trees can be made out, with one tree artfully framed as the dominant contrast. We are kept in the dark in this sequence, figuratively so when not literally so: we're given nothing resembling an establishing shot until the end – reversing the usual (and thus legible) order of close-up to establishing shot, and the sequence of images we get ostentatiously controls and limits our information, literally halting the flow via blackout before we would begin to get our bearings." (COLLIER. "'Our Silly Lies': Ideological Fictions in M. Night Shyamalan's *The Village*." 282–83.)

residents not from mysterious creatures but from the dangers and temptations of urban modernity".[44]

The idea that transgressing boundaries may be associated with danger is a notion that is also familiar from fairy tales. In his classic study of the fairy tale, Max Lüthi points out: "It is obvious that the fairytale hero is also one who *transgresses boundaries*, since he violates interdictions, and especially since he opens forbidden doors."[45] The heroine in *The Village* is the blind girl Ivy Walker, who exhibits the strength of character and determination that also tend to be the key to the success of fairytale heroes and heroines. Ivy's reasons for seeking to transgress the boundary are 'pure'; in other words, she is not led by mere curiosity, but wants to fetch medicine for the young man who has been seriously wounded by Noah. This 'purity' is supposed to provide her with a certain protection – a notion that also seems to echo the fairy tale. When Ivy, the quest heroine, is attacked by Noah, who has escaped from his prison and has donned one of the 'creature' costumes, the blind girl displays a remarkable resourcefulness by managing to trap Noah in a hole in the ground. Yet before she summons her courage and confronts what she presumably supposes to be one of the creatures she has heard about all her life, Ivy experiences intense fear. Her fear and confusion are captured by means of camera techniques; as Collier puts it, the "shocks are heightened by the frenetic editing, from hand-held shots to bird's-eye views to low-angle shots, in which the confrontation with the creature is shot".[46] The camera technique used in this climactic scene clearly invites the viewers to feel empathy with Ivy's fear.

In addition to the setting (the woods, the isolated location), *The Village* picks up a further feature that, at least in the nineteenth century, is characteristic of the American Gothic rather than the British Gothic tradition, namely the interest in insanity, one of the hallmark features of E.A. Poe's short stories, which time and again expose the reader to the musings of clearly insane narrators.[47] Already in one of the first scenes of *The Village* the viewers are introduced to the irrational behaviour displayed by Noah. Interestingly enough, Noah's irrationality is made apparent by the fact that he is the only one in the group who does *not* display any signs of discomfort when strange noises echo from the woods. Instead of being disturbed by the noise, he reacts with wild glee, which offers the viewers a very

---

44 COLLIER. "'Our Silly Lies': Ideological Fictions in M. Night Shyamalan's *The Village*." 277.
45 LÜTHI, Max. *The Fairytale as Art Form and Portrait of Man.* Translated by Jon Erickson. Bloomington/Indianapolis: Indiana University Press, 1984 [1975]. 141.
46 COLLIER. "'Our Silly Lies': Ideological Fictions in M. Night Shyamalan's *The Village*." 281.
47 Many of Poe's narrators are not only insane, but are also unreliable narrators. This suggests a further parallel to *The Village*, which can be seen as an example of filmic unreliable narration, since the viewers – similar to the younger inhabitants of Covington Woods – are deceived with respect to the temporal setting and the status of the village.

first glimpse of his insanity. Later on the viewers find out that Noah is responsible for killing and skinning small animals, which are found within the settlement. In addition to these gratuitous acts of violence, which suggest that he
enjoys killing and perhaps even torturing animals, Noah attacks his closest
friend, Lucius Hunt, with a knife, an act that is motivated by jealousy. While the
mysterious creatures in the woods turn out to be mere bogeymen, the real danger
is a young man who is well known to all of the inhabitants of the village, someone
who has lived among them since the day he was born.[48]

Ivy Walker is certainly the character the viewers are invited to feel most
empathy with. She experiences intense fear when she is alone in the woods, but
she still manages to act rationally when confronted with real danger, i.e. when
Noah (in the guise of one of the creatures) is attacking her. Ivy's comparative
helplessness is reminiscent of the Gothic stock character of the 'damsel-in-
distress', a young woman who is pursued ruthlessly by the villain. Yet Ivy, despite
her apparent helplessness, proves that she is up to the challenge. Rational behaviour is what ensures her victory despite the enormous disadvantage of her
blindness. Noah, the attacker, is certainly a villain, but he presumably is also a
victim. Like the other younger inhabitants of the village he has been systematically deprived of knowledge and has been raised in an atmosphere saturated
with fear. One might perhaps even argue that the film raises the question of
whether Noah's deeds can at least to a certain extent be attributed to the peculiar
circumstances in which he has grown up and specifically to the lack of professional medical/psychological care.

Shyamalan's film does more than simply presenting individuals experiencing
fear in the framework of a social experiment that may appear more or less
plausible to the viewers; the experiment in and of itself clearly has complex
cultural and historical resonances. The movie alludes to different periods of
American history. The tombstone that can be seen in one of the first scenes
obviously suggests that the story is set at the end of the nineteenth century.
Likewise,

> Colonial, Puritan America is cited in viewers' encounters with this community early in
> the film. At the communal meal following Daniel Nicholson's burial, Edward Walker
> prefaces his prayer with the question, 'Did we make the right decision to settle here?'
> Immediately after the prayer, the villagers hear an otherworldly howling coming from

---

48 The choice of a well-known and clearly human villain in *The Village* corresponds to a
tendency that is also characteristic of the modern horror film according to Davis: "While
more ethereal enemies once allowed viewers to distance themselves from the sources of daily
anxiety personified in vampires or ghosts, modern fears seem inclined to wear human
masks." (DAVIS. "The Character of Fear." 68.)

the woods, a none-too-subtle reference to the 'howling wilderness' of Puritan captivity narratives and exploration tracts.[49]

The Village can clearly be seen as a study of the fear experienced and generated in 'frontier' situations; thus it picks up a historical constellation that has been extremely important for American history and identity. Founding small settlements in a potentially hostile environment and trying to defend these against real or imagined intruders is a consequence of colonising a continent already inhabited by indigenous people, who presumably know much more about the natural environment than the newcomers do. Lauren Coats et al. point out that The Village reiterates ideas that are familiar from early accounts of encounters with the indigenous population in North America; Shyamalan's movie echoes those "stories about fear, violence, and inevitable triumph [that] underwrote the conquest of North America and the transformation of British into United States imperialism".[50] Puritan narratives as well as countless Westerns address situations that bear a strong resemblance to the predicament of the (younger) settlers in The Village: the fear caused by the presence of potentially hostile beings whose aims and motivations are largely unknown to the inhabitants.[51]

Beyond the historical resonances that are evoked by the situation depicted in The Village and specifically by the way of life voluntarily chosen by the Elders, the representation of a community separated from modern life is also reminiscent of groups who refuse to blend into modern American society, such as the Amish. Moreover, many critics comment on the references to the political situation in the United States at the beginning of the twenty-first century one can identify in The Village. Patrick C. Collier, for instance, points out that "the film was written and shot in the aftermath of the World Trade Center attacks on Sept. 11, 2001, and debuted in early 2004, 10 months after the United States launched a war in Iraq on premises that turned out to be just as fictional as the monsters in Shyamalan's woods".[52] In more general terms, The Village, being "a

---

49 COATS, Lauren et al. "Those We Don't Speak of: Indians in The Village." In: PMLA 123,2 (2008): 358–74, 363.
50 COATS et al. "Those We Don't Speak of." 359.
51 Although the frontier experience has been particularly significant for US-American culture, other 'settler colonies' have also been influenced by this type of experience. The novel Remembering Babylon (1993) by the Australian writer David Malouf, for instance, presents an Australian version of the frontier situation.
52 COLLIER. "'Our Silly Lies': Ideological Fictions in M. Night Shyamalan's The Village." 273. Cf. also COATS et al. "Those We Don't Speak of." 361: "The consensus reading of the movie [...] is that it is an allegory of contemporary United States foreign policy. [...] Resonating with an interpretation of Bush-administration policy following the events of 9/11, the community of Covington Woods is sustained by terror and by a story that is fabricated to create and sustain that terror (the village's leader shares the name Walker with George Walker Bush)."

story about the power of stories to construct our sense of reality", "emphasizes the way in which narrative can be used as a tool of political control".[53] One should add that *The Village* does not just explore the function of *narrative* as a political tool, but, more specifically, the power *narratives of fear* may exert both on the individual level and on the collective level.[54]

*****

A number of the articles in the present volume are based on papers that were delivered in the context of a conference which took place at the University of Bonn in September 2010. Thus, thanks are due to the people who helped organise this conference – Anna Coogan, Anja Drautzburg, Miriam Halfmann, Hatice Karakurt and Klaus Scheunemann. In addition I would like to thank Elena Baeva, Anna Coogan and Hatice Karakurt for their help with the editing and proof-reading of this volume.

References

ADAMS, James Eli. *A History of Victorian Literature*. Malden, MA/Oxford: Wiley-Black-well, 2009.

AUSTEN, Jane. *Northanger Abbey*. Harmondsworth: Penguin, 1985 [1818].

BROWNSTEIN, Rachel M. "*Northanger Abbey, Sense and Sensibility, Pride and Prejudice*." In: Edward Copeland and Juliet McMaster (eds.). *The Cambridge Companion to Jane Austen*. Cambridge: Cambridge University Press, 1997. 32 – 57.

COATS, Lauren, Matt COHEN, John David MILES, Kinohi NISHIKAWA and Rebecca WALSH. "Those We Don't Speak of: Indians in *The Village*." In: *PMLA* 123,2 (2008): 358 – 74.

COLLIER, Patrick C. "'Our Silly Lies': Ideological Fictions in M. Night Shyamalan's *The Village*." In: *Journal of Narrative Theory* 38,2 (2008): 269 – 92.

DAVIS, Jason. "The Character of Fear: Writing the Horror Film." In: *Creative Screenwriting* 13,5 (2006): 66 – 70.

DICKENS, Charles. *Great Expectations*. Harmondsworth: Penguin, 1994 [1861].

FOER, Jonathan Safran. *Extremely Loud and Incredibly Close*. London: Penguin, 2006 [2005].

GASKELL, Elizabeth. *North and South*. Oxford/New York: Oxford University Press, 1982 [1854 – 55].

HANICH, Julian. *Cinematic Emotion in Horror Films and Thrillers: The Aesthetic Paradox of Pleasurable Fear*. New York/London: Routledge, 2010.

---

53 WEINSTOCK. "Introduction." xxi.

54 For an exploration of narratives of fear and their political implications in the context of English Renaissance literature and culture, cf. the contribution by Uwe Baumann in the present volume.

Heelas, Paul. "Emotion Talk across Cultures." In: Rom Harré (ed.). *The Social Construction of Emotions*. Oxford: Blackwell, 1986. 234–66.

Hentschel, Frank. *Töne der Angst: Die Musik im Horrorfilm*. Berlin: Bertz + Fischer, 2011.

Hock, Michael and Carl-Walter Kohlmann. "Angst und Furcht." In: Veronika Brandstätter and Jürgen H. Otto (eds.). *Handbuch der Allgemeinen Psychologie – Motivation und Emotion*. Göttingen et al.: Hogrefe, 2009. 623–32.

Hoth, Stefanie. *Medium und Ereignis. 9/11 im amerikanischen Film, Fernsehen und Roman*. Heidelberg: Winter, 2011.

Kaye, Heidi. "Gothic Film." In: David Punter (ed.). *A Companion to the Gothic*. Oxford: Blackwell, 2000. 180–92.

Krohne, Heinz Walter. *Psychologie der Angst*. Stuttgart: Kohlhammer, 2010.

Lloyd-Smith, Allan. "Nineteenth-Century American Gothic." In: David Punter (ed.). *A Companion to the Gothic*. Oxford: Blackwell, 109–21.

Lüthi, Max. *The Fairytale as Art Form and Portrait of Man*. Translated by Jon Erickson. Bloomington/Indianapolis: Indiana University Press, 1984 [1975].

Punter, David. *The Literature of Terror: A History of Gothic Fictions from 1765 to the Present Day*. London: Longman, 1980.

Purchase, Sean. *Key Concepts in Victorian Literature*. Houndmills, Basingstoke: Palgrave Macmillan, 2006.

Radcliffe, Ann. *The Romance of the Forest*. Oxford: Oxford University Press, 2009 [1791].

Seeßlen, Georg and Fernand Jung. *Horror: Geschichte und Mythologie des Horrorfilms*. Marburg: Schüren, 2006.

Shyamalan, M. Night, dir. *The Village*. Touchstone Pictures, 2004.

Stöber, Joachim and Ralf Schwarzer. "Angst." In: Jürgen H. Otto, Harald A. Euler and Heinz Mandl (eds.). *Emotionspsychologie: Ein Handbuch*. Weinheim: Beltz, 2000, 189–98.

Voßkamp, Wilhelm. "Gattungen als literarisch-soziale Institutionen." In: Walter Hinck (ed.). *Textsortenlehre – Gattungsgeschichte*. Heidelberg: Quelle & Meyer, 1977. 27–42.

Weinstock, Jeffrey Andrew. "Introduction: Telling Stories about Telling Stories – The Films of M. Night Shyamalan." In: Jeffrey Andrew Weinstock (ed.). *Critical Approaches to the Films of M. Night Shyamalan: Spoiler Warnings*. Houndmills, Basingstoke: Palgrave Macmillan, 2010. ix–xxix.

Wright, Angela. "Disturbing the Female Gothic: An Excavation of the *Northanger Novels*." In: Diana Wallace and Andrew Smith (eds.). *The Female Gothic: New Directions*. Houndmills, Basingstoke: Palgrave Macmillan, 2009. 60–75.

Uwe Baumann

Ruling by Fear / Ruled by Fear: Representations of Political Violence and Political Fear in English Renaissance Culture and Literature

I.   Prologue

"A spectre is haunting humanity: the spectre of fear. Death stares unblinkingly at us. Danger dallies in everyday environs. Sometimes a scary person or menacing object can be identified: the flames searing patterns on the ceiling, the hydrogen bomb, the terrorist. More often, anxiety overwhelms us from some source 'within': there is an irrational panic about venturing outside, a dread of failure, a premonition of doom. There often seems no limit to the threats".[1] With these striking words that outline the main features of contemporary mentality, Joanna Bourke opens the introductory chapter of her cultural history of fear, which is divided into five main sections (I: "Worlds of Doom", 23 ff; II: "Spheres of Uncertainty", 79 ff; III: "Whorls of Irrationality", 165 ff; IV: "Zones of Confrontation", 195 ff; V: "Realms of Anxiety", 293 ff; "Conclusion: Terror", 357 ff). Following an almost four hundred pages long *tour de force* of the history of politics and mentality primarily of the nineteenth and twentieth centuries, she also stresses the civilizing and empowering functions of fear towards the end of her extensive analysis, as it were as a last consolatory appraisal:

> [...] fear is a great and glorious stimulant that works in direct opposition to attempts to rigidly control our environment. We are right to fear. A world without fear would be a dull world indeed. It is sobering to contemplate a world where parents did not fear for their children or where death was as insignificant as eating a meal. In the words of a woman living in Britain during the First World War when under attack by Zeppelins: 'I was dreadfully frightened and said my prayers ... I could never get used to raids, they frightened me terribly, as much for my two boys who were fighting in France as for myself. 'If it is like this here, what must it be there?' I used to ask myself'. A world without fear would be a world without love. Fear has been one of the most significant driving forces in history, encouraging individuals to reflect more deeply and

---

1 Bourke, Joanna. *Fear. A Cultural History.* London: Virago Press, 2005. 1.

prompting them to action. Indeed, much of the human urge to creativity depends upon fear [...].[2]

It may be difficult at times to realize this quality of fear, which to all intents and purposes is capable of stimulating positive, creative developments; for example in the international agreements and treaties concerning a protraction or prevention of the climate disaster triggered by global warming, inadequate as they still may be, or in the recent attempts at preventing a collapse of the European currency. What remains unchallenged, however, is that fear has always been one of the crucial factors in historical developments.[3] In general, however, the fundamental ambivalence of fear, as well as the role of emotions in history, has only begun to attract increased scholarly attention in historical studies within the last decades.[4] These studies, no matter which one of various topics they analyse and

---

2 BOURKE. *Fear.* 1 (with a quotation from Dorothy Constance Peel. *How We Lived Then 1914 – 1918.* London: John Lane, 1929).

3 Cf. ROBIN, Corey. *Fear. The History of a Political Idea.* Oxford: Oxford University Press, 2004. 1: "It is seldom noted, but fear is the first emotion experienced by a character in the Bible. Not desire, not shame, but fear. Adam eats from the tree, discovers he is naked, and hides from God, confessing, 'I was afraid, because I was naked.' [Genesis 1 – 3]. Before this admission, God creates and sees that his creations are good. [...] But these are reports of antiseptic perception, with no warming murmur of appreciation or aversion. Everyone looks, everyone sees. Does anyone feel? Not until they eat the forbidden fruit do we hear of felt experience. And when we do, it is fear. Why fear? Perhaps it is because, for the authors of the Bible, fear is the most electric of emotions. Prior to being afraid, Adam and Eve exist and act in the world, but without any palpable experience of it. Afraid, they are awash in experience, with God promising even more – for Eve the pain of childbirth, for Adam the duress of work, for both the dread knowledge of death. Unafraid, Adam and Eve have only the laziest appreciation of the good and haziest apprehension of the bad. Their dim cognizance of evil makes them spectators to their own lives, semiconscious actors at best. Adam names, Eve succumbs, but neither really knows what it is that they do. Afraid, they know. Shallow temptation gives way to dramatic choice, inertial motion to elected action. Their story – our story – is ready to begin".

4 Cf. e. g. ASCHMANN, Birgit (ed.). *Gefühl und Kalkül. Der Einfluss von Emotionen auf die Politik des 19. und 20. Jahrhunderts.* Stuttgart: Franz Steiner, 2005; BERGSDORF, Wolfgang. "Politik und Angst." In: Franz Bosbach (ed.). *Angst und Politik in der europäischen Geschichte.* Dettelbach: Röll, 2000. 13 – 28; BORMANN, Patrick, Thomas FREIBERGER and Judith MICHEL (eds.). *Angst in den Internationalen Beziehungen.* Göttingen: Bonn University Press, 2010; FUREDI, Frank. *Politics of Fear.* London: Continuum, 2005, esp. 123ff; GLASSNER, Barry. *The Culture of Fear. Why Americans Are Afraid of the Wrong Things.* New York: Basic Books, 1999; HEBBLETHWAITE, Kate and Elizabeth MCCARTHY (eds.). *Fear. Essays on the Meaning and Experience of Fear.* Dublin: Four Courts Press, 2007; HORN, Klaus and Volker RITTBERGER (eds.). *Mit Kriegsgefahren leben. Bedrohtsein, Bedrohungsgefühle und friedenspolitisches Engagement.* Opladen: Westdeutscher Verlag, 1987; KAESELITZ, Hella. "Die Ängste der Margaret Thatcher. Einige Aspekte der britischen Haltung zur deutschen Vereinigung." In: *Utopie kreativ* 105. Rosa Luxemburg Stiftung. Juli 1999, 61 – 67; RITTER, Gerhard. *Angst als Mittel der Politik in der Ost-West-Auseinandersetzung.* Berlin: Duncker & Humblot, 1986; ROBIN, Corey. *Fear. The History of a Political Idea.* Oxford: Oxford University Press, 2004; SCHILDT, Axel. "'German Angst': Überlegungen zur Mentalitätsgeschichte der Bundesrepublik." In: Daniela Münkel and Jutta Schwarzkopf (eds.). *Geschichte als Experiment:*

take stock of – the fears surrounding World War One, the policy of deterrence in the Cold War, British fears of a reunified Germany, American politics and the fear after September 11, 2001, or specifically American fears at large –, have one thing in common: almost without exception, they are limited to roughly the past one hundred years.[5] In the following, I intend to retreat into my *provincia*, my very own field of expertise and analyze some exemplary texts (political epigrams, tragedies) and cultural representations (political trials and the politics of Henry VIII) of the English Renaissance which concentrate on the differing functions of fear in the government, the governing and the governed. These exemplary analyses will necessarily be highly selective. Nevertheless, it will also be useful by way of introduction to briefly summarize some aspects that reach back to the classical era. It is here that the general argumentative contexts for the representation of political fear in the culture and literature of the English Renaissance are generated.

## II.	Representations of Political Fear: Facets of the Classical Tradition

While trying not to become entangled in the difficult problems of anthropological continuities and discontinuities, it is imperative, at the outset of this study, to state that fear was ubiquitous in the myth, history, and politics of classical antiquity.[6] Bearers and messengers of fear were the Erinyes or Furies,[7] from whose gaze one would flee in horror-struck confusion. 'Fear' and 'flight' were homonymously known in Ancient Greek as 'phobos'. In Aeschylus' *Eumenides*, the oppressively haunting words of the prophetess, who encountered the Erinyes in the temple of Apollo, still attest to her horror: "[…] but these are wingless, sable, and altogether detestable. Their snorting nostrils blow forth

---

Studien zu Politik, Kultur und Alltag im 19. und 20. Jahrhundert. Festschrift für Adelheid von Saldern. Frankfurt/Main: Campus-Verlag, 2004. 87–97; SCHRECKER, Ellen (ed.). *Cold War Triumphalism: The Misuse of History After the Fall of Communism.* New York: The New Press, 2004; SCHULTZ, Nancy L. (ed.). *Fear Itself: Enemies Real and Imagined.* West Lafayette: Purdue University Press, 1999; SCHWARZ, Urs. *Die Angst in der Politik.* Düsseldorf/Wien: Econ, 1967; SENGHAAS, Dieter. "Angst in der Politik." In: Hans Jürgen Schultz (ed.). *Angst.* Stuttgart: Kreuz-Verlag, 1987. 248–60; STEARNS, Peter N. "Fear and Contemporary History: A Review Essay." In: *Journal of Social History* 40,2 (2006): 477–84; STEARNS, Peter N. *American Fear. The Causes and Consequences of High Anxiety.* New York/London: Routledge, 2006; SVENDSEN, Lars. *A Philosophy of Fear.* London: Reaction Books, 2007, esp. 102 ff.

5 Cf. the following footnotes for some remarkable exceptions (esp. fts. 10, 12, 15, 17, 23, 24, 31, 32 and 34).

6 Cf. SCHWARZ. *Die Angst in der Politik.* Esp. 140 ff.

7 Cf. HUNGER, Herbert. *Lexikon der griechischen und römischen Mythologie.* 6th edn. Reinbek: Rowohlt, 1974. 127–28, s. v. 'Erínyen'.

fearsome blasts, and from their eyes oozes a loathly rheum."[8] In his grand historical drama *The Persians*, Aeschylus systematically utilizes fear in order to foreshadow the military defeat of the Persian army when, in the wake of a night full of ominous nightmares, the queen dowager Atossa reports the circumstances of her matutinal sacrifice:

> But when I had risen and dipped my hands in the clear-flowing water of a spring, I drew nigh unto an altar with incense in my hand, minded to make oblation of a sacrificial cake unto the divinities that avert evil, even unto those to whom these rites are due. But I saw an eagle fleeing for safety to the altar of Phoebus – and from terror, my friends, I stood reft of speech. And thereupon I spied a falcon rushing at full speed with out-stretched pinions and with his talons plucking at the eagle's head; while it did naught but cower and yield its body to his foe. These are the terrors I beheld, and terrors are they for you to hear.[9]

Just how intimately classical antiquity was acquainted with the knowledge of fear and the psychological mechanisms of fear is illuminated by the fascinating fact that "it employed a symbol of fear as a defense against the onslaught of fear"[10]: the Gorgoneion. The head of Medusa,[11] adorned with twisting serpents in place

---

8 AESCHYLUS. *Eumenides.* Translated by Herbert Weir Smyth. Loeb Classical Library No. 145 & 146, 2 Vols. London: Heinemann, 1956–1957. 51–54.

9 AESCHYLUS. *The Persians.* Translated by Herbert Weir Smyth. Loeb Classical Library No. 145 & 146, 2 Vols. London: Heinemann, 1956–1957. 201–11.

10 SCHWARZ. *Die Angst in der Politik.* 141. Cf. the classical myth in Francis Bacon's summary (*De Sapientia Veterum / The Wisedome of the Ancients, written in Latine by the Right Honourable Sir Francis Bacon, Knight, Baron of Verulam, and Lord Chancelor of England, Done into English by Sir Arthur Gorges Knight* [London: Iohn Bill, 1619 / Reprint: New York/ London: Garland Publishing, 1976]. VII, 38 – 40): "*Perseus* is said to haue beene employed by *Pallas* for the destroying of *Medusa*, who was very infectious to the western parts of the world, and especially about the vtmost coasts of *Hyberia*. A monster so dire and horrid, that by her onely aspect shee turned men into stones. This *Medusa* alone of all the *Gorgons* was Mortall, the rest not subiect to death. *Perseus* therefore preparing himself for this noble enterprise had armes, and guifts bestowed on him by three of the Gods: *Mercury* haue him wings annexed to his heeles, *Pluto* a helmet, *Pallas* a shield and a looking Glasse. Not-winthstanding (although hee were thus furnished) hee went not directly to *Medusa*, but first to the *Greae* which by the mother side were sisters to the *Gorgons*. These *Greae* from their birth were hoare-headed, resembling old women. They had but one onely eye, and one tooth among them all, both which shee that had occasion to goe abroad was wont to take with her, & at her returne to lay them downe againe. This eye and tooth they lent to *Perseus:* and so finding himself thoroughly furnished for the effecting of his designe hastens towards *Medusa.* Her hee found sleeping, and yet durst not present himself with his face towards her, least shee should awake, but turning his head aside beheld her in *Pallases* glasse, and (by this meanes directing his blowe) cut of her head, from whose blood gushing out instantly came *Pegasus* the flying horse. Her head thus smit of, *Perseus* bestows on *Pallas* her shield, which yet retained his virtue, that whosoeuer looked vpon it should become as stupid as a stone or like one plannetstrucken".

11 Cf. HUNGER. *Lexikon der griechischen und römischen Mythologie.* 144 – 45; s. v. 'Gorgonen';

of hair, decorated and protected anchors, domestic appliances, armour and shields: thus, famously, the shield of Agamemnon, the cuirass of Alexander the Great, as well as the armour of the Roman Emperors and their high-ranking officers.

Just as a symbol of fear was converted into the classical symbol of defense against fear, reinterpreting it for a productive positive effect, the Erinyes, too, would in later times become the Eumenides (the kind-hearted ones): guardians of safety and legal order. This modified conception of the Erinyes, which is possibly even too euphemistically accentuated in the process, may be taken to forebode the progressive development of the penal law system (as in the Athenian state, which had assumed the punitive function of the Erinyes). If this is the case, it also points to the indissoluble relationship between state organization and governance on the one hand and the conceptualization and functionalization of political fear on the other one.

References to fear as an incentive for human and government actions are remarkably numerous in Greek historiography, especially in Thucydides' writings.[12] Most notably, militaristic Sparta intentionally utilized fear as a means of political rule – in particular in order to keep the Messenian helots in bondage and slavery.[13] There was even a Spartan temple consecrated to fear, as handed down by Plutarch in his *Parallel Lives*:

> Now, the Lacedaemonians have temples of Death, Laughter, and that sort of thing, as well as of Fear. And they pay honours to Fear, not as they do to the powers which they try to avert because they think them baleful, but because they believe that fear is the chief support of their civil polity. [...] And the men of old, in my opinion, did not regard bravery as a lack of fear, but as fear of reproach and dread of disgrace. For the men who feel most dread of the laws have most courage in facing their enemies; and those shun death least who most fear ill fame. Therefore it has been well said:
>
> '... for where dread is, there also is reverence.'
>
> [...] For by the multitude reverence is most apt to be felt towards those whom they also fear. For this reason, too, the Lacedaemonians erected a temple to Fear alongside the mess-hall of ephors, after they had endowed this magistracy with almost absolute powers. (Cleomenes, IX, 1 – 4)

WALTHER, Lutz (ed.). *Antike Mythen und ihre Rezeption, Ein Lexikon*. Stuttgart: Reclam, 2003. 136 – 44, s. v. 'Medusa (Gorgo)'. Cf. also plate I.

12 Cf. CALABRESE, Brian E. *Fear in Democracy: A Study of Thucydides' Political Thought*. Diss. University of Michigan, 2008; cf. also Walter Russel MEAD's essay "Is Fear The Father Of Us All?" *http://blogs.the-american-interest.com/wrm/2011/02/14*.

13 Cf. SCHWARZ. *Die Angst in der Politik*. 142 – 43; cf. also CLAUSS, Manfred. *Sparta. Eine Einführung in seine Geschichte und Zivilisation*. Munich: Beck, 1983, esp. 112 – 14.

Thucydides recounts how, in the Athenian summer of 415 BC, the opponents of Alcibiades and the Sicilian Expedition deliberately excited a climate of collective fears with the mutilation of the hermae[14] and brought charges against Alcibiades in order to try to prevent the exit of the army and the fleet:

> In the midst of these preparations all the stone Hermae in the city of Athens, that is to say the customary square figures, so common in the doorways of private houses and temples, had in one night most of their faces mutilated. [...] The matter was taken up the more seriously, as it was thought to be ominous for the expedition, and part of a conspiracy to bring about a revolution and to upset the democracy. (VI, 27)

With the exit of the fleet, the mutilation of the hermae had missed one potential political end. Collective agitation, however, was by no means past: everyday life was now dominated by denunciations, arrests, tortures, and blatant law-breaking, while grotesque falsifications of history intensified the climate of collective fear:

> The commons had heard how oppressive the tyranny of Pisistratus and his sons had become before it ended, and further that that had been put down at last, not by themselves and Harmodius, but by the Lacedaemonians, and so were always in fear and took everything suspiciously. (VI, 53)

When only a few years later, in 411 BC, a small group of conspirators overthrew the Athenian democracy, the brutal evocation of collective fears became a crucial historical factor. This is attested by the vivid report of Thucydides, which particularly emphasizes both collective paralysis and individual helplessness in the face of this rogue regime:

> [...] Fear, and the sight of the conspirators, closed the mouths of the rest; or if any ventured to rise in opposition, he was presently put to death in some convenient way, and there was neither search for the murderers nor justice to be had against them if suspected; but the people remained motionless, being so thoroughly cowed that men thought themselves lucky to escape violence, even when they held their tongues. (VIII, 66)

While it may seem both alluring and rewarding to compare the effects of fear on the individual (isolation, unsettlement, paralysis) and the state (panic, law-breaking, up to the suspension of traditional and guaranteed civic rights) as vividly portrayed by Thucydides with reactions to scenarios of fear and panic over the epochs and times, it is necessary to systematically approach the texts we actually intend to analyze. For this reason, a short look at the Roman transmission and conceptualization of fear is due.

Just like its Greek counterpart, Roman historiography keeps evoking con-

---

14 Cf. in general MEIER, Christian. *Athen: Ein Neubeginn der Weltgeschichte*. Berlin: Siedler Verlag, 1993, esp. 620 ff.

ceptions of collective fear or classifying fear as the motive for particular actions.[15] Thus, the day of the Roman defeat through the Celts at the Allia in 387 BC was retained in the Roman calendar as *dies ater*, an ominous day of disaster,[16] and, at the same time, became a benchmark for Roman fear of external foes (*metus externus* or *metus hostilis*). This fear subsequently manifested itself time and again, triggered by events such as further Celtic attacks, the menace of Rome through Hannibal, and, finally, the conquering expeditions of the Cimbri and the Teutons.[17] Accordingly, it seemed obvious from both conceptual and rhetorical points of view to villainize the domestic political enemy using traditional experiences of fear in order to win over the senate and/or legislative assembly and provoke them into opposition. This holds particularly true from the first decades of the first century BC onwards, when Rome had been conquered three times by civil war troops and the exploitation of fears for political ends had become an almost everyday experience and routine. One speech from the fragments of Sallust's *Histories* summarizes the tenor and the terror of the political routine in the simple formula "habendus metus est aut faciendus" (to fear or to impose fear).[18] Besides Sulla and Cinna it was Caesar, in particular, who was apostrophized, on crossing the Rubicon in early 49 BC, as the new Brennus and the new Hannibal.[19]

In place of a good many more examples, here is a last concise instance of the political and rhetorical exploitation of fear in the political conflicts of the late Roman republic. In his account of the Catilinian conspiracy, Sallust has Caesar and Cato appear in an exposed position as orators in front of the senate (Sall. Cat. 51 – 52). Caesar eloquently cautions against a predominance of emotion at the expense of reason and pleads for a comparatively lenient punishment of the conspirators. Cato, on the other hand, cunningly calls upon the fundamental fears of the senators when he imagines and meticulously paints all kinds of threats to the state and the body and life of the individual, as may be documented in a short excerpt from his speech (Sall. Cat. 52, 24 – 29), in the translation of Thomas Heywood:

> Our fellow-Cittizens, and those discended of most Noble families, have conspired the
> invasion of their Countrey! They have done their utmost in the quarrell, to ingage the

---

15 Cf. e.g. HEINZ, Wolff-Rüdiger. *Die Furcht als politisches Phänomen bei Tacitus.* Heuremata Vol. 4. Amsterdam: B.R. Grüner, 1975.

16 Cf. Gell. V,17,2.

17 Cf. BELLEN, Heinz. *Metus Gallicus – Metus Punicus. Zum Furchtmotiv in der römischen Republik.* Stuttgart: Steiner, 1985; KNEPPE, Alfred. "Metus und Securitas. Angst und Politik in der römischen Kaiserzeit." In: Franz Bosbach (ed.). *Angst und Politik in der europäischen Geschichte.* Dettelbach: Röll, 2000. 53 – 66, esp. 55 ff.

18 Sall. Hist. Fr. 1,55,10.

19 Cf. Cic. Att. 7,11,1;3.

French, a Nation alwaies in deadlie hatred of the Roman name. The Captaine of the Warre, in person braveth you at your gates: and yet, you stand looking one uppon another; doubtfull and irresolute what to do, with those whom you have apprehended within your wals. Shall I enforme you? Then thus: They are young Gentlemen, deceived through foolish Ambition: Let them find favour: yea, let them depart armed; without doubt, this your lenity, and pittie, upon the next occasions, shall turne you to miserie.

The maine is bitter, ful of horror, but you feare it not! Yes iwis; and that extreamelie: why then like cowards and men of basest mould stand you still, straining curtesie who shal march formost? Well, I know the reasons. Now, as in former times, in most imminent dangers you trust that the immortall Goddes will turne all to the best. Fooles that wee are! To think that the Gods will be won by Womanish vowes and idle Sacrifices, without watching, without painstaking, and good Counsel. Where these stand joyntly imployed, al things come to happie ends. At Sloth and Cowardice the heavenly powers are offended.[20]

Cato's plea, designed to evoke fears and to target the audience's affects, is crowned with success: those conspirators that have been seized in Rome are executed (Sall. Cat. 53,1). Sallust's speech of Cato observes the rhetorical practice of the late republic in many details; a rhetoric which Aristotle had already demanded in his *Rhetoric*, in the passage on fear:

[...] when it is advisable that the audience should be frightened, the orator must make them feel that they really are in danger of something, pointing out that it has happened to others who were stronger than they are, and is happening, or has happened, to people like themselves, at the hands of unexpected people, in an unexpected form, and at an unexpected time.[21]

This rhetorical recommendation refers back to the definitional passages in the *Rhetoric*, where Aristotle brings forward some reflections and distinctions on the nature of fear and its general political relevance that are hardly to be overestimated in their relevance for our purposes:

Fear may be defined as a pain or disturbance due to a mental picture of some destructive or painful evil in the future. [...] And even these only if they appear not remote but so near as to be imminent: we do not fear things that are a very long way off: for instance, we all know we shall die, but we are not troubled thereby, because death is not close at hand. From this definition it will follow that fear is caused by whatever we feel has great power of destroying or of harming us in ways that tend to cause us great pain. Hence the very indications of such things are terrible, making us feel that the terrible thing itself is close at hand; the approach of what is terrible is just what we

---

20 SALLUST. *The Conspiracy of Catiline and The War of Jugurtha.* Translated by Thomas Heywood, Anno 1608, with an Introduction by Whibley, Charles. The Tudor Translations. London: Constable and Co, 1924. Chapter XVI (109).
21 ARISTOTLE. *Rhetoric.* Translated by William Rhys Roberts (1954). New York: Random House, 1984. Rhet. II, 5 (1383a9 – 13).

mean by 'danger'. Such indications are the enmity and anger of people who have power to do something to us; for it is plain that they have the will to do it, and so they are on the point of doing it. Also injustice in possession of power; for it is the unjust man's will to do evil that makes him unjust. Also outraged virtue in possession of power; for it is plain that, when outraged, it always has the will to retaliate, and now it has the power to do so. Also fear felt by those who have the power to do something to us, since such persons are sure to be ready to do it. And since most men tend to be bad – slaves to greed, and cowards in danger – it is, as a rule, a terrible thing to be at another man's mercy; and therefore, if we have done anything horrible, those in the secret terrify us with the thought that they may betray or desert us. [...] We also fear those who are to be feared by stronger people than ourselves: if they can hurt those stronger people, still more can they hurt us; and for the same reason, we fear those whom those stronger people are actually afraid of. Also those who have destroyed people stronger than we are. Also those who are attacking people weaker than we are: either they are already formidable, or they will be so when they have thus grown stronger. Of those we have wronged, and of our enemies or rivals, it is not the passionate and outspoken whom we have to fear, but the quiet, dissembling, unscrupulous; since we never know when they are upon us, we can never be sure they are at a safe distance. All terrible things are more terrible if they give us no chance of retrieving a blunder either no chance at all, or only one that depends on our enemies and not ourselves. Those things are also worse which we cannot, or cannot easily, help. Speaking generally, anything causes us to feel fear that when it happens to, or threatens, others cause us to feel pity.[22]

In light of the high significance, as outlined above, of affects in general and of fear in particular for rhetorical schooling, representations of fear became an important object of instruction and study in the rhetorical schools. This holds particularly true for the training of the *suasoriae*, i.e. speeches that were held in front of the senate and the legislative assemblies, and the *controversiae*, i.e. speeches that were held in court by the prosecutor or the defense.[23] This, again, encouraged the development and establishment of descriptive topoi.[24] Seneca's *Controversiae* with their emphasis on fear of tyrants afford concise examples of this, as do the *Sententiae* of Publilius Syrus (first century BC), which were likewise very popular during antiquity and the Renaissance. The *Sententiae* hand down more than 20 polished maxims on fear in proverbial style, a number of which refer to the power political implications, e.g.:

> 379: Multos timere debet quem multi timent. (Many must fear whom many fear); 398: Metus improbos compescit non clementia. (Fear, not clemency, restrains the wicked); 471: Nemo timendo ad summum pervenit locum. (Fear never brought one to the top);

---

22 ARISTOTLE. Rhet. II,5 (1382a21 – 1382b27).
23 Cf. KNEPPE, Alfred. "Metus und Securitas." esp. 54 ff. Cf. also FUHRMANN, Manfred. *Die antike Rhetorik, Eine Einführung.* Munich: Artemis, 1990, esp. 79 – 80.
24 Cf. KNEPPE, Alfred. *Metus temporum. Zur Bedeutung von Angst in Politik und Gesellschaft der römischen Kaiserzeit des 1. und 2. Jhdts. n. Chr.* Stuttgart: Steiner, 1994, esp. 43 ff.

704: Ubi nihil timetur, quod timeatur nascitur. (When nothing is feared, something arises to fear); 728: Virtutis omnis impedimentum est timor. (All virtue finds an obstacle in fear)[25]

Once Octavian/Augustus had successfully put an end to the chaotic civil war state of "habendus metus est aut faciundus" (Sall. Hist. Fr. 1,55,10) and institutionalized the monarchy, he made a point of claiming, in the res gestae – his famous record of deeds – that he had accomplished (by means of his expenditures and care) to free the whole city from fear and imminent danger within only a few days (RGDA 5,2: "[...] intra dies paucos metu et periclo praesenti civitatem universum liberarem inpensa et cura mea."). Even though the word metus in this sentence referred exclusively to the capital's plebs in the specific crisis of 23/22 BC,[26] Augustus' cura brought relief and provided freedom from fear as well as safety (securitas). This idea was subsequently adopted and consistently expanded for propagandistic ends in Augustan poetry.[27] At the same time, however, it also demonstrates that, through the political dominance of the princeps, the power to arouse fear or to determine its degree was concentrated almost exclusively in the princeps. This particularly turned regime changes into potential times of crisis when political discontinuities naturally generated fears for life and career, as documented, for instance, in the massive uncertainties of the regime changes of 69 AD.[28] Emperors such as Tiberius, Caligula, Nero, Domitian, Commodus, Caracalla, Elagabal, or, in late antiquity, Valentinian III spread fear and terror through their cynical waywardness and were stylized into classical tyrants by Roman historiography and biography.[29] These portrayals were in consistent continuation of the traditional Hellenistic and republican topical rhetoric of tyranny. Imposing lines of tragedy such as Caligula's favorite dictum "Oderint, dum metuant (Let them hate me, so they but fear me)"[30] thus turn into catchy proverbial self-characterizations, which, notwithstanding their topic, enduringly determine the historical judgment of the emperor.

Let us conclude the – potentially endless – chain of examples of classical

---

25 PUBLILIUS SYRUS. Sententiae. In: Minor Latin Poets. Translated by J. Wight Duff and Arnold M. Duff. Loeb Classical Library. Cambridge/MA: Harvard University Press, 1982.
26 Cf. KIENAST, Dietmar. Augustus. Prinzeps und Monarch. Darmstadt: WBG, 1982, esp. 92–93.
27 Cf. Prop. 4,6,37; 4,6,41; Hor. Carm. 4,14,41 ff; 4,15,17 ff (cf. Alfred KNEPPE. "Metus und Securitas." Esp. 63).
28 Cf. Tac. Hist. 2,52 ff; cf. FUHRMANN, Manfred. "Das Vierkaiserjahr bei Tacitus. Über den Aufbau der Historien Buch I – III." In: Philologus 104 (1960): 250–78; cf. also WELLESLEY, Kenneth. The Long Year A. D. 69. London: Elek, 1975.
29 Cf. sources and literature in BAUMANN, Uwe. "Thomas More and the Classical Tyrant." In: Moreana Vol. 86: Thomas More and the Classics. Edited by Ralph Keen and Daniel Kinney (1985): 108–26, esp. 108–13.
30 Suet. Cal. 30,1 (SUETONIUS. With an English Translation by J.C. ROLFE (1913). London: Heinemann, 1970).

representations of political fear at this point, leaving out similar instances from medieval historiography, and completely omitting the history of institutions such as the Holy Inquisition that were primarily based on fear and deterrence, and draw attention to the following points: descriptive topoi and representations of political fear, which had mostly already been formed in classical antiquity, were – not least due to the reception of classical rhetoric – well-known during the European Renaissance. Above all, functionalized scenarios of fear played a vital role in the justification of preemptive wars under international law,[31] where the imagined fear of a universal monarchy might already suffice.[32] Emblematics, too, offers several memorable instances: one emblem by Juan de Horozco y Covarrubias (1589) depicts Pandora opening the box, where hope and fear constitute the two poles of human existence,[33] while another one by Guillaume de la Perrières from 1539 shows a dog (love/faithfulness) and a rabbit (fear) jointly holding up a crown and thus declaring love and fear in equal parts as the central pillars of monarchical rule.[34] One of the classical, albeit controversial, texts of the theoretical discussions of politics in the Renaissance, Niccolò Machiavelli's *Il Principe / The Prince*, analyses the political role of fear *en detail:* thus, chapter XVII starts as if it were a commentary on Caligula's notorious "Oderint, dum metuant" and implicitly harks back to the definitional distinctions and conceptualizations of human nature in Aristotle:

> Upon this a question arises: whether it be better to be loved than feared or feared than loved? It may be answered that one should wish to be both, but, because it is difficult to unite them in one person, it is much safer to be feared than loved, when, of the two, either must be dispensed with. Because this is to be asserted in general of men, that they are ungrateful, fickle, false, cowardly, covetous, and as long as you succeed they are yours entirely; they will offer you their blood, property, life, and children, as is said above, when the need is far distant; but when it approaches they turn against you. And that prince who, relying entirely on their promises, has neglected other precautions, is ruined; because friendships that are obtained by payments, and not by greatness or nobility of mind, may indeed be earned, but they are not secured, and in time of need cannot be relied upon; and men have less scruple in offending one who is beloved than

31 Cf. Oschmann, Antje. "Der *Metus Iustus* in der deutschen Kriegsrechtslehre des 17. Jahrhunderts." In: Franz Bosbach (ed.). *Angst und Politik in der europäischen Geschichte.* Dettelbach: Röll, 2000. 101–31; cf. also Leinsle, Ulrich G. "Kasuistik der Angst. *Metus* in der Moralphilosophie und -theologie der Frühen Neuzeit." In: Franz Bosbach (ed.). *Angst und Politik in der europäischen Geschichte.* Dettelbach: Röll, 2000. 85–99.
32 Cf. Bosbach, Franz. "Angst und Universalmonarchie." In: Franz Bosbach (ed.). *Angst und Politik in der europäischen Geschichte.* Dettelbach: Röll, 2000. 151–66.
33 Cf. Henkel, Arthur and Albrecht Schöne (eds.). *Emblemata. Handbuch zur Sinnbildkunst des XVI. und XVII. Jahrhunderts.* Stuttgart: Metzler, 1967 [1789].
34 Cf. Henkel and Schöne. *Emblemata.* 555 (plate II); cf. in general Paulette Choné. "Angst im Spiegel der Emblematik (16.-17. Jahrhundert)." In: Franz Bosbach (ed.). *Angst und Politik in der europäischen Geschichte.* Dettelbach: Röll, 2000. 133–49.

one who is feared, for love is preserved by the link of obligation which, owing to the baseness of men, is broken at every opportunity for their advantage; but fear preserves you by a dread of punishment which never fails.

Nevertheless a prince ought to inspire fear in such a way that, if he does not win love, he avoids hatred; because he can endure very well being feared whilst he is not hated, which will always be as long as he abstains from the property of his citizens and subjects and from their women. But when it is necessary for him to proceed against the life of someone, he must do it on proper justification and for manifest cause, but above all things he must keep his hands off the property of others, because men more quickly forget the death of their fathers than the loss of their patrimony. [...] Returning to the question of being feared or loved, I come to the conclusion that, men loving according to their own will and fearing according to that of the prince, a wise prince should establish himself on that which is in his own control and not in that of others; he must endeavour only to avoid hatred, as is noted.[35]

III. Representations of Fear in the *Declamatio*, the *Epigrams* of Thomas More and the Politics of Henry VIII

In November 1506, Badius Ascensius in Paris published a book which immediately established Thomas More (1477/8–1535) as a brilliant translator and distinguished authority in classical rhetoric in the *res publica litterarum* of European humanism: *Luciani viri quam disertissimi compluria opuscula longe festiuissima ab Erasmo Roterodamo & Thoma Moro interpretibus optimis in latinorum linguam traducta.* This *editio princeps* of Erasmus' and More's translations of Lucian's dialogues contained 28 renditions by Erasmus, four by More, as well as one original *declamatio* of each of the friends.[36] More had chosen the dialogues *Cynicus, Menippus seu Necromantia, Philopseudes* and the *Ty-rannicida* and had explicated his choice in detail in a dedicatory letter to Thomas Ruthall, secretary to Henry VII. The translations pose no problems whatsoever. They are – just like the ones done by Erasmus – precise renditions of the Greek source and in this differ strongly from some of the earlier translations of Lu-

---

35 MACHIAVELLI, Niccolò. *The Prince.* Translated by W.K. Marriott. Chicago et al.: William Benton, 1952, Chap. XVII: "Concerning Cruelty and Clemency, and whether it is better to be Loved than Feared", 23–24. Cf. in general also HOEGES, Dirk. *Niccolò Machiavelli. Die Macht und der Schein.* Munich: Beck, 2000, esp. 171 ff; MÜNKLER, Herfried. *Machiavelli. Die Begründung des politischen Denkens der Neuzeit aus der Krise der Republik Florenz.* Frankfurt M.: Fischer, 1984, esp. 241 ff.

36 Cf. THOMPSON, Craig R. (ed.). Thomas More, *Translations of Lucian,* The Complete Works of St. Thomas More (CW) Vol. 3, Part I. New Haven/London: Yale University Press, 1974, esp. xxviii. Cf. also BAUMANN, Uwe. "Lukianübersetzungen." In: Uwe Baumann and Hans Peter Heinrich (eds.). *Thomas Morus. Humanistische Schriften.* Darmstadt: WBG, 1986. 40–54.

cian.[37] The only text relevant to our discussion is Lucian's *Tyrannicida*, a *declamatio*, i. e. one of the exercise speeches that were primarily used in the antique rhetorical schools of Greek provenance. It is a fictive civil case speech preserved in large number, in which legal problems relating to the tyranny laws were presented to students for practice.[38] Regardless of the objections that had already been brought forward in classical antiquity against a mode of education thus out of touch with reality,[39] which More certainly was familiar with, he chose the *Tyrannicida* for his translation and furthermore authored – in friendly competition with Erasmus – a reply to Lucian's *declamatio*.[40] The initial situation in Lucian's *Tyrannicida* illustrates how complex and complicated a judicial assessment can be: there is a law that allots a high reward to tyrannicides in a city-state subdued by a tyrant. After a fierce struggle with some guards, one citizen succeeds in entering the tyrant's castle. His intention is to dispatch the tyrant. He does not, however, locate him but only his son, whom he slays. He leaves his sword sticking in the corpse (or throws it down next to the corpse).[41] At the sight of his slain son, the father is overcome by grief and anguish and takes his own life with the same sword that has already killed his son. The citizen who had executed the tyrant's son now lays claim to the reward for the tyrannicide. More's reply to the detailed argumentation of this *declamatio* is entirely devised according to the rules of classical rhetoric.[42] In his *exordium*, following a short sketch of the facts of the disputed case (CW 3, I, 96/4 ff), he states that he intends to prove (CW 3,I, 100/1 – 4) that only Fortune and the mercy of the gods are to be held responsible for the events (the tyrant's death in particular). More refutes every single one of the claimant's reasons for his pretense to the reward in the *confirmatio* and *refutatio* of his speech: 1. because he killed the son, 2. because he tried to kill the father, and 3. because the father committed suicide with the sword left behind by the claimant.[43] In his confutation of the claimant's arguments More drafts a sketch of the tyrant that adopts many topoi of the antique topic of tyranny (e. g. the tyrant's crimes: robbery, murder, rape; the tyrant as a wild beast; non-

---

37 Cf. BAUMANN, Uwe. "Übersetzungstheorie und Übersetzungspraxis im englischen Früh-humanismus: Sir Thomas More und Sir Thomas Elyot." In: Karl-Egon Lönne (ed.). *Kultur-wandel im Spiegel des Sprachwandels*. Tübingen/Basel: Francke, 1995. 107 – 37, esp. 109 – 16.
38 Cf. BONNER, S.F. *Roman Declamation in the Late Republic and Early Empire*. Liverpool: Liverpool University Press, 1949, esp. 84 – 132.
39 Cf. e. g. Petr. Sat. 1; Tac. Dial. 35,5; Juv. Sat. 7, 150 – 51.
40 Cf. BAUMANN. "Lukianübersetzungen." 44.
41 Cf. on this decisive difference CW 3, I, 118/15 – 120/6 and 122/32 – 124/1.
42 Cf. THOMPSON. CW 3, I, 153 ff. Cf. also RAYMENT, C.S. "The 'Tyrannicide' of Erasmus: Translated Excerpts with Introduction and Commentary." In: *Speech Monographs* 26 (1959): 233 – 47 and BAUMANN, Uwe. "Thomas More and the Classical Tyrant." In: *Moreana* 22 (1985): 108 – 27.
43 Cf. BAUMANN. "Lukianübersetzungen." Esp. 46 – 49.

existence of laws in a tyranny)[44] and he avails himself of the same rhetoric
strategy that Sallust's Cato (Cat. 51 – 52), for instance, had so spectacularly
employed in the Roman senate: the oppressively realistic staging of scenarios of
fear.[45] More particularly takes the thought of what could have happened had the
tyrant not taken his own life on seeing his slain son as his point of departure.
Time and again, he demonstrates drastically to the judges the danger and suffering which would have befallen the city had the tyrant acted according to his
nature as a tyrant:

> Quod si Tyrannus id uoluisset, quod tute haud dubie fecisses, & quod illum quoque
> facturum longe uerisimilius quam quod fecit fuit: conclamasset satellites, coegisset
> sicarios, armasset carnifices, ac prolato filij cadauere, & natura crudelis, & tam atroci
> spectaculo irritatus, iram ac furorem illum effudisset, primum in te, per quem filius
> occisus, deinde in urbem uniuersam, propter quam occisus est, quae si contigissent (ut
> tua dementia propemodum contigerant) neque tu miser hodie uiueres, qui hoc prae-
> mium peteres, neque nos Rempublicam ullam a qua peti posset haberemus. (CW 3, I,
> 120/21 – 29)

> [What if the tyrant had been disposed to do what you yourself would doubtless have
> done, and what it is far more likely he would have done than what he actually did –
> summon his guard, call his ruffians together, arm his scoundrels; and, when the body of
> his son was brought before him, his cruel nature and his rage at so horrid a sight would
> have caused him to vent his wrath and fury first of all on you, by whom his son was slain,
> and then on the entire city for which he was slain? Had these things happened (as,
> thanks to your folly, they came close to happening), you would not be alive today, you
> miserable wretch, to seek this reward, nor would we have any commonwealth of which
> it could be sought.]

A citizen who has subjected the whole city to a dreadful threat such as this cannot
claim a reward for this deed, whose consequences, imagined in violently graphic
words, did not ensue only due to the mercy of the immortal gods. The city and
each single citizen had barely escaped political chaos and bloody destruction by
the skin of their teeth:

> Patrem ergo fingamus (ut dixi) uiuentem, ac filio quidem unico orbatum, sed satel-
> litum tamen caterua cinctum, caedem filij lachrymantem: sed interfectori minantem,
> atque omnia suppliciorum genera destinantem, in forum uultu tristi quidem, sed
> tamen truci procurrere, & prolato quem tu reliquisti gladio, ingentia polliceri praemia,
> si quis eius ensis dominum prodiderit: hic tu foro iam ab illo, atque eius satellitibus
> occupato, & in caput tuum quaestione iam haberi coepta, in publicum fortis Tyran-
> nicida procurre, & in medios globos irruens Tyrannum te occidisse proclamita, lib-
> ertatem omnibus denuncia, ac Tyrannicidij praemium postula. Quid fugis? Quid la-

---

44 Cf. the analysis, the discussion of sources and scholarly literature in BAUMANN. "Thomas
    More and the Classical Tyrant." 108 – 27.
45 Cf. e.g.: CW 3, I, 104/4 – 18; 110/18 – 23; 118/4 – 11; 120/21 – 29; 122/12 – 32; 124/15 – 31.

tebras quaeris? Quid Tyrannicida metuis? An non libera est respublica? An non Tyrannus occisus est? Neque ergo is quem peremisti Tyrannus erat. Sed quidam potius
Tyranni satelles, neque eius morte ciuitas libertati restituta est, quod solum pauloante
dicebas huius legis spectasse latorem. (CW 3, I, 104/4 – 18)

[Let us therefore, as I said, imagine the father living and bereft of his only son, but
nevertheless surrounded by his palace guard; bewailing the murder of his son, yet
threatening the murderer and intending all kinds of punishments. Let us imagine him
with mournful but grim countenance rushing into the forum and, displaying the sword
you left behind, promising vast rewards if anyone makes known the owner of that
sword. With the forum here already occupied by him and his retinue, and inquiry
already directed towards you, rush forward, brave tyrannicide, and, dashing into the
midst of the crowd, announce that you have killed the tyrant, proclaim liberty for all,
and demand a tyrannicide's reward! Why do you run away? Why look for a hiding-
place? Why are you, the tyrannicide, afraid? Is not the commonwealth free? Has not the
tyrant been killed? – Then the one you slew was not the tyrant but rather some
accomplice of the tyrant; nor was the city by his death restored to liberty, which, as you
said a short time ago, was the sole end the proposer of this law had in view.]

More receives and varies the same topoi of the antique topic of tyranny as in the
Declamatio [...] Lvcianicae Respondens in some twenty of his Latin epigrams
(1519).[46] Together with the *History of King Richard III* and the *declamatio*, these
epigrams strikingly validate Erasmus of Rotterdam's assertion concerning his
friend's incentives in choosing these topics: More had always conceived great
abhorrence for tyranny.[47] Alongside several epigrams that effectively vary
classical proverbs on the paralyzing futility of fear (cf. CW 3, II, no. 50 and
no. 69), two of these epigrams are of special interest here: they unveil, in judi-
cious distinctions and concise, trenchant language, the logical and rhetorical
relationship between political fear, rule, and the ideal sovereign (CW 3, II,
no. 120):

---

46 Cf. MILLER, Clarence H., Leicester BRADNER, Charles A. LYNCH and Revilo P. OLIVER (eds.).
   Thomas More, *Latin Poems*, The Complete Works of St. Thomas More (CW), Vol. 3, Part II.
   New Haven/London: Yale University Press, 1984; cf. also BAUMANN, Uwe. *Die Antike in den
   Epigrammen und Briefen Sir Thomas Mores*. Paderborn et al.: Schöningh, 1984, esp. 54 – 57.
47 Cf. ALLEN, Percy Stafford, Helen Mary ALLEN and H.W. GARROD (eds.). *Opus Epistolarum
   Des. Erasmi Roterodami*, 12 vols. Oxford: Oxford University Press, 1906 – 1958. IV, 999, 87 –
   99 (Erasmus to Ulrich von Hutten). Cf. also FENLON, Dermot. "Thomas More and Tyranny."
   In: *Journal of Ecclesiastical History* 32 (1981): 453 – 76; BAUMANN. "Thomas More and the
   Classical Tyrant." Esp. 113 ff.

Regem Non Satellitivm Sed
Virtvs Reddit Tvtvm

Non timor inuisus, non alta palatia regem,
Non compilata plebe tuentur opes,
Non rigidus uili mercabilis aere satelles
Qui sic alterius fiet ut huius erat.
Tutus erit, populum qui sic regit, utiliorem
Vt populus nullum censeat esse sibi.

[A King is protected, not by a
corps of guards, but by his own good qualities.

Not fear (accompanied by hatred), not towering palaces, not wealth wrung from a
plundered people protects a king. The stern bodyguard, hired for a pittance, offers no
protection, for the guard will serve a new master as he served the old. He will be safe
who so rules his people that they judge none other would promote their interests
better.]

Where this quite conventional epigram could still be read as a humanistic reply
to the question of how security can be granted to both sovereign and sovereignty,
as discussed contemporaneously by others such as Niccolò Machiavelli (in
chapter XVII of his *Il Principe / The Prince*), epigram no. 238 explicates the
nature of rule, and effectively every sovereign, as fundamentally endangered and
subject to a range of fears and apprehensions:

De Sollicita Potentvm Vita.

Semper habet miseras immensa potentia curas,
Anxia perpetuis sollicitudinibus.
Non prodit, multis nisi circumseptus ab armis,
Non nisi gustato uescitur ante cibo.
Tutamenta quidem sunt haec, tamen haec male tutum
Illum, aliter tutus qui nequit esse, docent.
Nempe satellitium, metuendos admonet enses,
Toxica praegustans esse timenda docet.
Ergo timore locus quisnam uacat hic? ubi gignunt
Haec eadem, pellunt quae metuenda, metum. (CW 3, II, no. 238)

[On the Anxious Life of Rulers

Immense power always brings miserable worries, tormented as it is by ever-present
fears. Such a person does not venture out unless surrounded by a large armed guard,
does not eat food which has not been tasted in advance. Certainly these precautions are
aids to safety; yet they show that a man is not safe if he cannot be safe without them.
Thus a bodyguard reveals fear of an assassin's sword. A food-taster manifests fear of

poison. And so what place is without fear in such a life? - where even the very means of repelling what is to be feared themselves engender fear.]

While this epigram can still primarily be read as a general abstract analysis in terms of moral philosophy and political theory, two different epigrams focus on concepts of fear from a considerably more specific historical perspective. These two epigrams form part of the five epigrams that Thomas More presented Henry VIII with immediately after his coronation (1509) in a – arguably somewhat clumsily illustrated – manuscript (CW 3, II, no. 19–23). They are typical specimen of panegyrics that, praising the young sovereign, ask to be read simultaneously as credentials for the author himself.[48] Their ebullient praise of Henry can by all means be called conventional, albeit ornamented with a multitude of flattering comparisons with heroes of the ancient world.[49] Tacitly, this once more accentuates their author's excellent and comprehensive humanistic education. In distinction from his contemporaries[50] and also in deliberate departure from the rhetorical traditions of the *panegyricus*, where explicit criticism of the predecessors was not reconcilable with the *decorum*, More praises Henry VIII for having immediately expelled general fear from England; a fear that had paralyzed the entire political, social, and economic life (CW 3, II, no. 19/26–45):

Nobilitas, uulgi iamdudum obnoxia faeci,
Nobilitas, nimium nomen inane diu,
Nunc caput attollit, nunc tali rege triumphat,
Et merito causas unde triumphet, habet.
Mercator uarijs deterritus ante tributis,
Nunc maris insuetas puppe resulcat aquas.
Leges inualidae prius, imo nocere coactae,
Nunc uires gaudent obtinuisse suas.
Congaudent omnes pariter pariterque rependunt
Omnes uenturo damna priora bona.

---

48 Cf. Lüsse, Beate. "Panegyric Poetry on the Coronation of King Henry VIII: The King's Praise and the Poet's Self-Presentation." In: Uwe Baumann (ed.). *Henry VIII. in History, Historiography and Literature.* Frankfurt M. et al.: Lang, 1992. 49–77. Cf. also Grace, Damian. "Thomas More's *Epigrammata:* Political Theory in a Poetic Idiom." In: *Parergon* N.S. 3 (1985): 115–29.

49 Cf. the sources and details in Baumann. *Die Antike in den Epigrammen und Briefen Sir Thomas Mores.* Esp. 50 ff.

50 Cf. and compare e.g. Skelton, John. "A Lawde and Prayse Made for Our Sovereigne Lord the Kyng." In: John Scattergood (ed.). John Skelton, *The Complete English Poems.* New Haven/London: Yale University Press, 1983. 110–12 and Hawes, Stephen "A Ioyfull meditacyon to all Englonde of the coronacyon of our moost naturall souerayne lorde kynge Henry the eyght." In: Florence W. Gluck and Alice B. Morgan (eds.). Stephen Hawes, *The Minor Poems,* Early English Text Society. London/Toronto: Oxford University Press, 1974. 84–91. Cf. also Lüsse. "Panegyric Poetry on the Coronation of King Henry VIII." Esp. 50 ff.

Iam quas abdiderat caecis timor ante latebris,
Promere quisque suas gaudet et audet opes.
Iam iuuat O, potuit tot furum si qua tot uncas
Tam circumspectas fallere praeda manus.
Non iam diuitias ullum est (magnum esse solebat)
Quaesitas nullo crimen habere dolo.
Non metus occultos insibilat aure susurros,
Nemo quod taceat, quodue susurret, habet.
Iam delatores uolupe est contemnere, nemo
Deferri, nisi qui detulit ante, timet.

[The nobility, long since at the mercy of the dregs of the population, the nobility, whose title has too long been without meaning, now lifts its head, now rejoices in such a king, and has proper reason for rejoicing. The merchant, heretofore deterred by numerous taxes, now once again plows seas grown unfamiliar. Laws, heretofore powerless – yes, even laws put to unjust ends – now happily have regained their proper authority. All are equally happy. All weigh their earlier losses against the advantages to come. Now each man happily does not hesitate to show the possessions which in the past his fear kept hidden in dark seclusion. Now there is enjoyment in any profit which managed to escape the many sly clutching hands of the many thieves. No longer is it a criminal offense to own property which was honestly acquired (formerly it was a serious offense). No longer does fear hiss whispered secrets in one's ear, for no one has secrets either to keep or to whisper. Now it is a delight to ignore informers. Only ex-informers fear informers now.]

Alongside the continually varied praise of the outstanding physical, intellectual, and political excellence of the youthful sovereign, King Henry VIII as warrantor of reclaimed civil and economic liberty is positively turned into the leitmotif of sovereign praise in this epigram no. 19 (cf. CW 3, II, no. 19, 120ff, cf. also no. 20 – 22), which at the same time explicitly celebrates the disappearance of fear (CW 3, II, no. 19/86 – 89): "Quod sic afficimur, quod libertate potimur, / Quodque abiere timor, damna, pericla, dolor, / Quod rediere simul, pax, commoda, gaudia, risus, / Eximij uirtus principis inde patet. [In that we are treated thus and gaining our liberty, in that fear, harm, danger, grief have vanished, while peace, ease, joy, and laughter have returned – therein is revealed the excellence of our distinguished prince]". This triumph over general fear as a first manifest proof of Henry's superior virtues as a sovereign naturally only holds true for England: external foes are certainly entitled (and supposed) to fear Henry. More than that, being loved by his own subjects and feared by his enemies bestows peace and security upon Henry's rule (cf. CW 3, II, no. 19, 128ff). The last one of the coronation epigrams (CW 3, II, no. 23) substantiates – from a perspective that seems almost sibylline – the historical opportunity proffered by this emphatically celebrated accession to power: Henry VIII,[51] the natural son of Elizabeth of York and Henry Tudor, unites the bloodlines of the white and the red rose. He becomes warrantor of the universal yearning for peace and bliss, even though their realization may come at a price, too:

> Scilicet huic uni species, decor, atque uenustas,
> Et color, et uirtus, est utriusque rosae.
> Alterutram ergo rosam uel solam quisquis amauit,
> Hanc in qua nunc est, quicquid amauit amet.
> At qui tam ferus est, ut non amet, ille timebat.
> Nempe etiam spinas flos habet iste suas. (CW 3, II, no. 23/9 – 14)

[In other words, this one rose has the beauty, grace, loveliness, color, and strength which used to belong to both. Therefore, if anyone loved either one of these roses, let him love this one in which is found whatever he loved. But if anyone is so fierce that he will not love this rose, then he will fear it, for this flower has its own thorns, too.]

The image of England under Henry's father, Henry VII, as an unfree and as it were politically and economically paralyzed commonwealth covered by a spider's web of spies, financial agents in particular, in More's account (CW 3, II, no. 19) culminates in a collective fear, for which, ultimately, the king himself is supposed to bear responsibility. More was by no means isolated in his assessment of Henry VII as a ruthless miser and exploiter who squeezed money out of his subjects in any way he could – by means of recourse to long forgotten feudal laws, exorbitantly high fines, and an exceedingly complicated taxation system. This is forcefully verified by a multitude of contemporary statements in the same tenor.[52] Henry VIII already demonstrated with his very first measures that he did not intend to follow in the steps of his father, who had left behind thoroughly secure state finances at his death, in his fiscal policy. On the one hand, he suggested a concrete amendment (*An Act that Informations upon Penal Statutes shall be made within three years*)[53]. On the other hand, he had his father's two

---

51 Cf. e.g. BAUMANN, Uwe. *Heinrich VIII. Mit Selbstzeugnissen und Bilddokumenten.* Reinbek: Rowohlt, 2010, esp. 20 ff; GUY, John A. *Tudor England.* Oxford/New York: Oxford University Press, 1990, esp. 80 ff; SCARISBRICK, J.J. *Henry VIII.* Berkeley/Los Angeles: University of California Press, 1968, esp. 3 ff.

52 Cf. a variety of sources in LOCKYER, Roger. *Henry VII.* Seminar Studies in History. London: Longman, 1968, esp. 108 – 44.

53 Cf. esp. the introductory lines of the act, which focus on a historical analysis: "Where in times past have been made divers and many acts and statutes penal … the great number of which statutes penal have not been put in execution till now of late, by mean whereof many and divers good and well disposed persons ignorant of any such statutes, their heirs and executors, have been put to great loss of goods, vexation and trouble by action, information and indictments for offences surmised to be done contrary to the same statutes many years after the offences were surmised to be done; upon which delaying of so long time, much perjury,

most hated tax collectors, Sir Richard Empson and Edmund Dudley, incarcerated as soon as April 23, during the general jubilance for the new king. The
official version stated that they had exceeded their authorities in the past and
lined their own pockets. This charge, however, just as the charge of having
planned a *coup d'etat*, could not be proven. Regardless of quite possible diverging assessments when it comes to details of single aspects in the trials,
biographers and historians are largely agreed in their political evaluation: Sir
Richard Empson and Edmund Dudley were charged as allegedly being responsible for the generally abhorred fiscal policy of Henry VII and executed in
the late summer of 1510; in truth, they were political scapegoats:

> Henry VII died on 21 April 1509, and Empson was arrested just three days later. He was
> indicted in both his private and public capacities before oyer and terminer commis-
> sions appointed later that year. Treason was read into his summons (for his own
> protection) of armed men to London as and after the king lay dying: for this he was
> charged before a special commission which met at Northampton on 8 August 1509.
> Taken from the Tower of London to Northampton Castle, Empson pleaded his own case
> at the bar of the court on 1 October, but was convicted and sentenced to the death of a
> traitor. He was attainted in the parliament of January-February 1510, and beheaded,
> along with Dudley, on Tower Hill on 17 August following.
>
> At Henry VII's death Dudley had many enemies and few friends even among his fellow
> councillors. Henry died late on 21 April 1509, but the fact was not announced until the
> evening of the 23rd. Early on the 24th Dudley and Empson were arrested and sent to the
> Tower of London, blamed for the oppressions of the late reign. Dudley was tried in
> London in July and convicted of treason on the 18th, the charge being that on 22 April he
> had conspired to 'hold, guide and govern the King and his Council' by summoning a
> force of men to London under the leadership of various named associates [...]. He may
> well have summoned the men, a prudent and possibly widespread precaution at a time
> of political uncertainty, but it is highly unlikely he intended such a *coup d'état*. In the
> parliament of 1510, when several statutes blamed him for the injustices of the previous
> regime, a bill to attaint him and Empson passed the Commons but failed in the Lords.
> Unaware of its failure, Dudley made an unsuccessful attempt to escape from the Tower.
> [...] His fate was finally settled when Henry VIII's progress took him through the
> midlands in summer 1510. There the king heard a fresh wave of complaints about the
> injustices of his father's ministers, and resolved on their execution. Dudley was be-
> headed on Tower Hill on 17 August 1510 and buried at the London Blackfriars. Dudley
> made a convenient scapegoat for Henry VII's exactions. Certainly he had exploited his
> position as the king's executive, but so to a less extreme degree had most of Henry's
> other councillors.[54]

---

great trouble, vexation and many inconveniences ensued to great number of the king's
  subjects" (LOCKYER. *Henry VII.* 145 [document no. 33]).
54 CONDON, M. M. "Empson, Sir Richard (c. 1450–1510)." In: *Oxford Dictionary of National
  Biography.* Oxford: Oxford University Press, 2004; Online Edition, January 2008; GUNN, S.J.
  "Dudley, Edmund (c. 1462–1510)." In: *Oxford Dictionary of National Biography.* Oxford:

In retrospect, the death sentences thus turn into acts of calculated political barbarity, which, on the one side, document Henry VIII's piety towards his father, while, on the other side, they were certainly designed as trendsetting political statements which illustrated that this seductively beautiful rose indeed had its thorns. Theo Stemmler quite rightly refers to Machiavelli's *Il Principe* / *The Prince* in this context, which was written not much later and offers quite an accurate general explanation for Henry's political reckoning:

> Therefore a prince, so long as he keeps his subjects united and loyal, ought not to mind the reproach of cruelty; because with a few examples he will be more merciful than those who, through too much mercy, allow disorders to arise, from which follow murders or robberies; for these are wont to injure the whole people, whilst those executions which originate with a prince offend the individual only.[55]

While, in his cynical political calculations, Henry VIII orchestrated a deterring example here, he still laid it down with at least a semblance of legality. This, again, was consistent with one of Machiavelli's demands: "But when it is necessary for him to proceed against the life of someone, he must do it on proper justification and for manifest cause, [...]".[56] In the populist staging of his power politics, Henry VIII time and again relied on political show trials, on both explicit and implicit threats of scenarios of terror and fear.[57] This, alongside his quite cynical concept of politics, is certainly one of the reasons why Henry VIII himself was controlled by fears and apprehensions for all of his life. In public, sure enough, he concealed these beneath his self-confident, radiant and chivalrous image as a sovereign. His accession to power had been, after all, the first one without bloodshed since almost a century. Less than 25 years ago, Richard III had lost the English crown to Henry Tudor (VII) in the wake of the battle of Bosworth (1485). Henry VIII regarded Tudor rule, emphatically and strategically celebrated in public as it was, as far from secured.[58] The menace of a relapse into

---

Oxford University Press, 2004; Online Edition, May 2010. Cf. also the short summary in SCARISBRICK, J.J. *Henry VIII.* 11–12; cf. also HOROWITZ, Mark R. "Richard Empson, Minister of Henry VII." In: *Bulletin of the Institute of Historical Research* 55 (1982): 35–49.

55 MACHIAVELLI. *The Prince.* Chap. XVII, 23. Cf. also STEMMLER, Theo (ed.). *Die Liebesbriefe Heinrichs VIII. an Anna Boleyn.* Zürich: Belser, 1988. 45.

56 MACHIAVELLI. *The Prince.* Chap. XVII, 24.

57 Cf. in general BAUMANN. *Heinrich VIII.* 30ff; GUY. *Tudor England.* 80ff; SCARISBRICK. *Henry VIII. passim.*

58 Cf. a variety of sources in BAUMANN, Uwe. "Politik, Propaganda und Mythologie. Zur politischen Mythologiedeutung in der englischen Renaissance." In: Bodo Guthmüller and Wilhelm Kühlmann (eds.). *Renaissancekultur und antike Mythologie.* Tübingen: Niemeyer, 1999. 207–29, esp. 210ff; BAUMANN, Uwe. "Artus-Stoff und Arturische Motive in der Geschichte, Kultur und Literatur Englands der Tudor- und Stuartzeit." In: Stefan Zimmer (ed.). *König Artus lebt! Eine Ringvorlesung des Mittelalterzentrums der Universität Bonn.* Heidelberg: Winter, 2005. 273–96, esp. 281 ff. Cf. also LOADES, David. *Henry VIII. Court, Church and Conflict.* Richmond: The National Archives, 2007; STARKEY, David. *Henry. Virtuous*

the horrid civil war conditions of the Wars of the Roses seemed quite real to him. These kinds of apprehensions entailed ghastly ramifications: to begin with, the systematic elimination of potential pretenders to the throne (e. g. Edmund de la Pole [1513]; Edward Stafford, Duke of Buckingham [1521]). Another consequence was the almost obsessive, albeit politically reasonable desire for a legitimate son: a male heir to the throne would be the one order of succession most difficult to challenge.[59] These apprehensions of the king's undoubtedly also contributed to the intricate and much discussed complex of motives that, beginning in 1525/27, led to a chain of events: the annulment of Henry's marriage to Catherine, the split with the Pope and the Roman Catholic church, the marriage to Anne Boleyn, and the revolutionary legislation of 1532–1534.[60]

The new legislation, as well as the Act of Succession (30 March 1534), and basically all reforms that had taken place between 1532 and 1534, were reinforced by means of a general oath that all subjects had to take. The Act of Succession itself was an extraordinary document[61] in that it laid down specific penalties for any violations of this law: actions or writings against the king, his title as Supreme Head of the Church of England, and his marriage would be prosecuted as high treason, while speaking against any of these would be judged as misprision of treason. In summary: with the Act of Succession and the power to bind all subjects to it – although the wording of the oath was not even specified –, the government had the perfect instrument to enforce the controversial reforms for good. And just as he did at the very start of his reign,

---

Prince. London et al.: Harper Perennial, 2009; WILSON, Derek. *A Brief History of Henry VIII. Reformer and Tyrant.* London: Constable & Robinson, 2009; cf. esp. the wealth of sources in *Henry VIII. Man & Monarch,* Catalogue edited by Susan DORAN, Exhibition guest curated by David Starkey. London: British Library, 2009.

59 Cf. e. g. SCARISBRICK. *Henry VIII.* 150: "Had Henry been able to glimpse into the second half of the century he would have had to change his mind on queens regnant, for his two daughters were to show quality that equaled or outmeasured their father's; [...]. But English experience of the queen regnant was remote and unhappy, and Henry's conventional mind, which no doubt accorded with his subjects', demanded a son as a political necessity. [...] There was, therefore, a real fear of a dynastic failure, of another bout of civil war, perhaps, or, if Mary were paired off as the treaty of 1525 provided, of England's union with a continental power". Cf. also MURPHY, Beverley A. *Bastard Prince. Henry VIII's Lost Son.* Phoenixmill: Sutten, 2001.

60 Cf. sources, evaluations of details and literature in SCARISBRICK. *Henry VIII.* esp. 163ff; BAUMANN. *Heinrich VIII.* Esp. 58ff and GUY. *Tudor England.* Esp. 116ff; cf. also BAUMANN, Uwe. "Der Kampf um den rechten Glauben, die Verfolgung von Ketzern und Hochverrätern und die tödlichen Grenzen der Streitkultur im England der (frühen) Tudorzeit." In: Uwe Baumann, Arnold Becker and Astrid Steiner-Weber (eds.). *Streitkultur. Okzidentale Traditionen des Streitens in Literatur, Geschichte und Kunst.* Super alta perennis. Studien zur Wirkung der Klassischen Antike. Vol. 2. Göttingen: Bonn University Press, 2008. 233–63, esp. 236 ff.

61 Cf. ELTON, Geoffrey R. (ed.). *The Tudor Constitution. Documents and Commentary.* Cambridge: Cambridge University Press, 1960 / Reprint 1972. Document no. 4, 6–12.

Henry VIII again relied on the deterring effect of exemplary show trials against those who refused to take the oath: some Carthusian and Franciscan monks, John Fisher, Bishop of Rochester, and Thomas More, his former friend, faithful servant, and erstwhile Lord Chancellor.[62] A summary survey of the trial reveals some interesting factors: the modification or rather aggravation of the high treason laws, which only made possible a death sentence against the accused, who had, in a perversion of justice, already been incarcerated for their refusal to take the oath; Cromwell's handwritten notes, which laid down sentences of death in advance of the trials against John Fisher and Thomas More;[63] the fact that in the case of Thomas More in particular an act of explicit perjury by Sir Richard Rich, Solicitor General, was required to obtain the desired verdict.[64] There is every indication that these death sentences, too, pronounced and executed as they were, are to be judged as cynically arranged and machiavellistically calculated political statements which were barely capable of sustaining a pretense to legality. They demonstrated in appalling brutality what those were in for who dared to defy the king's will. From an ethical point of view, these verdicts could by no means be justified; and Henry VIII could have had no delusions about that. In terms of politics, however, they yielded the desired result: whereas the Roman Catholic Church and humanists all over Europe might cry out in indignance,[65] the political situation in England remained calm. Indeed, people had only now

---

62 Cf. in general BAUMANN. *Heinrich VIII.* 89 ff; GUY. *Tudor England.* Esp. 116 ff; SCARISBRICK. *Henry VIII.* Esp. 305 ff. Cf. also the wealth of sources in MARIUS, Richard. *Thomas More. A Biography.* London/Melbourne: Knopf. 1984, esp. 461 ff. Cf. also the convincingly succinct analysis of Thomas More's last Tower-work, *De tristitia Christi*, by Richard Marius (*Thomas More*, 483): "More follows the scriptural texts from the gospels, and like a careful medieval university lecturer, he comments on them, sometimes explaining, sometimes relating a little history, sometimes making a guess or two, but mostly drawing devotional lessons from the example of Christ. Above all, these devotions deal with fear and how to overcome it by meditation on the sufferings and the love of Jesus. Like the *Dialogue of Comfort*, *De tristitia Christi* is art brought to the service of life, a literary discipline to strengthen his mind against the horrors of his imagination. Taken as a whole, the amazing variety of the work offers a stunning display of More's calm spirit at a time when he was both terribly afraid and indomitably resolute".

63 Cf. the absolutely convincing interpretation of the scanty evidence by SCHULTE HERBRÜGGEN, Hubertus. "The Process against Sir Thomas More." In: *The Law Quarterly Review* 99 (1983): 113–36, esp. 126: "The document thus gives direct evidence that More's condemnation and execution was a foregone conclusion, decided by Henry and implemented by Cromwell about a week before the judicial court was assigned and about a fortnight before the prisoner's trial".

64 Cf. the variety of sources and the generally convincing analysis in SCHULTE HERBRÜGGEN. "The Process against Sir Thomas More." 113–36, esp. 128 ff.

65 Cf. e.g. SCHULTE HERBRÜGGEN. "The Process against Sir Thomas More." 113–36, esp. 116 (sources).

truly realized the meaning of the formula of the king's supremacy over the church,[66] but England remained calm.[67]

IV.   Representations of Political Violence and Political Fear on the English Renaissance Stage

During the Renaissance, dramatic performances were – besides sermons – the mass medium in England. Plays were important multipliers of traditional, but also of innovative concepts or even revolutionary ideas, especially because performances allowed for reaching a mostly illiterate audience.

Despite strict observation by London's municipal authorities and efficient control by the censor, the Master of Revels, theatres became a most popular institution from around 1570/80 onwards: They not only supplied entertainment and were a profitable business for those who ran playhouses; theatres also provided the stage to be experimental with regard to philosophical, moral and political issues. Undoubtedly, Tudor and Stuart drama played a major role in the development and reinforcement of an English national identity. Particularly the history plays of the Tudor era are regarded as important means to propagate the Tudor myth, while such 'subversive' plays as William Shakespeare's *Richard II* and *Henry V* cannot be overlooked.[68] To give some more outstanding examples: Shakespeare's *Henry VI*, Parts I – III, as well as Thomas Lodge's *The Wounds of Civil War, or Marius and Scilla*,[69] warn most emphatically of the cruelties inflicted by civil war; the brutal consequences of an exclusively male society of warriors are pointed at in Shakespeare's *Troilus and Cressida*.[70] Above all, histories or tragedies raised a wide range of fundamental questions regarding the

---

66   Cf. the sources and details in ELTON (ed.). *The Tudor Constitution*. Esp. 329 ff.
67   It is one of the most fascinating ironies of history that some ten months after the beheading of Sir Thomas More (6 July 1535), Henry VIII's second wife, Anne Boleyn, a decisive cause of the English revolutionary developments 1527 – 1534, became another arguably 'innocent' victim of a political trial (execution: 19 May 1536). She proved "her innocence by dying 'boldly'" (WARNICKE, Retha M. *The Rise and Fall of Anne Boleyn*. Cambridge et al.: Cambridge University Press, 1989. 232). Cf. in general, sources and scholarly debates in WARNICKE. *The Rise and Fall of Anne Boleyn*. Esp. 191 ff; IVES, Eric William. *Anne Boleyn*. Oxford: Blackwell, 1986, esp. 335 ff.
68   Cf. e. g. ISER, Wolfgang. *Shakespeares Historien. Genesis und Geltung*. Konstanz: Universitätsverlag, 1988; LEGGATT, Alexander. *Shakespeare's Political Drama. The History Plays and the Roman Plays*. London/New York: Routledge, 1992.
69   Cf. GENTILI, Vanna. "Thomas Lodge's *Wounds of Civil War*: An Assessment of Context, Sources and Structure." In: *REAL* 2 (1984): 119 – 64.
70   Cf. KRIPPENDORFF, Ekkehart. *Politik in Shakespeares Dramen. Historien, Römerdramen, Tragödien*. Frankfurt M.: Suhrkamp, 1992, esp. 67 ff; BAUMANN, Uwe. *Shakespeare und seine Zeit*. Stuttgart et al.: Klett, 1998, esp. 46 ff.

state, the sovereign's virtues and the relationship between ruler and subject. Further, the duty to obey and the duty of care were discussed as well as issues of legitimacy, powers of resistance or rights of objection. Even violent resistance against the ruler (tyrannicide) was considered in obviously controversial manner on stage.[71] Those tragedies which focused on a sovereign, who could be labelled as a tyrant, were politically most explosive. Such a ruler – whether he was Eastern potentate, Italian duke or Roman emperor – was usually vain, unpredictable, and cruel, addicted only to vice, and regarded the state as his personal possession. For the subjects this resulted in living in constant fear of the tyrant and his brutal henchmen.

Haunting examples of depictions of paralysing fear can be found in some of the English Roman plays:[72] In Ben Jonson's *Sejanus His Fall* (1603), Arruntius, Silius, Sabinus and some like-minded characters, who structurally resemble a Greek chorus, have to experience how the general atmosphere in their country changes to a climate of anxiety, accompanied by suspicion, denunciation, and servility. The looming disaster, brought upon the people by Sejan's agents, cannot be averted. Silius complains that ancestry, moral values and honour do not count in such times; everyone is corrupt and tries to win Sejan's favour (I,1,27 – 41):[73]

> [...] These can lie,
> Flatter, and swear, forswear, deprave, inform,
> Smile, and betray; make guilty men; then beg
> The forfeit lives, to get the livings; cut
> Men's throats with whisperings; sell to gaping suitors
> The empty smoke, that flies about the palace;
> Laugh, when their patron laughs; sweat, when he sweats;
> Be hot, and cold with him; change every mood,
> Habit, and garb, as often as he varies;
> Observe him, as his watch observes his clock;
> And true, as turquoise in the dear lord's ring,
> Look well, or ill with him: ready to praise
> His lordship, if he spit, or but piss fair,

---

71 Cf. e.g. Hogg, James (ed.). *Jacobean Drama as Social Criticism.* Lewiston/Salzburg: Edwin Mellen, 1995; Baumann, Uwe (ed.). *Basileus und Tyrann. Herrscherbilder und Bilder von Herrschaft in der Englischen Renaissance.* Frankfurt M. et al.: Lang, 1999.

72 Cf. in general Baumann, Uwe. *Vorausdeutung und Tod im englischen Römerdrama der Renaissance (1564 – 1642).* Tübingen/Basel: Francke, 1996; Baumann, Uwe. "Historia magistra vitae? Römische Geschichte im Drama der Shakespearezeit." In: Astrid Steiner-Weber, Thomas A. Schmitz and Marc Laureys (eds.). *Bilder der Antike.* Super alta perennis. Studien zur Wirkung der Klassischen Antike Vol. 1. Göttingen: Bonn University Press, 2007. 89 – 126.

73 Cf. Bolton, Whitney F. (ed.). Ben Jonson, *Sejanus His Fall*, The New Mermaids. London: Benn, 1966.

> Have an indifferent stool, or break wind well,
> Nothing can 'scape their catch.

Arruntius continues claiming that it is not times but the people that have changed.[74] Traditional Roman virtues ceased to exist ever since Cato, Brutus and Cassius had died (I,1,86 – 104). However, what is most disillusioning about this tragedy is the fact that the fall of the alarmingly powerful prefect Sejan does not lead to a change. Macro succeeds Sejan in office and acts as ruthlessly as he did:[75] He orders the execution of Sejan's son and of his little daughter, who – because law prohibited to put a virgin to death – has to suffer the torment and humiliation of being raped before she is killed (V,6,842 – 857). And a dangerous Sphinx[76] looms in the background, the shadowy emperor Tiberius, who is a brilliant imperial actor and an obvious disciple of Machiavelli, who knows how to make sure that he is not outplayed by any other favourite. Mistrust, hate, servility, violence, and hypocrisy – they are all generated by fear and they remain ruling the people at the end of this play.[77]

The anonymous author of the tragedy *Claudius Tiberius Nero* (1607)[78] paints a similarly dark picture of the Roman imperial court. Tiberius' reign (14 – 37 A.D.) is depicted as an orgy of bad intentions, sinister schemes, and bloody monstrosities. The play focuses on the two Machiavellian politicians Seian and Tiberius, who use any means to keep or improve their positions. Seian first functions as Tiberius' most willing tool and together they commit crime after crime. Thus, Germanicus, Sabinus, Asinius, and Iulia are poisoned at Tiberius's instigation. But Seian ultimately schemes against Tiberius and makes him kill his own son Drusus, whereupon Tiberius executes Seian by means of a burning crown. He also murders Agrippina and her sons, Drusus and Nero, not to mention five servants, all of whom Tiberius slaughters within three minutes.

---

74 Cf. esp. I,1,86 – 92: "Times: the men,/ The men are not the same: 'tis we are base,/ poor, and degenerate from th'exalted strain/ Of our great fathers. Where is now the soul/ Of god-like Cato: he, that durst be good,/ When Caesar durst be evil; and had power,/ As not to live his slave, to die his master". The panegyrical portrait of Germanicus as ideal ruler (I,1,120 – 174) by Arruntius, Silius, Sabinus and Cordus constitutes a timeless brilliant and virtuous ideal. Cf. EVANS, K.W. "Sejanus and the Ideal Prince Tradition." In: *SEL* 11 (1971): 249 – 64; WOLF, William D. *The Reform of the Fallen World: The 'Virtuous Prince' in Jonsonian Tragedy and Comedy.* SSEL JDS Vol. 27. Salzburg, 1973.
75 Cf. III,2,714 – 49; IV,2,77 – 92; IV,4,514 – 22 and esp. Arruntius' explicit prophecy (V,6,753 – 56): "I prophesy, out of this Senate's flattery,/ That this new fellow, Macro, will become/ A greater prodigy in Rome, than he/ That now is fall'n".
76 Cf. the succinct – aside – remark by Arruntius (III,1,64 – 65): "By Jove, I am not Oedipus enough, / To understand this Sphinx".
77 Cf. esp. V,6,756 – 835.
78 Cf. BAUMANN, Uwe (ed.). *Claudius Tiberius Nero. A Critical Edition of the Play Published Anonymously in 1607.* Bibliotheca Humanistica Vol. IV. Frankfurt M. et al.: Lang, 1990.

Life, a life in 'vertue', is not possible under the tyrant Tiberius: hence, Nerva, Celsus and Livia commit suicide.

When Tiberius is overthrown, Rome seems at first to have been saved, but the later development of the tragedy resembles Ben Jonson's *Sejanus His Fall:* here, the violent and bloody killing of Seian neither changed the political climate nor helped to end the wallowing in vice nor to overcome the rule of fear. In *Claudius Tiberius Nero*, Caligula also cheats, flatters, and deceives to reach his goal, which ultimately attests him to be as tyrannical a character as Tiberius. It seems as if the tyrant only changed his name; after all, Seian's political – or rather Machiavellian – pragmatism (II,2,90 – 91: "If thou doost meane the Empire to obtaine,/ Sweare, flatter, lye, dissemble, cog & faine") succeeds: with Caligula, the more cunning hypocrite, the better actor, the more docile disciple of Machiavelli, prevails. For the state and for the people only one thing changes: the reason for their collective fear, the one responsible for the reigning sycophancy and mistrust bears a different name.

Looking at other Roman tragedies of the times, their representation of the Roman imperial court clearly reminds one of *Sejanus His Fall* and *Claudius Tiberius Nero:* In Thomas May's (1628) and Nathanael Richards' (1635) plays about Agrippina and Messallina, respectively,[79] both Roman empresses are punished with death for their crimes against the laws of the Gods, nature and humanity. In the anonymous tragedy *Nero* (1624) the protagonist is equally brought to justice after committing countless cruelties.[80]

In each of these plays the imperial court is depicted as a hotbed of vice, where schemers and bootlickers are either mere puppets committing cruelties or they are consciously turning into ruthless criminals.[81] Philip Massinger's *The Roman Actor* (1626) or John Fletcher's *The Tragedy of Valentinian* (1614) are excellent examples of analogous depictions of tyranny. They expertly expose the base nature of this form of rule by staging the politically functionalized fear (though they are not offering structural novelties): myriads of murders, the abhorrent, unpredictable cruelty of the emperor, and the resulting fear, even terror, is

---

79 Cf. SCHMID, F. Ernst (ed.). *Thomas May's Tragedy of Julia Agrippina, Empresse of Rome.* Materialien zur Kunde des Älteren Englischen Dramas Bd. 43. Louvain, 1914 / Reprint: Vaduz, 1963. Esp. V,537 ff. and SKEMP, Arthur R. (ed.). *Nathanael Richards' Tragedy of Messallina, The Roman Empresse.* Materialien zur Kunde des Älteren Englischen Dramas Bd. 30. Louvain, 1910 / Reprint: Nendeln, 1970. Esp. V,2449 ff.

80 Cf. HILL, Eliott M. (ed.). *The Tragedy of Nero. A Critical Edition of the Work First Published Anonymously in 1624.* Renaissance Drama, A Collection of Critical Editions. New York/ London: 1979, esp. V,3.

81 Cf. the sources and details in BAUMANN, Uwe. "Tyrannen, Attentäter und Intrigen: Die Darstellung des Römischen Kaiserhofes in der Jakobäischen Tragödie." In: Baumann (ed.). *Basileus und Tyrann.* 419 – 40.

described as a paralyzing, enslaving condition for the (few) upright citizens, who have not succumbed to the barbaric rogue regime.[82]

To conclude, what makes these tragedies such explosive, politically subversive plays is that they bring a Machiavellian tyrant on the stage,[83] analysing in a moralizing manner how every citizen is affected by the life of vice at the imperial court, giving and discussing detailed descriptions of resistance against the rule of terror, even including the unthinkable: tyrannicide.

By going back to the degenerated tyrants of the Roman imperial era, English dramatists found a way of holding up a mirror to their own times as they relied on the principle of correspondences[84]. Thus circumventing restrictions, they offered to their audience general criteria for evaluating political and social conditions. By pointing out how rulers use fear to secure or expand their position and by highlighting which serious consequences such a policy has on the people, they challenged or even destroyed the mystical aura that the Tudors and Stuarts publicly created around themselves.[85]

Representations of functionalized political fear, which turn out to be variations on classical themes and which often share the context of brutal violence, do

---

82 Cf. EDWARDS, Philip and Colin GIBSON (eds.). *The Plays and Poems of Philip Massinger*, Vol. III. Oxford: Oxford University Press, 1976. 1–93: *The Roman Actor*; TURNER, Robert K. (ed.). *The Tragedy of Valentinian*. In: Fredson Bowers (ed.). *The Dramatic Works in the Beaumont and Fletcher Canon*, Vol. IV. Cambridge et al.: Cambridge University Press, 1979. 261–414. Cf. BAUMANN. *Vorausdeutung und Tod*. Esp. 342ff and 391ff; BAUMANN. "Historia magistra vitae?" 89–126, esp. 117ff.

83 Cf. the brilliant analysis by BUSHNELL, Rebecca W. *Tragedies of Tyrants. Political Thought and Theatre in the English Renaissance*. Ithaca/London: Cornell University Press, 1990. Cf. also ADAMS, Robert P. "Opposed Tudor Myths of Power: Machiavellian Tyrants and Christian Kings." In: Dale B.J. Randall and George W. Williams (eds.). *Studies in the Continental Background of Renaissance English Literature: Essays Presented to J.L. Lievsay*. Durham, 1977. 67–90; ARMSTRONG, William A. "The Elizabethan Conception of the Tyrant." In: *RES* 22 (1946): 161–81; ARMSTRONG, William A. "The Influence of Seneca and Machiavelli on the Elizabethan Tyrant." In: *RES* 24 (1948): 19–35; BAUMANN, Uwe. "Thomas More and the Classical Tyrant." In: *Moreana* 22 (1985): 108–27; BAYERL, Francis James. *The Characterization of the Tyrant in Elizabethan Drama*. Diss. University of Toronto, 1974.

84 Cf. e.g. the discussions of this hermeneutic concept in Ben Jonson's *Sejanus His Fall* II,2,303–312; III,1,384–388, 390–392, 401–404 and Philip Massinger's *The Roman Actor* I,3,36–43; I,3,96–140 (cf. also BAUMANN. "Historia magistra vitae?" 89–126, esp. 100ff). Cf. also Martin BUTLER's remarks on Ben Jonson's *Sejanus* in the RSC Program (Gunpowder Season [2005]) of Gregory Doran's remarkably vivid modern production of the play ([8]): "[...] *Sejanus* was crucial for Jonson, since it was the first of many plays to build on the machiavellian dictum that men are driven by self-interest and crooks tend to prevail. [...] And its radicalism, its scepticism about public life and its intellectual pessimism, do give it undeniable dramatic power. *Perhaps the present time, once again preoccupied with tyrants and statecraft, will recognize what a remarkable play it is*" (my emphasis).

85 Cf. in general sources and literature in STRONG, Roy. *Feste der Renaissance 1450–1650. Kunst als Instrument der Macht*. Freiburg/Würzburg: Ploetz, 1991 and BAUMANN. "Politik, Propaganda und Mythologie." 207–29.

also appear in dramatic genres other than Roman tragedies. The following three tragedies were chosen as further examples of dramatic representations of rulership on the Renaissance stage: Christopher Marlowe's *Tamburlaine*; William Shakespeare's *Macbeth* and Colley Cibber's *Xerxes*.

Christopher Marlowe, *Tamburlaine* (1587)

The full title of this tragedy by Christopher Marlowe, probably his earliest, already leaves no doubt that the protagonist earned his title "Scourge of God" from strategically using fear and terror in his politics: "*Tamburlaine the Great. Who, from a Scythian Shepheard by his rare and wonderfull Conquests became a most puissant and mightye Monarque. And (for his tyranny, and terrour in Warre) was tearmed, The Scourge of God*".[86]

The fast and unstoppable rising of Tamburlaine, a brave, titanic ruler,[87] whose personal charisma and captivating rhetoric do not give away his mean birth, is covered in the first part of the play, whereas the second part concentrates on Zenocrates' death and its consequences.[88] Part two of the tragedy, which is

---

86 HARPER, J.W. (ed.). Christopher Marlowe, *Tamburlaine*. The New Mermaids. London: Benn, 1971. Cf. also "The Prologue" (esp. 3–6): "[...] We'll lead you to the stately tent of war, / Where you shall hear the Scythian Tamburlaine / Threatening the world with high astounding terms / And scourging kingdoms with his conquering sword".

87 Cf. e.g. the summary of sources and scholarly debates in ANTOR, Heinz. "Herrscherfiguren in den Dramen Christopher Marlowes." In: Baumann (ed.). *Basileus und Tyrann*. 235–77. Cf. in addition also HARDIN, Richard F. "Apocalypse Then: Tamburlaine and the Pleasures of Religious Fear." In: *Baylor Journal of Theatre and Performace* 3,2 (2006): 31–41; KHOURY, Joseph. "Marlowe's Tamburlaine: Idealized Machiavellian Prince." In: Patricia Vilches and Gerald Seaman (eds.). *Seeking Real Truths: Multidisciplinary Perspectives on Machiavelli*. Leiden: Brill, 2007. 329–56; LOGAN, Robert A. "Violence, Terrorism and War in Marlowe's Tamburlaine Plays." In: Sara M. Deats, Lagretta T. Lenker and Merry G. Perry (eds.). *War and Words: Horror and Heroism in the Literature of Warfare*. Lanham: Lexington, 2004. 65–81; MacKENZIE, Clayton G. "Marlowe's Grisly Monster: Death in *Tamburlaine*, Parts One & Two." In: *Dalhousie Review* 87,1 (2007): 9–24; MARCUS, Leah. "Marlowe in tempore belli." In: Sara M. Deats, Lagretta T. Lenker and Merry G. Perry (eds.). *War and Words: Horror and Heroism in the Literature of Warfare*. 295–316; NEWMARK, Paige. "Marlowe, Maps, and Might." In: Andrew Lynch and Anne M. Scott (eds.). *Renaissance Poetry and Drama in Context: Essays for Christopher Wortham*. Newcastle upon Tyne: Cambridge Scholars, 2008. 129–44; SCHRAY, Kateryna A.R. "'Is This Your Crown?' Conquest and Coronation in Tamburlaine I, Act II, Scene 4." In: *Cahiers Elisabéthains* 68 (2005): 19–26; SZURAWITZKI, Michael. *Contra den 'rex iustus / rex iniquus'? Der Einfluss von Machiavellis 'Il Principe' auf Marlowes 'Tamburlaine', Shakespeares 'Heinrich V.' und Gryphius 'Leo Armenius'*. Würzburg: Königshausen & Neumann, 2005.

88 Cf. on the structure of the play WURMBACH, Hubert. *Christopher Marlowes Tamburlaine-Dramen. Struktur, Rezeptionslenkung und historische Bedeutung: Ein Beitrag zur Dramenanalyse*. Heidelberg: Winter, 1984.

divided into several episodes, provides insight from different perspectives revealing how Tamburlaine presents himself as well as how others characterise him. For instance, Techelles, King of Fez, greets Tamburlaine most reverentially, treating him as if he were a fearsome god:

> And mighty Tamburlaine, our earthly god,
> Whose looks make this inferior world to quake,
> I here present thee with the crown of Fez,
> And with an host of Moors trained to the war,
> Whose coal-black faces make their foes retire,
> And quake for fear, as if infernal Jove,
> Meaning to aid thee in these Turkish arms,
> Should pierce the black circumference of hell,
> With ugly furies bearing fiery flags,
> And millions of his strong tormenting spirits: (Part II, I,6,11 – 20)

This panegyrical public image corresponds with Tamburlaine's self-image, as the following scene, i. e. Techelles gets his crown back with flourish (Part II, I,6,23 – 40), and also the later development proves. But especially Tamburlaine's great speech to a few of his defeated enemies after he has killed his own son Calyphas may illustrate this point:

> Villains, these terrors and these tyrannies
> (If tyrannies war's justice ye repute)
> I execute, enjoined me from above:
> To scourge the pride of such as heaven abhors,
> Nor am I made arch-monarch of the world,
> Crowned and invested by the hand of Jove,
> For deeds of bounty or nobility:
> But since I exercise a greater name,
> The Scourge of God and terror of the world,
> I must apply myself to fit those terms,
> In war, in blood, in death, in cruelty,
> And plague such peasants as resist in me
> The power of heaven's eternal majesty. (Part II, IV,1,144 – 56)

In the following lines his cruel killing orders show how Tamburlaine creates his own myth ("Scourge of God and terror of the world") again (Part II, IV,1,147 – 65). No one can stop him;[89] he even bids the gods, Mahomet and Jove, defiance:

> I will persist a terror to the world,
> Making the meteors, that like armed men
> Are seen to march upon the towers of heaven,

---

89 Cf. the programmatic early hyperbolic verses in Part I,2,174 – 77: "I hold the Fates bound fast in iron chains, / And with my hand turn Fortune's wheel about, / And sooner shall the sun fall from his sphere, / Than Tamburlaine be slaine or overcome".

Run tilting round about the firmament,
And break their burning lances in the air,
For honour of my wondrous victories. (Part II, IV,198 – 203)

So Tamburlaine's self-fashioning leads consequently to violence and bloodshed, to the atrocities committed against the defeated opponents, such as Bajazeth and his son Callapine, or against the kings of Asia whom he yokes to his wagon. Even Tamburlaine's mere reputation has a baneful effect as the tragic episode about Olympia, wife of the Captain of Balsera, illustrates: Out of fear of Tamburlaine and his men, her husband dead, she decides to kill her little son:

Come back again, sweet Death, and strike us both:
One minute end our days, and one sepulcher
Contain our bodies: Death, why com'st thou not?
Well, this must be the messenger for thee.
Now ugly Death stretch out thy sable wings,
And carry both our souls, where his remains.
Tell me sweet boy, art thou content to die?
These barbarous Scythians full of cruelty,
And Moors, in whom was never pity found,
Will hew us piecemeal, put us to the wheel,
Or else invent some torture worse than that,
Therefore die by thy living mother's hand,
Who gently now will lance thy ivory throat,
And quickly rid thee both of pain and life. (Part II, III,4,12 – 25)

Marlowe's image of the mother, who kills her own child out of love, is a most impressive way of capturing how the immense fear of Tamburlaine results in the abandoning of all ethical values, in a loss of humanity.

Hence, there is no need to go into detail about how Tamburlaine, even when facing death, still demonstrates a boundless will to power, as he assigns his sons with the task of conquering the entire world (cf. Part II, V,3,115 ff). It is neither necessary to elaborate on Tamburlaine's meteoric rising in part I, even though the stages of his way up are carefully designed (1. Mycetes, King of Persia, 2. Bajazeth, Emperor of Turkey, and 3. at Damascus, the Soldan of Egypt) and though they provide further, terribly realistic representations of Tamburlaine's abhorrent cruelties.[90] Only one last, especially striking example of how the play

---

90 Cf. e.g. Part I, 1,2,34 – 43; III,3,66 ff; III,3,40 ff; and esp. the messenger's threats (IV,2,49 – 63): "The first day when he pitcheth down his tents, / White is their hue, and on his silver crest / A snowy feather spangled white he bears, / To signify the mildness of his mind, / That satiate with spoil refuseth blood: / But when Aurora mounts the second time, / As red as scarlet is his furniture, / Then must his kindled wrath be quenched with blood, / Not sparing any that can manage arms: / But if these threats move not submission, / Black are his colours, black pavilion, / His spear, his shield, his horse, his armour, plumes, / And jetty feathers menace death and hell. / Without respect of sex, degree or age, / He razeth all his foes with fire and

presented the political exploitation of fear may be given: the *ultima verba* of the
dying Persian prince Agydas:

> I prophesied before and now I prove,
> The killing frowns of jealousy and love.
> He needed not with words confirm my fear,
> For words are vain where working tools present
> The naked action of my threatened end.
> It says, Agydas, thou shalt surely die,
> And of extremities elect the least.
> More honour and less pain it may procure,
> To die by this resolved hand of thine,
> Than stay the torments he and heaven have sworn.
> Then haste Agydas, and prevent the plagues:
> Which thy prolonged fates may draw on thee:
> Go wander free from fear of tyrant's rage,
> Removed from the torments and the hell:
> Wherewith he may excruciate thy soul.
> And let Agydas by Agydus die,
> And with this stab slumber eternally. [*Stabs himself*] (Part I, III,2,90 – 106)

William Shakespeare, *Macbeth* (1605/1606)

The first scenes of Shakespeare's *Hamlet* present a country in a state of alarm, the
threat of war looms large, the atmosphere is one of insecurity, and rumours are
circulating.[91] The opening of *Macbeth*, Shakespeare's most mature and far-
reaching 'vision of evil',[92] however, immediately confronts the audience with a
bloody battle, about the course of which even King Duncan is not well-informed.
Blood, violence and chaos dominate the situation, but one man stands out in this
bloody fight with rebels and foreign enemies because of his bravery in the field
and his vigorous determination: Macbeth.[93] He is hailed by King Duncan as

---

sword" and finally (IV,4,1 – 9), the total destruction of Damascus and its inhabitants sparing
not a single soul (V,2,1 ff). Cf. esp. V,2,58 – 65: "I will not spare these proud Egyptians, / Nor
charge my martial observations, / For all the wealth of Gihon's golden waves, / Or for the love
of Venus, would she leave / The angry god of arms, and lie with me. / They have refused the
offer of their lives, / And know my customs are as peremptory / As wrathful planets, death, or
destiny".

91 Cf. in general KRIPPENDORFF. *Politik in Shakespeares Dramen.* Esp. 345 ff; BAUMANN.
    Shakespeare und seine Zeit. Esp. 87 ff.
92 Cf. WILSON KNIGHT, G. *The Wheel of Fire.* London/New York: Methuen, 1983 [1930]. 140.
93 Cf. MUIR, Kenneth (ed.). William Shakespeare, *Macbeth.* Arden Edition. London/New York:
    Routledge, 1984. Cf. esp. I,2,14 – 23: "And Fortune, on his damned quarrel smiling, / Show'd
    like a rebel's whore: but all's too weak; / For brave Macbeth (well he deserves that name), /
    Disdaining Fortune, with his brandish'd steel, / Which smok'd with bloody execution, / Like

"valiant cousin! worthy gentleman" (I,2,24); the Thane of Rosse celebrates him
as "Bellona's bridegroom" (I,2,54); and his manly prowess even pays off ma-
terially: When the king finds out that he was betrayed by the Thane of Cawdor,
he orders to confer title and tenure to loyal, "noble Macbeth" (I,2,69).[94]

Macbeth's own words when he first enters the stage (I,3,37: "So foul and fair a
day I have not seen") refer back to the opening lines and to the witches' chorus
(I,1,11: "Fair is foul, and foul is fair"). This already hints at the close connection
between Macbeth and the witches, the forces of fate, whom he meets shortly
afterwards: They greet him (I,3,48 – 50) as Thane of Glamis, as Thane of Cawdor
and as future king. Macbeth is deeply confused after this and shows signs of fear
(I,3,51 – 52: [Banquo] "Good Sir, why do you start, and seem to fear / Things that
do sound so fair?"). But while he is still puzzling with Banquo (who is predicted
to become a father of kings [I,3,63 – 67]) about the meaning of the prophecies,
Rosse and Angus arrive with the tidings that Macbeth has been appointed Thane
of Cawdor by King Duncan. Banquo – who will, full of naive good faith, remain
inactive throughout the following scenes, despite his gloomy premonitions
(I,3,120 – 27; II,1,5 – 9) – immediately recognizes the connection between the
news and the predictions. Macbeth, however, is disbelieving, insecure, and
scared. The idea of killing Duncan in order to get hold of the promised crown
arises unexpectedly quickly, yet, it seems to shock Macbeth and the thought
becomes a "horrid image" (I,3,133 – 142) as he explains in an aside:

Valour's minion, carv'd out his passage, / Till he fac'd the slave; / Which ne'er shook hands,
nor bade farewell to him, / Till he unseam'd him from the nave to th'chops, / And fix'd his
head upon our battlements".

94 Cf. I,2,65 – 67. Cf. in general sources, discussion and scholarly literature in BAUMANN, Uwe.
"Macbeth und Duncan als Herrscher in Shakespeares *Macbeth*." In: Uwe Baumann (ed.).
Basileus und Tyrann. Herrscherbilder und Bilder von Herrschaft in der Englischen Ren-
aissance. Frankfurt M.: Lang, 1999. 363 – 76, esp. 367 ff. Cf. in addition CRAIG, Leon H. *Of*
Philosophers and Kings: Political Philosophy in Shakespeare's 'Macbeth' and 'King Lear'.
Toronto: Toronto University Press, 2001; ERZGRÄBER, Willi. "Das Gewissen bei Shake-
speare." In: *Literaturwissenschaftliches Jahrbuch* 40 (1999): 95 – 114; HERMAN, Peter C.
"*Macbeth*: Absolutism, the Ancient Constitution, and the Aporia of Politics." In: Constance
Jordan and Karen Cunningham (eds.). *The Law in Shakespeare.* Basingstoke: Palgrave Mac-
millan, 2009. 208 – 32; HUNT, Maurice. "Duncan, Macbeth, and the Thane of Cawdor." In:
Studies in the Humanities 28 (2001): 1 – 30; MAPSTONE, Sally. "Shakespeare and Scottish
Kingship: A Case History." In: Sally Mapstone and Juliette Wood (eds.). *The Rose and the*
Thistle: Essays on the Culture of Late Medieval and Renaissance Scotland. East Lothian:
Tuckwell, 1998. 158 – 89; MOSCHOVAKIS, Nick (ed.). *Macbeth: New Critical Essays.* New York:
Routledge, 2008; NEELY, Carol Thomas. *Distracted Subjects: Madness and Gender in Shake-*
speare and Early Modern Culture. Ithaca: Cornell University Press, 2004; WILSON, Richard
"'Blood Will Have Blood': Regime Change in *Macbeth*." In: *Shakespeare Jahrbuch* 143
(2007): 11 – 35; WOLPERS, Theodor. "Der 'Sturz des Mächtigen' in Shakespeares *Richard II*,
Richard III und *Macbeth*." In: Theodor Wolpers (ed.). *Der Sturz des Mächtigen: Zu Struktur,*
Funktion und Geschichte eines literarischen Motivs. Göttingen: Vandenhoeck & Ruprecht,
2000. 203 – 47.

[…] I am Thane of Cawdor:
If good, why do I yield to that suggestion
Whose horrid image doth unfix my hair,
And make my seated heart knock at my ribs,
Against the use of nature? Present fears
Are less than horrible imaginings.
My thought, whose murther yet is but fantastical,
Shakes so my single state of man,
That function is smother'd in surmise,
And nothing is, but what is not.

Macbeth decides not to do anything but to yield to his fate (I,3,144 – 45: "If Chance will have me King, why, Chance may crown me / Without my stir"). The dramatist seems to present a virtuous, loyal Macbeth who is honoured for his deeds, but who is tempted by the witches' influence, or by fate, so that he even considers committing regicide. For now, he is strong enough in character to abandon his criminal ideas and leave it to fate to make the prophecies come true.

Before he finally kills Duncan – which entails the murdering of two of Duncan's servants – Macbeth endlessly reconsiders the same thoughts: He ponders over the unlawful usurpation of the crown and shies away from it because of moral scruples – especially his famous "If it were done"-monologue (I,7,1 – 28) is exemplary of his indecision. Macbeth only murders the king because his wife, who is driven by burning ambition, challenges him, in her famous, rhetorically brilliant persuasive speech (I,7,35 – 83), to kill Duncan as proof of his manliness. It takes her persuasive words to make him commit the cruel crime, to violate the laws of hospitality and to burden his conscience with the guilt of regicide. Macbeth appears to be corrupted by the witches and by his wife – his deed may satisfy his ambition but it actually seems to contradict the nature of his character.[95] But is Macbeth a victim of fate (the witches) and of his wife's power of persuasion? This would be too easy an explanation, especially since Macbeth came up with the idea of regicide rather quickly, once he thought he had understood the prophecies. This certainly does not fit the image of a loyal subject to

---

95 Cf. Lady Macbeth's remarkable analysis of her husband's character after reading his letter (I,5,15 – 30): "Glamis thou art, and Cawdor; and shalt be / What thou art promis'd. – Yet do I fear thy nature: / It is too full o'th'milk of human kindness, / To catch the nearest way. Thou wouldst be great; / Art not without ambition, but without / The illness should attend it: what thou wouldst highly, / That wouldst thou holily; wouldst not play false, /And yet wouldst wrongly win; thou'dst have, great Glamis, / That which cries, 'Thus thou must do,' if thou have it; / And that which rather thou dost fear to do, / Than wishest should be undone. Hie thee hither, / That I may pour my spirits in thine ear, / And chastise with the valour of my tongue / All that impedes thee from the golden round, / Which fate and metaphysical aid doth seem / To have thee crown'd withal".

the king; and there is another telling detail which further fuels some doubts
about Macbeth. Lady Macbeth accuses him of not keeping his promise:

> […] What beast was't then,
> That made you break this enterprise to me?
> When you durst do it, then you were a man;
> And, to be more than what you were, you would
> Be so much more the man. Nor time, nor place,
> Did then adhere, and yet you would make both:
> They have made themselves, and that their fitness now
> Does unmake you. I have given suck, and know
> How tender 'tis to love the babe that milks me:
> I would, while it was smiling in my face,
> Have pluck'd my nipple from his boneless gums,
> And dash'd the brains out, had I so sworn
> As you have done to this. (I,7,47 – 59)

As Lady Macbeth refers to an earlier instance – "then" – when "nor time nor
place" had been right to kill Duncan, Macbeth must have been scheming with his
wife to murder the king long before he met the soothsaying witches.[96] Going
back to the opening, then, Macbeth's first reaction to the prophecies appears in
an altogether different, darker twilight: Does his agitation actually originate
from the fear that the witches might reveal his most secret wishes in front of
Banquo, that is to say, in public?[97]

Once he has Duncan's blood on his hands and after he has been elected king,
Macbeth has reached all his ambitious goals, but he seems to be terribly haunted.
To secure his position, though it is objectively not threatened,[98] Macbeth orders
the killing of Banquo and his son (III,1,46 – 141). He now shows the brutal
coldness his wife could not see in him before: He makes his own decisions; he
does not talk to her about his cruel plans. He wants to save her, who had been the
driving force behind the murder of King Duncan, from unnecessary sorrows
(III,2,45 – 46: "Be innocent of the knowledge, dearest chuck, / Till thou applaud
the deed"). But Macbeth overestimates his own unscrupulousness. After he had
Banquo murdered, the dead friend's ghost appears at the evening banquet and
Macbeth almost collapses. Macbeth is saved, only because Lady Macbeth – with
admirable presence of mind – is able to persuade the other guests that Macbeth's

---

96 Cf. e.g. KRIPPENDORFF. *Politik in Shakespeares Dramen.* Esp. 403.
97 Cf. the details in BAUMANN. "Macbeth und Duncan als Herrscher." 369 – 70.
98 Cf. esp. the monologue which presents Macbeth's subjective fears to the audience (III,1,46 –
   56): "To be thus is nothing, but to be safely thus: / Our fears in Banquo / Stick deep, and in his
   royalty of nature / Reigns that which would be fear'd: 'tis much he dares; / And, to that
   dauntless temper of his mind, / He hath a wisdom that doth guide his valour / To act in safety.
   There is none but he / Whose being I do fear: and under him / My Genius is rebuk'd; as, it is
   said, / Mark Antony's was by Caesar".

strange demeanor is an unexceptional symptom of a sickness. (III,4,40*-120). At
the same time, she reveals (just to her husband and the audience?) that she
knows the true reason for Macbeth's fearful reaction to the apparition:

> [...] O proper stuff!
> This is the very painting of your fear:
> This is the air-drawn dagger, which, you said,
> Led you to Duncan. O! these flaws and starts
> (Imposters to true fear), would well become
> A woman's story at a winter's fire,
> Authoris'd by her grandam. Shame itself!
> Why do you make such faces? When all's done,
> You look but on a stool. (III,4,59 – 67)

Because Shakespeare places special emphasis on tracing the slow deadening of
Macbeth's conscience and on representing the conflict between Macbeth's
ambition and his 'better' self in the monologues, the audience is moved to feel
sympathy for the protagonist; even more so when he suffers a breakdown as he
faces the ghost of Banquo. The depiction of Macbeth's internal perspective of
how he is tormented by his guilt arouses pity, even for a murderer.[99]

What is particularly important for this paper, however, is that after the
banquet scene (at the latest), Macbeth becomes utterly controlled by his terrible
fears. He turns into a bloodthirsty tyrant, and Scotland is ruled by fear and
chaos.[100] Macbeth leads a war against his own subjects, rivers of blood flow. Not
even women and children are spared by his cruel butchers, as especially the
slaughtering of the MacDuff family illustrates (IV,2). Interestingly, the word
'fear' (noun and verb) appears most frequently in this tragedy in comparison
with all of Shakespeare's dramatic works.[101] Considering that Macbeth is one of
his shortest plays, this seeming statistical trifle gains in importance.

Coming back to the main character, Macbeth is shown to be trapped in his
dark and gloomy ruminations. Although he briefly allowed himself to be lulled

---

99 Cf. LENGELER, Rainer. "*Macbeth*. Vom Mitleiden am Leiden des Verbrechers." In: Werner
    Habicht and Ina Schabert (eds.). *Sympathielenkung in den Dramen Shakespeares*. Munich:
    Fink, 1978. 55 – 64.
100 Cf. e. g. esp. IV,3,4 – 8: [Macduff] "Each new morn, / New widows howl, new orphans cry;
    new sorrows / Strike heaven on the face, that it resounds / As if it felt with Scotland, and
    yell'd out / Like syllable of dolour" and IV,3,39 – 41: [Malcolm] "I think our country sinks
    beneath the yoke; / It weeps, it bleeds; and each new day a gash / Is added to her wounds".
    Cf. also IV,3,165 – 74.
101 Cf. the statistical data in BARTLETT, John. *A Complete Concordance or Verbal Index to
    Words, Phrases and Passages in the Dramatic Works of Shakespeare, With a Supplementary
    Concordance to the Poems*. London: Macmillan, 1956 [1894]. 507 – 12 and SPEVACK, Marvin.
    A Complete and Systematic Concordance to the Works of Shakespeare. 9 Vols., Vol. IV.: 'A –
    Hilding'. Hildesheim: Olms, 1968. 992 – 97.

into a false sense of security by – his interpretation of – the witches' prophecies (IV,1,1 – 156), he soon returns to brooding over horrors and fears:

> I have almost forgot the taste of fears.
> The time has been, my senses would have cool'd
> To hear a night-shriek; and my fell of hair
> Would at a dismal treatise rouse, and stir,
> As life were in't. I have supp'd full with horrors:
> Direness, familiar to my slaughterous thoughts,
> Cannot once start me. (V,5,9 – 15)

The description of what Macbeth's subjects experience is, of course, reminiscent of the classical topoi as known e. g. from the depiction of bloody tyranny in Thukydides' works: They live in fear and terror; their everyday life is overshadowed by distrust for each other. A longer conversation between Macduff and Malcolm arguably highlights this: Malcolm play-acts out of fear that Macduff might betray him, until Macduff's resentful reaction proves that he is sincere. In its political details, this dialogue presents significant criteria for a general, ethical and moral evaluation of rulership (IV,3,1 – 137).[102]

Macbeth in the end barely notices the death of his wife (V,5,17 – 28), who could not cope with her guilt (cf. V,1). It is already too late when he recognises that his interpretation of the prophecies was wrong. Still, Macbeth pulls himself together and fights one last time: Once more he is presented as the frightening, blood-spattered, brave and brutal warrior the audience was introduced to at the beginning of the play (V,7 and V,8). Thus, the playwright not only grants Macbeth a heroic death – just as the tyrannic Richard III – but he also provides further indication for the deeper political understanding of the tragedy.

Scotland is depicted as an exclusively male space, a world in which only brave warriors will prevail. In this world of bloody battles, the physical ability to slaughter the enemy appears to be the only virtue that really counts.[103] War is the father of all things in this dark and gloomy place. Even the tragic ending still celebrates war and fighting: Young Siward dies "like a man" (cf. V,7,5 – 11*); and his father, when informed of his son's death, only wants to be reassured that his son got his mortal wounds in a decent fight facing the opponent (V,9,11). This warrior mentality is the source of all evil; Macbeth was raised with it, it nourished his ambition and Scotland is threatened with falling back on this value system, even after Macbeth's bloody tyranny is overcome. The new king, Malcolm, gets rid of Macbeth's men (V,9,34 – 35), but bases his regime on the support of his father's *elite*, whom he quickly appoints as Earls. In the end, when Macbeth, the tyrant and murderer of the king, got his just punishment, the

---

102　Cf. the sources and details in Baumann. "Macbeth und Duncan als Herrscher." Esp. 363 ff.
103　Cf. Krippendorff. *Politik in Shakespeares Dramen.* Esp. 391 – 426.

audience gets to listen to Malcolm, who celebrates the historical moment: the collectively achieved victory and the atmosphere of friendship and harmony (V,9,25 – 41). But it is almost impossible to overlook that the same critical power relations as witnessed in the beginning of the tragedy are restored: a weak king (then Duncan, now Malcolm) opposed to a tough warrior-hero (Macbeth, Macduff) – and the audience has no reason to forget that the witches are still waiting in their cave. Who will be the next to receive one of their prophecies, which seemingly promise continuity and security? Who will take the chance to usurp the crown by means of war and fight, the only means accepted in this country? The death of the tyrant Macbeth – to conclude this brief analysis – does not mark the end of political fear: the monster is merely sleeping for a while.

Colley Cibber, *Xerxes, A Tragedy* (1699)

Colley Cibber's *Xerxes, A Tragedy* (1699)[104] is one of the few English plays of the sixteenth and seventeenth century which focus on a Persian ruler.[105] It is a typical "horror tragedy"[106], which was a particularly popular genre during the last three decades of the seventeenth century.[107] Details about scenery and costumes as well as about the elaborate masks in this tragedy will not be at the centre of attention; also the problematic history of performance and the merely moderate success of the play are rather irrelevant for our purposes.[108] Only one central aspect is to be analysed: the fear and anxiety that the tyrant generates in his subjects as well as those fears which haunt the tyrant himself.

Xerxes is called a tyrant right from the beginning of the play. He is depicted as

---

104 Cf. VIATOR, Timothy J. and William J. BURLING (eds.). *The Plays of Colley Cibber*, Vol. 1. Madison/London: Associated UP, 2001. 244 – 326.

105 Cf. e. g. Thomas Preston, *A Comedy of King Cambyses* (1561); Anon., *King Darius* (1565); Christopher Marlowe, *Tamburlaine the Great* (1587); Anon., *The Wars of Cyrus* (1594); William Alexander, *The Tragedy of Darius* (1603); Charles Saunders, *Tamerlane the Great* (1681).

106 Cf. HUME, Robert D. *The Development of English Drama in the Late Seventeenth Century*. Oxford: Clarendon Press, 1976, esp. 199.

107 Cf. VIATOR and BURLING (eds.). *The Plays of Colley Cibber*. 247: "[…] Cibber seems to have known exactly what he was creating in regard to stage displays of such evil, with *Xerxes* closely following in the footsteps of Settle's *Empress of Morocco* (1673), the most important example of this type; its sequel, *The Heir of Morocco* (1682); and the more recent spate of horror plays, including Banks's *Cyrus the Great* (1695), Pix's *Ibrahim* (1696), Manley's *The Royal Mischief* (1696), and even Southerne's *Oroonoko* (1695), with its explicit re-presentation of the execution of the African prince".

108 Cf. in general KOON, Helene. *Colley Cibber*. Lexington: Kentucky University Press, 1986; VIATOR, Timothy J. "The Stage History of Cibber's *Xerxes*." In: *Theatre Notebook* 46,3 (1992): 155 – 59.

a ruler who overestimates himself beyond all measure and who has obviously lost touch with reality.[109] Even though he fled from the battlefield in the fights against the Greeks, he celebrates the defeat that depresses his generals as a triumph. He rages against the gods (I,230 – 238); he orders to whip the winds and to shoot arrows at the sun (I,I,296 ff); he acts deaf against the Magi's warnings;[110] and in his madness he even denies the gods their rule over death and the after-world and claims it for himself:

> Away! ye senseless dreamers of the world to come,
> Who dare pretend to fright mankind with tales,
> Of what shall happen after death:
> But yet can give us no account of what
> The soul endured, before it put on flesh!
> Hence from my sight and thoughts forever! (I,329 – 34)

Such rage in a tyrant leads to the well-known consequences: Xerxes, too, fights his own loyal subjects, he surrounds himself with hypocrites and sycophants (cf. e. g. II,292 ff), who not only appreciate his cruelties but who also act as his willing tools. Xerxes breaks his kingly parole in front of everybody (IV,1,382 – 416); he even denies those who fled his tyranny by committing suicide the peace of death, which is a typical example of a tyrant's delusion (III,211 – 12): "O spiteful sullen traitors! Bring in the torture! / By heaven I'll have 'em racked to life again!" Cruel, bloody violence against his subjects, threats and false promises to reach his goals are Xerxes' political strategies. By such means he tries to – at the height of his lecherous desires – rape the charming embodiment of virtue: Tamira (cf. IV,3,308 – 15; IV,3,322 – 30; IV,3,340 – 55). But he is outwitted by the intelligent woman (cf. IV,3,415 – 33), who cleverly pretends to be far less virtuous and chaste.[111]

The tyrant's subjects are depicted as traditionally as Xerxes' fears and qualms of conscience. He constantly worries about his safety and hires watchmen for his

---

109 Cf. esp. I,118 – 22: [Artabanus] "[…] His vain, / His proud (and what the history of man / Could never parallel), his monstruous resolution / After flight: He says he made th'A-thenians fly, / He lost no battle! Greece still trembles at his name, […]".

110 Cf. I,324 – 28: [2d Magi] "While frantic passions talk so wild and loud, / The voice of reason is of little force: / But still remember, king, / Though while you live the gods retard your doom, / Yet after death, a sure revenge will come".

111 Cf. esp. IV,3,341 – 55*: [Tamira] "Can there be horror in so sweet a pleasure? / Can force be needful to the yielding fair? / I find, you think me, what I seemed, all ice! / Ah! Little! Little do you know of womankind! / Our lives! Our thoughts! Our very souls are love. / Our tears are softness, and our coyness fear; / Our frowns affected, and our tongues belie 'em: / Our wishes secret, and our eyes betray 'em; / We must be cruel, ere we can be kind; / And use resistance to be more desired: / But when our cruelty has done its part, / And kindly proved how ill the wretch can bear, / Then! Then! Our joy's secure – A look can cure despair! / *Looks wantonly on him*". Cf. also IV,3,371 – 89 and the hoped for tyrant's reaction IV,3,401 – 14.

protection. Nobody, not even his generals, is allowed to be armed when they approach him (cf. esp. II,99 – 101: [Mardonius] "Gods! That a man so great in arms, / Should ever know the guilt of fear! See where he comes, / Amidst his court of women now! O shameful change"). But it is not only the classic fear of assassination which haunts Xerxes, he also suffers from his guilty conscience, which cannot be silenced as easily as troublemakers, whom he threatens into silence, imprisons, or puts to death. Afraid of the unknown future and probably driven by the fear that he might be held responsible for his deeds, Xerxes decides to consult a fortune teller. In Aeschylus' tragedy, which serves as a model for this scene, Xerxes acknowledges his guilt (cf. Pers. 908 ff). Cibber's Xerxes, however, remains proud and stubbornly obtuse (IV,2,151 – 83); but despite his defiant words (IV,3,176 – 77: "Spirit, thou liest; I ne'er despised shall die: / I'll change my death, to prove that fate can lie") he cannot silence the voice of his conscience:

> Through all th' unmeasured bounds of wild delight,
> I never yet could taste substantial joy,
> Or know one pleasure more than common men.
> If I indulge my appetite, I'm cloyed;
> Uneasy now, with what I lately longed for:
> If when my blood is high I taste of beauty,
> I lose the bliss, because my power commands;
> The peasant there takes more delight than I
> That travels through despair to sweet possession.
> When deaf to injuries, I make my way
> Through others' ruin,
> Stern conscience stops me short, and will be heard.
> She keeps me waking, when the world's at rest,
> And stuffs my pillow with a thousand thorns! (V,1,1 – 14)

Just as classical as the representation of the political terror and as typical as the depiction of the tyrant's anxiety is Cibber's portrayal of the subjects' reactions. Xerxes always finds accomplices for his crimes; the fear of the tyrant makes Memnon, for example, a traitor (III,1 – 34). But these are not all of the stereo-typical effects of bloody tyranny presented in Cibber's play: right from the beginning he introduces some honest and upright generals, especially worth mentioning are Artabanus and Mardonius, who function as appealing charac-ters and who openly level criticism against almighty Xerxes:

> I ha' no king; 'tis merit, not a crown,
> That makes a king: when pride and sloth debase
> The soul of majesty, the crown's a toy,
> No more in worth, than what it weighs in gold:
> I scorn a king, whose robes can only speak him royal. (II,393 – 97)

A sovereign who rules as despotically as Xerxes not only risks meeting resistance (Cibber shows much sympathy for the honest men who oppose the tyrant) and has to fear being murdered. At the same time he implicitly puts autocracy, the institution of monarchy, up for political negotiation:

> ARTABANUS. Why! Why ye powers! has such a tainted soul
> The care of th'empire? Or if the gods have stamped
> Divinity on kings, fixing them far above
> The reach of common men; why then have we
> The eyes of reason to inspect their faults?
> Why are we born with souls to loathe dishonor,
> And yet by honour bound to bear it?
> ARANTHES. How! To bear it! No! That loyalty's dishonourable,
> That bids me bear dishonor: When subjects
> Are no more the care of kings, we then
> Have only left the laws of nature to protect us,
> And nature ties us all to self-defense. (II,437 – 48)

This – arguably revolutionary – criticism of autocracy is to be continued in Act III, and it is even intensified by a representation of a successful revolt, "surely a vivid reminder of the events of 1688 – 89".[112] The critique is morally grounded and well-founded by political theory – and it is most clearly expressed:

> ARTABANUS. Never was cause, my friends, more cheerfully
> Embraced, never were hands more fit for action,
> Nor ever greater glory waiting on success:
> 'Tis not the thirst of others' wealth, or dignities,
> Nor envy of a favoured faction, that inflames us,
> No mercenary end: 'Tis bleeding honour calls us
> To revenge her wounds; 'tis *Xerxes*, not the king
> That stands accused: If *Xerxes* can relent,
> Still let him wear the crown; if not, the crown
> By us removed, can dignify
> Another head for empire.
> ARANTHES. 'Tis not who reigns, but who reigns well is king.
> ARTABANUS. He that neglects the regal office,
> Should be compelled to lay it down;
> And we who feel the smart of that neglect,
> Are only proper judges, where to place it. (III,34 – 49)

In the end, Colley Cibber's *Xerxes* proves to aim at the same effects as the Roman tragedies of the English Renaissance, which challenged the mystical aura of the Tudors and Stuarts by staging tyrannical Roman emperors. The very last lines of Cibber's tragedy may concludingly illustrate this point; Mardonius's call for

---

112 VIATOR and BURLING (eds.). *The Plays of Colley Cibber*. 248.

patience and his remark about the comfort conveyed by the gods cannot diminish the explosive nature of these political, revolutionary thoughts:[113]

> Let kings and jarring subjects hence be warned,
> Not to oppress, or drive revenge too far:
> Kings are but men, and men by nature err.
> Subjects are men, and cannot always bear.
> Much should be borne before revenge is sought:
> Ever revenge on kings is dearly bought.
> Yet, to our woes, the gods this comfort give;
> From those that die, the living learn to live. (V,3,425 – 32)

V.   Epilogue

The deliberately few examples should have made clear that the literature and culture of the English Renaissance function as a multi-voiced echo chamber for representations of political fear, which were developed and rhetorically shaped in the culture, history and literature of classical antiquity. These classical concepts, ideas, and historical concretizations were adapted, modified, discussed and appropriated to the times and political circumstances of the English Renaissance in a variety of ways – and by the unique institution of the public theatre they were presented to the public at large. Thus, the literature and culture of the English Renaissance itself become a marvellously rich treasure hoard, a source of inspiration for the following centuries, whose far-reaching influence and multiplicity of voices cannot be overestimated.

The many different forms of reaction to political terror presented in Renaissance literature might even have served as comfort and guidance in everyday life, which was often characterised by fear, insecurity and anxiety: particularly the contingencies of the revolutionary years 1527 – 1534, the fear of the Spanish armada (1587/88), the great concern about the succession of Elizabeth I (from about 1598 onwards), the civil war between king and parliament (from 1642 onwards), the threat of war during the Commonwealth, and the tense situation between the sovereign and the people up to the Glorious Revolution (1688/89).

Another line of tradition has been deliberately neglected up to this point. On 5th April 1588 – at a time when rumours about a war had been spreading for months and the powerful Spanish armada was threatening England – a boy was

---

113 Cf. also VIATOR and BURLING (eds.). *The Plays of Colley Cibber.* 249: "The distinction between the office of the monarch and his person, is, of course, the factor that keeps the play from being utterly seditious; but even so, the strong language of critique and the extended presentation of treasonous rebellion, even justified as it seems to modern readers, may well have struck playgoers in 1699 as just a bit too uncomfortable".

born in Westport (Wiltshire), who would later write about his birth: "My mother was filled with such fear, that she bore twins, me and together with me fear".[114] This boy was a second child and he was christened after his father: Thomas Hobbes (1588 – 1679)[115], and he was to become one of the most famous state philosophers of all times. He, Thomas Hobbes, puts particular emphasis on the role of fear for the origin and historical development of the modern autocratic state: "[…] the original of great and lasting societies consisted not in mutual good will men had toward each other, but in the mutual fear they had of each other".[116] In *The Elements of Law* Hobbes claims that "[i]n the state of nature every man is his own judge, and differeth from other concerning the names and appellations of things, and from those differences arise quarrels, and breach of peace".[117] The modern, absolutist state, whose true nature is disguised rather than unveiled by the biblical image of the Leviathan, is grounded primarily on fear. But the state is supposed to allay this fear; its long-term purpose is to avoid the war of the individuals: "Of all Passions, that which enclineth men least to break the Lawes, is Fear. Nay, (excepting some generous natures,) it is the onely thing, (when there is apparence of profit, or pleasure by breaking the Lawes,) that makes men keep them".[118]

Giambattista Vico shares these basically positive connotations and consequences of fear in his *opus magnum*, *The New Science*. He conceptualizes fear as the origin of the gods and myths:[119]

> [191] These things give the right sense to the saying, 'Fear first created gods in the world' (*Primos in orbe deos fecit timor*) [Statius, *Thebaid* 3.661]: false religions were born not of imposture but of credulity. […]

---

114 Cf. the sources in MARTINICH, Aloysius P. *Hobbes: A Biography.* New York: Cambridge University Press, 1999. 1 – 2.

115 Cf. in general MALCOLM, Noel. "Hobbes, Thomas (1588 – 1679), Philosopher." In: *Oxford Dictionary of National Biography* (2004), Online-Edition 2010.

116 HOBBES, Thomas. *De Cive.* In: *Man and Citizen.* Edited by Bernard Gert. Indianapolis: Hackett, 1991. I,2. 113.

117 HOBBES, Thomas. *The Elements of Law: Natural & Politic.* Edited by Ferdinand Tönnies. London: Frank Cass, 1969. II,10,8. 188.

118 HOBBES, Thomas. *Leviathan.* Edited by Kenneth R. Minogue. London et al.: Dent, 1973. II,27. 158. Cf. also EICH, Peter, Sebastian SCHMIDT-HOFNER and Christian WIELAND (eds.). *Der wiederkehrende Leviathan. Staatlichkeit und Staatswerdung in Spätantike und Früher Neuzeit.* Heidelberg: Winter, 2011; MAIER, Hans. "Hobbes." In: Hans Maier, Heinz Rausch and Horst Denzer (eds.). *Klassiker des politischen Denkens.* Vol. 1. *Von Plato bis Hobbes.* Munich: Beck, 1968. 351 – 75. Esp. 371 ff; BERMBACH, Udo and Klaus-M. KODALLE (eds.). *Furcht und Freiheit. Leviathan-Diskussion 300 Jahre nach Thomas Hobbes.* Opladen: Westdeutscher Verlag, 1982; ROBIN. *Fear. The History of a Political Idea.* Esp. 31 ff.

119 *The New Science of Giambattista Vico.* Revised Translation of the Third Edition (1744), by Thomas Goddard Bergin and Max Harold Fisch. Ithaca/New York: Cornell University Press, 1968.

[221] [...] the fables originating among the first savage and crude men were very severe, as suited the founding of nations emerging from a fierce bestial freedom. Then, with the long passage of years and change of customs, they lost their original meanings and were altered and obscured in the dissolute and corrupt times [708] [beginning] even before Homer [814 f]. Because religion was important to them, the men of Greece, lest the gods should oppose their desires as well as their customs, imputed these customs to the gods, and gave improper, ugly, and obscene meanings to the fables. [...]

[382] All the things here discussed agree with that golden passage of Eusebius [i.e. Lactantius] on the origins of idolatry: that the first people, simple and rough, invented the gods 'from terror of present power' [188]. Thus it was fear which created gods in the world; not fear awakened in men by other men, but fear awakened in men by themselves [191].

As these few quotes might have proved, it is equally possible to write another essay on representations of political fear in theories of culture and state, and that paper would – just as this article on the representation of political fear in the literature and culture of the English Renaissance[120] – analyse some of the multifarious facets of humankind's endless struggle with the monster of "Political Fear". However, none of these endeavours would ever qualify or tame the initially quoted statement: "A spectre is haunting humanity: the spectre of fear".

---

120 Last but not least I would like to thank the following friends, colleagues, research assistants and students, who read, discussed and commented upon this manuscript and its interpretations, whether in class, draft, or article form: Katharina Engel, Marion Gymnich, Wolfram Hogrebe, Marc Laureys, Silke Meyer, Vera Nickele, Imke Lichterfeld, Rachel Ramsay, Gislind Rohwer-Happe, Elisabeth Rüb, Konrad Vössing, and Friederike Wolfrum.

Plate I: Henkel, Arthur and Albrecht Schöne (eds.). *Emblemata. Handbuch zur Sinnbildkunst des XVI. und XVII. Jahrhunderts.* Stuttgart: Metzler, 1967. 1248

IN MORTEM PRAEPROPERAM

Qui teneras forma allexit, torsitque puellas,
Pulchrior, et tota nobilis urbe puer,
Occidit ante diem. nulli mage flendus (Aresti)
Quam tibi, cui casto iunctus amore fuit.
Ergo illi tumulum tanti monumenta doloris
Astruis: et querulis uocibus astra feris.
Me sine abis dilecte? neque amplius ibimus una?
Nec mecum in studijs ocia grata teres?
Sed te terra teget. sed fati, Gorgonis ora,
Delphinesque, tui signa dolenda dabunt.

Plate II: HENKEL, Arthur and Albrecht SCHÖNE (eds.). *Emblemata. Handbuch zur Sinnbildkunst des XVI. und XVII. Jahrhunderts.* Stuttgart: Metzler, 1967. 555

Prince qui ueult que sa uertu fleuronne,
Et que son bruit soit en tous lieux famé:
Pour asseurer son sceptre et sa couronne,
Fault que des siens il soit crainct et aymé.
Par ce moyen sera bien reclamé,
Et des subiectz honoré nuict et iour.
Le lieure crainct, le chien à grand amour.
Deux ennemys, ferme paix entretiennent,
Craincte et amour tiennent roys en seiour.
Lieures et chiens les couronnes soustiennent.

References

ADAMS, Robert P. "Opposed Tudor Myths of Power: Machiavellian Tyrants and Christian Kings." In: Dale B.J. Randall and George W. Williams (eds.). *Studies in the Continental Background of Renaissance English Literature: Essays Presented to J.L. Lievsay*. Durham: Duke University Press, 1977. 67 – 90.

AESCHYLUS. *Eumenides*. Translated by Herbert Weir Smyth. Loeb Classical Library No. 145 & 146. 2 Vols. London: Heinemann, 1956 – 1957.

– *The Persians*. Translated by Herbert Weir Smyth. Loeb Classical Library No. 145 & 146. 2 Vols. London: Heinemann, 1956 – 1957.

ALLEN, Percy Stafford, Helen Mary ALLEN and H.W. GARROD (eds.). *Opus Epistolarum Des. Erasmi Roterodami*, 12 vols. Oxford: Oxford University Press, 1906 – 1958.

ANTOR, Heinz. "Herrscherfiguren in den Dramen Christopher Marlowes." In: Uwe Baumann (ed.). *Basileus und Tyrann. Herrscherbilder und Bilder von Herrschaft in der Englischen Renaissance*. Frankfurt M.: Lang, 1999. 235 – 77.

ARISTOTLE. *Rhetoric*. Translated by William Rhys Roberts (1954). New York: Random House, 1984.

ARMSTRONG, William A. "The Elizabethan Conception of the Tyrant." In: *RES* 22 (1946): 161 – 81.

– "The Influence of Seneca and Machiavelli on the Elizabethan Tyrant." In: *RES* 24 (1948): 19 – 35.

ASCHMANN, Birgit (ed.). *Gefühl und Kalkül. Der Einfluss von Emotionen auf die Politik des 19. und 20. Jahrhunderts*. Stuttgart: Franz Steiner, 2005.

BARTLETT, John. *A Complete Concordance or Verbal Index to Words, Phrases and Passages in the Dramatic Works of Shakespeare, With a Supplementary Concordance to the Poems*. London: Macmillan, 1956 [1894].

BAUMANN, Uwe. *Die Antike in den Epigrammen und Briefen Sir Thomas Mores*. Paderborn et al.: Schöningh, 1984.

– "Thomas More and the Classical Tyrant." In: *Moreana 86: Thomas More and the Classics*. Edited by Ralph Keen & Daniel Kinney (1985): 108 – 26.

– "Lukianübersetzungen." In: Uwe Baumann and Hans Peter Heinrich (eds.). *Thomas Morus. Humanistische Schriften*. Darmstadt: WBG, 1986. 40 – 54.

– (ed.). *Claudius Tiberius Nero. A Critical Edition of the Play Published Anonymously in 1607*. Bibliotheca Humanistica Vol. IV. Frankfurt M.: Lang, 1990.

– "Übersetzungstheorie und Übersetzungspraxis im englischen Frühhumanismus: Sir Thomas More und Sir Thomas Elyot." In: Karl-Egon Lönne (ed.). *Kulturwandel im Spiegel des Sprachwandels*. Tübingen/Basel: Francke, 1995. 107 – 37.

– *Vorausdeutung und Tod im englischen Römerdrama der Renaissance (1564 – 1642)*. Tübingen/Basel: Francke, 1996.

– *Shakespeare und seine Zeit*. Stuttgart et al.: Klett, 1998.

– "Politik, Propaganda und Mythologie. Zur politischen Mythologiedeutung in der englischen Renaissance." In: Bodo Guthmüller and Wilhelm Kühlmann (eds.). *Renaissancekultur und antike Mythologie*. Tübingen: Niemeyer, 1999. 207 – 29.

– "Tyrannen, Attentäter und Intrigen: Die Darstellung des Römischen Kaiserhofes in der Jakobäischen Tragödie." In: Uwe Baumann (ed.). *Basileus und Tyrann. Herrscherbilder*

und Bilder von Herrschaft in der Englischen Renaissance. Frankfurt M.: Lang, 1999.
419 – 40.

– (ed.). *Basileus und Tyrann. Herrscherbilder und Bilder von Herrschaft in der Englischen Renaissance.* Frankfurt M.: Lang, 1999.

– "Macbeth und Duncan als Herrscher in Shakespeares *Macbeth.*" In: Uwe Baumann (ed.). *Basileus und Tyrann. Herrscherbilder und Bilder von Herrschaft in der Englischen Renaissance.* Frankfurt M.: Lang, 1999. 363 – 76.

– "Artus-Stoff und Arturische Motive in der Geschichte, Kultur und Literatur Englands der Tudor- und Stuartzeit." In: Stefan Zimmer (ed.). *König Artus lebt! Eine Ringvorlesung des Mittelalterzentrums der Universität Bonn.* Heidelberg: Winter, 2005. 273 – 96.

– "Historia magistra vitae? Römische Geschichte im Drama der Shakespearezeit." In: Astrid Steiner-Weber, Thomas A. Schmitz and Marc Laureys (eds.). *Bilder der Antike.* Super alta perennis. Studien zur Wirkung der Klassischen Antike Vol. 1. Göttingen: Bonn University Press, 2007. 89 – 126.

– "Der Kampf um den rechten Glauben, die Verfolgung von Ketzern und Hochverrätern und die tödlichen Grenzen der Streitkultur im England der (frühen) Tudorzeit." In: Uwe Baumann, Arnold Becker and Astrid Steiner-Weber (eds.). *Streitkultur. Okzidentale Traditionen des Streitens in Literatur, Geschichte und Kunst.* Super alta perennis: Studien zur Wirkung der Klassischen Antike Vol. 2. Göttingen: Bonn University Press, 2008. 233 – 63.

– *Heinrich VIII. Mit Selbstzeugnissen und Bilddokumenten.* 6th edn. Reinbek: Rowohlt, 2010.

BAYERL, Francis James. *The Characterization of the Tyrant in Elizabethan Drama.* Diss.: University of Toronto, 1974.

BELLEN, Heinz. *Metus Gallicus – Metus Punicus. Zum Furchtmotiv in der römischen Republik.* Stuttgart: Steiner, 1985.

BERGSDORF, Wolfgang. "Politik und Angst." In: Franz Bosbach (ed.). *Angst und Politik in der europäischen Geschichte.* Dettelbach: Röll, 2000. 13 – 28.

BERMBACH, Udo and Klaus-M. KODALLE (eds.). *Furcht und Freiheit. Leviathan-Diskussion 300 Jahre nach Thomas Hobbes.* Opladen: Westdeutscher Verlag, 1982.

BOLTON, Whitney F. (ed.). Ben Jonson, *Sejanus His Fall.* The New Mermaids. London: Benn, 1966.

BONNER, S.F. *Roman Declamation in the Late Republic and Early Empire.* Liverpool: Liverpool University Press, 1949.

BORMANN, Patrick, Thomas FREIBERGER and Judith MICHEL (eds.). *Angst in den Internationalen Beziehungen.* Göttingen: Bonn University Press, 2010.

BOSBACH, Franz. "Angst und Universalmonarchie." In: Franz Bosbach (ed.). *Angst und Politik in der europäischen Geschichte.* Dettelbach: Röll, 2000. 151 – 66.

BOURKE, Joanna. *Fear. A Cultural History.* London: Virago Press, 2005.

BRADNER, Leicester, Charles A. LYNCH, Clarence H. MILLER and Revilo P. OLIVER (eds.). Thomas More, *Latin Poems*, The Complete Works of St. Thomas More (CW), Vol. 3, Part II. New Haven/London: Yale University Press, 1984.

BUSHNELL, Rebecca W. *Tragedies of Tyrants. Political Thought and Theatre in the English Renaissance.* Ithaca/London: Cornell University Press, 1990.

CALABRESE, Brian E. *Fear in Democracy: A Study of Thucydides' Political Thought.* Diss. University of Michigan, 2008.

CHONÉ, Paulette. "Angst im Spiegel der Emblematik (16.–17. Jahrhundert)." In: Franz Bosbach (ed.). *Angst und Politik in der europäischen Geschichte.* Dettelbach: Röll, 2000. 133–49.

CLAUSS, Manfred. *Sparta. Eine Einführung in seine Geschichte und Zivilisation.* Munich: Beck, 1983.

CONDON, M.M. "Empson, Sir Richard (c. 1450–1510)." In: *Oxford Dictionary of National Biography.* Oxford: Oxford University Press, 2004.

CRAIG, Leon H. *Of Philosophers and Kings: Political Philosophy in Shakespeare's 'Macbeth' and 'King Lear'.* Toronto: Toronto University Press, 2001.

EDWARDS, Philip and Colin GIBSON (eds.). *The Plays and Poems of Philip Massinger,* Vol. III. Oxford: Oxford University Press, 1976.

EICH, Peter, Sebastian SCHMIDT-HOFNER and Christian WIELAND (eds.). *Der wiederkehrende Leviathan. Staatlichkeit und Staatswerdung in Spätantike und Früher Neuzeit.* Heidelberg: Winter, 2011.

ELTON, Geoffrey R. (ed.). *The Tudor Constitution. Documents and Commentary.* Cambridge: Cambridge University Press, 1960.

ERZGRÄBER, Willi. "Das Gewissen bei Shakespeare." In: *Literaturwissenschaftliches Jahrbuch* 40 (1999): 95–114.

EVANS, K.W. "Sejanus and the Ideal Prince Tradition." In: *SEL* 11 (1971): 249–64.

FENLON, Dermot. "Thomas More and Tyranny." In: *Journal of Ecclesiastical History* 32 (1981): 453–76.

FUHRMANN, Manfred. "Das Vierkaiserjahr bei Tacitus. Über den Aufbau der Historien Buch I–III." In: *Philologus* 104 (1960): 250–78.

– *Die antike Rhetorik, Eine Einführung.* Munich: Artemis, 1990.

FUREDI, Frank. *Politics of Fear.* London: Continuum, 2005.

GENTILI, Vanna. "Thomas Lodge's *Wounds of Civil War:* An Assessment of Context, Sources and Structure." In: *REAL* 2 (1984): 119–64.

GLASSNER, Barry. *The Culture of Fear. Why Americans Are Afraid of the Wrong Things.* New York: Basic Books, 1999.

GRACE, Damian. "Thomas More's *Epigrammata:* Political Theory in a Poetic Idiom." In: *Parergon,* N.S. 3 (1985): 115–29.

GUNN, S.J. "Dudley, Edmund (c. 1462–1510)." In: *Oxford Dictionary of National Biography.* Oxford: Oxford University Press, 2004.

GUY, John A. *Tudor England.* Oxford/New York: Oxford University Press, 1990.

HARDIN, Richard F. "Apocalypse Then: Tamburlaine and the Pleasures of Religious Fear." In: *Baylor Journal of Theatre and Performance* 3,2 (2006): 31–41.

HARPER, J.W. (ed.). Christopher Marlowe, *Tamburlaine.* The New Mermaids. London: Benn, 1971.

HAWES, Stephen. "A Ioyfull meditacyon to all Englonde of the coronacyon of our moost naturall soue2rayne lorde kynge Henry the eyght." In: Florence W. Gluck and Alice B. Morgan (eds.). Stephen Hawes, *The Minor Poems.* Early English Text Society. London/Toronto: Oxford University Press, 1974.

HEBBLETHWAITE, Kate and Elizabeth McCARTHY (eds.). *Fear. Essays on the Meaning and Experience of Fear.* Dublin: Four Courts Press, 2007.

HEINZ, Wolff-Rüdiger. *Die Furcht als politisches Phänomen bei Tacitus.* Heuremata Vol. 4. Amsterdam: B.R. Grüner, 1975.

HENKEL, Arthur and Albrecht SCHÖNE (eds.). *Emblemata. Handbuch zur Sinnbildkunst des XVI. und XVII. Jahrhunderts.* Stuttgart: Metzler, 1967.

HERMAN, Peter C. "*Macbeth:* Absolutism, the Ancient Constitution, and the Aporia of Politics." In: Constance Jordan and Karen Cunnigham (eds.). *The Law in Shakespeare.* Basingstoke: Palgrave Macmillan, 2009. 208–32.

HILL, Eliott M. (ed.). *The Tragedy of Nero. A Critical Edition of the work first published anonymously in 1624.* Renaissance Drama, A Collection of Critical Editions. New York/ London, 1979.

HOBBES, Thomas. *De Cive.* In: *Man and Citizen.* Edited by Bernard Gert. Indianapolis: Hackett, 1991.

– *Leviathan.* Edited by Kenneth R. Minogue. London et al.: Dent, 1973.

– *The Elements of Law: Natural & Politic.* Edited by Ferdinand Tönnies. London: Frank Cass, 1969.

HOEGES, Dirk. *Niccolò Machiavelli. Die Macht und der Schein.* Munich: Beck, 2000.

HOGG, James (ed.). *Jacobean Drama as Social Criticism.* Lewiston/Salzburg: Edwin Mellen, 1995.

HORN, Klaus and Volker RITTBERGER (eds.). *Mit Kriegsgefahren leben. Bedrohtsein, Bedrohungsgefühle und friedenspolitisches Engagement.* Opladen: Westdeutscher Verlag, 1987.

HOROWITZ, Mark R. "Richard Empson, Minister of Henry VII." In: *Bulletin of the Institute of Historical Research* 55 (1982): 35–49.

HUME, Robert D. *The Development of English Drama in the Late Seventeenth Century.* Oxford: Clarendon Press, 1976.

HUNGER, Herbert. *Lexikon der griechischen und römischen Mythologie.* 6th edn. Reinbek: Rowohlt, 1974.

HUNT, Maurice. "Duncan, Macbeth, and the Thane of Cawdor." In: *Studies in the Humanities* 28 (2001): 1–30.

ISER, Wolfgang. *Shakespeares Historien. Genesis und Geltung.* Konstanz: Universitätsverlag, 1988.

IVES, Eric William. *Anne Boleyn.* Oxford: Blackwell, 1986.

KAESELITZ, Hella. "Die Ängste der Margaret Thatcher. Einige Aspekte der britischen Haltung zur deutschen Vereinigung." In: *Utopie kreativ* 105. Rosa Luxemburg Stiftung. Juli 1999, 61–67.

KHOURY, Joseph. "Marlowe's Tamburlaine: Idealized Machiavellian Prince." In: Patricia Vilches and Gerald Seaman (eds.). *Seeking Real Truths: Multidisciplinary Perspectives on Machiavelli.* Leiden: Brill, 2007. 329–56.

KIENAST, Dietmar. *Augustus. Prinzeps und Monarch.* Darmstadt: WBG, 1982.

KNEPPE, Alfred. "Metus und Securitas. Angst und Politik in der römischen Kaiserzeit." In: Franz Bosbach (ed.). *Angst und Politik in der europäischen Geschichte.* Dettelbach: Röll, 2000. 53–66.

– *Metus temporum. Zur Bedeutung von Angst in Politik und Gesellschaft der römischen Kaiserzeit des 1. und 2. Jhdts. n. Chr.* Stuttgart: Steiner, 1994.

KOON, Helene. *Colley Cibber.* Lexington: Kentucky University Press, 1986.

KRIPPENDORFF, Ekkehart. *Politik in Shakespeares Dramen. Historien, Römerdramen, Tragödien.* Frankfurt M.: Suhrkamp, 1992.

LEGGATT, Alexander. *Shakespeare's Political Drama. The History Plays and the Roman Plays.* London/New York: Routledge, 1992.

LEINSLE, Ulrich G. "Kasuistik der Angst. *Metus* in der Moralphilosophie und -theologie der Frühen Neuzeit." In: Franz Bosbach (ed.). *Angst und Politik in der europäischen Geschichte.* Dettelbach: Röll, 2000. 85 – 99.

LENGELER, Rainer. "*Macbeth.* Vom Mitleiden am Leiden des Verbrechers." In: Werner Habicht and Ina Schabert (eds.). *Sympathielenkung in den Dramen Shakespeares.* Munich: Fink, 1978. 55 – 64.

LOADES, David. *Henry VIII. Court, Church and Conflict.* Richmond: The National Archives, 2007.

LOCKYER, Roger. *Henry VII.* Seminar Studies in History. London: Longman, 1968.

LOGAN, Robert A. "Violence, Terrorism and War in Marlowe's Tamburlaine Plays." In: Sara M. Deats, Lagretta T. Lenker and Merry G. Perry (eds.). *War and Words: Horror and Heroism in the Literature of Warfare.* Lanham: Lexington, 2004. 65 – 81.

LÜSSE, Beate. "Panegyric Poetry on the Coronation of King Henry VIII: The King's Praise and the Poet's Self-Presentation." In: Uwe Baumann (ed.). *Henry VIII. in History, Historiography and Literature.* Frankfurt M.: Lang, 1992. 49 – 77.

MACHIAVELLI, Niccolò. *The Prince.* Translated by W.K. Marriott. Chicago et al.: William Benton, 1952.

MACKENZIE, Clayton G. "Marlowe's Grisly Monster: Death in *Tamburlaine*, Parts One & Two." In: *Dalhousie Review* 87,1 (2007): 9 – 24.

MAIER, Hans. "Hobbes." In: Hans Maier, Heinz Rausch and Horst Denzer (eds.). *Klassiker des politischen Denkens.* Vol. 1. *Von Plato bis Hobbes.* Munich: Beck, 1968.

MALCOLM, Noel. "Hobbes, Thomas (1588 – 1679), Philosopher." In: *Oxford Dictionary of National Biography* (2004), Online-Edition 2010.

MAPSTONE, Sally. "Shakespeare and Scottish Kingship: A Case History." In: Sally Mapstone and Juliette Wood (eds.). *The Rose and the Thistle: Essays on the Culture of Late Medieval and Renaissance Scotland.* East Lothian: Tuckwell, 1998. 158 – 89.

MARCUS, Leah. "Marlowe in tempore belli." In: Sara M. Deats, Lagretta T. Lenker and Merry G. Perry (eds.). *War and Words: Horror and Heroism in the Literature of Warfare.* Lanham: Lexington Books, 2004. 295 – 316.

MARIUS, Richard. *Thomas More. A Biography.* London/Melbourne: Knopf, 1984.

MARTINICH, Aloysius P. *Hobbes: A Biography.* New York: Cambridge University Press, 1999.

MASSINGER, Philip. "The Roman Actor." In: Philip Edwards and Colin Gibson (eds.). *The Plays and Poems of Philip Massinger.* Vol. III. Oxford: Oxford University Press, 1976. 1 – 93.

MEAD, Walter Russel. "Is Fear The Father Of Us All?" *http://blogs.the-american-interest.com/wrm/2011/02/14.*

MEIER, Christian. *Athen. Ein Neubeginn der Weltgeschichte.* Berlin: Siedler Verlag, 1993.

MERTEN, Kai. "Medusa (Gorgo)." In: Lutz Walther (ed.). *Antike Mythen und ihre Rezeption, Ein Lexikon.* Stuttgart: Reclam, 2003. 136 – 44.

MOSCHOVAKIS, Nick (ed.). *Macbeth: New Critical Essays.* New York: Routledge, 2008.

MUIR, Kenneth (ed.). William Shakespeare, *Macbeth*. Arden Edition. London/New York: Routledge, 1984.

MÜNKLER, Herfried. *Machiavelli. Die Begründung des politischen Denkens der Neuzeit aus der Krise der Republik Florenz*. Frankfurt M.: Fischer, 1984.

MURPHY, Beverley A. *Bastard Prince. Henry VIII's Lost Son*. Phoenixmill: Sutten, 2001.

NEELY, Carol Thomas. *Distracted Subjects: Madness and Gender in Shakespeare and Early Modern Culture*. Ithaca: Cornell University Press, 2004.

NEWMARK, Paige. "Marlowe, Maps, and Might." In: Andrew Lynch and Anne M. Scott (eds.). *Renaissance Poetry and Drama in Context: Essays for Christopher Wortham*. Newcastle upon Tyne: Cambridge Scholars, 2008. 129 – 44.

The New Science of Giambattista Vico. Revised Translation of the Third Edition (1744) by Thomas Goddard Bergin and Max Harold Fisch. Ithaca/New York: Cornell University Press, 1968.

Opus Epistolarum Des. Erasmi Roterodami. Edited by Percy Stafford Allen, Helen Mary Allen and H.W. Garrod. 12 vols. Oxford: Oxford University Press, 1906.

OSCHMANN Antje. "Der *Metus Iustus* in der deutschen Kriegsrechtslehre des 17. Jahrhunderts." In: Franz Bosbach (ed.). *Angst und Politik in der europäischen Geschichte*. Dettelbach: Röll, 2000. 101 – 31.

PUBLILIUS SYRUS. "Sententiae." In: *Minor Latin Poets*. Translated by J. Wight Duff and Arnold M. Duff. Loeb Classial Library. Cambridge/MA: Harvard University Press, 1982.

RAYMENT, C.S. "The 'Tyrannicide' of Erasmus: Translated Excerpts with Introduction and Commentary." In: *Speech Monographs* 26 (1959): 233 – 47.

RITTER, Gerhard. *Angst als Mittel der Politik in der Ost-West-Auseinandersetzung*. Berlin: Duncker & Humblot, 1986.

ROBIN, Corey. *Fear. The History of a Political Idea*. Oxford: Oxford University Press, 2004.

SALLUST. *The Conspiracy of Catiline and The War of Jugurtha*. Translated into English by Thomas Heywood, Anno 1608, with an Introduction by Charles Whibley. The Tudor Translations. London: Constable and Co., 1924.

SCARISBRICK, J.J. *Henry VIII*. Berkeley/Los Angeles: University of California Press, 1968.

SCHILDT, Axel. "'German Angst': Überlegungen zur Mentalitätsgeschichte der Bundesrepublik." In: Daniela Münkel and Jutta Schwarzkopf (eds.). *Geschichte als Experiment: Studien zu Politik, Kultur und Alltag im 19. und 20. Jahrhundert. Festschrift für Adelheid von Saldern*. Frankfurt M.: Campus-Verlag, 2004. 87 – 97.

SCHMID, F. Ernst (ed.). *Thomas May's Tragedy of Julia Agrippina, Empresse of Rome*. Materialien zur Kunde des Älteren Englischen Dramas Vol. 43. Louvain, 1914 / Reprint: Vaduz, 1963.

SCHRAY, Kateryna A.R. "'Is This Your Crown?' Conquest and Coronation in *Tamburlaine* I, Act II, Scene 4." In: *Cahiers Elisabéthains* 68 (2005): 19 – 26.

SCHRECKER, Ellen (ed.). *Cold War Triumphalism: The Misuse of History After the Fall of Communism*. New York: The New Press, 2004.

SCHULTE HERBRÜGGEN, Hubertus. "The Process against Sir Thomas More." In: *The Law Quarterly Review* 99 (1983): 113 – 36.

SCHULTZ, Nancy L. (ed.). *Fear Itself: Enemies Real and Imagined*. West Lafayette: Purdue University Press, 1999.

SCHWARZ, Urs. *Die Angst in der Politik*. Düsseldorf/Wien: Econ, 1967.

SENGHAAS, Dieter. "Angst in der Politik." In: Hans Jürgen Schultz (ed.). *Angst*. Stuttgart: Kreuz-Verlag, 1987. 248 – 60.

SKELTON, John. "A Lawde and Prayse Made for Our Sovereigne Lord the Kyng." In: John Scattergood (ed.). John Skelton, *The Complete English Poems*. New Haven/London: Yale University Press, 1983.

SKEMP, Arthur R. (ed.). *Nathanael Richards' Tragedy of Messallina, The Roman Empresse.* Materialien zur Kunde des Älteren Englischen Dramas Vol. 30. Louvain, 1910 / Reprint: Nendeln, 1970.

SPEVACK, Marvin. *A Complete and Systematic Concordance to the Works of Shakespeare.* 9 Vols., Vol. IV.: 'A – Hilding'. Hildesheim: Olms, 1968.

STARKEY, David. *Henry. Virtuous Prince*. London et al.: Harper Perennial, 2009.

STEARNS, Peter N. "Fear and Contemporary History: A Review Essay." In: *Journal of Social History* 40,2 (2006): 477 – 84.

– *American Fear. The Causes and Consequences of High Anxiety*. New York/London: Routledge, 2006.

STEMMLER, Theo (ed.). *Die Liebesbriefe Heinrichs VIII. an Anna Boleyn*. Zürich: Belser, 1988.

STRONG, Roy. *Feste der Renaissance 1450 – 1650. Kunst als Instrument der Macht*. Freiburg/ Würzburg: Ploetz, 1991.

SUETONIUS. Translated by J.C. Rolfe (1913). London: Heinemann, 1970.

SVENDSEN, Lars. *A Philosophy of Fear*. London: Reaction Books, 2007.

SZURAWITZKI, Michael. *Contra den 'rex iustus / rex iniquus'? Der Einfluss von Machiavellis 'Il Principe' auf Marlowes 'Tamburlaine', Shakespeares 'Heinrich V.' und Gryphius 'Leo Armenius'*. Würzburg: Königshausen & Neumann, 2005.

THOMPSON, Craig R. (ed.). Thomas More, *Translations of Lucian*, The Complete Works of St. Thomas More (CW) Vol. 3, Part I. New Haven/London: Yale University Press, 1974.

TURNER, Robert K. (ed.). *The Tragedy of Valentinian*. In: Fredson Bowers (ed.). *The Dramatic Works in the Beaumont and Fletcher Canon*. Vol. IV. Cambridge et al.: Cambridge University Press, 1979. 261 – 414.

VIATOR, Timothy J. and William J. BURLING (eds.). *The Plays of Colley Cibber*. Vol. 1. Madison/London: Associated UP, 2001.

– "The Stage History of Cibber's *Xerxes*." In: *Theatre Notebook* 46,3 (1992): 155 – 59.

WARNICKE, Retha M. *The Rise and Fall of Anne Boleyn*. Cambridge et al.: Cambridge University Press, 1989.

WELLESLEY, Kenneth. *The Long Year A. D. 69*. London: Elek, 1975.

WILSON, Derek. *A Brief History of Henry VIII. Reformer and Tyrant*. London: Constable & Robinson, 2009.

WILSON, Richard. "'Blood Will Have Blood': Regime Change in *Macbeth*." In: *Shakespeare Jahrbuch* 143 (2007): 11 – 35.

WILSON KNIGHT, G. *The Wheel of Fire*. London/New York: Methuen, 1983 [1930].

WOLF, William D. *The Reform of the Fallen World: The 'Virtuous Prince' in Jonsonian Tragedy and Comedy*. SSEL JDS Vol. 27. Salzburg, 1973.

WOLPERS, Theodor. "Der 'Sturz des Mächtigen' in Shakespeares *Richard II, Richard III* und *Macbeth*." In: Theodor Wolpers (ed.). *Der Sturz des Mächtigen: Zu Struktur, Funktion und Geschichte eines literarischen Motivs*. Göttingen: Vandenhoeck & Ruprecht, 2000. 203 – 47.

WURMBACH, Hubert. *Christopher Marlowes Tamburlaine-Dramen. Struktur, Rezeptions-lenkung und historische Bedeutung: Ein Beitrag zur Dramenanalyse.* Heidelberg: Winter, 1984.

Andrea Rummel

Romanticism, Anxiety and Dramatic Representation

Sociologists, political scientists, historians and media scholars have concluded that we have for some time been living in a "culture of fear".[1] Many of the papers in this volume similarly trace horror and terror as significant categories in postmodern culture, clearly evidencing the aesthetic importance of fear. The paradoxical fascination of the fearful and horrible is a constant throughout cultural history – yet what culminates in contemporary explorations of the fearful and horrible frequently appears to have been anticipated in the philosophical and aesthetic discussions of the late seventeenth and eighteenth centuries.

A sizeable body of literary and aesthetic discussion in the eighteenth century turns to the fascination which fear and horror hold for the human psyche. The most notable contributions were certainly Edmund Burke's *A Philosophical Inquiry into the Origins of our Ideas of the Sublime and Beautiful* (1757) and Immanuel Kant's *Critique of the Power of Judgement* (1790). Writers such as Joseph Addison in "Why Terrour and Grief are Pleasing to the Mind when Excited by Descriptions" (1712) and John and Anna Laetitia Aikin in "On the Pleasure Derived from Objects of Terror" (1773) were interested more specifically by the aesthetic use of *terror* and *horror* in works of art, while texts such as David Hume's "Of Tragedy" (1757) and Friedrich Schiller's "On the Reason Why We Take Pleasure in Tragic Sujets" (1792) evidence how the general debate expands not only into literature and painting but characteristically also into the realm of tragic and sorrowful stage plays. As I would argue, the eighteenth century's oxymoronic expressions of 'terrible joy', 'pleasing horror', 'terreur agréable', 'schaudervolles Ergötzen' remain essential to what cultural theory today has identified as a contemporary culture of fear. Where many papers in this volume consider postmodern and contemporary expressions of these

---

1 See, for instance, GLASSNER, Barry. *The Culture of Fear. Why Americans Are Afraid of the Wrong Things.* New York: Basic, 1999; ALTHEIDE, David L. *Creating Fear. News and the Construction of Crisis.* New York: Aldine, 2002.

phenomena I will therefore turn to British writing of the Romantic period and seek to bridge the gap between dramatic representation at the end of the eighteenth century and cultural theory today.

Musing on tragic art, Friedrich Schiller confirmed the 'magic' fascination of the terrible and dreadful in 1792:

> Es ist eine allgemeine Erscheinung in unserer Natur, daß uns das Traurige, das Schreckliche, das Schauderhafte selbst mit unwiderstehlichem Zauber an sich lockt, daß wir uns von Auftritten des Jammers, des Entsetzens mit gleichen Kräften weggestoßen und wieder angezogen fühlen.[2]

Schiller's insistence on the power of horror to simultaneously attract and repulse encapsulates the eighteenth century's general interest in fear. What Schiller here formulates for the stage – the reason for me to single him out here – was expressed much more famously in Edmund Burke's conception of the sublime.[3] As opposed to the beautiful, the concept of the sublime opened the way to integrate the mis-formed, the monstrous, the uncanny into aesthetics, and Gothic writing is evidence of the productivity of the general trend informing this concept. While the Gothic novel may in this respect seem to epitomize the period's central aesthetic debate centring on horror and terror,[4] I will nevertheless steer away from this here into Romantic drama. For the topic of our discussion the drama of Romanticism appears to me more challenging and a more multilayered genre than the Gothic novel: as theatre provides dramatic as well as textual forms of representation and visualises as well as verbally expresses content, it formulates relationships with the public which are arguably more complex. At the same time, I believe that it is also the peculiar political dimension of these plays in a theatre marked by censorship that produces additional strategies of both staging and masking fear. Let us stay with Schiller therefore, and briefly explore some Romantic versions of terror on stage.

---

2 SCHILLER, Friedrich. "Über die tragische Kunst." In: *Werke*. Nationalausgabe. Begr. V. Julius Petersen. Weimar 1943 ff., NA 20. 148.
3 BURKE, Edmund. *An Inquiry into the Origin of our Ideas of the Sublime and Beautiful*. Edited by J.T. Boulton. London: Routledge, 1958.
4 Anne Radcliffe's famous differentiation of terror and horror is maybe the most famous example of this, cf. RADCLIFFE, Anne. "On the Supernatural in Poetry." In: *New Monthly Magazine and Literary Journal* 16 (1826): 145 – 52.

I.   Gothic Drama: George Colman the Younger, *Bluebeard*

Most Romantic stage dramas enact fear in one way or another. The diversity of different forms of contextualisation and representation is remarkable, however: due to the multiplicity of forms British Romantic drama takes, ranging from melodramatic productions to closet drama to Gothic tragedies, its strategies of staging and instrumentalising fear vary greatly. Looking at these dramatic forms, one would expect the productive and popular genre of Gothic drama to feature and functionalise fear and terror most prominently.

George Colman the Younger's *Bluebeard*, announced as a "Dramatick Romance" and thereby clearly aligning itself in the tradition of popular Gothic romance, to some extent confirms this. *Bluebeard*, a hugely successful play, premiered at Drury Lane in the place of a Christmas pantomime in January 1798. It closely followed the plot of the popular tale – but Colman the Younger had decided to transpose the story to Oriental Turkey, probably riding on the wave of popular taste for Eastern entertainments as well as using the Orient as a convenient Other. While this modification may indicate already that *Bluebeard* is more than a mere dramatisation of a fairy tale written because "English Children, both old and young, are disappointed without a Pantomime at Christmas",[5] the drama itself clearly shows its author turning to grotesque and Gothic modes. As one reviewer put it, "very little alteration is made in the main incidents of the original fable. But the story of Blue Beard is calculated chiefly to excite commiseration and terror".[6] While Colman's *Bluebeard* may have been a substitute or replacement piece for a Christmas harlequinade at Drury Lane, it was clearly also a play bent on maximising emotional effect, quite in line with the melodramatic tradition of the Haymarket and probably part of a general trend catering to popular demand and bringing the melodramatic even to Drury Lane.

The production of *Bluebeard* was hugely expensive. Cox and Gamer specify that over two thousand pounds were spent on the sets realised by the well-known prop-maker Alexander Johnston.[7] They included an immense animated panorama, mechanical animals and a moving skeleton – intricate stage machinery ensuring emotional effect and needed to propel the action which from the outset is typecast Gothic: set in "Romantick, Mountainous Country", against the backdrop of a "magnificent castle", *Bluebeard* turns into a Gothic romance. The play's characters, a tyrannical father, an unwanted bloodthirsty husband mut-

5 COLMAN THE YOUNGER, George. "Introduction." In: Jeffrey N. Cox and Michael Gamer (eds.). *The Broadview Anthology of Romantic Drama.* Peterborough, Canada: Broadview Press, 2003. 77.
6 ANON. "Review of the opening night performance of *Blue Beard*." In: *The Oracle and Public Advertiser* 19,833 (1798): 3.
7 Cox, Jeffrey N. and Michael GAMER (eds.). *The Broadview Anthology of Romantic Drama.* Peterborough, Canada: Broadview Press, 2003. 76.

tering "mystick spells and hellish incantations" (*Bluebeard* I.1.v.67 – 8), a beautiful and innocent young bride and a disregarded lover calling for revenge and retaliation, are Gothic types. Colman the Younger adapts the story of *Bluebeard* to include the stock settings and characters of any Gothic novel and imitates the Gothic's concern with heightened emotion, fear, terror and horror and supernatural effect – much more than a mere Christmas pantomime, *Bluebeard* targets popular taste for a fashionable mode.

Even in the popular fairy tale version, fear as a category is central in *Bluebeard:* already in Charles Perrault's 1697 *La Barbe bleue*, the violent nobleman Bluebeard cruelly punishes the curiosity of his several wives with the horrors of death. Perhaps the tale's emphasis on strong emotion was an additional reason that attracted Colman the Younger to his subject – also in his *Bluebeard*, fear and horror are the key emotions, effectively opposed to love and trust as suggested by the marriage plot and heightened in their intensity through this opposition. The functionalisation of the horrors of the blue chamber as instruments to punish the "female curiosity" of the play's subtitle is obvious, and the play has subsequently been read as "re-enacting masculinist stereotypes or as using conventional orientalist imagery to decry the subjugation of women to oppressive men."[8] While this gender subtext clearly informs both the original fairytale and Colman the Younger's *Bluebeard* plot, I would like to argue that in *Bluebeard* Colman the Younger appears to shift the focus from character and action to the stage and its spatial stimulation of strong emotional effect: the stage and its immensely elaborate props begin to dominate the play to an extent that seems to locate the primary function of horror and terror in spectacle on stage rather than in the ideology or prescriptive morality of its plotline.

This may be most readily illustrated by the depiction and use of the blue chamber, the *locus* of horror in both the tale and the play. In Colman the Younger's play, the blue chamber features centrally in the evocation of terror even in its absence: from Act I scene 2, Shacabac – Bluebeard's servant and unwilling agent – and other characters verbally voice their terror of the room long before it is visually part of the scene on stage – "Don't mention that Beda! – Never mention the Blue Chamber again!" (*Bluebeard* I.2.v.44 – 45). The secrecy and covert horror which they associate with the room intensifies until Shacabac at last verbally invokes what lies behind the "mysterious Portal" in Act I scene 3: "Flying Phantoms, sheeted Spectres, skipping Skeletons, and grinning ghosts at their gambols" (*Bluebeard* I.2.v.11 – 13) are the reason that "the Air of this Apartment chills" (*Bluebeard* I.2.v.4). Even then, however, the stage does not visually represent this, and the horrors of the blue chamber remain subject to the audience's imagination. It is only when Bluebeard and Shacabac enter the blue

---

8 Cox and GAMER (eds.). *The Broadview Anthology of Romantic Drama.* 76.

chamber that the stage directions convey to us what must have been a magnificent display of stage machinery in the original production,

> Shacabac puts the Key into the Lock; the Door instantly sinks, with a tremendous crash: and the Blue Chamber appears streaked with vivid streams of Blood. The figures in the Picture, over the door, change their position, and Abomelique is represented in the action of beheading the Beauty he was, before, supplicating. The Pictures, and Devices, of Love change to subjects of Horror and Death. The interior apartment (which the sinking of the door discovers), exhibits various Tombs, in a sepulchral building; – in the midst of which ghastly and supernatural forms are seen; – some in motion, some fix'd – In the centre, is a large Skeleton seated on a tomb… (*Bluebeard* I.3)

Thunder and lightning complete the scene, mysterious inscriptions appear as the scene continues and unfold before the audience a visual representation of the "subjects of Horror and Death". The blue chamber's Gothic effects must have been spectacular enough to dominate not only Act one, Scene three but the entire drama – and led one reviewer to call *Bluebeard* a "Spectacle of Action".[9] Complaining at the same time that "everything is addressed to the eye and the ear and so little to the judgement or the heart",[10] *The Morning Chronicle*'s impressions confirm the development of the play away from a focus on character and action to spatial spectacle: reading it today, the play abounds in "mystick ceremonies" (*Bluebeard* I.3.v.48) and supernatural machinery to an extent that seems to almost exclusively focus on exaggerated Gothic effect.

While Colman the Younger's *Bluebeard* thus obviously enacts strategies of staging fear, it may be taken to form part of the larger development outlined by Cox and Gamer which was to turn Gothic tragedy into melodrama.[11] The February 1811 revival of *Bluebeard*, staged at Covent Garden, clearly confirms this general trend: to heighten the spectacle real horses were introduced on the stage in place of Johnston's mechanical animals. This was successful enough to ensure that a second 'hippodrama', Matthew Gregory Lewis's *Timour the Tartar*, quickly followed in *Bluebeard*'s wake in the same year. The reviews of Lewis's drama maybe even more obviously than *Bluebeard*'s praise "splendid combat scenes", "eastern grandeur" and novel stage effects – and culminate in statements that single out horses rather than actors as the principal players on stage[12] and leave

---

9 ANON. "Review of the opening night performance of *Blue Beard*." In: *The Morning Chronicle* 8,939 (1798): 3.
10 ANON. "Review of the opening night performance of *Blue Beard*." 3.
11 Cox and GAMER (eds.). *The Broadview Anthology of Romantic Drama*. xxiii.
12 ANON. "Review of *Timour the Tartar*." In: *European Magazine* 59 (1811): 377–78: "The exertions of the horses have a wonderful effect. The white horse which carried the heroine (Mrs. H. Johnston) plays admirably. He kneels, leaps, tumbles, dances, fights, dashes into

the impression that the 'quadruped' rather than the 'biped' actors were at the heart of the performances. *The Sun* classified *Timour the Tartar* as "equestrian exhibition" rather than regular drama,[13] just as *Bluebeard* had been taken for a "Spectacle of Action" by *The Morning Chronicle*. One might conclude that Gothic drama – in spite of the fact that it clearly turns to fear and terror as central to the plot – increasingly develops into a pageant-like display of special stage effect. Colman the Younger's *Bluebeard* with its hugely expensive stage machinery clearly exemplifies this general trend: in its insistence on emotionalism and audience effect it seems to simplify horror into spectacle.

II.   Anti-Revolutionary Theatre: Edmund John Eyre, *The Maid of Normandy*

A totally different body of theatrical production I would like to briefly consider is the anti-revolutionary drama of the late eighteenth century: the plays written against the French Revolution during the 1790s are legion and virtually all of them dramatize the intersection of fear with power and politics.[14] One play that overtly does so is Edmund John Eyre's *The Maid of Normandy*. Already in its title Eyre's drama highlights the central importance of contemporary politics and its heroine Charlotte Corday, the infamous female assassin of the French Jacobin Jean-Paul Marat. In its dramatization of these contemporary political and cultural events, Edmund John Eyre's *The Maid of Normandy* appears typical as a piece of anti-revolutionary entertainment, emphasizing the horrors of the post-revolutionary regime and targeting an audience of Anti-Jacobin royalists. Eyre's tragedy was certainly not the first play to put revolutionary matters on stage; yet it was – as is evident already from its subject matter – particularly politically charged in its time and in spite of its royalist sympathies it was one of the dramas

---

water and up precipices, in a very superior style of acting, and completely astonished the audience".

13 ANON. "Review of *Timour the Tartar*." In: *The Sun* 5,814 (1811): 3. In spite of this allegorical allusion to political critique and anti-Napoleonic thought, *Timour the Tartar* seems to find its origin in sensational spectacle rather than in political content or an aesthetic of horror: it was actually commissioned by Henry Harris, then manager of Covent Garden, as a play featuring horses and live battles on the stage – Lewis himself remarked that it "was written merely to oblige Mr. Harris, who prest me very earnestly to give him a Spectacle, in which Horses might be introduced [...] for that [success] which it obtained in London, it was clearly indebted to the magnificence of the Scenery and Dresses, to the exertions of the Performers, and above all to the favour with which the Horses were received by the Public." LEWIS, Matthew G. "Advertisement to *Timour the Tartar*." In: Jeffrey N. Cox and Michael Gamer (eds.). *The Broadview Anthology of Romantic Drama*. 98.

14 See Cox, Jeffrey N. "Ideology and Genre in the British Antirevolutionary Drama of the 1790s." In: *English Literary History* 58,3 (1991): 579–610.

twice refused sanction by the Lord Chamberlain. It was also one of the earliest British literary representations of Charlotte Corday: Corday killed Marat in 1793, and the play was put on at the Theatre Royal, Bath, as early as 1794.

The obvious political functionalisation of the plot is patently evident throughout: the play is clearly royalist in outlook and the political sympathies of its author determine the portrayal of the characters to an extent that they at times appear reduced to mere stock characters in an allegory. Charlotte Corday is cast as an angelic liberator and heroine, and Eyre brings the death of Marie Antoinette into the drama at a time when the government was at war with France, giving a sympathetic, Burkean portrait of the queen. Conversely, Eyre casts the main agents of the revolution as quasi-Gothic villains: Robespierre is portrayed as a "Monster" (*The Maid of Normandy* I.1.v.107), Marat as "that vile assassin-fiend, that type of Hell" (*The Maid of Normandy* I.2.v.136). The portrayal of Marat as a monstrous despot in particular recalls Gothic horrors, and the play throughout seems little more than an enactment of anti-revolutionary anxiety in dramatic representation.

If Corday was an unsettling figure for many at the end of the eighteenth century – a violent woman, a female assassin who not at all corresponded to gender models which insisted on female passivity and women's benevolence[15] – the play thus mainly enacts the counterrevolutionary fears of an England involved in the struggle with France. *The Maid of Normandy* very clearly dramatizes this political struggle and brings issues of contemporary significance to the stage. It is not the first or the only play to do this – as Allardyce Nicoll records:

---

15 It is interesting to see that while Corday stands as the historical realization of violent or 'unsexed' literary women she becomes increasingly depersonalized and 'fictionalized' in literary accounts and an emblematic figure for both revolutionary and counterrevolutionary propaganda. Eyre's play is a significant example of this: whether Corday is cast as *femme forte* or *femme fatale* largely depends on perspective – and, as I have argued elsewhere, both the female ideal of fortitude and a negative and threatening vision can be seen oscillating in Eyre's play; see RUMMEL, Andrea. *Delusive Beauty. Femmes Fatales in English Literature.* Göttingen: V&R Unipress / Bonn University Press, 2008. 152 ff. For a general account of the literary uses of Corday by both Jacobins and Anti-Jacobins see CRACIUN, Adriana. "The New Cordays: Helen Craik and British Representations of Charlotte Corday, 1793–1800." In: Adriana Craciun and Kari E. Lokke (eds.). *Rebellious Hearts: British Women Writers and the French Revolution.* New York: State University of New York Press, 2001. 193–232, who traces the representation of Corday in British literary accounts (women writers). Inge STEPHAN outlines the same ambivalence in the German reception and highlights the mythologizing literarization of Corday, cf. STEPHAN, Inge. "'Die erhabne Männin Corday': Christine Westphalens Drama *Charlotte Corday* (1804) und der Corday-Kult am Ende des 18. Jahrhunderts." In: ibid. (ed.). *Inszenierte Weiblichkeit. Codierungen der Geschlechter in der Literatur des 18. Jahrhunderts.* Köln: Böhlau, 2004. 135–62.

numerous dramatic works of the nineties of the century are to be associated directly
with the chaos in France. As early as 1789 a spectacular *Bastille* was in rehearsal at
Covent Garden, while in August of that year the Royal Circus presented an entertainment entitled *The Triumph of Liberty, or the Destruction of the Bastille*. A year later, in
Aug. 1790, both Sadlers Wells and the Royal Grove were performing *Champ de Mars, or,
the Loyal Federation*, a description of the Grand National Fete held at Paris on July 14th
last, while the Royal Circus capped their efforts with *The French Jubilee*. Besides these,
there are several dramas written either on the tragic events taking place on the continent or on the political consequences arising therefrom.[16]

Coleridge's *The Fall of Robespierre*, written in the same year that Eyre published
the first edition of *The Maid of Normandy* (1794) may also serve as an example. I
would like to argue that for our analysis here the engagement of this particular
type of Romantic drama with national political debate and anxieties is significant in two respects:

Firstly, in this kind of anti-revolutionary theatre, there is a radicalisation of
terror vis-à-vis the Gothic: where Gothic drama as analysed above would typically and just as virtually any Gothic novel opt for past and remote situations –
the medieval era, Italy, Spain, or, in the case of *Bluebeard*, the Ottoman Orient –
the *Maid of Normandy* and its others turn on the contemporary and the political.
They dramatise anxieties much closer to their viewing public: in this type of
Romantic drama no convergence of temporalities free either audience or author
from their mimetic responsibility.

Secondly, this type of Romantic drama for me answers back to one thesis still
strong in critical discussion: in 1964 Richard Alewyn argued that the immense
popularity of terror and horror as an aesthetic category in eighteenth-century
discussion was indebted to a process of compensation. The aestheticisation of
the horrible for Alewyn is due to the fact that fear and terror were no longer
sufficiently present in real life. Alewyn argues for a necessary substitution of
these emotions: "Was aus dem Leben vertrieben war, rettete sich in die Literatur".[17] Alewyn's thesis has been controversial and has been contested by
Habermas, Ingeborg Weber, David Punter and others. As I would like to argue,
much of the drama put on stage in Romanticism also holds against Alewyn's
thesis – it appears to show that fear in some of the literature / theatre of the time
in fact mirrors and instrumentalises fear in real life, rather than substituting it
aesthetically. No matter whether it is the evocation of 'monstrous' women or the
horrors of tyrannical force, it is the very real threats following in the wake of the

---

16 NICOLL, Allardyce. *A History of English Drama 1660–1900. Vol. III, Late Eighteenth Century
    Drama 1750–1800*. Cambridge: Cambridge University Press, 1952. 54.
17 ALEWYN, Richard. "Die Lust an der Angst." In: ibid. *Probleme und Gestalten. Essays.*
    Frankfurt M.: Insel, 1974. 307–30, esp. 307–13.

French Revolution which become iconised in characters such as Charlotte Corday or Marat in plays such as Edmund John Eyre's *The Maid of Normandy*.

III.   Historical Tragedies: Percy Bysshe Shelley, *The Cenci*

Emphasizing yet another idea of fear and terror which links up more clearly to ideas of fear as discussed in cultural theory today, Percy Bysshe Shelley's first attempt at drama, *The Cenci*, was written in Italy in 1819. 250 copies were printed at an Italian press, and the play was popular enough to make a second edition in the following year. However, while Shelley had intended the tragedy explicitly for stage performance and written the part of Beatrice with a famous actress of the time, Miss O'Neil, in mind, *The Cenci* was rejected by Covent Garden and other playhouses on account of its content and never made it on stage.[18] One critic, writing in 1819, localizes the "disgust" and "horror" the drama incited due to its subject "utterly revolting to human nature":

> We have heard of Mr. Shelley's genius; and were it exercised upon any subject not utterly revolting to human nature, we might acknowledge it. But there are topics so disgusting [...] and this is one of them; there are crimes so beastly and demoniac [...] in which *The Cenci* riots and luxuriates, that no feeling can be excited by their obtrusion but those of detestation at the choice, and horror at the elaboration.[19]

The analysis reads like one of the reviews of scandalous Gothic novels such as *The Monk*, and the rejection of Shelley's play by its critical audience only begins its rather jagged reception history and a general reluctance towards the work shown by critics until today. Refused the official right to be staged for most of the nineteenth century, *The Cenci* has only lately and from the twentieth century onwards been working as a stage tragedy. It was first produced in 1886, during the founding festivities of the Shelley Society, yet only by amateurs and for a private circle of intellectuals. The real history of *The Cenci* on stage begins in 1922, almost a century after its original publication, and culminates in Artaud's use of it for his 'Theatre of Cruelty' in 1935.

---

18 SHELLEY, Mary. "Letter to Peacock, July 1819.": "What I want you to do, is to procure for me its presentation at Covent Garden. The principal character, Beatrice, is precisely fitted for Miss O'Neil, and it might even seem written for her, (God forbid that I should ever see her play it–it would tear my nerves to pieces,) and in all respects it is fitted only for Covent Garden. [...] The play was accordingly sent to Mr. Harris. He pronounced the subject to be so objectionable that he could not even submit the part to Miss O'Neil for perusal, but expressed his desire that the author would write a tragedy on some other subject, which he would gladly accept."

19 ANON. "Review of *The Cenci, a Tragedy in Five Acts*." In: *The Literary Gazette* 167 (1820): 209–10.

If this by itself already qualifies the tragedy for mention in this volume, its late performance history may indicate a modernist rather than late eighteenth-century realisation of central categories such as anxiety, cruelty, horror, fear. The 1922 production in Prague set the stage for *The Cenci* as follows:

> In ten of the fifteen scenes of the play appear one or two or three porphyry pillars [...] as high as the stage used [...] dull dappled red, and built of cubes laid one upon another, a small one between a large one and a large one. They act as a sort of architectural *leitmotif* in the play [...] always functioning importantly. For example, in the scene in which Beatrice begins to fear greatly half the stage is a sharply lit screen of red cubes, the other half is a yawning black entrance, and one of the porphyry pillars stands between [...]. For the banquet scene the three are put close together and form one huge block of cubes back of the judgment seat.[20]

The abstract stage props, dappled in red and black could almost be read as an early visualization of what Roger Blood termed Shelley's abstracted patterning of the tragedy many decades later.[21] At the same time, the strong impact of this spatial patterning may recall the suggested primacy of emotional effect over action in Colman the Younger's *Bluebeard*. However, in the case of the 1922 stage for *The Cenci*, the strong emotional effect evoked by lighting and scene only visually expresses the horror, emptiness and threat which lie at the heart of Shelley's drama and which, in the 1819 dedication and preface to *The Cenci*, Shelley contrasts with his earlier writings. While in his other writings, as he says, he concentrated on "apprehensions of the beautiful and the just", this newly written drama showed "the most dark and secret caverns of the human heart". If one recalls that Shelley had published his two Gothic novels *Zastrozzi* (1810) and *St Irvyne* (1811) almost a decade earlier this may be a surprise – but indeed *The Cenci*, as I would like to argue, represents a new dimension in the use of horror compared to both Gothic novels Shelley had written before.

Shelley himself summarizes the plotline of *The Cenci* as follows:

> The story is, that an old man, having spent his life in debauchery and wickedness, conceived at length an implacable hatred towards his children; which shewed itself towards one daughter under the form of an incestuous passion, aggravated by every circumstance of cruelty and violence. This daughter, after long and vain attempts to escape [...] at length plotted with her mother-in-law and brother to murder their common tyrant. The young maiden, who was urged to this tremendous deed by an impulse which overpowered its horror, was evidently a most gentle and amiable being, a creature formed to adorn and be admired [...]. The deed was quickly discovered and

---

20 CAMERON, Kenneth N. and Horst FRENZ. "Stage History of Shelley's 'The Cenci'." In: *PMLA* 60,4 (1945): 1084.
21 BLOOD, Roger. "Allegory and Dramatic Representation in 'The Cenci'." In: *Studies in Romanticism* 33,3 (1994): 355–89.

in spite of the mist earnest prayers made to the Pope by the highest persons in Rome, the criminals were put to death.[22]

Shelley's summary outlines the horrors of the play: parental tyranny and violation of his daughter, the daughter's parricide in an extreme psychological despair "which overpowered its horror". It also, however, stresses the play's characteristic ambivalence – the "tremendous deed" of parricide makes Beatrice clearly criminal; yet the crimes of her father appear to almost – but never quite – excuse her wrong. As Shelley stated in his preface, part of the strength of Cenci's story resides in the "romantic pity" Beatrice's story arouses and the "passionate Exculpation of the horrible deed" through horror itself – the even more horrible deeds of her father:

> It is in the restless and anatomizing casuistry with which men seek the justification of Beatrice, yet feel that she has done what needs justification; it is in the superstitious horror with which they contemplate alike her wrongs and their revenge; that the dramatic character of what she did and suffered, consists.[23]

This is a double-bind interesting enough for a topic such as that of our topic: *The Cenci* makes the theatre a place where conventional categories seem to break down. Here horror entails the breakdown of morality and appears to annihilate the meaning of good and evil. In the terms of Kristeva, it is not amoral but abject, recalling her conception of the *"pouvoir de l'horreur"* and her definition of abjection as that which "disturbs identity, system, order. What does not respect borders, positions, rules."[24]

Throughout, Shelley's play appears to stage Kristeva's thoughts on horror and abjection, on incest and the pre-verbal – a long time before Kristeva. Quite in contrast to Colman the Younger's Gothic melodrama, this is even more consistently presented in the total absence of horror from the stage. In what Roussetzki calls the Shelleyan "Theatre of Anxiety",[25] it is only on a "spiritual stage" that anxiety in *The Cenci* is experienced. In spite of the terrible crimes committed in the play, in spite of the violence which fuels its action, there is a total absence of the visual, the horror always happens off-stage and is – crucially – very often not even verbally represented. After Beatrice has been violated by

22 SHELLEY, Percy Bysshe. "Preface to *The Cenci.*" In: Jeffrey N. Cox and Michael Gamer (eds.). *The Broadview Anthology of Romantic Drama.* Peterborough, Canada: Broadview Press, 2003. 223.
23 SHELLEY. "Preface to *The Cenci.*" 224.
24 KRISTEVA, Julia. *Powers of Horror. An Essay on Abjection.* Edited and translated by Leon S. Roudiez. New York: Columbia University Press, 1982. 4.
25 ROUSSETZKI, Remy. "Theatre of Anxiety in Shelley's *The Cenci* and Musset's *Lorrenzaccio.*" In: *Criticism* 42,1 (2000): 31–57.

her father, for instance, she appears dishevelled on stage, doubting whether such horror can indeed be real, doubting her own identity, doubting perception itself:

> Do you know, / I thought I was wretched Beatrice / Men speak of, whom her father sometimes hales / From hall to hall by the entangled hair / At others pens up naked in damp cells / Where scaly reptiles crawl, and starves her there, / Till she will eat strange flesh. This woeful story / So did I overact in my sick dreams / That I imagined [...] no, it cannot be! / Horrible things have been in this wide world / Prodigious mixtures and confusions strange / Of good and ill; and worse have been conceived / Than ever there was found a heart to do. But never fancy imaged such a deed / As [...] (*Pauses, suddenly recollecting herself*) (*The Cenci* III.1.v.42 ff).

Almost systematically, Beatrice is here voicing what Kristeva terms self-abjection, that which is "beyond the scope of the possible, the tolerable, the thinkable".[26] In other passages, Beatrice refuses to recount anything at all – "What can I say?" – and the horrors of *The Cenci* remain wholly unspeakable, cannot be understood, comprehended, or even put into words.[27] As Roussetzki has argued, this propels much of the dialogue in *The Cenci* into soliloquies strewn with highly abstracted figures. At the same time, however, this 'unspeakability' recalls Kristeva's conclusion that the "non-distinctiveness of inside and outside would thus be unnameable"[28]: where Kristeva sees the advent of language as constituting the subjective history of each individual, the unspeakable crimes of Count Cenci make Beatrice not only doubt their existence but question her own self.

Totally opposed to the visually and spatially representable horrors of Colman the Younger's *Bluebeard* spectacle, *The Cenci* seems to be about the insistence of the irrepresentable – horror, cruelty, fear in their extreme – and the central characters' speech revolves around what exists perforce beyond language's – and the mind's – grasp. In this, one could argue, *The Cenci* is an example of what Soren Kierkegaard has termed a theatre "turned inward, not outward",[29] a theatre where the drama is concerned with what happens 'inside, not outside'.[30] Horror here is something which, as in Kristeva's 'abject', turns to the incomprehensible, the not-categorizable. And it is with equal horror and awe that the postmodern spectator sees Beatrice imagine herself, polluted, poisoned,

26 Kristeva. *Powers of Horror*. 1.
27 Curran, Stuart. *Shelley's Cenci: Scorpions Ringed with Fire*. Princeton: Princeton University Press, 1970. 90. Shelley forms "an entire play around an event that could not be named on stage" (50), see also Roussetzki. "Theatre of Anxiety".
28 Kristeva. *Powers of Horror*. 61.
29 Kierkegaard, Soren. *Either/Or*. Edited and translated by Howard and Edna Hong. Princeton: Princeton University Press, 1987. 155.
30 Roussetzki. "Theatre of Anxiety."

suffocated, mad – and dead, because of the incomprehensible horrors she has had to endure:

> My God! / The beautiful blue heaven is flecked with blood! The sunshine on the floor is black! The air / Is changed to vapours such as the dead breathe / In charnel pits! Pah! I am choked! There creeps / A clinging, black, contaminating mist / About me... 'tis substantial, heavy thick / I cannot pluck it from me, for it glues / My fingers and my limbs to one another / And eats into my sinews, and dissolves / My flesh to a pollution, poisoning / The subtle, pure, and inmost spirit of life! / My God! I never knew what the mad felt / Before; for I am mad beyond all doubt! / (more wildly) No, I am dead! These Putrefying limbs / Shut round and sepulchre the panting soul / Which would burst forth into the wandering air! (*The Cenci* III.1.v.12ff)

Where Kristeva's central image for the 'abject' in *Pouvoirs de l'horreur* always is the dead body, where "the corpse [...] is the utmost of abjection. It is death infecting life",[31] also the tragedy of Beatrice Cenci culminates in that central image where meaning collapses, the living 'I' overcome by the corpse.

IV. Enacting Fear on the Romantic Stage

Any book thinking about fear in literature will automatically debate the idea of fear being not only a negative but an aesthetically attractive category. This clearly leads into eighteenth-century philosophical thought and also into the literature of the Romantic period. While the Gothic novel is an obvious example, I would like to argue that British Romantic drama provides even more complex and above all more diverse treatments of fear, anxiety, or horror in their textual as well as visual realisation. Dramas drawing on the Gothic as a mode, exemplified in this paper by Colman the Younger's *Bluebeard*, clearly demonstrate this through their insistence on intense emotional and visual effect. The verbal and visual/spatial dramatisation of fear and terror here foreground the centrality of emotion to an extent that turns the theatre into a space for spectacle rather than argument. Conversely, anti-revolutionary drama as exemplified by Edmund John Eyre's *The Maid of Normandy* highlights fear and anxiety in its interrogation of contemporary politics and the corresponding political terrors, bringing the monstrous and the fearful into the social sphere of the London viewing public rather than evoking a remote Italy or Orient. In this, the play is an example of how Romantic drama can emphasize the very tangible nature of horror rather than enact strategies of an aestheticisation of the horrible as Alewyn has argued for the eighteenth century. This particular instrumentalisation of fear in real life, rather than its aesthetic substitute, however,

---

31 KRISTEVA. *Powers of Horror.* 4.

is only one of the Romantic drama's several connections to this volume's overarching topic *Fear in Literature*. Yet another example of an entirely different use of fear on stage might be a different group of plays, the more abstracted historical tragedies such as Percy Bysshe Shelley's *The Cenci*. Shelley's play appears singular here in that it seems to function only through an evocation of intense and painful feelings and is almost postmodern in the way it uses abhorrence as a central category – its strategies of polarising are reminiscent of the conception of 'powers of horror' as forwarded by twentieth-century theorists such as Julia Kristeva. In this, *The Cenci* also demonstrates the lasting relevance of late eighteenth-century aesthetic categories for postmodern cultural theory – while at the same time attesting to the complex relevance of a category such as 'fear' for British Romantic drama, something which this paper unfortunately was only tentatively able to explore.

References

ALEWYN, Richard. "Die Lust an der Angst." In: ibid. *Probleme und Gestalten. Essays.* Frankfurt M.: Insel, 1974. 307 – 30.

ALTHEIDE, David L. *Creating Fear. News and the Construction of Crisis.* New York: Aldine, 2002.

ANON. "Review of the opening night performance of *Blue Beard.*" In: *The Oracle and Public Advertiser* 19,833 (1798): 3.

ANON. "Review of *Timour the Tartar.*" In: *European Magazine* 59 (1811): 377 – 78.

ANON. "Review of *Timour the Tartar.*" In: *The Sun* 5,814 (1811): 3

ANON. "Review of *The Cenci, a Tragedy in Five Acts.*" In: *The Literary Gazette* 167 (1820): 209 – 10.

BLOOD, Roger. "Allegory and Dramatic Representation in 'The Cenci'." In: *Studies in Romanticism* 33,3 (1994): 355 – 89.

BURKE, Edmund. *An Inquiry into the Origin of our Ideas of the Sublime and Beautiful.* Edited by J.T. Boulton. London: Routledge, 1958.

CAMERON, Kenneth N. and Horst FRENZ. "Stage History of Shelley's 'The Cenci'." In: *PMLA* 60,4 (1945): 1084.

COLMAN THE YOUNGER, George. "Introduction." In: Jeffrey N. Cox and Michael Gamer (eds.). *The Broadview Anthology of Romantic Drama.* Peterborough, Canada: Broadview Press, 2003.

Cox, Jeffrey N. "Ideology and Genre in the British Antirevolutionary Drama of the 1790s." In: *English Literary History* 58,3 (1991): 579 – 610.

Cox, Jeffrey N. and Michael GAMER (eds.). *The Broadview Anthology of Romantic Drama.* Peterborough, Canada: Broadview Press, 2003.

CRACIUN, Adriana. "The New Cordays: Helen Craik and British Representations of Charlotte Corday, 1793 – 1800." In: Adriana Craciun and Kari E. Lokke (eds.). *Rebel-*

lious Hearts: British Women Writers and the French Revolution. New York: State University of New York Press, 2001. 193 – 232.

CURRAN, Stuart. *Shelley's Cenci: Scorpions Ringed with Fire.* Princeton: Princeton University Press, 1970.

GLASSNER, Barry. *The Culture of Fear. Why Americans are Afraid of the Wrong Things.* New York: Basic, 1999.

KIERKEGAARD, Soren. *Either/Or.* Edited and translated by Howard and Edna Hong. Princeton: Princeton University Press, 1987.

KRISTEVA, Julia. *Powers of Horror. An Essay on Abjection.* Edited and translated by Leon S. Roudiez. New York: Columbia University Press, 1982.

LEWIS, Matthew G. "Advertisement to *Timour the Tartar.*" In: Jeffrey N. Cox and Michael Gamer (eds.). *The Broadview Anthology of Romantic Drama.* Peterborough, Canada: Broadview Press, 2003. 98.

NICOLL, Allardyce. *A History of English Drama 1660 – 1900. Vol. III, Late Eighteenth Century Drama 1750 – 1800.* Cambridge: Cambridge University Press, 1952.

RADCLIFFE, Anne. "On the Supernatural in Poetry." In: *New Monthly Magazine and Literary Journal* 16 (1826): 145 – 52.

ROUSSETZKI, Remy. "Theatre of Anxiety in Shelley's *The Cenci* and Musset's *Lorrenzaccio.*" In: *Criticism* 42,1 (2000): 31 – 57.

RUMMEL, Andrea. *Delusive Beauty. Femmes Fatales in English Literature.* Göttingen: V & R Unipress / Bonn University Press, 2008.

SCHILLER, Friedrich. "Über die Tragische Kunst." In: *Werke.* Nationalausgabe. Begr. V. Julius Petersen. Weimar 1943 ff., NA 20. 148 – 70.

SHELLEY, Percy Bysshe. "Preface to *The Cenci.*" In: Jeffrey N. Cox and Michael Gamer (eds.). *The Broadview Anthology of Romantic Drama.* Peterborough, Canada: Broadview Press.

STEPHAN, Inge. "'Die erhabne Männin Corday': Christine Westphalens Drama *Charlotte Corday* (1804) und der Corday-Kult am Ende des 18. Jahrhunderts." In: Inge Stephan (ed.). *Inszenierte Weiblichkeit. Codierungen der Geschlechter in der Literatur des 18. Jahrhunderts.* Köln: Böhlau, 2004. 135 – 62.

Gislind Rohwer-Happe

The Dramatic Monologue and the Preservation of Victorian Fears

I. The Contextualization of the Dramatic Monologue

The genre of the dramatic monologue, which originated in the 1830s, can be regarded as a literary answer to the rise of the fairly new field of the science of the mind, i. e. psychology.[1] As such, the dramatic monologue functions as a translation of scientific insights into literature. Yet, the dramatic monologue in a way makes the findings of the new branch of science more approachable and understandable to a broader public while at the same time satisfying the public's clearly discernible interest in the matters of the mind and, more specifically, its obsession with the potential abyss of the human mind and soul.[2]

The dramatic monologue with its many different voices is influenced by the social and economic changes caused by the industrialisation. As Langbaum notes, the genre is "an appropriate form for an empiricist and relative age [...] which has come to consider value as an evolving thing dependent upon the changing individual requirements of the historical process"[3] since it explores unsettling topics of the Victorian age by granting a marginalized, frequently quite extreme, persona a voice, who thus is enabled to declare and communicate its position concerning dismaying and perturbing issues that could not be discussed openly. These highly idiosyncratic and varied accounts can be regarded as a representation of the newly acknowledged awareness that there is no such thing as a universal truth.[4] Instead, the dramatic monologue confronts its reader with the fact that all values and truths are merely relative, a point which is

---

1 Cf. FAAS, Ekbert. *Retreat into the Mind: Victorian Poetry and the Rise of Psychiatry.* Princeton: Princeton University Press, 1988. 4.
2 FAAS. *Retreat into the Mind.* 4 perceives an "unprecedented literary obsession" with the human mind: "[N]ever before had poets been more intent upon exploring the human psyche; nor had they ever evolved subtler techniques for doing so."
3 LANGBAUM, Robert. *The Poetry of Experience. The Dramatic Monologue in Modern Literary Tradition.* London: Chatto & Windus, 1957. 107–08.
4 Cf. BYRON, Glennis. *Dramatic Monologue.* London: Routledge, 2003. 33–34.

typically emphasized by contextualizing the perspective that is voiced historically and/or locally.[5] The disclosure of relative values and the presentation of
extreme, deviant viewpoints which, more often than not, hint at the speaker's
difficult psychological condition, necessarily involve challenging generally accepted rules and conventions. This exploration of "abnormal mental states", as
Ekbert Faas so fittingly described the subject matter of the dramatic monologue,[6] is made possible by the use of unreliable narration,[7] which allows for a
seemingly authentic representation of a given perspective, which nevertheless
can more or less easily be doubted or dismissed by the reader. The dramatic
monologue became a highly popular genre not only because of its portrayal of
singular and distorted positions but also because of the fact that its reader could
completely focus on the deviant disposition of the speaker of the monologue,
thus potentially even foregoing an analysis of himself by analysing others. On
that account, the dramatic monologue may even contribute to the mental health
of its readership since it offers a safe alternative to self-analysis. Instead of
"[g]azing inward on oneself",[8] which supposedly could cause madness,[9] the
individual has access to a harmless approach to introspection and a detached
investigation of abnormalities in the literary genre of the dramatic monologue.

While the dramatic monologue must predominantly be understood as a literary answer to the newly evolving discourse of psychology,[10] it not only deals
with "abnormal mental states"[11] as such, but uses them to elaborate on other
topics and questions of Victorian society and culture. Accordingly, the dramatic
monologue is not only a literary translation of common scientific knowledge
that serves to appease the Victorian appetite for sensational presentations of
abnormal mental states, but fulfills a distinctly social and cultural function as
well. As a genre, the dramatic monolgue deals with the principal cultural
questions and topics of the Victorian era, namely religion, crime, morality and
death, which were the source of much anxiety and were even perceived as a threat
to the order and well-being of Victorian society. While these topics of course
pose a more or less latent threat to each and every society and its members,
regardless of the historical period, they gained a special momentum since vari-

---

5 Cf. BYRON. *Dramatic Monologue.* 34.
6 FAAS. *Retreat into the Mind.* 51.
7 For an extensive introduction to the narrative phenomenon of unreliable narration cf.
   NÜNNING, Ansgar, Carola SURKAMP and Bruno ZERWECK (eds.). *Unreliable Narration:
   Studien zur Theorie und Praxis unglaubwürdigen Erzählens in der englischsprachigen Erzählliteratur.* Trier: WVT, 1998.
8 CARLYLE, Thomas. *Critical and Miscellaneous Essays.* Vol. IV. Boston: James Munroe and
   Company, 1839. 371.
9 Cf. CARLYLE. *Critical and Miscellaneous Essay.* 371.
10 Cf. FAAS. *Retreat into the Mind.*
11 FAAS. *Retreat into the Mind.* 51.

ous sciences, such as psychology, geology and (evolutionary) biology, unsettled people's beliefs and assumptions during the Victorian era.[12] These new fields of research offered insights into the age of the earth and the history of mankind which inevitably questioned or overruled common knowledge and the postulates of religion, thus destabilizing the previously agreed upon world view and challenging long-standing values and conventions.[13]

The exploration of these menacing cultural topics in the dramatic monologue functions as a means to stimulate the ongoing, mostly covert, debate on those topics and promotes criticism of well-established traditions since the genre's use of unreliable narration allows for the expression of nonstandard positions without discrediting either the author or the reader.[14] Accordingly, the dramatic monlogue could state opinions that, strictly speaking, were taboo, thus offering new and worthwhile, albeit rather subversive, contributions to the debates.

At the same time, the genre also always serves as an investigation of the influences of the distressing cultural themes religion, crime, hypocrisy and fear of death on the individual as it was assumed that the thorough scrutiny of one or more of these topics must result in negative psychological consequences. By allowing the reader to come face to face with individuals that suffer from the results of an intense exploration of those topics, which is markedly shown by their oddities, peculiarities, deviant behavior and abnormal perspectives, which are betrayed by the use of unreliable narration, the dramatic monologue vividly expresses predominant Victorian fears. At first glance, one might be tempted to argue that for this reason the genre serves as a means to channel and control those fears and to ultimately dissolve them, but actually the case is diametrically opposed. In fact, the dramatic monologue fosters and maintains society's anxieties by expressing deviant viewpoints and by showing the results of a thorough examination of those troublesome themes. Thus, the dramatic monologue serves as a warning to all 'normal' members of society not to become too much involved with disturbing thoughts lest they should suffer the consequences. Therefore, despite its innovative form, the dramatic monologue

---

12 Cf. Byron. *Dramatic Monologue.* 33.

13 Cf. Byron. *Dramatic Monologue.* 33 and Abrams, M.H. et al. *The Norton Anthology of English Literature.* 7th edn. Vol. 2. New York/London: Norton, 2000. 1050.

14 Morson, Gary Saul. *The Boundaries of Genre. Dostoevsky's 'Diary of a Writer' and the Traditions of Literary Utopia.* Austin: University of Texas Press, 1981. 44 describes the author's position as follows: "Because fictive utterances are not being said but rather represented, we *do* not hold their authors responsible in the same way that we might hold them for their nonfictional statements. We do hold them responsible for the act of *representing* certain statements, which is quite a different thing." Faas (*Retreat into the Mind.* 6) compares the position of the reader to that of a psychiatrist: "Despite our emphatic understanding for the person's character and dilemma, we are supposed to stand back, analyze, even judge the speaker the way an alienist (or psychiatrist) might diagnose his patient."

fulfills indeed a highly conventional function. By confronting the reader with unusual perspectives, voiced by unreliable narrators, who are unable to engage the reader's sympathy, it cultivates and promotes the reader's adherence to the norm. This can be demonstrated by an overview of the way the dramatic monolgue functions with regard to the four predominant cultural issues already referred to: religion, crime, hypocrisy and fear of death.

II. Religion and the Dramatic Monologue

Religious beliefs and in particular religious doubts strongly influenced Victorian thought and life. While at the beginning of Queen Victoria's reign the situation was still rather simple given the fact that it was common knowledge that "to be British was *ipso facto* to be Protestant",[15] religion became a major concern during the epoch. Especially the fact that the Roman Catholic faith was gaining more strength was perceived by many as a threat to British (national) identity, as "Roman Catholicism was alien to the national spirit"[16]; after all, "[t]he Roman Church may be a true church in Italy, but in England it is not only in error, but in heresy and schismatical."[17] Apart from the threat that was caused by a strong Catholic faith in England, religious peace was also at stake because of the ongoing disintegration of the Church of England, which led to three distinct tendencies: the High, Broad and Low Church.[18] While the High Church was closely related to the 'dangerous' Catholic faith with its strong emphasis on rituals and tradition, the Low Church was characterized by its strict Puritanism.[19] The Broad Church, finally, sought to combine these different ideas.[20]

Yet it was not only the organisation of the church as such that fostered skepticism regarding the Christian belief. The scientific findings of the Victorian era cast doubt on much of what is written in the Bible. In particular Darwin's evolutionary theory, but also the emerging sciences of geology and astronomy were hardly compatible with the Book of Genesis.[21] Moreover, the new ideas of the Higher Criticism stressed the fact that the Bible is a fictional text and has to be read as such.[22] Accordingly, the Bible's status as a holy text was ignored by

---

15 WILSON, A.N. *The Victorians.* London: Arrow Books, 2003. 64.
16 WILSON. *The Victorians.* 64.
17 BENSON, A.C. *The Life of Edward White Benson, Sometime Archbishop of Canterbury.* Vol. 1. London: Macmillan, 1899. 47.
18 Cf. ABRAMS. *The Norton Anthology of English Literature.* 1050.
19 Cf. ABRAMS. *The Norton Anthology of English Literature.* 1050.
20 Cf. ABRAMS. *The Norton Anthology of English Literature.* 1050.
21 Cf. ABRAMS. *The Norton Anthology of English Literature.* 1051–2.
22 Cf. ABRAMS. *The Norton Anthology of English Literature.* 1050.

Higher Criticism and its function as the foundation of the Christian faith was severely damaged.[23]

Religious doubts and fears thus provide the context in which the Victorian dramatic monologue deals with issues of faith. Yet the monologues written at the time are not concerned with the dominant Anglican faith, but almost exclusively with Catholicism. In spite of all the existing doubts in God, there apparently was no doubt as to the superiority of the Anglican faith, while certain Catholic rituals were perceived as blasphemous and Catholicism itself was seen as a possible reason for the psychological and moral degeneration of its followers. Catholic saints and believers were thus an obvious choice for the role of the speaker in a dramatic monologue; after all, the adherence to Roman Catholicism as such presupposed an extreme psychological situation according to many Victorians. The use of unreliable narration in the dramatic monologue serves as a means to reveal the alleged hypocrisy of the Catholic Church. By employing dramatic irony or discrepant awareness the utterances of so-called Catholic saints and worshippers in the dramatic monologue are endowed with an additional meaning that contradicts the one intended by the speaker. The speaker's belief in his own purity and holiness is unveiled as being nothing but delusion that originates in the speaker's arrogance and vanity. Since the function of the dramatic monologue is an involuntary revelation of the speaker's negative character traits, Catholic personas were a favourite subject of the dramatic monologue given the fact that the Victorians firmly believe that all Catholics suffered from delusion and that their piety served as a mere façade, used to hide a lack of morals and personality. The speakers of dramatic monologues with a religious topic regularly unmask themselves as superficial and malicious hypocrites whose whole existence revolves around appearances and the desire to become famous. By showing Catholics in such an unfavourable light, the dramatic monologue stirs Victorian fears concerning a possible strengthening of Catholicism in England, while at the same time, similar to a slandering pamphlet, warning people who are supposedly in a state of crisis of faith, not to fall for Catholicism and its spiritual void.

Examples of dramatic monologues that deal with religious speakers include Alfred Lord Tennyson's "St Simeon Stylites" (1833), Robert Browning's "Soliloquy of the Spanish Cloister" (1842) and "Bishop Blougram's Apology" (1855), Charles Kingsley's "Saint Maura. A.D. 304" (1852), Augusta Webster's "A Preacher" (1866) and Mathilde Blind's "The Mystic's Vision" (1891).

---

23 Cf. ABRAMS. *The Norton Anthology of English Literature.* 1050.

III.   Crime, Madness and the Dramatic Monologue

Dramatic monologues presenting mad and criminal speakers satisfy society's
obvious interest in sensational stories,[24] while at the same time cautioning their
readership against indulging their own illicit desires. Crime and madness are
topics that appear to be nearly inseparable in the Victorian era, since it was
assumed that crime and madness are closely linked. To be categorized as a
'madman' was fairly easy during the Victorian age, as even minimal deviations,
such as somnambulism, were regarded as a sign of insanity.[25] People exhibiting
such symptoms were often sent to asylums in order to isolate them and protect
the public from the threat alleged madmen might constitute.[26] Yet it was most of
all the state of "moral insanity"[27] which was thought to be menacing to society at
large, since it linked madness with moral degeneration,[28] and those that suffered
from moral insanity were regarded as being extremely clear-sighted and as
revealing a strong affinity to criminal deeds.[29]

   In 1863 James Fitzjames Stephens published his *General View of the Criminal
Law of England*, which was based on the idea that the individual is able to
distinguish between right and wrong and suggested that British law should be
guided by the individual's ability to judge his doings morally.[30] Stephen's position created a direct connection between crime and madness, which became
also obvious in the hearing of psychiatrists as experts and witnesses in court.[31]

   Dramatic monologues dealing with crimes such as rape, murder, or a combination thereof nevertheless are not so much interested in the crime itself; the
criminal deed is at best mentioned perfunctorily. Instead, the monologues exploring madness and crime offer an insight into the workings of the mind and
focus on speakers who suffer from so-called rational lunacy, which means that
"the speaker is 'morally insane', that is, apparently sane and rational, yet com-
pelled by sudden impulse to commit an atrocious act".[32] The authors of dramatic
monologues respond to the Victorian reader's taste for scandal and his ob-

---

24 This interest is also evident in the highly popular Victorian sensation novel. Cf. MORAN,
    Maureen. *Victorian Literature and Culture*. London: Continuum, 2006. 23.
25 Cf. PURCHASE, Sean. *Key Concepts in Victorian Literature*. Palgrave Key Concepts. Basing-
    stoke: Palgrave Macmillan. 2006. 93.
26 Cf. WILSON. *The Victorians*. 38.
27 FAAS. *Retreat into the Mind*. 44–5.
28 Cf. HARRISON, James Bower. "The Human Mind Considered in Some of its Medical Aspects."
    In: *The Journal of Medicine and Mental Pathology* 3 (1850): 246–62, 258.
29 Cf. PINEL, Philippe. *A Treatise on Insanity*. New York: Hafner, 1962 [1806]. 151.
30 Cf. PURCHASE. *Key Concepts in Victorian Literature*. 93.
31 Cf. FAAS. *Retreat into the Mind*. 165.
32 GRIBBLE, Jennifer. "Subject and Power in 'Porphyria's Lover'." In: *Sydney Studies in English*
    29 (2003): 17–29, 21.

session with crime and madness. By employing unreliable narration the dramatic monologue achieves an illusion of authenticity, which allows the reader to make himself believe that he is actually listening to the immediate and genuine confession of a murderer or a madman. Interestingly enough, all these 'confessions' of criminal or mad speakers reveal the same reasons for committing the deed: all speakers were driven by motives that were constantly repressed in the Victorian age – such as sexual lust or deviance – and they almost always direct their violence against women.

Dramatic monologues dealing with crime and madness thus serve to verbalize sexual urges and to satisfy the Victorian appetite for sensation and scandal. They function as an illustration of the criminal energy exhibited by the speaker as well as a demonstration of madness in all of its forms that may trigger the criminal tendencies of the speaker. Unreliable narration in these monologues suggests a seemingly instantaneous, albeit quite detached confrontation with evil and mad personas, while offering approachable perspectives related to the newly evolved science of psychology. Dramatic monologues featuring mad and criminal speakers offer a detailed insight into the workings of the mind and try out forbidden emotions and inacceptable behaviour. Having read such a monologue, the reader (hopefully) can distance himself from such feelings and therefore be assured of his own sanity. As a result, dramatic monologues with mad and criminal speakers function as an implicit warning not to give way to any latent, forbidden, unnatural urges.

Dramatic monologues presenting mad and criminal speakers include Robert Browning's "Porphyria's Lover" (1836) and "A Laboratory" (1844), William Morris's "The Wind" (1858), Charles Algernon Swinburne's "The Leper" (1866), Edmund Ollier's "The Wife-Slayer" (1867), Robert Bulwer-Lytton's "Trial by Combat" (1868), Robert W. Buchanan's "Fra Giacomo" (1884) and George Barlow's "A Southern Vengeance" (1889).

IV.   Death and the Dramatic Monologue

Like religion, crime and madness, death was felt to be a major threat in Victorian times. Nowadays, of course, death is still a cause of fear; yet the special attitude towards death in the Victorian period is due to dramatic changes corncerning the way death was perceived during this period. Charles Darwin's *The Origins of Species* (1859) was certainly a crucial contribution to this change of perception, but it was by no means the only text which altered the attitude towards mankind's position in the history of the earth and questioned the Bible's authenticity concerning the genesis of man:

[M]ost readers recognized that Darwin's theory of natural selection conflicted not only with the concept of creation derived from the Bible but also with long-established assumptions of the values attached to humanity's special role in the world.[33]

Since the Victorian age was particularly fond of scientific aproaches to a wide range of subjects, the Bible also became the object of closer scrutiny and came to be treated like any other text, with no higher claim to truthfulness.[34] The newly gained scientific insights as well as the changed reading of biblical texts fostered a profound skepticism regarding God's existence as such and made the belief in life after death a doubtful concept. In the Victorian age death thus no longer promises relief and eternal comfort. Instead, it loses its function as a passageway between earthly and heavenly life and becomes simply the termination of human existence.

Because of the uncertainties associated with this new perception of death, death became one of the major topics of the Victorian age: "[T]he Victorians were obsessed with death, and above all with the ways and means of coping with it."[35] Funerals became highly ritualised affairs, which hint at the Victorians' wish to exercise at least some control over the end of human existence:

> [The Victorians] are [...] often credited with the invention of British funeral rites, and especially the black pomp and splendour associated with the deaths of popular state figures and celebrities. [...] Victorians also ritualized the wearing of black clothes by mourners, in which changes of ensemble were supposed to correspond with the various stages of bereavement.[36]

The Victorians' obsession with death is also mirrored in Victorian literature.[37] The dramatic monologue, in contrast to the very public and elaborate funerals characteristic of the time, focuses on the individual coping with death: "[The dramatic monologue] stress[es] how each persona confronts the same experience in a particular manner and under special circumstances."[38] Even though all of the so-called "deathbed-monologues"[39] ultimately share the same cause for their speaker's utterances, they constitute a very heterogenous group of texts in terms of the presentation of the situation.[40] Still, what many of the "deathbed-monologues" have in common is the way they employ unreliable narration, which is used first and foremost as a means of manipulating and controlling the

---

33 ABRAMS. The Norton Anthology of English Literature. 1052.
34 Cf. ABRAMS. The Norton Anthology of English Literature. 1051.
35 PURCHASE. Key Concepts in Victorian Literature. 35.
36 PURCHASE. Key Concepts in Victorian Literature. 35.
37 PURCHASE. Key Concepts in Victorian Literature. 36.
38 Cf. FAAS. Retreat into the Mind. 153.
39 Cf. FAAS. Retreat into the Mind. 153.
40 Cf. FAAS, Egbert. Poesie als Psychogramm. Die dramatisch-monologische Versdichtung im viktorianischen Zeitalter. München: Fink, 1974. 80.

listener in this kind of dramatic monologue. The speaker's wish to subject the listener to his will is much stronger and more palpable than in any of the other types of monologues discussed here. The reason for the speaker's excessive desire to influence the listener on his behalf is caused by his loss of faith in a life after death; the speaker at least wishes to ascertain that he will be remembered after his death, and he wants to make sure that this remembrance will be performed in a way he would approve of. The speaker mercilessly exploits the threat of his impending death in order to make the listener feel guilty and make him act in accordance with the speaker's wishes. By the attempt at controlling the listener's doings even after the speaker's death, the speaker is arguably depicted in a very unfavourable light. The idea that one ought to behave respectfully towards the dying is dramatically subverted by revealing the speaker to be a manipulative, self-righteous egocentric, whose character does not improve in the face of imminent death.

Despite the negative depiction of a dying speaker, dramatic monologues dealing with death verbalize major fears and hopes of the Victorian age: the fear of death and the hope of being remembered by the living. The disadvantageous portrait of the speaker does not alleviate the fear of death; however, the fact that the speakers in the "deathbed-monologues" are invariably more or less corrupt and unpleasant at least allows the reader to try out emotions which are otherwise taboo; the dramatic monologues enable the reader to feel satisfaction in the face of the death of an unloved person. Apart from this, the dramatic monologues contain a very general warning. They ask the reader to improve his life and character as long as there is still time to do so – and are thus very similar to texts like Charles Dickens's *A Christmas Carol* (1843). The fear of God, whose existence becomes more and more doubtful for the Victorians, is replaced by the fear of death, which appears more threatening due to the fact that there is no certainty of a heavenly afterlife anymore.

Monologues dealing with death include Elizabeth Barrett Browning's "Bertha in the Lane" (1844), Robert Browning's "The Bishop Orders His Tomb at St Praxed's Church" (1845), Charlotte Brontë's "Apostasy" (1846), Robert Bulwer-Lytton's "Last Words of a Sensitive Second-Rate Poet" (1868), Eugene Lee-Hamilton's "The Mandolin" (1882), Rudyard Kipling's "The 'Mary Gloster'" (1894) and Arthur Conan Doyle's "The Dying Whip" (1898).

V.   'The Great Social Evil' and the Dramatic Monologue

Despite the fact that the Victorian age is known for its optimistic belief in progress and modernisation, the developments associated with this belief also have their darker sides. Industrialization and the expansion of the British Empire are certainly also responsible for major social problems. The industrialization has created a strong class consciousness in Britain, making the middle class the ideologically controlling class.[41] Morally, the middle class was governed by principles such as self-renunciation, self-improvement and duty;[42] principles which in turn made the members of the middle class believe that it was their duty to help the poor. Prostitutes were thought of as being particularly needful, since the number of women who sold their body for a living rose dramatically in the nineteenth century.[43] However, the desire to help the prostitutes was not only based on altruism. Instead, the middle class wished to eliminate prostitution completely, as prostitutes threatened the Victorian value system and were perceived as a menace to society's health and well-being.[44] Prostitutes thus "activat[ed] simultaneously complex associations of pity/redemption and fear/threat".[45]

The fact that prostitutes were considered a danger to the good citizen turned them into a major topic in literature as well: "'The Great Social Evil' [i.e. prostitution] became a national obsession which spawned [...] hundreds of public debates, thousands of pages in periodicals, books, novels, poems, plays, pamphlets, tracts and sermons".[46] There are also a number of dramatic monologues that address prostitution, such as the well-known monologue "Jenny" (1870) by Dante Gabriel Rossetti and Augusta Webster's "A Castaway" (1870). The form of the dramatic monologue and its use of unreliable narration provide a very immediate and apparently authentic depiction of the fallen women's hopeless situation. Both examples also illustrate the hypocrisy and double standards characteristic of the Victorian age: they show how on the one hand the fallen woman becomes a "figure of contagion, disease and death",[47] while, on the other hand, she is perceived as a "suffering and tragic figure"[48].

While the three thematic groups of monologues discussed above – those dealing with religion, crime and madness or death – serve as a more or less

---

41 Cf. PURCHASE. Key Concepts in Victorian Literature. 23.
42 Cf. NÜNNING, Vera. Der englische Roman des 19. Jahrhunderts. Stuttgart: Klett, 2000, 16–19.
43 Cf. NÜNNING. Der englische Roman des 19. Jahrhunderts. 18.
44 BARTLEY, Paula. Prostitution: Prevention and Reform in England, 1860–1914. London: Routledge, 2000. 25 states that "[p]rostitution, it was believed, would be eliminated if there were no prostitutes. Reformers therefore founded a variety of institutions, ranging from large penitentiaries and asylums to smaller homes, to rehabilitate prostitutes and make them respectable once more."
45 NEAD, Lynda. Myths of Sexuality: Representations of Women in Victorian Britain. Oxford: Blackwell, 1988. 106.
46 BROWN, Susan. "Economical Representations: Dante Gabriel Rossetti's 'Jenny,' Augusta Webster's 'A Castaway,' and the Campaign against the Contagious Disease Act." In: Victorian Review 17,1 (1991): 78–95. 78.
47 NEAD. Myths of Sexuality. 106.
48 NEAD. Myths of Sexuality. 106.

explicit warning to the readership, admonishing them to follow the right path, those monologues dealing with social problems such as prostitution provide at best a very subtle warning. By highlighting the moral hypocrisy of the ideologically dominant middle class, the monologue warns the reader not to accept the social norms and values associated with the 'Great Social Evil', although the breaking of taboos in the dramatic monologues dealing with social problems undermines the impact such a warning may have. Nevertheless, the dramatic monologues certainly do attack the middle class and its morals, a fact which definitely makes the texts subversive. Unreliable narration is used to reveal social problems and the dissimulation of Victorian society. The monologues do not seek to eliminate the fear of the readers in the face of a rising number of prostitutes in Britain, but instead serve to illuminate the reasons for the problem, thus criticizing society.

Apart from the dramatic monologues by Augusta Webster and Dante Gabriel Rossetti already mentioned above, there are a number of further monologues that share the function of social criticism. Among those there are Robert Williams Buchanan's "Attorney Sneak" (1866), Henry Austin Dobson's "A Virtuoso" (1873), Mathilde Blind's "The Russian Student's Tale" (1891), John Davidson's "Thirty Bob a Week" (1894) and Edith Nesbit's "The Sick Journalist" (1908).

VI. Conclusion

In conclusion it can be said that the dramatic monologue as a genre illustrates the dominant fears of the Victorian age. The dramatic monologues mentioned in this article are clearly not meant to alleviate and reduce fear; instead, they display taboo emotions and abnormal perspectives by offering, by means of unreliable narration, an insight into the psychological workings of the speaker's mind. By confronting the reader with opinions that are highly idiosyncratic, they admonish the recipient to follow norms, or, provided the underlying social rules are presented as dubious, to question them. Despite the fact that all dramatic monologues present the positions of social outsiders and minorities, of characters who are morally and ethically deviant, the genre as such has a moral function: it is meant to encourage the reader to stay on or to choose the right path.

All dramatic monologues mentioned above are concerned with major changes which were underway in the Victorian age. It is in this context that the genre makes use of unreliable narration, in other words, a narrative phenomenon the Victorian readership was not particularly familiar with. Regardless of this apparently progressive style, the dramatic monologue as such is a very conservative genre, since it is only interested in maintaining order and norms or, in the case of those monologues that address prostitution, in promoting a more altruistic attitude. After all, the dramatic monologue, in spite of being a new genre in the nineteenth century and in spite of employing an innovative narrative strategy, ultimately helps maintain the Victorian system of norms and values.

References

ABRAMS, M.H. et al. *The Norton Anthology of English Literature.* 7th edn. Vol. 2. New York/London: Norton, 2000.

BARTLEY, Paula. *Prostitution: Prevention and Reform in England, 1860–1914.* London: Routledge, 2000.

BENSON, A.C. *The Life of Edward White Benson, Sometime Archbishop of Canterbury.* Vol. 1. London: Macmillan, 1899.

BROWN, Susan. "Economical Representations: Dante Gabriel Rossetti's 'Jenny,' Augusta Webster's 'A Castaway,' and the Campaign against the Contagious Disease Act." In: *Victorian Review* 17,1 (1991): 78–95.

BYRON, Glennis. *Dramatic Monologue.* London: Routledge, 2003.

CARLYLE, Thomas. *Critical and Miscellaneous Essays.* Vol. IV. Boston: James Munroe and Company, 1839.

FAAS, Egbert. *Poesie als Psychogramm. Die dramatisch-monologische Versdichtung im viktorianischen Zeitalter.* München: Fink, 1974.

FAAS, Ekbert [sic]. *Retreat into the Mind: Victorian Poetry and the Rise of Psychiatry.* Princeton: Princeton University Press, 1988.

GRIBBLE, Jennifer. "Subject and Power in 'Porphyria's Lover'." In: *Sydney Studies in English* 29 (2003): 17–29.

HARRISON, James Bower. "The Human Mind Considered in Some of its Medical Aspects." In: *The Journal of Medicine and Mental Pathology* 3 (1850): 246–62.

LANGBAUM, Robert. *The Poetry of Experience. The Dramatic Monologue in Modern Literary Tradition.* London: Chatto & Windus, 1957.

MORAN, Maureen. *Victorian Literature and Culture.* London: Continuum, 2006.

MORSON, Gary Saul. *The Boundaries of Genre. Dostoevsky's 'Diary of a Writer' and the Traditions of Literary Utopia.* Austin: University of Texas Press, 1981.

NEAD, Lynda. *Myths of Sexuality: Representations of Women in Victorian Britain.* Oxford: Blackwell, 1988.

NÜNNING, Ansgar, Carola SURKAMP and Bruno ZERWECK (eds.). *Unreliable Narration: Studien zur Theorie und Praxis unglaubwürdigen Erzählens in der englischsprachigen Erzählliteratur.* Trier: WVT, 1998.

NÜNNING, Vera. *Der englische Roman des 19. Jahrhunderts.* Stuttgart: Klett, 2000.

PINEL, Philippe. *A Treatise on Insanity.* New York: Hafner, 1962 [1806].

PURCHASE, Sean. *Key Concepts in Victorian Literature.* Basingstoke: Palgrave Macmillan, 2006.

WILSON, A.N. *The Victorians.* London: Arrow Books, 2003.

Stella Butter

Cultural Constructions of Fear and Empathy: The Emotional Structure of Relationships in George Eliot's *Daniel Deronda* (1876) and Jonathan Nasaw's *Fear Itself* (2003)

Fear belongs to the basic emotions of humanity. Put in the technical terms of cognitive emotion theory, fear is an innate emotion with its "own distinctive signals in the brain" and which manifests itself in a "universal nonverbal expressio[n]"[1]. The notion of fear as an integral part of humanity's emotional repertoire is also frequently voiced in the realm of literature. A humorous example that comes to mind is a droll fairytale with the programmatic title "The Story of a Boy Who Went Forth to Learn Fear". In the tale by the Grimms, the hero goes to great lengths (e. g. sleeping in a haunted castle) in order to find out what it means to be afraid. Unfortunately, all of his efforts are to no avail. It is only when his newly wed wife, who is tired of his complaining that he knows no fear, tips a bucketful of live fish over him during the night that he learns how to shudder with fright.[2] The humour of the tale results from the reversal of our conventional expectations. Not only do we assume that the ability to feel fear is universal to the human, but we also usually consider fear to be a negative emotion and thus hardly an experience we would welcome, let alone actively seek.[3] This negativity harks back to the evolutionary origins of fear as a func-

---

1 JOHNSON-LAIRD, P.N. and Keith OATLEY. "Emotions, Music, and Literature." In: Lisa Barrett, Jeanette M. Haviland and Michael Lewis (eds.). *Handbook of Emotions*. New York/London: Guilford Press, 2008. 102–13, 104.
2 Critics have noted the sexual implications of the way our hero learns to shudder in bed. For interpretations of the fairytale by the Grimms see RÖLLEKE, Heinz. "Märchen von einem, der auszog, das Fürchten zu lernen. Zu Überlieferung und Bedeutung des KHM4." In: *Fabula* 20 (1979): 193–204 and MARSCHALL, Amy Horning. "Reflections on the Pedagogy of Fear. 'Märchen von einem, der auszog, das Fürchten zu lernen'." In: *Fabula* 36 (1995): 289–95.
3 The popularity of the fairytale "The Story of a Boy Who Went Forth to Learn Fear" is attested by its numerous retellings. A noteworthy example can be found in the widely-read *Asterix* comic series. *Asterix and the Normans* depicts the Normans desperate to "LEARN THE MEANING OF FEAR" (9). Chief Olaf Timandahaf's grandiose speech to his assembled men presents fear as initiation into valuable knowledge: "WE CAN'T GO ON LIKE THIS! EVEN THE WEAKEST OF NATIONS KNOW ABOUT FEAR AND BEING FRIGHTENED\UBUT NOT US! AND WE PRIDE OURSELVES ON KNOWING EVERYTHING! EVERYTHING!" (ibid.) As in the case of the fairytale by the Grimms, the humour results from the inversion of con-

tional response to a perceived threat.[4] While the view of fear as "an inevitable part of human existence"[5] stands uncontested, it is intriguing to trace the changing cultural conceptualizations and codings of fear throughout history.

Fear may be an "innate, biologically grounded [...] emotio[n]"[6] as naturalists argue, but it is part of emotion's complexity that it also allows for cultural variations. This is where emotionology comes in, "which concerns the collective emotional standards of a culture as opposed to the experience of emotion itself. Emotionologies are frameworks for conceptualizing emotions, their causes, and how participants in discourse are likely to display them."[7] Literature and media play a vital role in shaping emotion discourses.[8] One key example of how literature contributed to emotionology is its development of a language of interiority during the eighteenth century.[9] Practices of writing and reading helped forge a form of subjectivity attuned to its affective experientiality.[10] This brief example draws attention to two important points. First of all, aesthetic practices influence and transform dominant models of subjectivity.[11] The second point is that the perception and evaluative coding of emotions depend on the internalized model of subjectivity. Literature provides rich source material for the study of emotionology because it is concerned with the particular, especially the

---

ventional modes of thinking: fear not as something negative, but as enlightenment, a source of empowerment and the mark of the ultra-masculine warrior: "WE SHALL COME HOME TO TELL AN ADMIRING WORLD THE NORMANS KNOW THE MEANING OF FEAR! THE NORMANS ARE MORE FRIGHTENED THAN YOU!" (10). While most people "desperately wish to avoid [fear] in everyday life" (HANICH, Julian. *Cinematic Emotion in Horror Films and Thrillers. The Aesthetic Paradox of Pleasurable Fear.* New York/London: Routledge, 2010. 4.), much ink has been spilled on why so many people enjoy reading or viewing scary works of fiction. On the "aesthetic paradox of pleasurable fear" (HANICH. *Cinematic Emotion in Horror Films and Thrillers.*) cf. Christian KNÖPPLER's article in this volume.

4 Cf. ÖHMAN, Arne. "Fear and Anxiety. Overlaps and Dissociations." In: Lisa Barrett, Jeanette M. Haviland and Michael Lewis (eds.). *Handbook of Emotions.* New York/London: Guilford Press, 2008. 709–29, 710: "Basically, fear is a functional emotion with a deep evolutionary origin, reflecting the fact that earth has always been a hazardous environment to inhabit. Staying alive is a prerequisite for the basic goal of biological evolution – sending genes on to subsequent generations. Hence even the most primitive of organisms have developed defense responses to deal with life threats in their environment [...]. Viewed from the evolutionary perspective, fear is central to mammalian evolution."

5 ÖHMAN. "Fear and Anxiety. Overlaps and Dissociations." 709.

6 HERMAN, David. "Cognition, Emotion, and Consciousness." In: David Herman (ed.). *The Cambridge Companion to Narrative.* Cambridge: Cambridge University Press, 2007. 245–59, 254.

7 HERMAN. "Cognition, Emotion, and Consciousness." 255.

8 Cf. HERMAN. "Cognition, Emotion, and Consciousness." 255.

9 Cf. RECKWITZ, Andreas. *Das hybride Subjekt. Eine Theorie der Subjektkulturen von der bürgerlichen Moderne zur Postmoderne.* Weilerswist: Velbrück, 2006. 155 ff.

10 Cf. RECKWITZ. *Das hybride Subjekt.* 155 ff.

11 Cf. RECKWITZ. *Das hybride Subjekt.* 17–18.

affective experientiality of the subject. The polysemy of literary texts thereby endows the portrayals of affective experience, such as fear and empathy, with a multiplicity of meanings, which may undermine dominant cultural constructions of emotions.

The aim of this essay is to contribute to the study of emotionology by tracing changing cultural constructions of fear and empathy in the novel. I have chosen to focus on the pairing of these two emotions because ruptures in the ideological fabric of literary texts often become especially apparent when analysing the depicted interplay between fear and empathy (see below).[12] Two case studies serve for a contrastive analysis: a canonical novel from the nineteenth century, George Eliot's *Daniel Deronda* (1876), and a contemporary bestseller from the realm of popular fiction, namely Jonathan Nasaw's *Fear Itself* (2003).[13] The two novels make for an interesting comparison not only on account of their different socio-historical context, which informs their treatment of severe fear. The analysis of these novels serves, moreover, to illustrate the points made above about how literature participates in shaping emotion discourses. The following three theses are thereby central for my argument:

1. In both novels, the privileged form of subjectivity determines the understanding of fear. In *Daniel Deronda*, a conflict is played out between what Andreas Reckwitz terms the 'moral subject' and the 'speculative subject' (see

---

12 There is no consensus among scholars regarding the definition of empathy. In this article, I will be working with Amy COPLAN's conceptualization of empathy: "I understand empathy as a complex imaginative process involving both cognition and emotion. When I empathize with another, I take up his or her psychological perspective and imaginatively experience, to some degree or other, what he or she experiences." (COPLAN, Amy. "Empathic Engagement with Narrative Fictions." In: *The Journal of Aesthetics and Art Criticism* 62,2 (2004): 141 – 52, 143) "On my account of empathy, empathy requires the following four conditions: (1) the empathizer experiences psychological states that are either identical or very similar to those of the target, (2) perspective-taking – the empathizer imaginatively experiences the target's experiences from the target's point of view, (3) (1) is the case by virtue of (2), and (4) the empathizer maintains self-other differentiation." (COPLAN. "Empathic Engagement with Narrative Fictions." 144) In contrast to fear, empathy can be categorized as a 'complex emotion'. The distinction between basic and complex emotions goes back to the communicative theory of emotions. According to this theory, "[b]asic emotions [i.e. happiness, sadness, anger, and fear] can arise as a result of rudimentary appraisals, and they can be experienced for no known reason [...]. Basic emotions are the biological foundation of the *complex* emotions that appear to be unique to humans. Complex emotions depend on conscious appraisals that relate to our models of ourselves, and often to comparisons between alternative possibilities or between actual events and possibilities that we imagine in alternative histories. They therefore can be experienced only for known reasons. They include such emotions as empathy, jealousy, pride, and embarrassment." (JOHNSON-LAIRD and OATLEY. "Emotions, Music, and Literature." 104).

13 I am grateful to Marcus Menzel for having drawn my attention to Nasaw's novel as suitable material for the topic 'fear and empathy in literature'. In the following, *Daniel Deronda* will be abbreviated with '*DD*' and *Fear Itself* with '*FI*' when quoting from the text.

below). The dominant textual strategies present severe fear in a positive light because this emotion plays a crucial role in the transformation of the speculative subject into a moral subject. However, a psychoanalytical reading, which targets the polysemy of the text, reveals how the staging of severe fear translates into an indictment of the very form of subjectivity upheld as an ideal in the novel. *Fear Itself* features the Cartesian subject as the dominant subject model. In accordance with this model, fear is presented as an emotion to be controlled and exorcised.

2. Discourses on fear and empathy are closely intertwined in both novels. While *Daniel Deronda* presents severe fear as a realm beyond empathetic access, *Fear Itself* inverts this relationship. The shared experience of (phobic) fear is seen as a pre-condition for empathy with the Other. These markedly different emotional constellations follow from the diverging conceptualizations of fear.

3. While the authorial narrator in both novels parrots dominant cultural constructions of fear and empathy, the staging of these emotions undercuts the authorial discourse. This discrepancy between telling and showing in the literary texts highlights frissons in the ideological fabric.

In the following, I will substantiate these claims by analyzing each of the novels in turn before comparing their stance on fear and empathy in my conclusion.

I.   George Eliot: *Daniel Deronda* (1876)

In *Daniel Deronda*, the emotions of fear and empathy are clearly correlated with different forms of subjectivity. Severe fear and lack of empathy characterize the 'speculative subject'. In contrast, the 'moral subject' is not plagued by fear and displays a remarkable talent for empathy. These different forms of subjectivity are represented by Gwendolen Harleth and Daniel Deronda. Although the title of Eliot's novel grants Daniel Deronda centre stage, it is the wilful sylph Gwendolen Harleth who continues to fascinate the reading public and scholars alike. The opening scene of the novel presents Gwendolen as part of the emerging risk society, intent on breaking free from oppressive gender restrictions by means of her reckless gambling in Leubronn. Her captivating and enigmatic quality is foregrounded by the musings of Deronda, who is watching her in the casino:

> Was she beautiful or not beautiful? And what was the secret of form or expression which gave the dynamic quality to her glance? Was the good or the evil genius dominant in those beams? [...] Why was the wish to look again felt as coercion and not as a longing in which the whole being consents? (*DD* 7)

The novel may set up Deronda as a paragon of virtue and thus the ideal bour-geoise 'moral subject', but his erotically charged fascination with Gwendolen reveals an attraction to a form of subjectivity that challenges Victorian middle-class morality. In contrast to the Victorian moral subject, which presents itself as transparent (i.e. the body as transparent signifier), authentic and temperate,[14] Gwendolen is associated with intransparency (cf. Deronda's failure to read Gwendolen's body), artifice or theatricality, the parasitic, and different forms of excess (e.g. risk-taking).[15] All of Gwendolen's attributes conform to the codes of the 'speculative subject', i.e. a model of subjectivity linked with developments of market economy in the nineteenth century, especially speculative finance.[16] It is no coincidence that the first description of Gwendolen shows her gambling and thus connects her with the world of money and risk. The speculative subject is the Other of the moral subject.[17] At first glance, Gwendolen's inexplicable "fits of spiritual dread" (*DD* 63) or attacks of severe fear appear as a further instance of excess and thus as corresponding with the codes of the speculative subject. However, her fits of fear ultimately function as a catalyst for her transformation into a moral subject.

The following analysis of Eliot's novel is concerned with laying bare the ambivalence that lies at the heart of Gwendolen's re-education as a moral sub-ject. Eliot's novel introduces an existential notion of fear as an interpretative gloss on Gwendolen's dread, thereby highlighting the limits of empathy. What is striking about this framing of fear is what is not addressed: the problematic price the speculative female subject has to pay in order to mould herself into the shape

---

14 Cf. RECKWITZ. *Das hybride Subjekt.* 105.
15 For a full account of conflicting models of subjectivity in the nineteenth century cf. RECK-WITZ (*Das hybride Subjekt.* 97–274). In his seminal study *Das hybride Subjekt* ('The Hybrid Subject', 2006), Reckwitz traces the changing models of subjectivity from the eighteenth century onwards and shows how these 'subject cultures' interact with three fields of social practices: the realm of work with its 'economic subject', the realm of personal relationships (e.g. family, friends, sexuality) with its 'intimate subject', and the field of 'technologies of self' (e.g. the media's role in shaping the subject, consumer culture, etc.). Reckwitz's con-ceptualization of the 'moral subject' and its Other, the 'speculative subject', forms an im-portant basis for my reading of *Daniel Deronda.*
16 Cf. RECKWITZ. *Das hybride Subjekt.* 129 ff. For a detailed discussion of the codes that can be attributed to the speculative subject cf. ibid. Gwendolen's life is initially portrayed as a parasitic existence because she egoistically puts her social ambitions first, no matter what the price is others have to pay. One of the reasons why Deronda strongly disapproves of Gwendolen's gambling is its (alleged) parasitic logic, which he glosses as 'one's gain is another's loss'. He thus translates the monetary movements of gambling into moral terms (cf. McCOBB, E.A. "*Daniel Deronda* as Will and Representation: George Eliot and Scho-penhauer." In: *The Modern Language Review* 80,3 (1985): 533–49.). On artifice and theat-rality in *Daniel Deronda* see MARSHALL, David. *The Figure of Theatre: Shaftesbury, Defoe, Adam Smith, and George Eliot.* New York: Columbia University Press, 1986. 193–240.
17 Cf. RECKWITZ. *Das hybride Subjekt.* 105.

of the 'moral subject', i. e. into a partriarchal model of femininity, under Deronda's guidance. In order to outline the tension between the manifest and latent content of *Daniel Deronda*, I will first focus on the existential coding of fear in the novel. As this motif is linked to the rejection of the 'casino world' in Eliot's novel, I will begin by taking a closer look at the opening description of the casino. The existential reading of fear will then be contrasted with a psychoanalytical explanation of Gwendolen's dread. I will then tie back the findings of my analysis to the briefly outlined conflict between different models of subjectivity in the nineteenth century.

The world of the casino is a world of radical contingency. The narrator paints this alienated world in bleak and depressing colours. Personal relationships and intimacy have been replaced by indifferent monetary connections, casting the individual unit as interchangeable.[18] Accordingly, the players appear as indistinguishable in their "uniform negativeness of expression which had the effect of a mask" (*DD* 9). The individual is no longer embedded within traditional social structures and thus social bonds have been eroded.[19] The emphasis on contingency in the play of chance also has implications for the experience of time. If random chance rules, then the spectre of a meaningless universe arises. Time appears as empty and dehistoricized in the casino.

The attributes of this casino world tailor Gwendolen's experience of severe fear. The following description may serve as a point of departure to illustrate this interrelation between Gwendolen's affective experientiality and speculative market society:

> What she unwillingly recognised, and would have been glad for others to be unaware of, was that liability of hers to fits of spiritual dread, though this fountain of awe within her had not found its way into connection with the religion taught her or with any human relations. [...] Solitude in any wide scene impressed her with an undefined feeling of immeasurable existence aloof from her, in the midst of which she was helplessly incapable of asserting herself. The little astronomy taught her at school used sometimes to set her imagination at work in a way that made her tremble: but always when some one joined her she recovered her indifference to the vastness in which she seemed an exile; she found again her usual world in which her will was of some avail, and the religious nomenclature belonging to this world was no more identified for her with

---

18 On the connection between monetary equivalence and qualitative indifference cf. HÖRISCH, Jochen. *Kopf oder Zahl. Die Poesie des Geldes.* Frankfurt M.: Suhrkamp, 1998 [1996]. 203 – 04.

19 See also STONE, Wilfred. "The Play of Chance and Ego in *Daniel Deronda*." In: *Nineteenth-Century Literature* 53,1 (1998): 25 – 55, 32: "The scene is an emblem of the market society in its most alienated aspect, a money-state divorced from work, divorced from production, and – since anonymity has replaced personal relations – divorced from love. Money in its elemental function equals 'bread', the staff of life, but money abstracted from life, as here at the gaming table, is [...] sterile and dead." For a close reading of the opening casino scene, see also MARSHALL. *The Figure of Theatre.* 197.

those uneasy impressions of awe than her uncle's surplices seen out of use at the Rectory. (*DD* 63–64)

The vastness of space threatens Gwendolen's sense of self. With this depiction of Gwendolen's dread, Eliot continues romantic traditions of thought, drawing especially on Edmund Burke's philosophy with its listing of solitude, immensity, and darkness as inducing sublime experience. The signature of the sublime is its move towards transcendence by means of surpassing human scale. This confrontation with transcendence explains the recurring conflation of the sublime with religious-spiritual experientiality.[20] On the one hand, the sublime may offer a reunion with the spiritual as is highlighted by the explicit reference to religion in the passage above. On the other hand, an "identification of the transcendent with the Nothingness of death"[21] is also possible. It is the latter case which we find in Gwendolen's reaction. The activation of the self in face of the sublime, which results from the subject's attempts to grasp the unimaginable, is relinquished, leading to a gripping paralysis.

Of special significance in the quoted passage is the implicit link drawn between secularization and Gwendolen's incapability of drawing strength from this "fountain of awe".[22] With no meaningful "religious nomenclature" as a frame of reference, Gwendolen possesses no resources to draw on for self-preservation or for creating significance. In the light of this threatened loss of self, the connection to the casino scene comes prominently to the fore. Gwendolen is portrayed as a subject devoid of roots in an organic community and thus left adrift in the blighted world of market society. In such a world, "the feeling of dread just floats".[23]

Daniel Deronda depicts the loss of community as a process of decay and introduces an alternative model England may emulate to reverse its decay: "Judaism/Zionism as a culture that remains organically whole even though physically dispersed".[24] The subject model connected with this ideal of organic

---

20 Cf. FICK, Monika. "Pfeiler der klassischen Ästhetik: Das Erhabene." In: Monika Fick and Sybille Goessl (eds.). *Der Schein der Dinge. Einführung in die Ästhetik.* Tübingen: Attempto, 2002. 39–62, 54.

21 Cf. FICK. "Pfeiler der klassischen Ästhetik: Das Erhabene." 54 (my translation).

22 Cf. DURING, Lisabeth. "The Concept of Dread: Sympathy and Ethics in *Daniel Deronda.*" In: *Critical Review* 33 (1993): 88–111, 92.

23 DURING. "The Concept of Dread: Sympathy and Ethics in *Daniel Deronda.*" 92.

24 JACKSON, Tony E. "George Eliot's 'New Evangel': *Daniel Deronda* and the Ends of Realism." In: *Genre* 25 (1992): 229–48, 243. For a critical discussion of the ideal of community George Eliot presents in *Daniel Deronda* see GRAVER, Suzanne. *George Eliot and Community. A Study in Social Theory and Fictional Form.* Berkeley/Los Angeles/London: University of California Press, 1984. 224–43 and WINKGENS, Meinhard. *Die kulturelle Symbolik von Rede und Schrift in den Romanen von George Eliot. Untersuchungen zu ihrer Entwicklung, Funktionalisierung und Bewertung.* Tübingen: Narr, 1997. 354 ff.

wholeness is the previously outlined moral subject. This becomes especially clear when it turns out that Deronda, who was brought up as an Englishman, is of Jewish origin and destined to found the Jewish nation state. The replacement of chance by destiny in the Jewish part of the novel points to the religious function of nationalism[25] and thus its potential to combat the alienated casino world.

Eliot's organicist thinking arguably leads to essentialist notions of gender.[26] Accordingly, the codes of the moral subject, which inform the vision of social organicism, are deeply enmeshed with patriarchal gender stereotypes.[27] Mirah, for example, whose Jewish "religion was one fibre with her affections" (DD 362), is incapable of dissimulation and conforms to traditional notions of femininity ('angel in the house'). In contrast, the speculative or deviant subject Gwendolen is intent on breaking free from submissive femininity.

In keeping with this ideological outlook of Daniel Deronda, Gwendolen is punished for her 'speculative' stance towards life and attempts to usurp patriarchal power. In the "vastness in which she seemed an exile" (DD 64), Deronda acts as Gwendolen's sheet anchor, i. e. "in the stead of God" (DD 763). Therefore it is Deronda whom Gwendolen turns to when seeking a way to deal with her pressing and inexplicable fear. Deronda's reaction highlights the interdependency between cultural constructions of fear and models of subjectivity. It is in her fits of fear that Gwendolen ceases her theatrical self-stylization and is wrested out of her "usual world" (DD 64).[28] Critics have noted the connections that one may draw to Kierkegaard's and Heidegger's philosophy.[29] In Heideggerian diction, Gwendolen's existential dread cuts her off from the dictates and pressure of the Anyone (das Man) and compels her "to face the full range of

---

25 Cf. ANDERSON, Benedict. Imagined Communities: Reflections on the Origin and Spread of Nationalism. London: Verso, 1983. 51: "It is the magic of nationalism to turn chance into destiny." On this function of nationalism in Daniel Deronda see McCAW, Neil. George Eliot and Victorian Historiography. Imagining the National Past. Houndmills: Macmillan, 2000. 111.

26 Cf. WINKGENS, Meinard. "George Eliot und die Musik: Funktionsvarianten von Musik und Stimme in ihrem Romanwerk." In: Stefan Horlacher and Marion Islinger (eds.). Expedition nach der Wahrheit. Poems, Essays and Papers in Honour of Theo Stemmler. Festschrift zum 60. Geburtstag von Theo Stemmler. Heidelberg: Winter. 1996. 399–424.

27 For an analysis of the metaphysics of presence underpinning Eliot's organicist vision in Daniel Deronda cf. WINKGENS. Die kulturelle Symbolik von Rede und Schrift in den Romanen von George Eliot. 283–379. Winkgens' analysis also takes gender into account. For a feminist reading of the novel cf. SYPHER, Eileen. "Resisting Gwendolen's 'Subjection': Daniel Deronda's Proto-Feminism." In: Studies in the Novel 28,4 (1996): 506–24.

28 Cf. WINKGENS. Die kulturelle Symbolik von Rede und Schrift in den Romanen von George Eliot. 314.

29 Cf. McCOBB. "Daniel Deronda as Will and Representation: George Eliot and Schopenhauer." 546, and especially DURING. "The Concept of Dread: Sympathy and Ethics in Daniel Deronda.", who offers an extensive analysis of Daniel Deronda in the light of Heidegger's and Kierkegaard's philosophy.

[...] [her] freedom".[30] We see Gwendolen, however, withdrawing from this existential freedom by entering paralysis and seeking to cling to her known world. This defensive reaction corresponds with the authorial evaluation of her rebellious nature: "Gwendolen's daring was not in the least that of the adventuress; the demand to be held a lady was in her very marrow." (DD 272) Despite her desire for greater freedom and independence, she is firmly in the grip of the Anyone, i.e. highly susceptible to social pressure and prescriptions.

Deronda's failure to understand Gwendolen's fear points to the existential dimension of her fits of dread.[31] A key trait of Deronda is his "many-sided sympathy" (DD 364), which becomes manifest in his "habit of seeing things as they probably appeared to others" (DD 364). While we are repeatedly informed on the level of telling that Deronda successfully 'reads' Gwendolen, thus rendering her transparent, his perplexity in the face of her spiritual dread casts doubt on this alleged empathetic relationship. In phenomenological terms, the dread or existential anxiety of the Other resists empathetic access because in "dread all connection to others is cut off":[32] "Fear is the *principium individuationis:* through fear Dasein is disclosed as a whole";[33] i.e. Dasein is individualized and we are thus "stripped of our embeddedness in a community and our reliance upon a world that has been publicly interpreted".[34] This explains why Deronda is unable to empathize with Gwendolen's excessive dread. Existential fear resists empathetic access.

If existential dread confronts us with our 'ownmost ability-to-be', thus freeing us from the grip of social conventions and expectations, then this "breakdown experience"[35] may also liberate us in such a way that we are able to forge a form of subjectivity in conflict with the prescriptions of the Anyone. Deronda's advice to Gwendolen as to how to deal with her fear is, however, geared towards suppressing forms of subjectivity deviating from the moral identity model. As her fear remains impenetrable for him, he commends using her dread as a moral compass:

> Turn your fear into a safeguard. Keep your dread fixed on the idea of increasing that remorse which is so bitter to you. Fixed meditation may do a great deal towards

---

30 BLATTNER, William. *Heidegger's Being and Time. A Reader's Guide.* London/New York: Continuum, 2006. 167.
31 Cf. DURING. "The Concept of Dread: Sympathy and Ethics in *Daniel Deronda.*" 91.
32 DURING. "The Concept of Dread: Sympathy and Ethics in *Daniel Deronda.*" 91.
33 LUCKNER, Andreas. *Martin Heidegger: 'Sein und Zeit'.* Paderborn et al.: Schöningh, 2001 [1997]. 82 (my translation). The full quote reads in the original as follows: "Die Angst ist somit das *principium individuationis:* durch die Angst erschließt das Dasein sich als ein *ganzes*, d.h. im ursprünglichen Wortsinne individuelles, nämlich ungeteiltes."
34 BLATTNER. *Heidegger's Being and Time.* 144.
35 BLATTNER. *Heidegger's Being and Time.* 144.

defining our longing or dread. We are not always in a state of strong emotion, and when we are calm we can use our memories and gradually change the bias of our fear, as we do our tastes. Take your fear as a safeguard. It is like quickness of hearing. It may make consequences passionately present to you. Try to take hold of your sensibility, and use it as if it were a faculty, like vision. (*DD* 452)

His advice identifies her dread as a source of authentic emotional expressivity, i. e. as a means of re-establishing contact with her 'true self', which was previously submerged in the wake of her role-playing.[36] Due to this authenticity, fear may serve as a suitable 'faculty' to evaluate the rightness of one's action and to break with the world of artificiality and theatricality.[37] Deronda's words chime with the codes of the moral subject. On the one hand, Deronda's view of fear as a source of authenticity allows for connections with the notion of individualized *Dasein* in moments of dread. On the other hand, his focus on morality serves to counteract the moment of existential freedom. The interaction between Deronda and Gwendolen reads as a continuation of his efforts to inculcate her with the codes of the moral subject: fear as a moral safeguard and a source of authenticity. Due to the fact that Deronda ultimately is unable to understand Gwendolen's dread, his advice arguably bears no fruit, at least if one concentrates on the level of showing.[38]

Discrepancies between telling and showing regarding Gwendolen's development abound in Eliot's novel.[39] I will focus on the level of telling first.[40] According to the authorial narrator (cf. *DD* 763), Gwendolen's development is to be seen in a positive light because she successfully renounces her egoistic impulses under Deronda's guidance, who serves as her "outer conscience" (*DD* 763). This

---

36 Cf. WINKGENS. *Die kulturelle Symbolik von Rede und Schrift in den Romanen von George Eliot.* 321. Cf. also WINKGENS. *Die kulturelle Symbolik von Rede und Schrift in den Romanen von George Eliot.* 320: "In ihrer Wirkung und Funktion in vielerlei Hinsicht dem Ruf des Gewissens vergleichbar, mit dem in der Heideggerschen Existentialontologie das Selbst sich aus seiner Verfallenheit an das Man im Modus der Uneigentlichkeit zurück- und in den Modus der Eigentlichkeit hineinruft, ist Gwendolens zunehmende Bereitschaft, die Manifestationen ihrer 'fits of spiritual dread' anzunehmen, gleichbedeutend mit dem wiedergewonnenen Zugang zur Autorität ihres innerlichen Selbstgefühls, zur Authentizität ihrer expressiven Stimme; einen Zugang, den sie über ihre ausschließliche Orientierung an einer performativen Mündlichkeit in einem Prozeß wachsender Selbstentfremdung verdrängt und verloren hatte." For a detailed analysis of authenticity in *Daniel Deronda* cf. WINKGENS. *Die kulturelle Symbolik von Rede und Schrift in den Romanen von George Eliot.* 283 – 379, and WINKGENS. "George Eliot und die Musik."
37 Cf. WINKGENS. *Die kulturelle Symbolik von Rede und Schrift in den Romanen von George Eliot.* 321.
38 Cf. PARIS, Bernard J. *Rereading George Eliot. Changing Responses to Her Experiments in Life.* Albany: State University of New York, 2003. 157 ff.
39 For a detailed analysis of discrepancies between telling and showing in *Daniel Deronda* see PARIS. *Rereading George Eliot.* 111 – 208.
40 See also PARIS. *Rereading George Eliot.* 157 ff.

authorial judgment implies that Gwendolen is not responsible for her husband's death. Gwendolen had been harbouring a murderous rage against her husband Grandcourt for quite some time due to his oppressive and cruel behaviour. Her feeling of dread in response to a "picture of an upturned dead face, from which an obscure figure seemed to be fleeing with outstretched arms" (*DD* 27), early on in the novel reads as an uncanny example of precognition because it foreshadows Grandcourt's later death in a boating accident.[41] Gwendolen suffers from feelings of guilt because she hesitated to throw a rope to Grandcourt struggling in the water. Her feelings of guilt are aggravated to the point of psychological break-down due to the uncanny manner in which Grandcourt's drowning fulfilled her deepest desire: "I knew no way of killing him there, but I did, I did kill him in my thoughts. [...] I saw my wish [i.e. that Grandcourt drown] outside me" (*DD* 695 – 96). The reader cannot be sure what happened during the boating incident because there is no authorial description of the events. Deronda, who did not witness Grandcourt's death, is equally in the dark regarding this happening. He, however, is adamant in insisting that Gwendolen's "murderous will" (*DD* 699) played no part in Grandcourt's death (cf. *DD* 699). Deronda's reading of the boating incident is implicitly backed up by the authorial narrator, who em-pathically asserts Deronda's therapeutic influence on Gwendolen. The view of Gwendolen as a murderess is incompatible with the authorial claim of Deronda's 'unspoiled mission':[42]

> Would her remorse have maintained its power within her, or would she have felt absolved by secrecy, if it had not been for that outer conscience which was made for her by Deronda? [...] In this way our brother may be in the stead of God to us [...]. That mission of Deronda to Gwendolen had begun with what she had felt to be his judgment of her at the gaming-table. He might easily have spoiled it:– much of our lives is spent marring our own influence [...]. Deronda had not spoiled his mission. (*DD* 699)

All in all, Deronda is able to shape Gwendolen's moral development through his talent of "interpret[ing] her" (*DD* 434) when she herself cannot. Moreover, he is able to channel her remorse to positive ends. In this way, "his influence [enters] [...] into the current of that self-suspicion and self-blame which awakens a new consciousness" (*DD* 430).

Gwendolen surmounts the last shreds of her egoism when Deronda tells her of

---

41 At the time she sees the picture, Gwendolen has not yet met Grandcourt. For interpretations of Gwendolen's precognition see HORATSCHEK, Anna-Margaretha. "'Logicized' Taboo: Abjection in George Eliot's *Daniel Deronda*." In: Stefan Glomb, Lars Heiler and Stefan Horlacher (eds.). *Taboo and Transgression in British Literature from the Renaissance to the Present.* New York: Palgrave Macmillan, 2010. 193 – 210, SYPHER. "Resisting Gwendolen's 'Subjection': *Daniel Deronda's* Proto-Feminism." and EAGLETON, Terry. *The English Novel. An Introduction.* Malden, MA: Blackwell, 2008 [2005]. 185.

42 Cf. PARIS. *Rereading George Eliot.* 166 ff.

his impending departure to fulfill his historical destiny of founding the Jewish nation state. Although this news triggers another fit of dread as she sees her 'God' deserting her, she is finally able to accept "the separateness of his life" (*DD* 796) and her own decentred status. Gwendolen's successful and positive transformation into a moral subject is indicated not only by her awakened consciousness and her rediscovery of emotional authenticity,[43] but also by her return to Offendene, the place of her childhood. Offendene had been characterized by the authorial narrator as a place where Gwendolen could have developed an organically rooted and communally embedded sense of identity.[44] The return to Offendene thus implies a withdrawal from the 'casino world' and the possibility of developing a rooted sense of place.[45]

While such a reading is borne out on the level of telling, a different picture emerges when one concentrates on the level of showing. On the one hand, the level of showing does feature Gwendolen's fits of dread as a source of emotional authenticity. Her fear therefore constitutes a crucial element in her later adoption of the codes of the moral subject. On the other hand, her fits of dread also appear as a radical indictment of the very form of subjectivity held up as an ideal in the novel.[46] In order to substantiate this thesis, it is necessary to backtrack for a moment and to take a closer look at Gwendolen's resentment against patriarchal dominance.

From the very beginning, the female speculative subject is portrayed as in rebellion against patriarchal restrictions. The threatening force of Gwendolen's resistance to patriarchal dominance is foregrounded by her capacity to "infelonious murder" (*DD* 25). The first intimation of this disturbing female violence is offered in Gwendolen's childhood when she strangles her step-sister's canary. A psychoanalytical reading of the passage describing this childhood incident reveals that the killing of the bird is the result of displacement: Gwendolen transfers her murderous impulses against her stepfather onto the canary she associates with him. There are numerous textual elements pointing to displacement. It is, for example, highly significant that the canary belonged to

---

43 WINKGENS, Meinhard. *Die kulturelle Symbolik von Rede und Schrift in den Romanen von George Eliot.* 318

44 Cf. WINGKENS. *Die kulturelle Symbolik von Rede und Schrift in den Romanen von George Eliot.* 318.

45 Cf. WINGKENS. *Die kulturelle Symbolik von Rede und Schrift in den Romanen von George Eliot.* 318.

46 See also PARIS. *Rereading George Eliot.* 159: "It seems to me that there is a great dissonance between what George Eliot says about Gwendolen's transformation and what she concretely depicts. While we are being told that Gwendolen is undergoing a conversion in which she develops a new consciousness, a new soul, we are being shown a character who is full of rage, despair, and self-hatred, and who finds herself trapped in a situation from which she can find no other escape than the death of her husband."

her stepsister, i.e. the offspring of her hated step-father. This biological tie contributes to the metonymic continuity between 'stepfather – stepfather's daughter – stepsister's pet'. Moreover, the two topics (Gwendolen's hatred of her stepfather, her killing of the bird) closely follow each other on the level of narrative discourse, thus strengthening the impression of a metonymic relation. Moreover, Gwendolen's murderous impulse in the instance of the bird may be seen in parallel to her later desire to kill her husband. Against this foil, the bird appears as a surrogate for a patriarchal figure. Last but not least, this psycho-analytic reading helps to explain the curious choice of the word "murder" with reference to the killing of an animal.[47] Given the force of Gwendolen's aggression, great psychic energy is needed to suppress these violent impulses in order to comply with what is expected of a lady.

Against this backdrop, Gwendolen's fits of dread can be explained as a return of the repressed. It is no coincidence that she experiences paralytic fear "in the very moments she reaches out imaginatively to secure an identity in perfect compliance with the social norms of her society".[48] Her posing as Hermione in the *tableau vivante* of *The Winter's Tale* is a case in point.[49] The very moment she stylizes herself as an embodiment of female virtue (according to patriarchal gender stereotypes), her illicit desire to eliminate patriarchal authority is externalized in the picture of the corpse that comes to haunt her.[50] This psycho-analytic reading necessitates a re-evaluation of the sublime dimension attributed to Gwendolen's fits of dread.

In the context of patriarchy, Gwendolen's desire to kill the Father is the ultimate taboo. The fact that her murderous impulses "signify a moment of transgression into tabooed territories"[51] of the Real (*sensu* Lacan), i.e. the realm beyond (patriarchal) Law, is signalled by the presence of death in the picture.[52]

---

47 For a discussion of Gwendolen's murderous impulses against her stepfather see also PARIS. *Rereading George Eliot.* 148–49: "Gwendolen must have had death wishes toward her stepfather [...]. It is a psychological commonplace that people often experience intense, irrational feelings of guilt when their wish for someone's death is fulfilled, even if they had nothing to do with bringing the death about. The picture of the dead face may be so terrifying to Gwendolen because it taps into her unconscious guilt over wishing Captain Davilow [= her stepfather] dead [...]." I discuss the implications of Gwendolen's fearful reaction to the picture further below.

48 HORATSCHEK. "'Logicized' Taboo: Abjection in George Eliot's *Daniel Deronda.*" 197.

49 Cf. HORATSCHEK. "'Logicized' Taboo: Abjection in George Eliot's *Daniel Deronda.*" 197 ff.

50 Cf. HORATSCHEK. "'Logicized' Taboo: Abjection in George Eliot's *Daniel Deronda.*" 197 ff.

51 HORATSCHEK. "'Logicized' Taboo: Abjection in George Eliot's *Daniel Deronda.*" 197.

52 HORATSCHEK offers a detailed psychoanalytical reading of Gwendolen's fear based on Julia Kristeva's theory of abjection. Drawing on Kristeva, she explains the interconnection between the taboo and the abject (or in Lacanian terms: the Real). My Lacanian interpretation follows hers in positing the picture of the corpse as "represent[ing] all those 'things which were meant to be shut up' (*DD* 20), namely a psychic reality the young woman has un-

The loss of the Symbolic means the death of self for the Real is the realm of de-differentiation. This psychic dynamic not only explains why Gwendolen experiences the return of the repressed as an existential threat to self. It also reveals the logic that underpins the conflation of the sublime with the return of the repressed illicit desire: "a taboo is a prohibition justified by the sacredness of what is prohibited, and this sacredness, in turn, is embodied by 'puissances redoutables'".[53]

Furthermore, the transgressive nature of Gwendolen's aggressive impulses endows added significance to the often noted frisson in the realist or English part of Eliot's novel:[54]

> Both the intensity of her wishing and the compliance of the plot, however welcome, are a lapse from the realism of the novel. [...] Gwendolen's anger is [...] a superfluity of emotion, that Eliot has not been able to probe through the realist frame that has worked to contain her representation of extreme female emotion.[55]

Due to the fact that Gwendolen's fits of fear remain inexplicable within the textual world, i.e. their roots in the taboo remain secret, she herself ultimately cannot be rendered transparent by patriarchal readings of her body. It is, for example, far from clear what really happened during the boating accident because we are never granted an authorial description of the events. We therefore do not know whether Gwendolen's hesitation to help Grandcourt was decisive for his death or not, despite Deronda's clear pronouncement to the contrary and the gushing comments of the authorial narrator on Deronda's positive role in Gwendolen's life.[56]

The analysis of Gwendolen's fits of fear shows the full extent to which she is Other to the ideal version of self and nationhood in *Daniel Deronda*. Her (initial) 'speculative subjectivity' is explicitly presented by the authorial narrator as part of communal decay (level of telling). In accordance with the above-mentioned intertwinement of subject models with gender stereotypes, the female speculative subject harbours a murderous resentment for being forced to comply with the dictates of patriarchy. The challenge posed by Gwendolen's hysterical fear

---

consciously known and tried to repress for years: To be a princess means to be a 'princess in exile' (*DD* 32)" (HORATSCHEK. "'Logicized' Taboo: Abjection in George Eliot's *Daniel Deronda*." 199.).

53 Emile Durkheim, quoted in HORLACHER, Stefan. "Taboo, Transgression, and Literature: An Introduction." In: Stefan Glomb, Lars Heiler and Stefan Horlacher (eds.). *Taboo and Transgression in British Literature from the Renaissance to the Present*. New York: Palgrave Macmillan, 2010. 3–21, 6–7.

54 Scholars frequently characterize *Daniel Deronda* as falling into two parts: the 'realist English part' with its focus on Gwendolen and the 'epic Jewish part' that revolves around Deronda's gradual discovery of his Jewish identity and destiny.

55 SYPHER. "Resisting Gwendolen's 'Subjection': *Daniel Deronda's* Proto-Feminism." 518.

56 See also PARIS. *Rereading George Eliot*. 156.

becomes especially manifest in her destabilization of Mordecai's prophetic function, which in turn throws a dubious light on the organicist ideal in the shape of Judaism/Zionism (level of showing):

> Although Eliot continues throughout the novel to valorize Gwendolen and Deronda's bond of conscience and to grant Mordecai the official role of prophet, the form of Gwendolen's hysteria finally challenges and mimics the dominant narrative structure. Gwendolen's power to make her 'inner visions' come true, to see her wishes take shape outside her body, constitutes a spiritual and prophetic dimension to her character that is in conflict with the novel's authorized spiritual voice.

> [...] Gwendolen's spectral experiences [...] carry a potential challenge to Mordecai's prophetic authority because, like medical correlations between saints and hysterics, Eliot's rhetoric encodes the possibility that all visionary powers are a function of nervous disease.[57]

If Gwendolen is a threatening Other to the ideals expounded in the novel, then her transformation into a moral subject becomes all the more pressing. The high price Gwendolen has to pay for this transformation is staged in the final scenes of the novel (level of showing): her hysterical crying and outbursts "I will try – try to live" (*DD* 806) point to a complete psychological collapse of self.[58] As we are not granted access to her inner life after her breakdown, the reader is left with the impression of lasting psychological damage in the wake of Deronda's or her 'God's' departure. While the transformation of the speculative subject is presented in terms of a positive moral development on the level of telling, what is staged on the level of showing is the deathly wounding of a self. This tension cannot be resolved, despite the dominant textual strategies (e.g. authorial comments) geared towards a positive coding of Gwendolen's transformation. Depending on what level one focuses on, one will arrive at radically different interpretations of Gwendolen's development.

The effect of this ambivalence is to draw attention to ideological fissures and dubious argumentative moves within Eliot's novel. A closer look reveals that the outlined ambivalence is a direct result of Eliot's problematic fusion of patriarchal gender politics with a rejection of egoism. Throughout the novel, female efforts to gain autonomy are repeatedly characterized as a form of egoism and thus de-legitimized. This value scheme has an impact on the staging of empathy. While the authorial narrator is quick to assure us of Deronda's pronounced empathetic ability, one cannot help but notice that empathy for an assertive woman is apparently only possible if she suffers for her attempts to attain a position of power. Gwendolen had married Grandcourt on the assumption that

---

57 VRETTOS, Athena. "From Neurosis to Narrative: The Private Life of the Nerves in *Villette* and *Daniel Deronda*." In: *Victorian Studies* 33,4 (1990): 551 – 79, 574 – 75.
58 Cf. PARIS. *Rereading George Eliot.* 174 – 77.

he was a pliable man whose wealth would ensure her greater social liberty. She had entered marriage in the full knowledge of her 'gain being another's loss' for Grandcourt's mistress had hoped to become a respectable woman for the sake of their children. With this in mind, Deronda is only able to empathize with Gwendolen if her gamble in marriage does not pay off:

> Gwendolen knowing of that woman and her children, marrying Grandcourt, and showing herself contented, would have been among the most repulsive of beings to him; but Gwendolen tasting the bitterness of remorse for having contributed to their injury was brought very near to his fellow-feeling. (*DD* 434)

Telling passages such as the above imply that the willingness to imagine what the Other experiences pre-conditions allegiance. Such a feeling of allegiance in turn requires the perception of a shared similarity, as is indicated by the reference to "fellow-feeling".[59] Against this backdrop, a different explanation for Deronda's inability to understand Gwendolen's fits of dread begins to emerge.

Deronda's failure to empathize with Gwendolen's fear results from the lack of shared 'world', i. e. the radical experiential difference of being a woman or a man in patriarchal society. As his mother (Princess Halm-Eberstein) bitterly states, "You are not a woman. You may try – but you can never imagine what it is to have a man's force of genius in you, and yet to suffer the slavery of being a girl." (*DD* 631) One can read these words as "express[ing] the same sympathetic principle Deronda eventually does: the belief that a specific group identification is a prerequisite for sympathy".[60] It is also, however, possible to go a step further. Her harsh rebuttal of her son's attempts to empathize with her draws attention to the fine line between empathy and the eradication of alterity in the name of perceived similarity.[61] Empathy, a key trait of the moral subject, starts to take on

---

59 This view of empathy accords with contemporary theories of empathy that postulate "some minimum shared experience" (HAROLD, James. "Empathy with Fictions." In: *British Journal of Aesthetics* 40,3 (2000): 340–55, 346) as a pre-condition for an empathetic response. The question of allegiance plays a crucial role in Fritz Breithaupt's conceptualization of empathy. He defines empathy as "a decision for partisanship that is legitimized in emotional and rational terms through narrative strategies" (BREITHAUPT, Fritz. *Kulturen der Empathie.* Frankfurt M.: Suhrkamp, 2009. 175; my translation). (Original quote: *"Empathie ist eine Entscheidung zur Parteinahme für den einen (und nicht den anderen), die durch narrative Strategien emotional und rational legitimiert wird."*) One may also draw connections to research on empathetic responses of readers or viewers to works of fiction. Dolf ZILLMANN, for example, claims that "positive affective dispositions toward models [i.e. characters] allow empathic reactions, whereas negative affective dispositions impair, prevent, or hedonically reverse them" (ZILLMANN, Dolf. "Mechanisms of Emotional Involvement with Drama." In: *Poetics* 23 (1994): 33–51, 44.)

60 JAFFE, Audrey. *Scenes of Sympathy: Identity and Representation in Victorian Fiction.* Ithaca/ London: Cornell University Press, 2000. 144.

61 For George Eliot sympathy is a moral emotion because it entails altruism. Critics have been quick to point out that Eliot explores the limits of sympathy in *Daniel Deronda*, highlighting

darker hues when concentrating on ideological tensions within the text. The fine line between empathy and narcisstic projections also gives rise to ideological fissures in *Fear Itself*, which tries to reconcile the equation of empathy and altruism with the vampiric empathy of the serial killer.

II.   Jonathan Nasaw: *Fear Itself* (2003)

Over 120 years separate Eliot's *Daniel Deronda* from Jonathan Nasaw's serial killer novel *Fear Itself*. The approach to fear adopted in Nasaw's novel is clearly indebted to the accelerating processes of rationalization and domestication (i. e. control of inner and outer nature) that drive modernization. In keeping with a rationalistic world-view, *Fear Itself* heavily draws on scientific and psycho-analytic discourses on fear. These discourses serve to render fear transparent and to banish the spectre of losing control. In the following, I will trace the ways in which the drive towards retaining control shapes the novel's stance on fear. Ruptures within the ideological fabric of the text will be highlighted by means of a close reading of passages that correlate fear and empathy.

A brief plot synopsis of Nasaw's novel is already sufficient to draw attention to its obsession with pathological fear. *Fear Itself* is about a psychopathic serial killer, Simon Childs, who kills people suffering from phobia. He is especially sadistic in the way he kills because his chosen method always entails making the phobic's nightmare come true:[62]

---

the danger of paralysis resulting from excessive sympathy: "His [= Deronda's] imagination had so wrought itself to the habit of seeing things as they probably appeared to others, that a strong partisanship, unless it were against immediate oppression, had become an insincerity for him. [...] A too reflective and diffusive sympathy was in danger of paralysing in him that indignation against wrong and that selectness of fellowship which are the conditions of moral force [...]." (*DD* 364) See also DURING. "The Concept of Dread: Sympathy and Ethics in *Daniel Deronda*." 89, on Eliot's treatment of sympathy in *Daniel Deronda*: "Given the social implications of the modernity she analyses here [= in *Daniel Deronda*], the road to a triumphant reign of sympathy was never going to be smooth. But George Eliot felt she had to go to great lengths to save sympathy as an idea. As Nietzsche would have complained, she had to make it Jewish." When discussing sympathy or empathy in *Daniel Deronda*, it is important to keep the difference between these two overlapping concepts in mind. George Eliot stands in the tradition of eighteenth century moralists who link sympathy with "compassion and active benevolence" (KEEN, Suzanne. *Empathy and the Novel*. Oxford: Oxford University Press, 2007. 44; cf. 53 – 54). Strictly speaking, empathy and sympathy are not synonyms: while both entail adopting the perspective of another, empathy arguably does not necessarily lead to altruism (cf. KEEN. *Empathy and the Novel*. 16 – 26). For an overview of conceptual-izations of sympathy and empathy cf. KEEN. *Empathy and the Novel*. 4 – 5; 37 – 64.

62 An earlier variant of this theme can be found in an episode of *The Avengers* ("The Fear Merchants", 1967), in which a 'business efficiency bureau' literally eliminates competition

Two: Kimberly Rosen. Chicago. Pnigophobia. Fear of suffocation. On June 15th, her mother found her in the bathtub of her apartment with a plastic bag over her head. [...]

Three: Mara Agajanian. Fresno. Hemophobia. Fear of blood. Found in the bathtub on August 17th, with her wrists slit. (*FI* 31)

Due to this method of torture and murder, Simon sees himself as embodying 'fear itself' for his victims. Phobia also features prominently in Simon's motivation to kill because, to put it in the profiler's words,

our man is a phobophobe. [...] Fear of fear: a phobophobe is afraid of fear itself. But this subject's phobia would seem to be manifesting counterphobically – in other words, he seeks out that which he's afraid of – which in turn fits hand in glove with the psychopathy: he fights his boredom by feeding on fear. (*FI* 50)

The multiperspective structure of the novel with its different focalizers, which include Simon, his victims and criminal investigators, foregrounds differences and similarities between the characters' relation to fear. While figural narration dominates the novel, there are also instances where an authorial narrator intrudes, often to instruct the reader and to direct his or her sympathies and judgments. I will start out my analysis by focusing on the pervasive scientific or rationalistic discourses in the novel because they fundamentally shape the novel's stance on fear and empathy.

Apparently all of Simon's victims have been in therapy and are therefore well-informed about the physiological side of fear and possibilities of fear management:

Wayne knew he could forestall a panic-induced blackout (or, as Dr. Taylor called it, a vasovagal syncope) by breathing slowly from the diaphragm while tensing and relaxing his muscles. (*FI* 2)

She knew what was happening – her sinoaortic baroreflex arc, the mechanism responsible for the vasovagal syncope, was overcompensating for the sudden increase in blood pressure by dropping the pressure just as suddenly. But she also knew, after all these years, how to take charge, how to reverse the process. (*FI* 18)

This medical or therapeutical approach to fear serves the phobic's goal of regaining control ('taking charge') as is repeatedly emphasized: "all phobics were afraid of [...] loss of control" (*FI* 133). Control or domestication of fear entails an objectification of the body in this passage. The body appears as a separate object to be described in medicalese (e.g. "sinoartic baroreflex"). This scientific discourse distances affective experientiality by turning it into an object that can be rationally analysed. Distancing and control go hand in hand. On the one hand,

---

for its client by frightening his competitors to death. I am indebted to Stefan Glomb for drawing my attention to this.

the novel indicates the limits of such a scientific approach to fear by granting access to the phobic's experiential dimension which eludes scientific terminology.[63] Moreover, knowledge of scientific explanations of fear cannot ward off the phenomenon itself, thus highlighting the *"cognitive impenetrability"*[64] of fear, i.e. the fact that the subject's phobia cannot be affected by rational arguments or beliefs.

Despite staging the discrepancy between scientific discourses on fear and *qualia*, the novel, on the other hand, is dominated by a scientific stance to the phenomenon. It is striking to note how often the narrator adopts a classificatory and statistic approach to phobia. A brief quote from the beginning of a long authorial comment may serve to illustrate this point:

> Of the approximately thirty million Americans who suffer from phobia disorders serious enough to require professional consultation at some point in their lives, forty-two percent are afraid of illness and/or injury, eighteen percent are afraid of thunderstorms [...]. (*FI* 16)

The narrator then goes on to talk about one of the main protagonists whom Simon targets as a witness: "Dorie Bell, age fifty-two, of Carmel-by-the-Sea, California, had been a prosoponophobe since age three." (*FI* 16). This sentence could easily feature as an introduction to a clinical case study. And what is one to make of the following description of how Dorie met Wayne Summers, a friend of hers:

> They had met the previous spring, in Las Vegas, [...], where nearly a hundred phobics (or, as they preferred to be called, Persons with Specific Phobia Disorder) had gathered for the PWSPD convention, and the two had become fast friends despite some rather striking differences between them, *including age, race, religion, and sexual orientation.* (*FI* 16–17)

The latter list of categories introduces a level of abstraction typical of scientific discourse. The more one reads on, the stronger the suspicion grows that the narrator is intent on distancing the threatening quality of pathological fear or phobia by adopting a scientific outlook.

This suspicion is strengthened by two further factors. First of all, one finds parallel shifts in register on the level of characters whenever they are intent on

---

63 The unbridgeable gap between scientific discourse and the experientiality of the subject is the macabre topic of conversation between the serial killer and one of his victims: "'Yes, I know how she died. Coral snake, neurotoxin, respiratory failure. So you can save *yourself* the trouble.' 'But it sounds so clinical, the way you put it. It wasn't clinical at all.' [...] And he was right; it wasn't clinical at all. He made Gloria's death throes come alive; he acted out the pain [...].'" (*FI* 285)

64 GOLDIE, Peter. *The Emotions. A Philosophical Exploration.* Oxford: Clarendon Press, 2002 [2000]. 76.

suppressing sources of fear. For the killer Simon, his impotency is an unacknowledged source of anxiety because he perceives it as undermining his
claims to phallic masculinity. In contrast, his murderous "fear game" affirms his
claim to omnipotence. In the following passage, the marked shift of register in
the free indirect speech correlates with these two contrasting positions:

> [...] Simon was only mildly disappointed. Because the ejaculatio praecox that had
> plagued him since early adolescence rendered penile insertion problematical and ex-
> tended intercourse all but impossible, he was incapable of enjoying prolonged sexual
> gratification, *but when it came to the fear game*, Simon Childs was an all-night, do-
> right, sixty-minute man. The longer he could make a game last, the better he felt about
> himself. (*FI* 90; emphasis added)

As one can see, there is a striking transition from high register or medicalese to
low register or colloquial English beginning with the phrase "when it came to the
fear game".[65] The second factor nourishing suspicion of the narrator's com-
plicity with strategies of distancing is the introduction of a clear "us/them"
distinction:

> So Nelson gathered up his courage (and it would be a mistake to think that severe
> phobics are lacking in courage: it took more nerve for Nelson to leave his house once a
> week than it would *for most of us* to bungee-jump off the Golden Gate Bridge) [...]. (*FI*
> 133 – 34; emphasis added)

If non-phobics are "us", then phobics are clearly deemed Other, no matter that
our sympathies for these Others are explicitly enlisted. In this way, the phenomenon of pathological fear is distanced to a certain extent despite its emotionally charged staging in the extensive descriptions of the phobic's experientiality. It is in keeping with this implicit Othering that the radical version of
phobia – fear of phobia or 'fear itself' – takes on the shape of a psychopathic
killer.

The drive towards distancing fear by coding it as Other and turning it into an
object of scientific discourse point to a Cartesian notion of the self. For the
Cartesian subject, control over inner and outer nature is of utmost importance.
The Cartesian privileging of the mind devaluates affective experientiality. The
body appears as merely an entity under the control of the mind (e. g. it is the
object of scientific investigation). An overwhelming of the thinking mind by the
emotions is consequently seen as a threat to the self. The rationalistic outlook to

---

65 On language and fear see also *FI* 99: "*predicament* was the second word that came to mind;
 the first had been *nightmare*. But since for the moment words were the only thing Dorie had
 any degree of control over, she chose the less charged one. *Predicament* was a good word, the
 kind of word you could use to stave off panic. Because predicaments, after all, were things you
 figured your way out of, she told herself, closing her eyes again. All you could do with a
 nightmare was wake up from it. Or not."

the world adopted by the authorial narrator ties in with such a Cartesian subject model. Ironically, the serial killer may be seen embodying a key trait of Cartesian subjectivity in its extreme form, namely the emphasis on mastery. The parallels between the serial killer and a Cartesian model of self introduce an important fissure within the ideological stance of Nasaw's novel. While the Cartesian self is the privileged subject model in *Fear Itself* (see also below), the parallels to the serial killer imply that Cartesian subjectivity has pathological hues. Against this backdrop it is telling to note the wealth of textual strategies introduced in order to Other the serial killer, thus maintaining a positive coding of the Cartesian self.

The extent to which the serial killer is Othered rests crucially on the question of whether he is able to empathize with his victim's fear. In a similar vein to Eliot's novel, glaring discrepancies between telling and showing can be spotted when concentrating on textual passages that deal with the interplay of fear and empathy. A familiar strategy of Othering the serial killer is to portray him as incapable of empathy. In contemporary discourses on empathy, this emotion ranks high "in the [...] roster of virtues"[66] because it is frequently seen as the basis of altruism. While this view continues to be highly controversial within the scientific community,[67] in "the popular culture view, lack of empathy spells social problems, danger to others, criminality, and inhumanity".[68] Therefore, "lacking empathy often correlates with sociopathic behaviour"[69] in works of popular crime fiction, such as *Fear Itself:*

> But on another, deeper level, down where the personality takes root, Simon's grandiose sense of himself, the preternatural confidence of the psychopath, and the *inability to empathize with others* [...] or to appreciate that others lived on the same plane of consciousness as himself, with the same interior life, all combined to render Simon constitutionally incapable of imagining the universe continuing after his death. In this regard, for all his intelligence and awareness, Simon was like an infant, unable to establish any boundaries between itself and the outside world [...]. (*FI* 199–200)

The above judgment on Simon is voiced by the authorial narrator, who quotes dominant cultural discourses on empathy. However, a closer look at the figural narrative passages that depict Simon's 'fear game' with his victims reveals a more nuanced version. In stark contrast to the authorial pronouncement, Simon is convinced that he is imaginatively experiencing what the other thinks and feels:

---

66 KEEN. *Empathy and the Novel.* 11.
67 Cf. the overview of the critical debate within the scientific community provided by KEEN. *Empathy and the Novel.* 16–26. See also COPLAN. "Empathic Engagement with Narrative Fictions." 144–46.
68 KEEN. *Empathy and the Novel.* 10.
69 KEEN. *Empathy and the Novel.* 10.

With Dorie, [...] [who has a phobic fear of masks; Stella Butter], the relationship was both enhanced and skewed by the unfamiliar presence of a third party – the lurid Kabuki mask. Wearing it took Simon outside himself, somehow. It was as if he were seeing himself approach through *her* eyes and hearing the whispering rasp of his slippers on the rough cement [...], and her own shallow panting through *her* ears. He felt the shock down to his bones when she saw the mask; when her terror peaked, when her thoughts shut down, he knew, and understood.

He was even glad for her when her vasovagal reflex kicked in, causing her to lose consciousness. He was glad for himself as well – the connection was too intense to be endured for extended periods [...]. (*FI* 109 – 10)

If Simon himself is a phobic, then this is an important realm of shared experience with his victims that allows him to 'know and understand' their phobic fear. Simon's empathetic understanding of their fear arguably gives him power over the Other because he knows what buttons to push in order to trigger over-whelming terror in his victims. For the serial killer, fear functions as a means of controlling the Other. It seems safe to say that Simon is not mistaken in his empathetic imagining of Dorie's experience because it ties in with the inside view we were granted of her only shortly before: "a glimpse of the Kabuki mask covering his face propelled her into an alternate universe where there were no thoughts, only wordless terror" (*FI* 109). In adopting Dorie's perspective, Simon not only understands what she is going through, but he also experiences her emotions: "He felt the shock down to his bones when she saw the mask". Thus, the "cognitive and affective processes"[70] integrated in the empathetic encounter also shape Simon's relationship to Dorie.

The fact that Simon's empathy with his victims plays a crucial role in the kick he gains from his 'fear game' is rendered explicit later on in the novel:

Surprisingly, it was the first time he'd ever played a game on X [= Ecstasy] – surprising because, now that he thought about it, the empathy drug seemed like a natural fit. The game was all about empathy – fear and empathy. (*FI* 237)

What strikes me as surprising about this passage is the amount of effort taken to reconcile Simon's empathetic ability with the earlier authorial statement that psychopaths lack empathy. Science comes to save the day: the characterisation of Ecstasy as an "empathy drug" refers to scientific studies whose results show that the "most salient feature of MDMA [= Ecstasy] is actually empathy".[71] This is then followed by a second strategic move. Simon may be able to empathize, but

---

70 COPLAN. "Empathic Engagement with Narrative Fictions." 143.
71 The quote is taken from an interview given by the psychiatrist Dr. Charles Grob (cf AVNI, Sheerly. "Ecstasy begets empathy: Psychiatrist and drug researcher Dr. Charles Grob sees value in MDMA – when it's taken in therapy, not at a rave." http://dir.salon.com/mwt/feature/2002/09/12/grob_interview (accessed 17 July, 2011)).

he is only prepared to indulge this feeling in the context of his fear game. When his mother, whom he blames for having abandoned him and his sister as children, pleads for empathy ("Try to put yourself in my shoes, Simon"; *FI* 264), he fights against "that unfamiliar feeling – the tug of empathy" (*FI* 265). Simon's reaction implies that he is only able to brutally murder his mother because he resists empathizing with her. In this way, Nasaw's novel tries to maintain the linkage between empathy and pro-social behaviour, despite the key role empathy plays in Simon's sadistic murders.

The depiction of the serial killer draws attention to the fine line between empathy and narcissism. Simon's narcissistic world-view explains why his empathetic response is restricted to his victim's fear. Empathy is "a threshold concept"[72], allowing "for degrees of involvement".[73] While the interaction with Dorie was an example of a strong empathetic response, for the most part Simon does indeed only display a low degree of empathy. This has to do with his psychological make-up. As already indicated in the plot synopsis, Simon cannot acknowledge his own repressed phobias, and therefore unconsciously displaces them onto the Other, using the Other or rather 'the game' as a controlled safe zone to live out his repressed fears. In accordance with clichés of serial killer literature, the obligatory childhood trauma and abuse is introduced as an explanatory framework for the roots of evil. We learn that Simon developed a fear of water after his father drowned in an accident. His abusive grandfather used beatings and drastic shock tactics (e. g. dunkings) to 'cure' Simon of his phobia, only thereby setting off a chain of endless displacements. Fear of drowning was followed by fear of the dark, the fear of dogs and so forth. Simon's repressed polyphobia thus returns as a "compensatory counterphobia" or phobophobia (cf. *FI* 220). When interacting with his victims, Simon is only interested in empathetically tapping into the experiential dimension of fear, all the while retaining control. As empathy entails a self/other-differentiation,[74] Simon is able to experience fear via empathy with the victim (other), without being overwhelmed by terror (self). In this way, he achieves control over his (suppressed) fear by turning into "that which he's afraid of" (*FI* 50)[75] and dictating the rules of the fear game.

As Simon perceives his victims solely as phobics (and not as individuals), he is only able to empathetically access one facet of their rich inner lives, namely their experience of severe fear. His tormenting and killing of Wayne Summers, who

---

72 HAROLD. "Empathy with Fictions." 346.
73 HAROLD. "Empathy with Fictions." 346.
74 Cf. COPLAN. "Empathic Engagement with Narrative Fictions." 144.
75 This motif of 'turning into that which he's afraid of' is taken to an extreme when Simon morphs into Grandfather Childs: "'It's you,' he [= Simon] said to the grim-visaged old man in the mirror. 'It's you,' Grandfather Childs replied." (*FI* 228)

suffers from ornithophobia, is a case in point. Wayne uses music, i.e. his
imaginary playing of Bach's Six Suites for Cello Solo, as a strategy of psychic
survival when he is captured and held prison in a room full of birds: "in his mind
his bowing action had never been freer, or more joyous, or, paradoxically
enough, *more under control*" (*FI* 27; emphasis added). While imprisoned and
tortured, Wayne retreats into an inner world centred on completing his imaginary cello play of Bach's Suites. His love for music is an integral part of
Wayne's subjecthood, which eludes Simon due to his reduction of the individual
to the phobic. He is thus unable to interpret Wayne's twitching fingers as his
imaginary play on an instrument. If empathy requires "a minimum of shared
experience",[76] then there is always the danger of eradicating alterity, i.e. falsely
assuming similarity in a supposedly empathetic reaction. In other words, empathy can easily blur into narcissistic projection.[77] This danger of conflating
empathy with narcissism reveals empathy to be a 'success term';[78] i.e. one may be
completely mistaken in one's imagining of another's experience. In that case, the
result is not genuine empathy, but only an attempt to empathize.[79]

This danger of mistaking narcissism for empathy is prominently displayed in
Simon's fear games because the basis of his empathetic response rests on unconsciously perceiving the Other as similar to himself. Thus, his adoption of the
perspective of another is limited to the experientiality of phobic fear. Against this
backdrop, it is surely no coincidence that Wayne plays pieces of music, i.e.
Bach's Six Suites, famous for their so-called 'latent polyphony'.[80] In contrast,
Simon stands for a dominantly monological approach to the world and is
therefore unable to recognize this polyphonic dimension in the Other.

Earlier on, I mentioned that there is a distinct gap between scientific discourse
on fear and the experiential dimension of the subject. This also holds true for the
psychoanalytical commentary on Simon, which is granted scientific status in the
novel, and the way he himself experiences his fear games. In phenomenological
terms, fear brings Simon into contact with the sacred:

> But without the looming presence of the blind rat [= boredom], [...] he'd never have
> known the highs of the fear game, never have experienced a moment of such *radiant
> perfection* as last night, when Dorie looked up [...] and their eyes met through the
> mask. Darkness and light, cruelty and tenderness, fear and hope, *all in perfect equipoise*

76 HAROLD. "Empathy with Fictions." 346.
77 On this fine line between narcissism and empathy see BREITHAUPT. *Kulturen der Empathie.* 20.
78 Cf. HAROLD. "Empathy with Fictions." 344; FEAGIN, Susan. "Imagining Emotions and Appreciating Fiction." In: *Canadian Journal of Philosophy* 18 (1988): 485–500.
79 Cf. HAROLD. "Empathy with Fictions." 344.
80 I am indebted to Regina Schober for this information on Bach's Suites.

for once [...] – how in heaven had the world managed to keep turning, Simon wondered. (*FI* 77; emphasis added)

Her sense of shock and horror was almost palpable; it touched someplace deep inside Simon, someplace *deep and holy*. [...] The sensation was so intense, so exquisite, that it was almost painful, like being in love. [...] *Pure, intense*, virginal fear – [...] there's nothing to match it. (*FI* 82; emphasis added)

'Perfection', 'holy' and 'pure' all belong to the semantic field of the sacred. What is striking about this description is the emphasis on a moment of "perfect equipoise". A pattern begins to emerge. The striving for control correlates with the drive to reduce the complexity of world. After all, perfect equipoise means standstill in time and thus the elimination of change. 'Purity' also stands in contrast to the messiness of a complex world. The coupling of purity with the sacred also connects with Simon's experiencing intimacy with his victims. This intimacy results from his belief that fear strips the subject down to its raw being:[81] "It wasn't so much Corky's fear as it was the way the fear had transformed her, stripped her more naked than naked, until her soul was as bare as her sad, pale, skinny little body." (*FI* 194) The choice of the word "soul" continues the religious register and implies an essentialist view of identity, again eliminating complexity. For Simon, the heterogeneous individual is first reduced to 'the phobic', who is in a second step stripped down to the soul. Moreover, if fear lays bare the soul, then it is a source of authenticity – a motif familiar from Eliot's novel, albeit given dark overtones in *Fear Itself*.

It is not only Simon who associates fear with a stripping down of the subject. The same can be said of the authorial narrator, who, however, prefers a scientific framework. When Dorie sees Simon wearing a mask, "wordless terror well[s] up from [...] in the dark region of the brain stem where the lizard-self still ruled, and the human mind never ventured" (*FI* 109). The "lizard-self" is a reference to Paul MacLean's triune model of the brain, according to which different structures or layers were added to the brain in the evolutionary process. It is not only the evolutionary origins of fear that are highlighted.[82] The distinction between "lizard-self" and "human mind" appears in the authorial comment as one between the non-verbal instinctual and the thinking human mind. Put in more abstract terms, a nature/culture-divide is implied that firmly places fear within the realm of nature. If fear is a source of authenticity and partakes of nature, then

---

81 It is also possible to offer a psychoanalytical explanation, based on Simon's narcissism, for his feeling of intimacy. The fear of his victims allows him to tap into submerged elements of his self so that the intimacy he experiences is not with the Other, but with himself. Simon's sexual arousal in the wake of his fear games can be seen as resulting from his claim to phallic dominance during the fear game.
82 MacLean, Paul D. *The Triune Brain in Evolution: Role in Paleocerebral Functions.* New York: Plenum Press, 1990.

this may be read as an implicit equation of the two terms. Fear takes you outside of culture – that is the decisive point.

Fear is a threat to forms of subjectivity modelled on Cartesian notions of the self because it is Other to the thinking human mind. As the Cartesian self aspires to absolute mastery, its nightmare consists in powerlessness. It is this Cartesian nightmare that *Fear Itself* stages: loss of control as the ultimate source of fear is programmatic for the novel as a whole. The loss of control thereby not only relates to the phobic's fear. An explicit parallel is also drawn between the fears of the phobic and the fears of an FBI agent, Linda Abruzzi, suffering from Multiple Sclerosis:

> What if she had an attack while she was driving? Or in the office, or at lunch? Wouldn't it be better to stay home [...]. Then it struck her: this was what classic agoraphobia was like [...]. (*FI* 234)

The fact that a host of characters are afraid of losing control does not in itself signify Cartesian identity politics. The crucial factor is instead what drives the textual strategies of Nasaw's novel. *Fear Itself* is shaped by a logic geared towards establishing control, by domesticating and exorcising fear. First, by personifying fear in the shape of a serial killer, fear is objectified and can then be eliminated by killing the bad guy. Second, Simon's sadistic 'flooding' of his victims seems to function inadvertently, more often than not, as a means of effectively curing them of their phobia.[83] Third, Linda, whose physical deterioration progresses, dies a heroine and will be remembered in the "Hall of Honor" with "the Service Martyr plaque" (*FI* 325). The nightmare of being in the grip of an uncontrollable illness is thus effectively killed off and eclipsed by honour and glory. Last but not least, *Fear Itself* features an authorial narrator intent on controlling the reader's value judgements and flouting strategies of distancing fear. All of these elements 'quadruple-knot' the lesson that fear can be confronted, dealt with and ultimately expelled. Fear is fingered, but it is not allowed to render the world foreign and impenetrable.

---

83 See for example Wayne's and Linda's development: "It might have been the result of such an extreme application of Dr. Taylor's desensitization therapy. *Flooding*, the technical term for overwhelming a phobic with the object of his fear, was considered by some psychiatrists to be the most effective form of phobia therapy, but few patients or psychiatrists had the stomach for it [...]. Or perhaps it had something to do with the fact that he and the birds were all fellow captives, but whatever the reason, Wayne's ornithophobia had vanished [...]" (*FI* 24); "She [= Linda] *had* been afraid of snakes her whole life [...] – but she was afraid of them no longer. Must have worked through it when Childs was thrusting the coral into her face. [...] Flooding, they called it: the most extreme and successful form of counterphobic programming." For Dorie's cure cf. *FI* 128.

III. Conclusion

As *Daniel Deronda* and *Fear Itself* are rooted in dominant discourses of their time, both offer a very different cultural construction of severe fear. In Eliot's novel, the authorial narrator identifies Gwendolen's fits of dread as a "fountain of awe" and interprets her experience of fear as a manifestation of the sublime. A social critique is introduced by highlighting how a communion with the spiritual inevitably fails in modern market or risk society. Gwendolen's fear is endowed with a positive coding, not only because it is linked to the sublime, but also because her dread serves as a 'moral faculty' and a source of authenticity. This positive evaluation of Gwendolen's fits of fear follows the codes of the moral subject. In contrast, *Fear Itself* establishes extreme or "unreasonable fear" (*FI* 24) in scientific categories, i. e. as a psychic disorder that can be classified, analyzed in physiological terms and captured by statistics. Psychoanalysis is introduced as a framework to explain the origins of 'fear itself' or phobophobia. However, this psychologising is more a token gesture at explaining the phenomenon of the serial killer than it is about exploring the psychic roots of phobia. Accordingly, there is no speculation about the psychological causes for the phobia of Simon's victims. This in turn confirms Dorie's emphatic pronouncement that the origin of her phobia is "irrelevant" (*FI* 58), not lastly because the experts themselves offer radically different theories, e. g. trauma, genetics, brain chemistry, etc. (cf. *FI* 58).

These different conceptualizations of fear explain the diverging interplay of fear and empathy in each of the novels. In *Daniel Deronda*, severe fear is presented as an existentialist moment of freedom and thus as a *principuum individuationis* that eludes the empathetic access of the Other. As *Fear Itself* shies away from such an existentialist understanding of fear, this emotion may function as the basis for the killer's empathy with his victims because he perceives phobic fear as a similarity between self and Other.

Fear Itself is about confronting, controlling and ultimately exorcising fear. This stance is rooted in Cartesian identity politics. Accordingly, a positive coding of fear, as can be identified in Eliot's novel, is completely missing, unless one were prepared to accept the trivial observation that you "can't be fearless [i.e. courageous] until you've been afraid" (*FI* 18) as a counter-argument. The rationalistic worldview expounded in Nasaw's novel goes a far way in explaining why the only intertwinement of fear with the sacred occurs with regard to the serial killer. It is he who experiences his victim's fear as a holy moment. The internal view of his victims shows that for them pure terror is anguish devoid of a sacral dimension. The configuration 'fear and the sacred' thus represents not a potentially valuable fountain of spirituality, but is the signature of a psychopathological worldview.

Despite their very different evaluative codings of fear, *Daniel Deronda* and *Fear Itself* share two important similarities in their treatment of fear. The dominant textual strategies in both novels are geared towards containing excessive fear. This point has already been elaborated in great detail with regard to *Fear Itself*. In *Daniel Deronda*, the characterization of fear as a moral faculty and a source of emotional authenticity can equally be seen as a move to neutralize the disturbing implications of Gwendolen's fits of extreme fear. This conceptualization of fear is tailored to suit the codes of the moral subject. In keeping with the view of fear voiced by the moral subject, Gwendolen's dread is portrayed by the authorial narrator as an important factor in her moral development. The inexplicable, i. e. severe fear, is thus transformed into a moral vehicle on the level of telling. The second similarity concerns the presentation of fear as manifestation of our raw being. In *Daniel Deronda*, fear shatters Gwendolen's artificial role-playing, while in Nasaw's novel fear belongs to the lizard-brain, an older stage of evolution correlated with the realm of nature.

The analysis of the interplay between empathy and fear revealed that both texts are shot through with ideological fissures. A host of textual signals in the scenes portraying Gwendolen's actual fits of dread indicate that her dread is rooted in the return of the repressed. A psychoanalytic and feminist reading translates her fits of dread as an indictment of patriarchal gender stereotypes. As the moral subject is implicated in patriarchal gender politics, this indictment also targets the moral subject. Due to the lack of shared 'world', the male moral subject (Deronda) is unable to empathize successfully with women who rebel against patriarchal oppression (Gwendolen, Princess Halm-Eberstein). This psychoanalytical reading means that the interplay between fear and empathy may not be that different between Eliot's and Nasaw's novel after all. Shared similarity functions as a pre-condition for empathy in both texts. While both novels insist that empathy is a core moral value, their depiction of empathy draws attention to the fine line between empathy and narcissism. Perceived similarity may be nothing but the result of narcissistic projection. This blurring of empathy with narcissism also gives rise to ideological fissions in *Fear Itself*, which tries to maintain the tenuous link between empathy and altruism despite the killer's fear games.

All in all, the analysis of *Daniel Deronda* and *Fear Itself* has shown how literature contributes to the changing "cultural and rhetorical grounding of emotion discourse".[84] An important dimension of literature's contribution resides in its exploration of "the role emotions play in the course of unfolding encounters between people".[85] As outlined above, Eliot's and Nasaw's novel do

---

84 HERMAN. "Cognition, Emotion, and Consciousness." 255.
85 PARKINSON, Brian, Agneta H. FISCHER and Antony S.R. MANSTEAD. *Emotion in Social*

not just show fear and empathy "as intensely personal experiences".[86] Instead, both novels draw attention to how social relations are affected and (re)structured by these emotions.[87] In the light of these findings, literature can be seen as staging an understanding of emotion that has only recently become state-of-the art within contemporary scientific studies: "In Western psychological studies emotions are more and more being seen not just as states that occur in individual minds and bodies, but as processes that give structure and shape to relationships."[88] This comparison between literary and scientific discourses on emotion underscores the valuable contribution literature may make towards exploring the role of emotions in society.[89]

References

ANDERSON, Benedict. *Imagined Communities: Reflections on the Origin and Spread of Nationalism.* London: Verso, 1983.

Asterix. Vol. 9: *Asterix and the Normans.* Text written by René Goscinny, drawings by Albert Uderzo. English translations by Anthea Bell and Derek Hockridge. London: Hodder & Stoughton, 1978.

AVNI, Sheerly. "Ecstasy begets empathy: Psychiatrist and drug researcher Dr. Charles Grob sees value in MDMA – when it's taken in therapy, not at a rave." http://dir.salon.com/ mwt/feature/2002/09/12/grob_interview (accessed 17 July, 2011)

BLATTNER, William. *Heidegger's Being and Time. A Reader's Guide.* London/New York: Continuum, 2006.

BREITHAUPT, Fritz. *Kulturen der Empathie.* Frankfurt M.: Suhrkamp, 2009.

COPLAN, Amy. "Empathic Engagement with Narrative Fictions." In: *The Journal of Aesthetics and Art Criticism* 62,2 (2004): 141–52.

DURING, Lisabeth. "The Concept of Dread: Sympathy and Ethics in *Daniel Deronda.*" In: *Critical Review* 33 (1993): 88–111.

EAGLETON, Terry. *The English Novel. An Introduction.* Malden, MA: Blackwell, 2008 [2005].

ELIOT, George. *Daniel Deronda.* Edited with an introduction and notes by Terence Cave. London: Penguin, 2003 [1876].

FEAGIN, Susan. "Imagining Emotions and Appreciating Fiction." In: *Canadian Journal of Philosophy* 18 (1988): 485–500.

FICK, Monika. "Pfeiler der klassischen Ästhetik: Das Erhabene." In: Monika Fick and

---

Relations: Cultural, Group, and Interpersonal Processes. New York/Hove, East Sussex: Psychology Press, 2005. 2.

86 PARKINSON, FISCHER and MANSTEAD. *Emotion in Social Relations: Cultural, Group, and Interpersonal Processes.* 2.

87 See PARKINSON, FISCHER and MANSTEAD. *Emotion in Social Relations: Cultural, Group, and Interpersonal Processes.*

88 OATLEY, Keith. *Emotions. A Brief History.* Malden, MA et al.: Blackwell, 2005 [2004]. 155.

89 I am grateful to Regina Schober for her helpful comments on an earlier version of this paper.

Sybille Goessl (eds.). *Der Schein der Dinge. Einführung in die Ästhetik.* Tübingen: Attempto, 2002. 39 – 62.

GOLDIE, Peter. *The Emotions. A Philosophical Exploration.* Oxford: Clarendon Press, 2002 [2000].

GRAVER, Suzanne. *George Eliot and Community. A Study in Social Theory and Fictional Form.* Berkeley/Los Angeles/London: University of California Press, 1984.

HANICH, Julian. *Cinematic Emotion in Horror Films and Thrillers. The Aesthetic Paradox of Pleasurable Fear.* New York/London: Routledge, 2010.

HAROLD, James. "Empathy with Fictions." In: *British Journal of Aesthetics* 40,3 (2000): 340 – 55.

HERMAN, David. "Cognition, Emotion, and Consciousness." In: David Herman (ed.). *The Cambridge Companion to Narrative.* Cambridge: Cambridge University Press, 2007. 245 – 59.

HÖRISCH, Jochen. *Kopf oder Zahl. Die Poesie des Geldes.* Frankfurt M.: Suhrkamp, 1998 [1996].

HORATSCHEK, Anna-Margaretha. "'Logicized' Taboo: Abjection in George Eliot's *Daniel Deronda.*" In: Stefan Horlacher, Stefan Glomb and Lars Heiler (eds.). *Taboo and Transgression in British Literature from the Renaissance to the Present.* New York: Palgrave Macmillan, 2010. 193 – 210.

HORLACHER, Stefan. "Taboo, Transgression, and Literature: An Introduction." In: Stefan Horlacher, Stefan Glomb and Lars Heiler (eds.). *Taboo and Transgression in British Literature from the Renaissance to the Present.* New York: Palgrave Macmillan, 2010. 3 – 21.

JACKSON, Tony E. "George Eliot's 'New Evangel': *Daniel Deronda* and the Ends of Realism." In: *Genre* 25 (1992): 229 – 48.

JAFFE, Audrey. *Scenes of Sympathy: Identity and Representation in Victorian Fiction.* Ithaca/London: Cornell University Press, 2000.

JOHNSON-LAIRD, P.N. and Keith OATLEY. "Emotions, Music, and Literature." In: Michael Lewis, Jeannette M. Haviland-Jones and Lisa Barrett (eds.). *Handbook of Emotions.* 3rd edn. New York/London: Guilford Press, 2008. 102 – 13.

KEEN, Suzanne. *Empathy and the Novel.* Oxford: Oxford University Press, 2007.

LUCKNER, Andreas. *Martin Heidegger: 'Sein und Zeit'.* Paderborn et al.: Schöningh, 2001 [1997].

MacLEAN, Paul D. *The Triune Brain in Evolution: Role in Paleocerebral Functions.* New York: Plenum Press, 1990.

MARSCHALL, Amy Horning. "Reflections on the Pedagogy of Fear. 'Märchen von einem, der auszog, das Fürchten zu lernen'." In: *Fabula* 36 (1995): 289 – 95.

MARSCHALL, David. *The Figure of Theatre: Shaftesbury, Defoe, Adam Smith, and George Eliot.* New York: Columbia University Press, 1986.

McCAW, Neil. *George Eliot and Victorian Historiography. Imagining the National Past.* Houndmills: Macmillan, 2000.

McCOBB, E.A. "*Daniel Deronda* as Will and Representation: George Eliot and Schopenhauer." In: *The Modern Language Review* 80,3 (1985): 533 – 49.

NASAW, Jonathan. *Fear Itself.* New York et al.: Simon & Schuster, 2003.

NESTOR, Pauline. *George Eliot.* Houndmills/Basingstoke: Palgrave, 2002.

OATLEY, Keith. *Emotions. A Brief History.* Malden, MA et al.: Blackwell, 2005 [2004].

ÖHMAN, Arne. "Fear and Anxiety. Overlaps and Dissociations." In: Michael Lewis, Jeannette M. Haviland-Jones and Lisa Barrett (eds.). *Handbook of Emotions*. 3rd edn. New York/London: Guilford Press, 2008. 709–29.

PARIS, Bernard J. *Rereading George Eliot. Changing Responses to Her Experiments in Life.* Albany: State University of New York, 2003.

PARKINSON, Brian, Agneta H. FISCHER and Antony S.R. MANSTEAD. *Emotion in Social Relations: Cultural, Group, and Interpersonal Processes.* New York/Hove, East Sussex: Psychology Press, 2005.

RECKWITZ, Andreas. *Das hybride Subjekt. Eine Theorie der Subjektkulturen von der bürgerlichen Moderne zur Postmoderne.* Weilerswist: Velbrück, 2006.

RÖLLEKE, Heinz. "Märchen von einem, der auszog, das Fürchten zu lernen. Zu Überlieferung und Bedeutung des KHM4." In: *Fabula* 20 (1979): 193–204.

STONE, Wilfred. "The Play of Chance and Ego in *Daniel Deronda*." In: *Nineteenth-Century Literature* 53,1 (1998): 25–55.

SYPHER, Eileen. "Resisting Gwendolen's 'Subjection': *Daniel Deronda's* Proto-Feminism." In: *Studies in the Novel* 28,4 (1996): 506–24.

VRETTOS, Athena. "From Neurosis to Narrative: The Private Life of the Nerves in *Villette* and *Daniel Deronda*." In: *Victorian Studies* 33,4 (1990): 551–79.

WINKGENS, Meinard. "George Eliot und die Musik: Funktionsvarianten von Musik und Stimme in ihrem Romanwerk." In: Stefan Horlacher and Marion Islinger (eds.). *Expedition nach der Wahrheit. Poems, Essays and Papers in Honour of Theo Stemmler. Festschrift zum 60. Geburtstag von Theo Stemmler.* Heidelberg: Winter, 1996. 399–424.

– *Die kulturelle Symbolik von Rede und Schrift in den Romanen von George Eliot. Untersuchungen zu ihrer Entwicklung, Funktionalisierung und Bewertung.* Tübingen: Narr, 1997.

ZILLMANN, Dolf. "Mechanisms of Emotional Involvement with Drama." In: *Poetics* 23 (1994): 33–51.

Sara Strauß

Facets of Children's Fears in Twentieth- and Twenty-First-Century Stream-of-Consciousness Fiction

Anxiety and fear are emotional states which, by and large, every human being experiences. Research in evolutionary psychology has long identified certain fears and anxieties as originating from prehistoric times, since "[t]he evolutionary history of all species has included a world of threatening events".[1] With regard to these evolutionary biological insights, psychologists point out that "[f]ear and anxiety are normal responses in everyday life. To some extent, they are experienced by virtually all people. These emotions are an important part of being human."[2] Being important aspects of human life, fear and anxiety have also been taken into account in literature. On the one hand, narratives, in oral, written and audiovisual form, have always been used to tell stories in order to create situations of suspense. On the other hand, authors who concentrate on a mimetic portrayal of human life present anxieties as an integral part of human existence. They disclose how people are psychologically affected by fear and anxiety and explore the ways in which individuals cope with these emotions. As a kind of literature which concentrates on the inner life of its protagonists, stream-of-consciousness fiction seeks to permit an insight into the consciousness of human beings, their subjective perceptions of the outside world and their different emotions. Of course, the various sensations people experience in everyday life also include states of fear and anxiety, and these are consequently portrayed in stream-of-consciousness fiction, too. It is by giving an insight into the consciousness of the protagonists that different narrative techniques, like free indirect style and interior monologue, disclose the fictional characters' intimate thoughts, their worries, emotional distress, etc.

1 BLANCHARD, Robert J., D. Caroline BLANCHARD, Guy GRIEBEL and David NUTT. "Introduction to the Handbook on Fear and Anxiety." In: Robert J. Blanchard, D. Caroline Blanchard, Guy Griebel and David Nutt (eds.). *Handbook of Fear and Anxiety*. London/New York et al.: Academic Press, 2008. 3–7, 3.
2 MCNEIL, Daniel W., Cynthia L. TURK and Barry J. RIES. "Anxiety and Fear." In: V.S. Ramachandran (ed.). *Encyclopedia of Human Behavior: Vol. I*. London/New York et al.: Academic Press, 1994. 151–63, 153.

Both psychological research and literary fiction not only concentrate on the manifestations of fear in adults, but also focus on the psyche of children. With regard to the extreme case of anxiety disorders, Deborah C. Beidel points to a crucial problem involved in the diagnosis and comprehension of children's anxieties:

> Anxiety disorders can occur at any age and children as well as adults can suffer from any of the conditions. [...] The core features of anxiety disorders in children are similar to those seen in adults who suffer from the same disorder, but children often do not discuss their experience in the same fashion.[3]

While children's inability or reluctance to discuss their experience affects psychoanalytical diagnosis, it also constitutes a particular challenge to authors of literary texts to imagine the way in which children experience situations of fear and anxiety and to create a fictional representation of their inner life. In this regard, stream-of-consciousness fiction is exceptional in its pronounced interest in children's perception of the world as an addition and an alternative to the perspective of adults. For this reason, this article focuses on the literary representation of children's anxiety and fear in stream-of-consciousness fiction of the twentieth and twenty-first centuries. It examines the young protagonists' responses to frightening situations in the story "At the Bay" by Katherine Mansfield, in Elizabeth Bowen's short story "Coming Home" and in a passage taken from Ian McEwan's novel *Atonement*. The article does not specifically concentrate on the depiction of anxiety disorders but primarily on different facets of children's 'normal' fear as experienced in everyday life.

Although the terms 'fear' and 'anxiety' are used synonymously in everyday language, psychologists distinguish these emotional states. *"[F]ear* is often defined as a response to a clearly identifiable danger, whereas *anxiety* is conceptualized as a response to an unidentifiable threat or an anticipated danger."[4] Both emotional states are characterised by particular physiological as well as cognitive symptoms and can be accompanied by specific behaviours.

> Anxiety is an emotion characterized by heightened autonomic system activity, specifically activation of the sympathetic nervous system (i. e., increased heart rate, blood pressure, respiration, and muscle tone), subjective feelings of tension, and cognitions that involve apprehension and worry. Although the subjective experience of anxiety is not necessarily accompanied by particular behaviors, behavioral indicators are often

---

3 BEIDEL, Deborah C. "Anxiety Disorders." In: Alan E. Kazdin (ed.). *Encyclopedia of Psychology: Vol. I.* Oxford/Washington et al.: Oxford University Press and American Psychological Association, 2000. 212–16, 213.

4 KOWALSKI, Robin M. "Anxiety." In: Alan E. Kazdin (ed.). *Encyclopedia of Psychology: Vol I.* Oxford/Washington et al.: Oxford University Press and American Psychological Association, 2000. 209–12, 209.

present, such as speech dysfluencies, avoidance of the focal object or event, immobilization, or observable tremor.[5]

Fear is an emotional state similar to anxiety, involving comparable physiological symptoms. Whereas anxiety is characterised by "more cognitive symptoms and less visceral activation [...], [f]ear, however, involves greater mobilization for physical action. Typically, it is triggered by specific objects or situations."[6]

As the definition of anxiety already suggests, these emotional states are highly subjective experiences. While a particular situation or object works as a stimulus for anxiety for one individual, it may not affect another one. Just as these situations are experienced subjectively, the responses vary from one person to another. Moreover, the stimuli correlate with the individual's developmental stage. "What human beings fear and find anxiety-provoking changes across the lifespan."[7] During infancy and childhood several types of fears are very common because "virtually all children display a large number of fears (e. g., of injections, doctors, darkness, and strangers), most of which are transitory or short-lived".[8] The following analysis focuses on different facets of these fears of children. Since fear and anxiety are always experienced subjectively, the literary representation of these emotions will be examined in fiction which is particularly dedicated to the introspection into the minds of its young protagonists.

One of the earliest fears of children is their fear of separation from their parents, particularly from their mother.[9] It develops in early infancy when it "can emerge as early as 4 months and peaks between 13 and 18 months".[10] Later this emotional distress can once again peak during the first years at kindergarten and school because "[t]he beginning of school may be one such threatening experience [of separation], involving as it does a partial disruption of the child's previous closeness with the mother".[11] Separation anxiety is also related to children's gradual understanding of the concept of death and their fear of death, which usually emerges during subsequent phases of the child's cognitive development. Robert Kastenbaum emphasises that

---

5 KOWALSKI. "Anxiety." 209.
6 MCNEIL, TURK and RIES. "Anxiety and Fear." 151.
7 MCNEIL, TURK and RIES. "Anxiety and Fear." 156.
8 MCNEIL, TURK and RIES. "Anxiety and Fear." 156.
9 For a concise overview of children's fears at different developmental stages see figure 1.2 in SCHNEIDER, Silvia. "Entwicklungspsychopathologische Grundlagen." In: Silvia Schneider (ed.). *Angststörungen bei Kindern und Jugendlichen: Grundlagen und Behandlung.* Berlin/New York et al.: Springer Verlag, 2004. 3–16, 10.
10 MCNEIL, TURK and RIES. "Anxiety and Fear." 155.
11 JOHNSON, Ronald C. and Gene R. MEDINNUS. *Child Psychology: Behavior and Development.* London/New York et al.: John Wiley & Sons, [2]1969. 584.

[...] children do think of loss, separation, abandonment, and death a lot more than most adults realize. Trying to make sense out of death is a significant part of mental and emotional development from early childhood onward.[12]

The fears of separation and death, which thoroughly engage children during different phases of their mental and emotional development, are presented in fiction in various contexts. In Katherine Mansfield's story "At the Bay" the little girl Kezia is afraid of being separated from her grandmother, who fulfils the mother role in the family. When her grandmother tells her about an uncle of Kezia's who is dead, Kezia, who is about four years old, learns about death:

> 'Does everybody have to die?' asked Kezia.
> 'Everybody!'
> '*Me?*' Kezia sounded fearfully incredulous.
> 'Some day, my darling.'
> 'But, grandma.' Kezia waved her left leg and waggled the toes. They felt sandy. 'What if I just won't?' ("At the Bay" 226)

Kezia instantly transposes her newly acquired knowledge about death to her own existence and concludes that if everybody has to die, she has to die, too. This frightens her although she still remains incredulous. The little girl already has a limited idea of death but does not yet understand its complexity. Her childish misconception is obvious in her refusal to die. In her seminal studies of children's ideas of death Sylvia Anthony – with reference to Freud – describes a child's denial of death, like the one exemplified by Mansfield's fictional character Kezia, as one of children's "mechanisms of defense" against death anxiety:

> An unpleasant theme may be initially admitted to consciousness by its negation. The child who says, 'I shall never die' is by this very statement refusing to repress the knowledge that he himself is mortal, though he cannot yet consciously assent to it.[13]

Thus, according to this psychoanalytical explanation, Kezia's refusal to accept her own mortality is a common reaction of children at her developmental stage. The conversation about death engages Kezia in deep contemplation: "Kezia lay still thinking this over. She didn't want to die. It meant she would have to leave here, leave everywhere, for ever, leave – leave her grandma." ("At the Bay" 227) Kezia's ruminations prove that despite her young age she has a clear idea of death. Twentieth-century studies in children's cognitive development by psychologists like Sylvia Anthony and Jean Piaget give evidence that children's

---

12 KASTENBAUM, Robert. *On our Way: The Final Passage through Life and Death.* London/ Berkeley et al.: University of California Press, 2004. 26.
13 ANTHONY, Sylvia. "The Child's Idea of Death." In: Toby Talbot (ed.). *The World of the Child: Clinical and Cultural Studies from Birth to Adolescence.* New York: Jason Aronson, 1974. 315–28, 325.

understanding of concepts such as death develops in a sequence of several stages.[14] Late twentieth-century research adds that the question of when a child reaches a certain stage "is essentially a developmental issue, not a chronological one".[15] Thus, the ability to reach the next developmental stage is not restricted by the child's age but may vary according to the child's individual development, which is also essentially influenced by social factors. Katherine Mansfield portrays her fictional character Kezia in the middle of this developmental process of acquiring an accurate concept of death. Kezia understands that death is eternal and irreversible, but she only gradually becomes aware of the universality of death. She has never thought about the consequences of death and finally realises that death means a separation from her grandmother, who is a mother-substitute for the girl. Kezia hesitates to draw this conclusion. Her hesitation to finish this train of thought reveals that it causes great distress to the young girl. It is the prospect of a separation from her grandmother which threatens Kezia more than her previous hypothetical consideration of her own death:

> 'Grandma,' she said in a startled voice.
> 'What, my pet!'
> '*You're* not to die.' Kezia was very decided.
> 'Ah, Kezia' – her grandma looked up and smiled and shook her head – 'don't let's talk about it.'
> 'But you're not to. You couldn't leave me. You couldn't not be there.' This was awful.
> 'Promise me you won't ever do it, grandma,' pleaded Kezia.
> The old woman went on knitting.
> 'Promise me! Say never!'
> But still her grandma was silent.
> Kezia rolled off the bed; she couldn't bear it any longer [...]. ("At the Bay" 227)

Kezia experiences the thought of being separated from her grandmother as "awful" and cannot "bear it any longer". She refuses to accept the inevitability of death and begs her grandmother for comfort in order to alleviate her anxiety regarding a possible separation. Sylvia Anthony observes this as behaviour that is typical during children's development towards an accurate idea of death: "Separation of mother from child often seems to be the first concept and concern of the child in his thinking about death. He may then assure himself, half in

---

14 See ANTHONY, Sylvia. *The Child's Discovery of Death.* London: Routledge, 1940 and PIAGET, Jean. "Piaget's Theory." In: Paul H. Mussen (ed.). *Carmichael's Manual of Child Psychology: Vol. I.* New York/London et al.: John Wiley & Sons, ³1970. 703–32. For a concise overview of Piaget's theory of the cognitive development of the child as well as a critical response to his theory see SCHARLAU, Ingrid. *Jean Piaget zur Einführung.* Hamburg: Junius Verlag, 2007.
15 DAVIES, Betty. *Shadows in the Sun: The Experience of Sibling Bereavement in Childhood.* London/Philadelphia: Taylor & Francis, 1999. 32.

fantasy, that there will be no such separation."[16] Katherine Mansfield renders the worries of the young girl in a convincing way. Kezia not only admits her distress in a conversation with her closest intimate, but Mansfield also incorporates free indirect style in order to represent the child's train of thought and the feelings aroused by it. By combining the narrative modes of direct style, free indirect style and thought report the author, thus, succeeds in giving an insight into the perturbed state of mind of the child. It is noteworthy that Katherine Mansfield, who composed her story in 1921, imagines the psychological processes of her fictional character in accordance with the psychoanalysis of Sigmund Freud, which was seminal at that time and had great influence on modernist artists.

Another situation of children's separation anxiety is exemplified in Elizabeth Bowen's short story "Coming Home". It illustrates the way in which a school girl, who is some years older than Katherine Mansfield's protagonist Kezia, experiences the fear of separation from her mother. On her way home from school twelve-year-old Rosalind eagerly anticipates seeing her mother again after some hours of being apart. The dramatic effect the separation has on the girl's emotional life and behaviour becomes evident in Rosalind's excitement about the eventual reunion. Rosalind runs all the way home lamenting that "it was sometimes terrible to live so far away" ("Coming Home" 95). All the day, her attention is exclusively directed towards her mother, whom she constantly refers to by the pet name Darlingest. At school Rosalind concentrates neither on the teacher nor on the subject taught, but entirely focuses on the attention she receives from other pupils and will later receive from her mother. Thus, during the lesson "[s]he [is] beginning already to feel about for words for Darlingest" ("Coming Home" 95). When she finally approaches their house, Rosalind is at first relieved:

> The houses grew scarcer and the roads greener, and Rosalind relaxed a little; she was nearly home. She looked at the syringa bushes by the gate, and it was as if a cold wing had brushed against her. Supposing Darlingest were out...? ("Coming Home" 96)

At this moment Rosalind's anticipation and gradual relaxation immediately turn into severe anxiety. The sudden realisation of the mere possibility of her mother's absence threatens Rosalind to such a degree that she is unable to finish her thought. She is paralysed by this spontaneous intuition and "slow[s] down her running steps to a walk" ("Coming Home" 96). The closer Rosalind gets to the house, the more persuaded she is of her worst apprehension. When she discovers the house to be empty, the initial feeling of anxiety develops into extreme fear. Rosalind's fear is evident in her extreme physical arousal, which impairs her normal behaviour: the girl rushes through the rooms in search of

---

16 ANTHONY. "The Child's Idea of Death." 321.

her parent, she sobs and cries, and finally she falls to her knees next to her mother's bed.

In this situation Rosalind's senses are highly perceptive. All over the house she hears clocks ticking, which emphasises the absence of human sounds and thereby confirms the emptiness of the rooms. At the same time, the references to the ticking of the clocks convey Rosalind's feeling of time standing still, in which a few minutes appear to be eternal. Although Rosalind just entered the house and can hear the maid's movements in the kitchen, she feels like having been alone for hours. In addition to her acute sense of hearing, Rosalind is very sensitive to the scent of several flowers. She immediately notices the syringa bushes, anemones, daffodils and above all primroses in the house and garden. The smells of these flowers affect Rosalind in a very subjective way and arouse feelings of horror: "The whole house was full of the scent and horror of the primroses." ("Coming Home" 97) The reason for this intimidating effect on Rosalind is that these scents conjure up associations with death:

> The hall was chilly; she could not think why the primroses gave her such a feeling of horror, then she remembered the wreath of primroses, and the scent of it, lying on the raw new earth of that grave... ("Coming Home" 96)

The smell of the primroses arouses the girl's memory of attending a funeral. It is likely that Rosalind recalls the death of her father since the memory evokes great emotional distress. Moreover, she lives alone with her mother as an only child and her egoistic thoughts reveal that she enjoys as well as demands her mother's whole attention: "But Darlingest, so exclusively one's own..." ("Coming Home" 96) Research on trauma and loss provides evidence of a correlation between children's, adolescents' and adults' experience of the death of a close relative and separation anxiety.[17] Consequently, Rosalind's immediate association between the scents of the flowers and death suggests that it is the girl's previous experience of loss which increases her fear of separation from the remaining parent. As a result of her bereavement, Rosalind's sense of security is disturbed. She entirely focuses on her mother as the person who provides her with security and confidence and is afraid of losing her, too.

In this context, Rosalind blames her mother for being inconsiderate with respect to her daughter's emotions:

> Darlingest had spent the morning doing those deathly primroses, and then taken up her grey gloves and gone out, at the end of the afternoon, just when she knew her little girl

---

17 See RAPHAEL, Beverly and Matthew DOBSON. "Bereavement." In: John H. Harvey and Eric D. Miller (eds.). *Loss and Trauma: General and Close Relationship Perspectives.* Abingdon/New York: Taylor & Francis, 2000. 45–61, 47–51.

would be coming in. A quarter-past four. It was unforgivable of Darlingest [...].
("Coming Home" 96)

Free indirect style here represents how Rosalind mentally retraces every step her
mother might have taken before leaving the house. Rosalind's subjective assessment of her mother's behaviour as inexcusable reveals the girl's self-centred
worldview. She vividly imagines the adult paying attention to "those deathly
primroses" instead of thinking of her daughter. Rosalind's feelings are deeply
hurt and she condemns her mother's behaviour. Her attitude towards her parent
is typical of children suffering from separation anxiety disorder:

> Kinder mit einer Störung mit Trennungsangst zeigen häufig eine ausgeprägte Angst vor
> Krankheiten, dem Sterben und vor dem Tod. Von ihren Eltern werden sie oft als sehr
> fordernd und aufmerksamkeitsbedürftig beschrieben.[18]

In consequence of her subjective interpretation that the parent's absence results
from disinterest in her daughter, the young adolescent immediately loses any
self-confidence:

> Darlingest could never have really believed in her. She could never have really believed
> in that Rosalind would do anything wonderful at school, or she would have been more
> careful to be in to hear about it. ("Coming Home" 96–97)

Rosalind begins to doubt her mother's love. This growing uncertainty and lack of
security provided by the mother ends up in usual responses to fear and anxiety:
anger and aggression. Elizabeth Bowen here also alludes to the implications of
anxiety for a child's performance at school. "It is likely that anxiety impairs a
child's intellectual functioning – as though so much of his attention and effort is
diverted to coping with his problems that he cannot apply himself sufficiently to
other tasks. In this sense the child is certainly emotionally handicapped."[19]
During the lesson Rosalind's anticipation of the reunion with her mother discloses that her attention is diverted from her tasks at school. Furthermore, the
insight into Rosalind's consciousness hints at an underlying conflict between the
pupil and her mother due to Rosalind's performance at school. Rosalind experiences an exceptionally successful day at school, which seems to be in contrast to her usual achievements. This becomes obvious through Rosalind's intense satisfaction with her essay having been read out in class. Her defiant
attitude shows that this exceeds her mother's usual expectations regarding her
daughter's work at school.

The girl's anger soon gives way to a deep feeling of guilt. Hence, Rosalind

18 SCHNEIDER, Silvia and Tina IN-ALBON. "Störung mit Trennungsangst." In: Schneider, Silvia
   (ed.). Angststörungen bei Kindern und Jugendlichen: Grundlagen und Behandlung. Berlin/
   New York et al.: Springer Verlag, 2004. 105–32, 110.
19 JOHNSON and MEDINNUS. Child Psychology. 585.

reproaches herself: "How could she ever have left Darlingest? She might have known, she might have known." ("Coming Home" 97) She finally comes to the conviction that her mother will never return:

> Tea was spread on the table by the window, tea for two that the two might never... [...] All the afternoon she had sat there waiting and working, and now – poor little Darlingest, perhaps she had gone out because she was lonely. People who went out sometimes never came back again. Here she was, being angry with Darlingest, and all the time... ("Coming Home" 97)

Rosalind gradually convinces herself of her mother's death. This idea is so threatening to the adolescent that once again she is unable to finish her thought. She does not let her subconscious come to the surface of her consciousness but tries to suppress her worst fear. In this regard, Rosalind grows more and more desperate. Elizabeth Bowen renders the extreme despair which impinges on the protagonist's reasoning in an interior monologue:

> 'I can't bear it, I can't bear it. What have I done? I did love her, I did so awfully love her.' 'Perhaps she was all right when I came in; coming home smiling. Then I stopped loving her, I hated her and was angry. And it happened. She was crossing a road and something happened to her. I was angry and she died. I killed her.' ("Coming Home" 98)

Rosalind's sense of guilt increases so much that she even believes she killed her mother. This is an assumption about the causality of death and the power of their own thoughts typical of children. Such a misconception and a feeling of guilt usually affect children who do not yet understand "the generality and impersonality of death".[20]

During the minutes between her realisation of the parent's absence and her eventual return the girl works herself up into a state of extreme fear. Her reaction is so excessive that it suggests that Rosalind might suffer from a pathological condition of separation anxiety disorder. The adolescent's behaviour is inadequate for her age and meets the different criteria which contrast it from normal separation anxiety by definition of the American Psychiatric Association:

> The essential feature of Separation Anxiety Disorder is excessive anxiety concerning separation from the home or from those to whom the person is attached (Criterion A). This anxiety is beyond that which is expected for the individual's developmental level. The disturbance must last for a period of at least 4 weeks (Criterion B), begin before age 18 years (Criterion C), and cause clinically significant distress or impairment in social, academic (occupational), or other important areas of functioning (Criterion D).[21]

---

20 ANTHONY. "The Child's Idea of Death." 327.
21 AMERICAN PSYCHIATRIC ASSOCIATION. *Diagnostic and Statistical Manual of Mental Disorders: DSM-IV-TR.* Washington, DC: American Psychiatric Association, [4]2000, text revision. 121.

The likelihood that Rosalind's separation anxiety correlates with a previous experience of loss suggests that she may have already been suffering from this distress for a longer period. Moreover, it does not only impair her in the acute state of fear, but her anxiety also affects her everyday life; she is, for example, unable to concentrate at school but is constantly troubled by thoughts about home.

Rosalind's responses to a separation from her parent exemplify different facets of her fear. It develops from an anticipation of the threatening situation, over anxiety, loss of self-confidence, anger and aggression, horror and excessive fear to feelings of guilt and despair. Elizabeth Bowen succeeds in rendering these emotions very convincingly by means of different narrative modes of presenting consciousness. Whereas the narratorial report of the protagonist's behaviour and outward appearance already exposes her physical arousal as well as her anger and aggression, free indirect style and interior monologue give an insight into the character's emotional life. The more desperate the protagonist gets, the less narratorial mediation is employed. When Rosalind's anxiety reaches fever pitch as a result of her misconception that she might be responsible for the death of her mother, the author represents the girl's despair in an interior monologue. It is by a combination of these narrative techniques that Elizabeth Bowen succeeds in representing both different aspects which characterise children's fears and their heightened sensitivity to situations which provoke anxiety and fear.

In addition to separation anxiety, children's daily life regularly includes other occurrences which give rise to fear and anxiety. A classic example of specific situational anxiety of children is their fear of the dark. It usually affects infants at early developmental stages and grows in intensity from the age of two until five.[22] In Ian McEwan's novel *Atonement* the adolescent protagonist still experiences fear of the dark although she already reached a later phase in her individual development. In this case, the fear of the dark resurfaces in a particular situation which constitutes a decisive rite of passage in the protagonist's progress from childhood to maturity.

In *Atonement* the thirteen-year-old Briony is unsettled by the frightening darkness when walking through the park around her parents' mansion at night. She is in search of her two younger twin cousins, who ran away from their relatives' house in the evening. Whereas Briony's adult brother and sister, her cousin Lola and friends of the family departed in search parties to other areas of the large estate, Briony walks through the park on her own and "[u]nlike the adults, she ha[s] no torch" (*Atonement* 208). Although the scenery is familiar to her by daylight, Briony is afraid of it at night. She is not used to being outside in

---

22 See GRAY, Jeffrey Alan. *The Psychology of Fear and Stress*. Cambridge/New York et al.: Cambridge University Press, ²1987. 10–11.

the dark and presumably has never been alone in the garden at night. Therefore she hurries through passages of extremely intimidating darkness:

> She stumbled as she hurried through the darkness of the bamboo tunnel, and emerged onto the reassuring geometry of the paving stones. The underwater lights, installed [in the pond] that spring, were still a novelty. The upward bluish gleam gave everything around the pool a colorless, moonlit look, like a photograph. (*Atonement* 203)

At night the garden has an atmosphere which is unknown to Briony. The newly installed underwater lights of the pond do not comfort the young girl but rather illuminate the familiar landscape by a strange, artificial light. Thereby the scenery appears bizarre and unreal to her. Things look different in the dim light and therefore frighten her. At the same time, Briony is aware of the dangers darkness implies, for example the difficulties "of keeping to the path or ducking the branches that [hang] low over it" (*Atonement* 204). These and other potential dangers at night explain children's fear of the dark to originate from evolutionary biology.[23] Throughout evolution human beings as well as diurnal animals adapted to a dangerous environment, such as darkness. That is to say, fear of the dark worked as a natural mechanism for survival. A classic danger of the dark, then and now, is the advantage darkness offers to possible assailants. This also constitutes Briony's major worry in *Atonement*. The shadows do not only distort her perspective on the familiar garden; Briony is also aware that they enable persons who do not want to be seen to hide:

> The dark shapes of the widely spaced trees across the park made her hesitate. [...] The nearer trees, or at least their trunks, had a human form. Or could conceal one. Even a man standing in front of a tree trunk would not be visible to her. (*Atonement* 207)

The distorted appearance of the trees is presented by free indirect style closely to the way in which Briony perceives her environment. Her perception of the trees is impaired by the darkness as well as by the girl's powers of imagination. Hence, she discerns a human form in the trunks. This delusion is essentially caused by Briony's subconscious fear of being ambushed by a man behind a tree. As a result of the girl's misunderstanding of adult affairs earlier that evening, Briony is under the misconception that her family's close friend Robbie, who also searches for the twins somewhere in the park, is a maniac. This misapprehension motivates and increases her anxious anticipation of an encounter with someone in the dark. Therefore, she instantly concludes that the plants might conceal a person. It is this situation which Briony is most afraid of. Stylistically, her reasoning is presented by an incomplete sentence in order to represent the sudden

---

23 See PAUL, Andreas. "Wer hat Angst vorm bösen Wolf? – Evolutionsbiologische Grundlagen kindlicher Ängste." In: Schneider. *Angststörungen bei Kindern und Jugendlichen.* 41–53, 46–47.

realisation when she becomes aware of this potential danger. The incomplete syntax of free indirect style conveys the logic and spontaneity of Briony's conclusions as well as the anxiety they impose upon her.

In addition to visual delusions resulting from the darkness, the nocturnal sounds are also strange to the inexperienced girl:

> [S]he forced herself to walk on and cross the bridge. From beneath her, amplified by the stone arch, came the hiss of the breeze disturbing the sedge, and a sudden beating of wings against water which subsided abruptly. These were everyday sounds magnified by darkness. And darkness was nothing – it was not a substance, it was not a presence, it was no more than an absence of light. (*Atonement* 208)

Here, free indirect style reveals that Briony constantly tries to reassure herself. She does not allow the fear to overpower her. Instead, she is aware of the distorting quality of darkness and by logical reasoning reminds herself to calm down. This is one strategy by which Briony suppresses her fear.

Nevertheless, Briony's behaviour inevitably shows that she is afraid. Although she reassures herself, her physical reactions to the frightening atmosphere are telling: she stumbles, she hurries, she hesitates and she forces herself to walk on (see quotes above). This behaviour reveals her insecurity as well as typical strategies of avoidance versus the wish to overcome the fear. At the same time, Briony does not admit her fear to herself: "It was the steepness of the bank, of course, which held her back" (*Atonement* 209). Here, free indirect style conveys narrative irony as it discloses the way in which Briony searches for excuses for her misgivings. She does not admit her cowardice to herself but convinces herself that "of course" there are objective reasons for it. The reader however understands these reasons to be of completely subjective origin.

Although Briony persistently seeks to assess the situation in an objective way, her senses are deluded by the unknown situation and, above all, by her subconscious. While she earlier almost mistook the trees for a person, she later believes the shape of a man to be a plant. Besides, she mistakes human noise for the natural sounds of the garden at night:

> [N]earer, in the center of the grassy stretch, there was a shrub she did not remember. Or rather, she remembered it being closer to the shore. The trees were not right either, what she could see of them. The oak was too bulbous, the elm too straggly, and in their strangeness they seemed in league. As she put her hand out to touch the parapet of the bridge, a duck startled her with a high, unpleasant call, almost human in its breathy downward note. (*Atonement* 209)

Briony is unable to trust her senses anymore. However, she does not realise this but explains the delusion to herself by the inaccuracy of her own memory. She has reassured herself to such a high degree of the natural origin of all strange sounds and misperceptions that now she does not realise their human origin anymore. This is a common process of repression. It is only when the bush moves and she finds her cousin Lola, who has been attacked by an assailant, that Briony becomes aware of the fact that what she considered to be a bush is a man. In addition, she has to realise that instead of a duck she heard a cry by Lola.

In these passages of *Atonement* Ian McEwan exemplifies people's usual responses to threatening situations. Yet Briony resorts to different strategies in order to cope with her fear: on the one hand, she wants to prove her courage and face her fears, on the other hand, she shows typical symptoms of avoidance. Briony considers her experiences of this day as initiation into adult life. The evening spent alone outside means another proof of her coming of age to her. Hence, initially "she [is] trying not to be afraid" (*Atonement* 201) and enjoys being outside at night: "They [the twins] were safe, [...] and she, Briony, was free to wander in the dark and contemplate her extraordinary day. Her childhood had ended, she decided" (*Atonement* 204). Yet, the adolescent only acts courageously as long as she is able to explain any strange occurrences to herself. As soon as she perceives unusual phenomena, she lapses into strategies of avoidance:

> As she passed it [the fountain] she thought she heard a faint shout, and thought she saw from the corner of her eye a point of light flash on and off. She stopped, and strained to hear over the sound of the trickling water. [...] She walked in that direction for half a minute, and stopped to listen again. But there was nothing, nothing but the tumbling dark mass of the woods just discernable against the grayish-blue of the western sky. After waiting a while she decided to turn back. In order to pick up her path she was walking directly to the house, toward the terrace where a paraffin globe lamp shone among glasses, bottles, and an ice bucket. (*Atonement* 205)

Instead of trying to find out about the happenings in the distance Briony repeatedly stops and finally decides to turn back. This proves Briony's search for her cousins to be mere pretence. Actually, she is afraid of either encountering someone in the dark or finding the twins, whom she earlier already imagined "floating [on the water of the pond] facedown in death, indistinguishable to the last" (*Atonement* 199). However, Briony does not admit this pretence to herself but finds an excuse why she heads towards the illuminated house.

When Briony is finally unable to deny her timidity any longer, she convinces herself of the social and moral acceptability of her conduct: "Nothing was expected of her, she was a child after all in their [the adults'] eyes. The twins were not in danger." (*Atonement* 208) After this psychological reassurance Briony considers different options:

> She remained on the gravel for a minute or two, not quite frightened enough to turn back, nor confident enough to go on. She could return to her mother and keep her company in the drawing room while she waited. She could take a safer route, along the driveway and back, before it entered the woods – and still give the impression of a serious search. (*Atonement* 208)

Here, free indirect style reveals the persistence of Briony's inner conflict. Although she now admits her timidity and her feigned search to herself, she shies away from confessing it to other people. Instead, she ponders a compromise: she considers to take a route which does not frighten her but offers the possibility to adhere to the pretence of seriously searching for the twins. All in all, Briony's intimate thoughts convey the inner conflict people experience with regard to fear and anxiety. Briony's personal approaches to coping with her fear include psychological processes of reassuring herself as well as attempts at confrontation with the frightening situation.

Beside the fear of the dark the short passage of *Atonement* relates to anxiety with regard to death. Like Kezia in Katherine Mansfield's story "At the Bay" and Elizabeth Bowen's character Rosalind, Ian McEwan's protagonist Briony also considers questions of death when confronted with situations she fears. She unconsciously connects her anxious mood and the surrounding darkness with the subconsciously ever-present anxiety of death. First of all, Briony is afraid of finding her two younger cousins dead. What is more, when she observes her mother through a window, the girl imagines the bereavement of her mother:

> Briony indulged herself by looking through the window in a spirit of farewell. Her mother was forty-six, dispiritingly old. One day she would die. There would be a funeral in the village at which Briony's dignified reticence would hint at the vastness of her sorrow. (*Atonement* 206)

As Robert Kastenbaum observes: "The dark is a natural proxy for death. Lying motionless is another."[24] It is therefore not surprising that in these surroundings of intimidating darkness Briony's consciousness engages with questions of death when she sees her mother lying motionless on the settee. However, it is less an anxiety of separation from the mother which perturbs Briony; at the beginning of adolescence she has achieved a developmental stage at which she has overcome the childish dependence on her parents. Moreover, Briony's way of imagining the funeral gives proof of her narcissistic attitude. She imagines herself the centre of attention during the funeral. Although in her phase of increasing maturity Briony should have realised her own mortality, she does not relate her mother's mortality and the transience of her own life. Instead, Briony imagines her mother's death in an emotionally detached and very theatrical way.

All in all, Ian McEwan's use of free indirect style and internal focalisation through the young protagonist Briony illustrates various aspects of human anxieties and fears. It conveys Briony's subjective responses to intimidating darkness, such as her uncertainty and nervousness as regards the distorted appearance of the environment at night. Furthermore, the fictional character's

---

24 KASTENBAUM, Robert. *On our Way.* 39.

attitude reveals two extremes of coping with fear: avoidance and confrontation. As regards narrative mediation, free indirect style fulfils the function of giving an insight into Briony's consciousness as well as into her unconscious. It discloses the discrepancy between the character's unconscious and her deliberately admitted thoughts. In this way free indirect style enables the author to employ narrative irony. As a result, the reader is able to recognise the girl's strategies of self-deception with regard to her fears.

On the whole, the fictional narratives by Katherine Mansfield, Elizabeth Bowen and Ian McEwan provide compelling insights into children's experiences of fear and anxiety. They portray classic fears between infancy and maturity, like the fear of separation, fear of the dark and anxiety relating to the inevitability of death. It is remarkable that the literary texts disclose a whole spectrum of the various aspects which are characteristic of these emotional states, such as the physical and psychological symptoms people suffer from, specific strategies of coping as well as alluding to the origins of some fears in evolutionary biology or in the individual's personal history. Thereby the texts give an impression of the multidimensional facets of fears. Besides, it is noteworthy that the different authors' portrayal of children's fears is, of course, influenced by psychological paradigms of their respective times. Whereas effects of the studies in psychoanalysis by Sigmund Freud, which were seminal during the modernist period, are evident in Katherine Mansfield's representation of the child's mind, contemporary author Ian McEwan depicts his protagonist's emotional life in keeping with today's conceptions of psychology. From a narratological point of view, the analysis of Mansfield's and Bowen's stories as well as McEwan's novel exemplifies that the use of narrative techniques of introspection, like free indirect style and interior monologue, enables authors to render a vivid representation of children's mental life in fiction. Of course, one should keep in mind that these are fictional accounts. They can, however, enable adult readers to engage imaginatively with the psyche of children and understand the implications of fears and anxieties for children's daily life.

References

AMERICAN PSYCHIATRIC ASSOCIATION. *Diagnostic and Statistical Manual of Mental Disorders: DSM-IV-TR.* Washington, DC: American Psychiatric Association, [4]2000, text revision.

ANTHONY, Sylvia. "The Child's Idea of Death." In: Toby Talbot (ed.). *The World of the Child: Clinical and Cultural Studies from Birth to Adolescence.* New York: Jason Aronson, 1974. 315–28.

– *The Child's Discovery of Death.* London: Routledge, 1940.

BEIDEL, Deborah C. "Anxiety Disorders." In: Alan E. Kazdin (ed.). *Encyclopedia of Psychology: Vol. I.* Oxford/Washington et al.: Oxford University Press and American Psychological Association, 2000. 212–16.

BLANCHARD, Robert J., D. Caroline BLANCHARD, Guy GRIEBEL and David NUTT. "Introduction to the Handbook on Fear and Anxiety." In: Robert J. Blanchard, D. Caroline Blanchard, Guy Griebel and David Nutt (eds.). *Handbook of Fear and Anxiety.* London/New York et al.: Academic Press, 2008. 3–7.

BOWEN, Elizabeth. "Coming Home." In: *The Collected Stories of Elizabeth Bowen.* With an Introduction by Angus Wilson. London: Jonathan Cape, 1980. 95–100.

DAVIES, Betty. *Shadows in the Sun: The Experience of Sibling Bereavement in Childhood.* London/Philadelphia: Taylor & Francis, 1999.

GRAY, Jeffrey Alan. *The Psychology of Fear and Stress.* Cambridge/New York et al.: Cambridge University Press, [2]1987.

JOHNSON, Ronald C. and Gene R. MEDINNUS. *Child Psychology: Behavior and Development.* London/New York et al.: John Wiley & Sons, [2]1969.

KASTENBAUM, Robert. *On our Way: The Final Passage Through Life and Death.* London/Berkeley et al.: University of California Press, 2004.

KOWALSKI, Robin M. "Anxiety." In: Alan E. Kazdin (ed.). *Encyclopedia of Psychology: Vol I.* Oxford/Washington et al.: Oxford University Press and American Psychological Association, 2000. 209–12.

MANSFIELD, Katherine. "At the Bay." In: *The Collected Stories of Katherine Mansfield.* With an Introduction by Ali Smith. London/New York et al.: Penguin, 2007. 205–45.

MCEWAN, Ian. *Atonement.* New York: Anchor Books, 2003.

MCNEIL, Daniel W., Cynthia L. TURK and Barry J. RIES. "Anxiety and Fear." In: V.S. Ramachandran (ed.). *Encyclopedia of Human Behavior: Vol. I.* London/New York et al.: Academic Press, 1994. 151–63.

PAUL, Andreas. "Wer hat Angst vorm bösen Wolf? – Evolutionsbiologische Grundlagen kindlicher Ängste." In: Silvia Schneider (ed.). *Angststörungen bei Kindern und Jugendlichen: Grundlagen und Behandlung.* Berlin/New York et al.: Springer Verlag, 2004. 41–53.

PIAGET, Jean. "Piaget's Theory." In: Paul H. Mussen (ed.). *Carmichael's Manual of Child Psychology: Vol. I.* New York/London et al.: John Wiley & Sons, [3]1970. 703–32.

RAPHAEL, Beverly and Matthew DOBSON. "Bereavement." In: John H. Harvey and Eric D. Miller (eds.). *Loss and Trauma: General and Close Relationship Perspectives.* Abingdon/New York: Taylor & Francis, 2000. 45–61.

SCHARLAU, Ingrid. *Jean Piaget zur Einführung.* Hamburg: Junius Verlag, 2007.

SCHNEIDER, Silvia (ed.). *Angststörungen bei Kindern und Jugendlichen: Grundlagen und Behandlung.* Berlin/New York et al.: Springer Verlag, 2004.

– "Entwicklungspsychopathologische Grundlagen." In: Silvia Schneider (ed.). *Angststörungen bei Kindern und Jugendlichen: Grundlagen und Behandlung.* Berlin/New York et al.: Springer Verlag, 2004. 3–16.

SCHNEIDER, Silvia and Tina IN-ALBON. "Störung mit Trennungsangst." In: Silvia Schneider (ed.). *Angststörungen bei Kindern und Jugendlichen: Grundlagen und Behandlung.* Berlin/New York et al.: Springer Verlag, 2004. 105–32.

Marcel Inhoff

Fearing, Loathing: Robert Lowell, Hunter S. Thompson and the Rise of Richard Nixon

It is hard to imagine two writers more dissimilar than Hunter S. Thompson and Robert Lowell. On the one hand, we have Robert Traill Spence Lowell IV, with his emphasis on form and tradition, the great establishment poet from Boston, educated at Harvard and at Kenyon College, a man about whose family John Collins Brossidy concocted the familiar Boston verses:

> And this is good old Boston,
> The home of the bean and the cod,
> Where the Lowells talk to the Cabots,
> And the Cabots talk only to God.[1]

On the other hand, we have Dr. Hunter S. Thompson, with his doctorate in divinity from a fringe Christian institution, the perennial outlaw journalist, who rode with the Hell's Angels, talked about football with President Nixon, and, when he died, had his ashes fired from a cannon atop a tower by American actor Johnny Depp. But in the late 1960s and early 1970s, their career paths crossed briefly. Within four years of each other, each had produced a highly original literary work about an election year.[2] Responding to the same stimuli, these two vastly different writers wrote books that have similar foci: personal and political fears in an age dominated by Richard Milhous Nixon. One worked from within poetic traditions, the other from within the conventions of journalism. In 1969, Lowell published *Notebook 1967–68*, a long poem consisting of over three hundred free blank verse sonnets. In 1973, Thompson published *Fear and Loathing on the Campaign Trail '72*, an account of Nixon's re-election bid. Lowell and Thompson gave voice to the fear that catastrophic political developments

---

1 He declaimed the verses in a 1910 toast at a Holy Cross College Alumni Dinner (ALVAREZ, A. "Robert Lowell in Conversation." In: Jeffrey Meyers (ed.). *Robert Lowell, Interviews and Memoirs*. Ann Arbor: University of Michigan Press, 1988. 78, n 1).

2 Lowell's book, which covers 1967 and 1968 chronologically, is about more than the election year 1968. Lowell's concerns also extend beyond the campaigns, the primaries, and the presidential election, and are therefore broader than Thompson's.

had aroused in them, and each wrote a book so as to make sense of it all. The two books resemble each other in their poetics and in the motivation that drives each; both represent ways of dealing with fear and anxiety. Lowell and Thompson produced works that markedly differed from the sort of writing they were known for, and both wrote during a period significantly shaped by Nixon, extending back long before he became President of the United States. Finally, both intensely disliked Nixon. As early as 1954, Lowell called one of Nixon's speeches "the most servile mush you ever heard" (Letters 225), and Thompson's hatred of Nixon was legendary.

Lowell's and Thompson's contempt for Nixon might strike one as nothing unusual. Given the abundance of mid-1960s satire directed at Nixon, one might assume that everybody hated him. Ridicule[3] was mixed with a strong dose of passionate loathing of the man who had been, as Hunter S. Thompson remarked in an interview, "the national boogeyman [for] 15 or 20 years", "always evil, always ugly".[4] Fear and hate seem grafted onto many resumés of his career. Today, we may associate Nixon primarily with the six years of his presidency and the Watergate scandal that ended it, but for those on the left he remained above all the arch-representative of almost three decades of red-baiting politics. Despite this hostility, the historical fact is that Nixon was actually a remarkably effective and popular politician who ran for office successfully seven out of nine times. The reason for his success at the polls is as simple as it was scary for people like Thompson: in his speeches throughout his career, as Farber records, "Nixon created a land of endless local pride [...]. That land was called Middle America and it was populated with people called the 'silent majority'",[5] i.e. people who were seized by a fear of disorder and a fear of Communist infiltration. These fears were fanned by Nixon, who would call protesters "violent thugs" whenever he was down in the polls.[6] This silent majority was not a rhetorical invention of Nixon's, it really existed, and it was highly instrumental in his electoral triumphs and in sustaining his popularity.

Nixon's political career began in 1946 with his work on the infamous House Un-American Activities Committee, which helped him quickly gain national prominence. He was divisive from the start, and purposefully so, since it worked in his favor. He was easily re-elected to the House of Representatives, and he won

---

3 It wasn't all that easy to ridicule Nixon, since "Richard Nixon defied lampooning by his very blandness" (WHITFIELD, Stephen J. "Richard Nixon as a Comic Figure." In: American Quarterly 37,1 (1985): 114 – 32, 119).

4 VETTER, Craig. "Playboy Interview: Hunter Thompson." In: Anita Thompson (ed.). Ancient Gonzo Wisdom: Interviews with Hunter S. Thompson. Cambridge: Da Capo, 2009. 31 – 56, 50.

5 FARBER, David. Chicago '68. Chicago: University of Chicago Press, 1988. 256.

6 LUKAS, J. Anthony. Nightmare: The Underside of the Nixon Years. New York: Viking Press, 1976. 4.

a seat in the US Senate just as easily. It was his senatorial campaign that earned him the nickname 'Tricky Dick'. In 1952, he became Vice President under Eisenhower and one of the youngest men ever to hold that office. Four years later, he was re-elected on the Eisenhower/Nixon ticket,[7] and in 1960 he ran for President himself, losing narrowly to John F. Kennedy. This defeat became a turning point in how many regarded Nixon, thanks to Theodore H. White's pro-Kennedy campaign coverage in *The Making of the President, 1960* (1961). "Nixon had lost that election by a whisper. In the book by which most people would remember it, his loss felt inevitable."[8] After another close defeat in a contest for the governorship of California, things quieted down for a while. It was not until five long years later that Nixon ran for President again, this time winning both the nomination and the general election in 1968 by comfortable margins, and four years later he was re-elected in a landslide victory against George McGovern. His eventual fall from grace capped a period of upheaval that radically changed America. Rick Perlstein argues persuasively that during the decades of Nixon's political career the American political climate took a decided turn for the worse, spawning race riots, a culture of paranoia, and a rancorous political division between the left and the right that dominates American politics to this day. Perlstein notes that "the complex set of forces unleashed by [the] Watts [riots] and the final rise [...] of Richard Milhous Nixon [came] to be seen as synonymous".[9] For whole generations of poets and other writers, becoming politically active meant taking a stand against Nixon and everything he epitomized. As Hunter S. Thompson observed in a letter written in 1971: "those, who instinctively identified with the mad angst of *Howl* [...] also understood [...] the importance of beating Nixon" (*Fear and Loathing in America* 421).

In Thompson's prose work, this "mad angst" manifests itself in a mixture of private fears and observations about the political system. *Fear and Loathing on the Campaign Trail '72* contains frequent personal, sometimes embarrassingly private comments, such as Thompson's indignant remark that his "body is turning to wax and bad flap" and that "impotence looms" (*Campaign Trail* 219). He voices political outrage again and again, as in his reference to elections as "these big bogus showdowns" (*Campaign Trail* 56) or when he gives advice to

---

7 This may not seem like much, but although Eisenhower had always enjoyed great personal popularity, Nixon was a great help in getting Ike elected in 1952. Painfully aware of this, in the next election Eisenhower played mind games, debasing and practically insulting Nixon in public, "trying to create the myth that he didn't owe Nixon anything for having got to be president." (BLACK, Conrad. *Richard M. Nixon: A Life in Full.* New York: PublicAffairs, 2007. 326).

8 PERLSTEIN, Rick. *Nixonland: The Rise of a President and the Fracturing of America.* New York: Scribner, 2008. 59.

9 PERLSTEIN. *Nixonland.* 19.

George McGovern in "a casual conversation between two people standing at adjoining urinals" (*Campaign Trail* 366). Both his public and his private observations are driven by an anxiety that Thompson describes as feeling "The Fear coming on" (*Campaign Trail* 57). By contrast, in the "Afterthought" to *Notebook 1967–68* Lowell dismisses any notion that his book is "a chronicle or almanac", and maintains: "[t]his is not my diary, my confession, not a puritan's too literal pornographic honesty, glad to share private embarrassment, and triumph." (*Notebook 1967–68* 159) The most interesting phrase in his denial is the qualifying expression "too literal". As we will see, Lowell makes more use of connections and allusions than of blunt statements in order to convey to his readers the extent of his anxieties. After revising and expanding his poetic sequence and publishing it simply as *Notebook* (1970), he altered the earlier disclaimer and declared, less coyly: "[i]t is less an almanac than the story of my life." (*Notebook* 262)

In Lowell's *For the Union Dead* (1964), *Near the Ocean* (1967) and *Notebook 1967–68* (1969), the interconnection of private and political fears culminates in sonnets such as the two titled "The March", where personal fears and a climate of political anxiety sometimes co-exist within the same densely woven line. This will not strike careful readers of Lowell's oeuvre as a surprise. Like Thompson, Lowell had always been interested in the interconnections of personal and public anxiety. One earlier instance is the poem "Inauguration Day: January 1953", from *Life Studies* (1959), which depicts an old, derelict New York creaking under the weight of a snow storm laying siege to the city. Like Lowell's poems in *Notebook 1967–68* a variation on sonnet form,[10] it closes with what almost amounts to a sestet:

> Ice, ice. Our wheels no longer move.
> Look, the fixed stars, all just alike
> as lack-land atoms, split apart,
> and the Republic summons Ike,
> the mausoleum in her heart. (*Collected Poems* 117)

Lowell invests this description of the city with enough anxiety[11] to make it difficult to go along with the traditional readings of the decade as 'tranquil' and

---

10 SMITH, Ernest J. "'Approaching Our Maturity': The Dialectic of Engagement and Withdrawal in the Political Poetry of Berryman and Lowell." In: Suzanne Ferguson (ed.). *Jarrell, Bishop, Lowell, & Co.: Middle-Generation Poets in Context*. Knoxville: University of Tennessee Press, 2003. 287–302, 292–93.

11 For a thorough discussion of the political anxieties and implications in this small, but prominently placed poem in Lowell's most famous collection of poetry, see BEARDSWORTH, Adam. "Learning to Love the Bomb: Robert Lowell's Pathological Poetics." In: *Canadian Review of American Studies/Revue canadienne d'études américaines* 40,1 (2010): 95–116, 101–04.

uneventful. "Inauguration Day: January 1953" might seem to address only public fear, but in other poems written in the 1950s Lowell overtly interfuses public themes and personal observations, some of which reveal surprising similarities between Lowell and Thompson. Thompson's comments on the ills of society are famously peppered with descriptions of substance abuse, and he has become well known as a drug fiend whose symbol was a fist clutching a peyote button. Lowell's legal vice is prescription drugs. In "Memories of West Street and Lepke", also from *Life Studies*, he declares:

> These are the tranquilized Fifties,
> and I am forty. [...] (*Collected Poems* 187)

Lowell invokes the notion 'tranquil fifties', a common but misleading epithet for the decade when Cold War fears arose and Allen Ginsberg was writing not only about them but also about anal sex and drug use, even as the House Un-American Activities Committee went about its manic witch-hunting. By altering the tranquil fifties to the "tranquilized Fifties", Lowell associates the decade with the new, widespread use of sedatives, i.e., tranquilizers. Lowell used them himself and in "Man and Wife", another *Life Studies* poem, he remembers lying on a bed, "[t]amed by Miltown" (*Collected Poems* 189), 'Miltown' being a brand name for meprobamate, an anxiolytic drug and minor tranquilizer. A combination of public anxieties and personal observations had marked Lowell's poetry all along. Not until the late 1960s, however, did his poetry become fully engaged with the tumultuous political events unfolding. Both private fears and political anxieties moved to the center of his writing, culminating in the various incarnations of the *Notebook* poems.

The turbulent 1960s shook American society to its roots. Protests and controversies surrounding the civil rights movement were front and center in the news and in the public mind. And while the silent majority and politicians like Nixon and Barry Goldwater caused Thompson and those like him to be fearful, something very similar happened at the other end of the political spectrum. Race riots proved to be especially divisive. As Warren E. Miller and Teresa E. Levitin record:

> [w]hites who had been indifferent to or even sympathetic with the nonviolent civil rights movement [...] were opposed to, and frightened by, this new black militancy. Backlash was no longer limited to [...] southern whites.[12]

Patterson, in his mammoth study of US history between 1945 and 1974, points to the result of this backlash: "a major development of the mid-1960s: rapidly

---

12 MILLER, Warren E. and Teresa E. LEVITIN. *Leadership and Change: Presidential Elections from 1952 to 1976*. Cambridge, MA: Winthrop, 1976. 57.

rising polarization along class, generational and racial lines,"[13] and he notes that "the rising numbers of people who became part of the backlash [...] used the word 'squeeze' to capture their plight".[14] He concludes with an evaluation of "these angry people" as "a political force to be reckoned with".[15] The most immediate consequence of their anger was a new rise in the fortunes of Richard Nixon in 1967. Unlike Thompson, who vociferously allied himself with a particular political camp, Lowell's stance was more complicated. But in the late 1960s, his political preference seemed clearer than usual.

On October 21, 1967, he took part in the march on the Pentagon along with other prominent writers, "seasoned veterans of the defiant gesture",[16] as Paul Mariani called Norman Mailer, Paul Goodman, Dr. Benjamin Spock and the others. The Pentagon March capped a year of upheavals and a decade of fear and violence. In 1967 alone, major riots occurred in Newark, Detroit, Plainfield and Buffalo. Robert Lowell, the preeminent American poet of the time, had publicly rejected an invitation to the White House on account of what was happening in Vietnam. Nor was he aloof to what was happening in America itself. Lowell, who had recently been featured on the cover of *Time*, was now viewed as "chic",[17] and he became increasingly involved in the public sphere and in politics.[18] As Flanzbaum remarks, "Lowell became a sensation: an American celebrity and a figure of political influence."[19]*Near the Ocean*, published in 1967, in the midst of

---

13 PATTERSON, James T. *Grand Expectations: The United States, 1945–1974*. New York/Oxford: Oxford University Press, 1996. 676.

14 PATTERSON. *Grand Expectations*. 676.

15 PATTERSON. *Grand Expectations*. 677.

16 MARIANI, Paul. *Lost Puritan: A Life of Robert Lowell*. New York/London: W.W. Norton, 1994. 354.

17 FLANZBAUM, Hilene. "Surviving the Marketplace: Robert Lowell and the Sixties." In: *The New England Quarterly* 68,1 (1995): 44–57, 45. FLANZBAUM's article describes the events involving Lowell rather precisely, but imbues them with an utter disdain for Lowell's public persona and his skill in "mastering the formula for media attention". See SULLIVAN's study of the same phenomena for a less acidulous treatment of Lowell's capturing of public attention and the spotlight in the late 1960s (SULLIVAN, James. "Investing the Cultural Capital of Robert Lowell." In: *Twentieth Century Literature* 38,2 (1992): 194–213).

18 Adam BEARDSWORTH's study of Lowell's confessional poetry is worth acknowledging here, because BEARDSWORTH maintains that Lowell's confessional poems "renegotiat[e] the containment and conformity characteristic of the early Cold War era" (BEARDSWORTH. "Learning." 113) and are generally better read as political commentary than as private soliloquies. Obviously, on that reading, the changes I point to in Lowell's work would not be all that sudden. BEARDSWORTH makes his case by using almost exclusively texts connected to mental instability, which are exceptional in several ways and cannot be brought to bear on a general assessment of the political content of Lowell's work. BEARDSWORTH does show, however, that a study looking at the relationships between Lowell's politics, theology, and his poetry of madness on the one hand, and Agamben, Foucault and Deleuze/Guattari on the other, is well worth undertaking, and one hopes to read its like in the near future.

19 FLANZBAUM. "Surviving." 44.

tumultuous events at home and abroad, marks a fitting departure in his work. It contains public poetry at its most vehement, quotations of political slogans, passionate oratory and stern pronouncements of doom. "The message [could not] be missed: the poems do not hide their meanings in dense metaphors or obscure references."[20] Instead, the tone reverberates with pathos, and the references to "commonplaces circulating in oppositional editorials, opinion pieces, and conversations"[21] are easy to decode and understand. While many of Lowell's collections strike some balance between private and public, *Near the Ocean* never quite finds it, opting instead for powerful, engaged poetry addressing the general public.

Poem after poem in *Notebook 1967–68* demonstrate that at the height of his celebrity as a public figure, Lowell was fearful and was ready to retreat to a more private mode of writing. A flurry of poems beginning 1967 were attempts to regain private poetic ground while recording "personal happenings, moods [and] brushes with the great events", as he put it in a letter to A. Alvarez (*Letters* 501–02). Fear of what the future would hold and personal anxiety had already been palpable in *Near the Ocean*, nowhere more so than in the opening poem, "Waking Early Sunday Morning", which concludes:

> Pity the planet, all joy gone
> from this sweet volcanic cone;
> peace to our children when they fall
> in small war on the heels of small
> war – until the end of time
> to police the earth, a ghost
> orbiting forever lost
> in our monotonous sublime. (*Collected Poems* 386)

This is a grand, serene, ominous statement, befitting the poetic elder statesman that Lowell had become by 1967. Additionally, "Waking Early Sunday Morning" is not as simple a poem as it might initially seem. Although it may sound resigned and gloomy, Lowell chose to publicly read it at a gathering in Washington two nights before the march. He was loudly applauded because the poem may appear to be resigned to the awfulness it describes, but it "distinctly disapproves. That code of protest [...] resonated through the audience."[22] Whether Lowell chose the role of wise man and seer, or the role of speaker who rallied the troops "with an axe in his hand and a Cromwellian light in his eye",[23] he was

---

20 FLANZBAUM. "Surviving." 51.
21 AXELROD, Steven Gould. "Robert Lowell and the Cold War." In: *The New England Quarterly* 72,3 (1999): 339–61, 357.
22 SULLIVAN. "Investing." 199.
23 MAILER, Norman. *The Armies of the Night.* New York: New American Library, 1968. 46.

successful in both, but these roles increasingly conflicted with his subjective view of the time and his place in it. The closeness of Lowell's work prior to *Near the Ocean* to Baudelaire's, in its fears and anxieties, has been pointed out by critics who show that Lowell's poems frequently are, as Steven Axelrod states, "painful examinations of the spiritual emptiness which afflicts the poet as representative man."[24] *Near the Ocean* is different, however. It turns the poet from that "representative man" into someone who teaches, writes about and fires up that "representative man". At the same time, Lowell's need to become once again that figure of the "poet as representative man" became more insistent, as evidenced by his speech introducing the Russian poet Andrei Voznesensky:

> This is a hard time to be a poet [...]. It is almost impossible [...] to be directly political and remain inspired. Still the world presses in as never before, prodding, benumbing. [...] It's too much, it's too tense. (*Collected Prose* 121)

This anxiety is not new to his work. It is on display in much of *Life Studies*, and even earlier in the fervently Catholic *Lord Weary's Castle* (1946) his fears underlie many of the book's tensions.[25] Neither is politics something new in his work. In a 1954 letter to then CBS anchor Blair Clark, Lowell wrote that he was "amazed" by one of Adlai Stevenson's speeches (*Letters* 225), and Alan Williamson has referred to Lowell's attempts to create "an image of moral political action"[26] in "For the Union Dead". Before 1967, instances of direct political engagement crop up only occasionally in his poetry. However, when Lowell marches with the protesters, is almost arrested and gets involved in Eugene

---

24 AXELROD, Steven Gould. "Baudelaire and the Poetry of Robert Lowell." In: *Twentieth Century Literature* 17,4 (1971): 257–74, 268. Interestingly, this assertion occurs in AXELROD's lucid discussion of Lowell's early to middle period poems, specifically those in *For the Union Dead*. BEARDSWORTH's more political and more postmodern reading enlists Kristeva, Derrida and Freud to help make the case I touched on above in footnote 18. AXELROD's discussion of "Waking Early Sunday Morning" in the same essay (AXELROD. "Baudelaire." 271–73) is also penetrating and casts light on the confluence of several influences on Lowell, notably Baudelaire and Milton, who helped him create this powerhouse of a poem. MACKINNON's study of the role of Baudelaire in Lowell's, Auden's and Eliot's work makes a pertinent additional point: reading Lowell as a Baudelairean dandy, he suggests that "straightforward satire is not a form in which [Lowell] can operate with ease" (MACKINNON, Lachlan. *Eliot, Auden, Lowell: Aspects of the Baudelairean Inheritance*. London: Macmillan, 1983). Following both AXELROD and MACKINNON, one may see *Notebook 1967–68* as a necessary development of Lowell's poetry after the declamatory rhetoric of *Near the Ocean*.
25 In his study of Catholic influence on American culture, Paul GILES argues however that Catholicism encourages a "skeptical attitude toward the whole idea of lyrical or subjective intuition" (GILES, Paul. *American Catholic Arts and Fictions: Culture, Ideology, Aesthetics*. Cambridge/New York: Cambridge University Press, 1992. 50), which is a far cry from the focus on "personal happenings [and] moods" (*Letters* 501) that would so dominate *Notebook 1967–68*.
26 WILLIAMSON, Alan. *Pity the Monsters: The Political Vision of Robert Lowell*. New Haven/London: Yale University Press, 1974. 106.

McCarthy's campaign for the Democratic nomination for the presidency, this changes.

Lowell now tried his hand at a more immediate style of writing, and he decided, as he put it in a letter to Elizabeth Bishop, "to write with such openness and not hold[] back" (*Letters* 494). The very same year he began composing a long poem, in "a coma of sloth or industry" (*Letters* 489). In "a hard time to be a poet", he tried to be a poet in a different way and created, as one reviewer perspicaciously put it, "a provisional book written in a provisional time".[27]

Alex Calder has demonstrated that Lowell's shaping of the book came along slowly. Occasional poems, including drafts of birthday poems and drafts of poems dedicated to his daughter, slowly fed into a larger project,[28] which he originally conceived of as three long poems. In his letters, he first discussed his writing in terms of lines[29] rather than sections or individual poems. It was only gradually that he imposed a form on them, but once he started working on the long poem in earnest, he soon settled on the sonnet composed in free blank verse.[30] After Lowell had settled on writing free blank verse sonnets he began crafting his irregular lines about various people, including, prominently, himself and his family.

Many of the brief poems were written like dramatic monologues, and whereas the rhythms of *Near the Ocean* amplified Lowell's declamatory voice, the blank verse in the new sonnets created the impression of listening to characters on a

---

27 COOLEY, Peter. "Reaching out, Keeping Position: New Poems by James Wright and Robert Lowell." In: *The North American Review* 254,3 (1969): 67–70, 70. COOLEY was right in different ways of course; the label of "provisional poem" proved to be utterly correct when Lowell started revising and republishing the poems from *Notebook 1967–68* as *Notebook* and still later as *History* and *For Lizzie and Harriet*.

28 CALDER is especially excellent on the early period of the poem's gestation, cf. CALDER, Alex. "*Notebook 1967–68*: Writing the Process Poem." In: Steven Gould Axelrod and Helen Deese (eds.). *Robert Lowell: Essays on the Poetry*. Cambridge/New York: Cambridge University Press, 1986. 120–26.

29 He would tell his correspondent, for example: "My summer's poem is now 800 lines" (*The Letters* 492).

30 One reason for Lowell's choice might be the kinship Lowell had always felt to Milton's work, cf. BURT, Stephen. "Rebellious Authority: Robert Lowell and Milton at Midcentury." In: *Journal of Modern Literature* 24,2 (2001): 337–47. However, although BURT's focus is primarily on early Milton, for example "Lycidas", his general point extends well beyond this. Especially since BURT's attention is devoted to early Lowell, as well. There are several Miltonic lines in the *Notebook* sonnets, and BURT's essay is immensely helpful for explaining them, and Lowell's use of the sonnet in general. As AXELROD points out in his discussion of "Waking Early Sunday Morning" and other poems, the Miltonic line continues to be important in Lowell's work even after his 'rebellious' early writing, cf. AXELROD. "Baudelaire." 272. Meanwhile, WALLINGFORD has suggested what the reason for the continuing relevance of Milton for Lowell was and argues that Lowell "works through his rebellious act in [...] new context[s]" (WALLINGFORD, Katharine T. "Robert Lowell's Poetry of Repetition." In: *American Literature* 57,3 (1985): 424–33, 432).

stage. In fact, several other long poems composed in sonnets or variations on the form share this effect.[31] Both Berryman's *Sonnets to Chris* and *Dream Songs*, for example, profit greatly from being read aloud, as well as Ted Berrigan's *The Sonnets* (1964), Tony Harrison's *School of Eloquence* (1981) and Edwin Morgan's *Sonnets from Scotland* (1984). In Lowell's case, this effect is very likely connected to his work in drama, as "[b]etween 1960 and 1970 [...] Lowell was almost continuously involved in some dramatic project".[32]

The poems in *Notebook 1967–68* do not pontificate. Unlike "Waking Early Sunday Morning", they are not meant to strike fear in the hearts of their readers. They were carefully crafted to be read as the poet's experience of private fear in public settings. The period given in the title, "1967–68", provides the general context, and a page-long appendix headed "Dates" lists historical events alluded to in the sonnets. An initial sentence reads: "Dates fade faster than we do" (*Notebook 1967–68* 163).

The most frequently cited instances of Lowell's "brushes with the great events" (*Letters* 501–02) are the two sonnets about the March on the Pentagon. Originally published as two halves of one poem (and ultimately returned to that state in *History*), Lowell integrated them as sonnets three and four in a six-sonnet sequence titled "October and November". The poems invoke two separate feelings. The first sonnet recreates initial enthusiasm, when the protesters "step[ped] off like green Union Army recruits" to confront the soldiers, "the other army, the Martian, the ape, the hero" (*Notebook 1967–68* 27). But even before the protesters come into contact with the soldiers, Lowell suggests that fear is one prevailing feeling.

The poem lacks a sonnet rhyme scheme, but is structurally divided into an octet and two tercets. The first tercet begins with the act of stepping off, but at the end of the tercet, the syntax peters out, and Lowell ends the line with "fear, glory, chaos, rout" (*Notebook 1967–68* 27), separated from the rest of the poem by two ellipses at either end. The second tercet again begins with the act of walking, but Lowell replaces "to step off" with "staggered out" (*Notebook 1967–68* 27), marking a change from brisk marching to more uncoordinated movement. The second tercet and the sonnet ends with a description of the soldiers' equipment, their weapons and their "green new steel helmet[s]" (*Notebook 1967–68* 27). This particular detail is one of several places where Lowell merges private

---

31 However, RAFFEL correctly points out that Lowell's sonnets combined form "a mass of poetry, over 850 printed pages in length" (RAFFEL, Burton. *Robert Lowell*. New York: Frederick Ungar, 1981. 74), and he compares this page count to other book length poems, like Berryman's *Dream Songs*, and demonstrates that Lowell's output of sonnets that starts with *Notebook 1967–68* dwarfs that of his peers and colleagues.

32 LINDSAY, Geoffrey. "Drama and Dramatic Strategies in Robert Lowell's *Notebook 1967–68*." In: *Twentieth Century Literature* 44,1 (1998): 53–81, 55.

anxieties with his remarks about public events and fears. The helmet recalls similar headgear that the reader of *Notebook 1967 – 68* encountered earlier, in the third sonnet of the sonnet sequence "Long Summer". The sonnet describes a breakdown, and ends with an enumeration of impressions:

> I have to brace myself against a wall
> to keep myself from swaying – swaying wall,
> straitjacket, hypodermic, helmeted
> doctors, one crowd, white-smocked, in panic, hit,
> stop, bury the runner on the cleated field. (*Notebook 1967 – 68* 6)

The field bearing traces of cleats anticipates the walking protesters, and the enumeration of impressions resembles that of "fear, glory, chaos, rout" (*Notebook 1967 – 68* 27). The most salient point for our purposes is the "helmeted / doctors". They connect the "panic" that Lowell felt in contending with his psychological disorders and the fear felt by the protesters as they walked up to the menacing soldiers on the lawn of the Pentagon. In a January 1968 letter to Elizabeth Bishop, Lowell reported that the medication he was taking was helping, and he remarked that "[o]rdinarily I would certainly have been in the hospital by now" (*Letters* 494). He likened the apprehension he had felt to being "in danger of falling with every step [he] took" (*Letters* 494). The similarity of the imagery is striking.

Often the topic of fear and anxiety is not pursued head-on, but suggested indirectly. Sometimes, however, Lowell writes very explicitly about the doubts plaguing him, as in the second sonnet on the March.

>   sadly
> unfit to follow their dream, I sat in the sunset
> shade of their Bastille, the Pentagon,
> nursing leg- and arch-cramps, my cowardly,
> foolhardy heart; (*Notebook 1967 – 68* 27)

Already, it is "their dream" and "their Bastille". The sonnet ends with Lowell fleeing the scene, helped by "kind hands".

Taken together, the two sonnets show the poet embroiled in public events but unable to properly join in because of personal anxieties. Private fears lead to Lowell fleeing the scene. A conflict between what he wants to do and what he is able to, between what he knows and what he feels, is also reflected in the book's language. In stark contrast to the coherent and straightforward poetry of *Near the Ocean*, Lowell's writing becomes more fragmented, splitting up into adjectives and small phrases. Marjorie Perloff complained that "the new loose syntax is problematic".[33] Perloff points to Lowell's increased use of phrasal verbs

---

33 PERLOFF, Marjorie. *The Poetic Art of Robert Lowell.* Ithaca/London: Cornell University Press,

and adjectives, and she concludes that these stylistic traits have become "mere mannerisms" used "out of sheer habit".[34] The first "The March" sonnet shows, however, that Lowell can employ these "mannerisms" effectively. He breaks up syntax to mirror fear, and he piles up nouns to reproduce the claustrophobia inside a manic mind.

Lowell pairs private despair with public events time and again, sometimes, as in the first "The March" sonnet, by comparing his personal 'panic' in moments of mania with the fear that a marching crowd feels. Another example of this kind of comparison is "F.O. Matthiessen: 1902–1950", the twelfth sonnet in a sequence titled "Power". The sonnet begins:

> Matthiessen jumping from the North Station Hotel,
> breaking his mania barrier to despair;
> a prophet to the dead Czech-student torches? (*Notebook 1967–68* 101)

The connection of personal despair with public events, in this case the Russian occupation of Czechoslovakia, is obvious, but the reference is really more private than that. One does not even need to know about Lowell's personal history of mental breakdowns. The book itself offers us a two-sonnet poem called "Mania", which alludes to his relationship with Ann Adden.[35] A line from the first of the two sonnets, titled "1958", may serve as summary: "I mad, you mad for me" (*Notebook 1967–68* 89). "Mania" comes just a few pages before "Power" and Lowell can expect his readers to connect the two manias. Matthiessen's suicide becomes a violent act, a viable option maybe for Lowell himself, a violent act, moreover, that is equivalent to acts of political despair. This mirrors the scene in "The March": Lowell hunched over, brought low by his personal anxieties, fears and shame, while the political activists around him march on, impelled by their own necessities.[36]

But Lowell can also see how his personal environments may mirror larger political issues. Mark Rudman points to a particularly interesting example: the ninth sonnet of the "Long Summers" sequence describes a marina, but a hidden reference in it alludes to the Vietnam War. In the sonnet Lowell tells us, "I have counted the catalogue / of ships down half its length" (*Notebook 1967–68* 9). Rudman demonstrates that the sonnet as a whole, and this line in particular,

---

1973. 125.

34 PERLOFF. *The Poetic Art of Robert Lowell*. 126–27.

35 Ann Adden was "a young psychiatric fieldworker fresh out of Bennington" (MARIANI. *Lost Puritan*. 262) whom he met while in McLean's, a psychiatric hospital in Belmont, MA.

36 Jerome MAZZARO adds the factor of age: "[t]he youthful idealism and passionate convictions of both armies return Lowell to the sense of his exile from youth" (MAZZARO, Jerome. *Robert Lowell and America*. Bloomington, IN: Xlibris, 2002. 161).

allude to Mandelstam's poem "No. 78",[37] which in turn refers to reading the catalogue of warships in Homer's *Iliad*.[38] Of all of Lowell's political preoccupations, his opposition to the Vietnam War was most vehement.

The war also determined his political stance, notably in his support for the staunch anti-war candidate Eugene McCarthy in the 1968 Democratic primaries. The political debates were tumultuous because "[t]he events of the preceding four years had added a bitter and compelling edge [...] among [the candidates] and among voters themselves".[39] Lowell vividly renders this climate in "Five Hour Rally", the second sonnet in a ten-sonnet sequence titled "The Races", which treats the 1968 Democratic primaries and the Presidential election:

> All excel, as if they were the key-note speaker,
> first of the twenty first-ballerinas in the act,
> all original or at least in person...
> This acre of carpet is coal-on-cherry sunset,
> one figure to each ten feet, like the rich in his grave;
> its head is a broken pretzel, less head than gulf;
> the wings are fernshoots, done like ironwork
> for a Goya balcony, lure and bar to love.
> The belly is a big watermelon seed,
> the body is the belly's overcoat –
> poor vermin, it could only live for that...
> Sunrise comes. Who can live on breath alone?
> Insects and politicians grapple on the carpet,
> saying, 'You will swallow me. I you.' (*Notebook 1967–68* 136)

In accord with Perloff's analysis of Lowell's changed style, his expansive syntax has vanished and what is left is a fragmented recapitulation of impressions. After each period, a new observation starts, leading on to the next, until the dire image that terminates the poem. Despite the absence of a rhyme scheme, one can read the sonnet as composed of an octave framed by two tercets, one that begins the sonnet and another that concludes it. Although here as elsewhere in *Notebook 1967–68* iambic pentameter is the normative line, Lowell departs from it now and again for fluctuating tonal purposes. The first three lines are humorous, satirical, and at once critical and condescending. The octave conveys impressions of figures portrayed on a carpet. The narrator's reaction to the pitiful spectacle before him is to look down, in embarrassment, perhaps. And now,

---

37 For RUDMAN's discussion, cf. RUDMAN, Mark. *Robert Lowell: An Introduction to the Poetry.* New York: Columbia University Press, 1983. 156 ff.

38 Mandelstam's poem itself is a mixture of public and private elements, not dissimilar to what Lowell attempts in his *Notebook* poems. According to Ralph DUTLI, Mandelstam's poem discusses both the First World War and love. For more details, cf. DUTLI, Ralph. *Meine Zeit, Mein Tier: Ossip Mandelstam, eine Biographie.* Zurich: Amman, 2003. 128–29.

39 MILLER and LEVITIN. *Leadership and Change.* 58.

looking down, he sees hell opening. Whatever really is figured on that carpet, the narrator associates it with graves, with Goya and deformed bodies. He then either imagines insects to be depicted on the carpet, or he sees living insects scurrying over it. Lowell's abrupt syntax does not allow us to see exactly what he does. The final tercet, then, immerses the whole spectacle in the surreal and dark world he found figured on the carpet. The last two lines, which have an almost folksy rhythm, drag politicians onto the same level as insects, and they culminate in an image of cannibalism and mythical circularity.

The personal element here is not easy to detect, but correspondences throughout the book give the game away. In the sonnet "Reading Myself", the fourth and final sonnet in the sequence titled "We do what we are", Lowell writes in slightly surreal terms about the relationship of an artist to his work. Jonathan Veitch speaks of a "grim ontology"[40] which "spatializ[es] history in a surrealistic frieze".[41] The phrase "insect lives preserved in honey" (*Notebook 1967–68* 128) prepares us for the other use of the word 'insect' in "The Races", which provides a different kind of "surrealistic frieze", fewer than ten pages later. Lowell's use of similar images and phrases in the course of several sonnets creates a claustrophobic sense of sameness, so that it makes little difference whether the stage where things are taking place is public or private.

"Five Hour Rally" ends at "sunrise", a new day, but not a new beginning. The claustrophobia induced by the bracketing tercets, the syntax, the circular world view, all this is not much different from the goings on in Thompson's book, which ends with a bitter chant: "four more years!"

According to Godfrey Hodgson, Nixon's success was the beginning of an ascendency of conservatism, as "[s]uddenly, in 1968 and 1969, [...] journalists, social scientists, pollsters and politicians all discovered the new majority",[42] after having harbored fears "since the Goldwater debacle that no candidate with [conservative] views could ever get to the White House."[43] This was the status quo when Hunter Thompson began writing political journalism, but when Nixon campaigned for re-election in 1972, the situation in the liberal camp

---

40 VEITCH, Jonathan. "'Moondust in the Prowling Eye': The 'History' Poems of Robert Lowell."
    In: *Contemporary Literature* 33,3 (1992): 458–79, 459.
41 VEITCH. "'Moondust in the Prowling Eye'." 460. It's important to note that, although I follow
    Jonathan VEITCH's reading in this case, other readings of this sonnet have emphasized the
    self-referential, poetological and circular nature of this poem. Cf. for example KEARFUL,
    Frank. "Circling American Poetry." In: *Partial Answers* 1,2 (2003): 125–57 and YENSER,
    Stephen. *Circle to Circle: The Poetry of Robert Lowell.* Berkeley/London: University of Ca-
    lifornia Press, 1975. 282–83.
42 HODGSON, Godfrey. *In Our Time: America from World War II to Nixon.* London: Macmillan,
    1976. 415.
43 HODGSON. *In Our Time.* 414.

strongly resembled that of the early 1950s, when "liberal opinionmakers [were] feeling besieged and threatened."[44]

That emergent feeling of angst and a changing political landscape prompted many new writers, Hunter Thompson being one of them, to try out fresh and exciting literary techniques. Critics usually regard Thompson's oeuvre as part of a literary movement dubbed by Tom Wolfe 'New Journalism', which surfaced in the 1960s and 1970s and sought to combine fictional techniques with traditional journalistic tools in order to produce work that would be perceived as more relevant. "New Journalism [was] new for the same reason that [1960s] fiction [was] new", i. e., because of "an alteration in American experience".[45] Among the New Journalists one could find a broad array of writers and talents, ranging from Wolfe himself and Norman Mailer, to writers like Gay Talese and Joan Didion.

Despite their frequently outré subjects, most New Journalists should be regarded as more or less ordinary journalists who produced traditional quality journalism, embellished by frequent stylistic mannerisms and their books' structural quirks. To take two examples, *The Kingdom and the Power*, Talese's book about the *New York Times*, and *The Electric Kool-Aid Acid Test*, Wolfe's book about Ken Kesey and the Merry Pranksters, hold up well today as sober, clear-eyed accounts of the *New York Times* and a subset of the hippie community. In the introduction to his anthology *The New Journalism* (1973), Tom Wolfe himself focuses more on technical aspects of the journalist's trade than on anything else. After noting the "lumpenproles"[46] status of journalists, he showcases four novelistic techniques that have turned him and his fellow New Journalists into dominant literary figures, beating the novelists at their own game.[47] Much of what he sets out does not really amount to a revolution in form, merely to a tauter and more reliable and trustworthy framework: structuring your writing, using significant descriptions and making ample use of dialogues and interviews. John Hellmann, one of the leading critics on the genre, nevertheless was quick to label all New Journalism as fiction in the "more sophisticated and original sense of the word".[48] Dwight Macdonald once convincingly argued that Wolfe's books don't "stand up as fiction",[49] and the brilliance of his

---

44 CHAPPELL, David L. "The Triumph of Conservatives in a Liberal Age." In: Jean-Christophe Agnew and Roy Rosenzweig (eds.). *A Companion to Post-1945 America*. Malden/Oxford: Blackwell, 2007. 303–27, 307.
45 HELLMANN, John. *Fables of Fact: The New Journalism as New Fiction*. Urbana: University of Illinois Press, 1981. 18.
46 WOLFE, Tom. "The New Journalism." In: Tom Wolfe and E.W. Johnson (eds.). *The New Journalism: with an Anthology*. New York: Harper and Row, 1973. 25.
47 WOLFE. "The New Journalism." 31 ff.
48 HELLMANN. *Fables*. 17.
49 MACDONALD, Dwight. "Parajournalism, or Tom Wolfe and his Magic Writing Machine." In:

and Talese's books in fact stands out not through comparison to works of fiction, but to other journalism.

In an "Author's Note" to his acclaimed book about the 1988 presidential campaign *What It Takes* (1993), Richard Ben Cramer describes his methods[50] along lines that closely resemble the four pillars of New Journalism that Wolfe erected decades earlier. In Cramer's own view, his methods do not lead a writer toward the realm of fiction and to literary heights, but to "trust" and "accuracy and fairness".[51] One might read this as a sign that New Journalism has been assimilated by mainstream journalism, but it makes more sense to take Wolfe's conception of New Journalism as an assessment of flaws in the journalism of his time, such as imprecise and inaccurate writing, and as an attempt to mend them. By contrast, Hunter Thompson's aesthetics fundamentally differ from both mainstream journalism and New Journalism.

Thompson himself said that the new Journalists were "much better reporters",[52] and he called his colleague Tom Wolfe, who made use of Thompson's research in his book on Kesey, "a hell of a reporter".[53] Unlike Wolfe, though, Thompson was under no illusions as to the limitations and possibilities of journalism. While his New Journalistic peers transmuted their material by use of fictive imagination, Thompson threw himself into his stories. "Instead of institutionalizing common knowledge [...], [Thompson] told a story that was only beginning to happen" (*Hell's Angels* 66).[54] While his fellow New Journalists were embracing subjectivity in order to attain "a higher kind of 'objectivity'",[55] Thompson eventually adopted the term 'Gonzo Journalism',[56] which he defined

---

Ronald Weber (ed.). *The Reporter as Artist: A Look at the New Journalism Controversy.* New York: Hastings House, 1974. 223–33, 227.

50 Cf. especially CRAMER, Richard Ben. *What It Takes: The Way to the White House.* New York: Vintage, 1993. viii-ix.

51 CRAMER. *What It Takes.* ix.

52 VETTER. "Playboy Interview." 47.

53 O'ROURKE, P.J. "Interview by P.J. O'Rourke for the 25th Anniversary of *Rolling Stone* Magazine." In: Anita Thompson (ed.). *Ancient Gonzo Wisdom: Interviews with Hunter S. Thompson.* Cambridge: Da Capo, 2009. 153–58, 154.

54 These comments refer to Laslo Benedek's movie *The Wild One*, but they can equally well serve as commentary on Thompson's own work and were presumably even intended as such. This does not, however, make Thompson's observations about *The Wild One* any less fitting, as many studies, written decades after Thompson's, demonstrate (cf. especially RUBIN, Martin. "'Make Love Make War': Cultural Confusion and the Biker Film Cycle." In: *Film History* 6,3 (1994): 355–81, 360–61). The more you read Thompson and compare him with later writers on the same events, you will be struck by the overall precision and exactness of many of his descriptions and observations, regardless of the tone and voice in which they are delivered.

55 HOLLOWELL, John. *Fact & Fiction: The New Journalism and the Nonfiction Novel.* Chapel Hill: University of North Carolina Press, 1977. 22.

56 Thompson did not coin the term himself, however. For a succinct discussion of the word

as "Total Subjectivity" (*Fear and Loathing in America* 406). The difference becomes more glaring insofar as his writing combined "Total Subjectivity" with a rapidly increasing sense of spontaneity.[57] Thompson's debut book *Hell's Angels* was a rather carefully composed affair, well structured, written in a measured style.[58] Although portions of it recount his personal adventures with the Hell's Angels, Thompson by and large portrays himself as being more on the sidelines. This first-book reticence gradually receded, until his interjection of himself culminated in *Fear and Loathing on the Campaign Trail '72*. Early in it, Thompson repudiates "objective journalism" as "a pompous contradiction in terms" (*Campaign Trail* 48). His first two books went through multiple drafts, but everything thereafter came, according to Thompson, straight from his reporter's writing desk. Even letters to his editor at *Rolling Stone* were incorporated into *Fear and Loathing on the Campaign Trail '72* (cf. *Fear and Loathing in America* 465 ff.).

Wolfe's poetics foregrounds observation, not participation. Talking to the major players and giving them enough room to stand out like well-rounded characters created such a strong impression of impartiality that "[s]ome have even wondered if Wolfe has a [...] social vision at all".[59] In sharp contrast, Thompson's early writing was highly political. In his essay "The Battle of Aspen", sometimes referred to as "Freak Power in the Rockies", he describes local political events that could serve equally well as national campaign material. By the time of Nixon's 1972 re-election bid, Thompson had been personally involved in politics for quite a while, as a man driven by fear of the 'silent majority' pressing in on him and on people like him. He had even run for Sheriff in Aspen, Colorado on a 'Freak Power' ticket, one year after his "The Battle of Aspen" article had appeared. On the campaign trail in 1972, he told Democratic candidate George McGovern that:

> if he had any real sense he would make drastic alterations in the whole style and tone of his campaign and re-model it along the lines of the Aspen freak power uprising,

---

'Gonzo' and its origins, cf. TAMONY, Peter. "On Gonzo." In: *American Speech* 58,1 (1983): 73 – 75.

57 It is, however, not correct to arrange Thompson's oeuvre on a rising scale of subjectivity and spontaneity or 'Gonzo': eventually, as he said in a 1986 interview, media attention and self-consciousness amounted to "a retreat from Gonzo journalism", taking "the fun out of it" (KAIHLA, Paul. "Thirty-Six Manic Hours in Toronto with Dr. Hunter S. Thompson, Guru of Gonzo Journalism." In: Anita Thompson (ed.). *Ancient Gonzo Wisdom: Interviews with Hunter S. Thompson*. Cambridge: Da Capo, 2009. 143 – 46, 144 – 45).

58 And yet its sections dealing with the general malaise of journalism are among the most potent attacks on the genre ever written by one of its own practitioners, easily surpassing Talese's book, for example, in insight and incisiveness.

59 LOUNSBERRY, Barbara. *The Art of Fact: Contemporary Artists of Nonfiction*. New York: Greenwood Press, 1990. 38.

specifically, along the lines of [Thompson's] own extremely weird and nerve-rattling campaign for Sheriff of Pitkin County, Colorado. (*Campaign Trail* 243)

Thompson's involvement in politics, his attempts to convince George McGov-ern, Walter Mondale, Eugene McCarthy, and members of Richard Nixon's staff of his own political vision, is highly reminiscent of the influence Robert Lowell exerted on Eugene McCarthy's campaign and of his attempts to influence Robert Kennedy. As with Lowell, the campaign was an environment that spurred Thompson to thrive as a writer.

In contrast to Lowell, though, Thompson's active involvement goes beyond discussions with political candidates and their campaign managers. Thompson used a variety of tactics and approaches that included lending his press cre-dentials to "a crazy sonofabitch" (*Campaign Trail* 104) and concocting various stories, among them the claim that Democratic candidate Ed Muskie got high on a dangerous South American drug. This was taken as real news at the time. In all his books and most of his articles, Thompson's treatment of his fellow jour-nalists and their *laissez faire* approach to truth is scathing and contemptuous,[60] but in this case he was astonished to find that "even some of the reporters who'd been covering Muskie for three of four months took it seriously".[61] The bulk of his book had been published during the campaign in *Rolling Stone* in install-ments that helped create the reality that they depicted. Wolfe and the others assumed that fictional techniques would provide a better way of ordering per-ceptions and observations, while Thompson saw how the mere act of writing about his subject was changing it already and that any 'ordering' would run the danger of misrepresenting its subject.

Thompson's writing is always explicitly personal. The interviews transcribed in the book seem only minimally trustworthy, and his artful precision and the cunning overall quality of his political journalism seem almost accidental. The basic idea of *Fear and Loathing on the Campaign Trail '72* can be summed up by

---

60 In his articles Thompson reserved his bile for mainstream media, but in the interviews he complains that his New Journalism peers have fallen to similar lows. Michael A. STAUB's study "Black Panthers, New Journalism, and the Rewriting of the Sixties." (In: *Representa-tions* 57 (1997): 52–72) similarly contends that New Journalists, especially Tom Wolfe and Gail Sheehy, introduce insinuations that rival right-wing mainstream media.

61 VETTER. "Playboy Interview." 46. However, this may be less surprising if we consider articles like SHAW and SPARROW's CDA study of campaign coverage "From the Inner Ring Out". While major, or 'elite' newspapers are frequently 'cue-givers' to the 'non-elite' or 'outer ring' papers, they are restrained as to the kind of news they can break, and would be dependent on an 'outer ring' journalist like Thompson to break a major story like Muskie's alleged drug use: "inner ring news stories with the greatest circulation should be ones that are more balanced and less 'edgy' or one-sided in their campaign coverage" (SHAW, Daron R. and Bartholomew H. SPARROW. "From the Inner Ring Out: News Congruence, Cue-Taking, and Campaign Coverage." In: *Political Research Quarterly* 52,2 (1999): 323–51, 340).

the phrase Lowell used to describe his nascent *Notebook* poems: 'Journal of a Year'. No narrative is imposed on the material that Thompson presents to his readers in the order in which it was originally written. In an "Afterthought" Lowell remarks: "Accident threw up subjects, and the plot swallowed them" (*Notebook 1967–68* 159), which is as good as any description of Thompson's own writing, although differences are naturally discernible. As a poet, Lowell carefully assembled his sonnets and while his narrative can be called frag-mented, there is a limit to how disjointed a text can be that consists of "fourteen line unrhymed blank verse sections" (*Notebook 1967–68* 160). Lowell published some individual sonnets before he completed the book, but the bulk of the volume was not previously published. Thompson's book, on the other hand, recounts his "tearing [his] Ohio primary notebook apart and sending about fifty pages of scribbled shorthand notes straight to the typesetter" (*Campaign Trail* 186), even as he was shaking with fear and the constant threat of failure hung over him. Lowell and Thompson adamantly stress the spontaneous nature of their endeavors, but dissimilarities follow upon the different genres they employ.

Differences and similarities can also be found in their uses of literary refer-ences and allusions. Lowell's influences, indicated in the "Afterthought", range from Thomas More to Herbert Marcuse and R.P. Blackmur, while Thompson's range is narrower. The most prominent reference in *Fear and Loathing on the Campaign Trail '72* is to T.S. Eliot's poem "The Hollow Men" (1925), which Thompson quoted in the epigraph: "Between the Idea and Reality... Falls the Shadow."[62] This poem and others by Eliot left traces throughout Thompson's work, and even the title of another book of his, *Kingdom of Fear* (2003), echoes "death's dream kingdom"[63] in "The Hollow Men". In *Fear and Loathing on the Campaign Trail '72*, Eliot's invocation of "the Shadow", often read as repre-senting death, lends Thompson's book its focus. The radically disjointed nature of his work necessitates this narrow focus, in order to make the intended pol-itical and rhetorical impact.[64]

Lowell and Thompson both have recourse to surrealistic devices to express their anxieties. Lowell himself admits that he is "devoted to surrealism" (*Note-book 1967–68* 159), and the surreal and the fantastic imbue his observations, dreams, and visions. Thompson also recurrently uses *doppelganger* or *revenant* characters, the most famous of which in his case are his *alter ego* Raoul Duke and

---

62 ELIOT, T.S. *Collected Poems 1909–1962*. London: Faber and Faber, 1989. 92.
63 ELIOT. *Collected Poems 1909–1962*. 89.
64 In a 1968 letter to Eugene McCarthy, Thompson offers his help, saying: "I'm not sure how I could help, but given the fact that I make my living as a writer, it would have to be in that area" (*Fear and Loathing in America* 11). Since he was similarly intent on helping McGovern's camp in the 1972 election, it's not difficult to assume that the articles that make up *Fear and Loathing on the Campaign Trail '72* are some kind of attempt to help.

the Samoan attorney Dr. Gonzo, who is a literary representation of his friend Oscar Zeta Acosta, Chicano lawyer and activist.

Perhaps the most important difference between *Notebook 1967–68* and *Fear and Loathing on the Campaign Trail '72* is their rendering of personal and public fears. Lowell combines personal and public fears through allusion, and in his "Afterthought" he rejects "too literal [...] honesty". Thompson is more direct. He says of the room in which he writes, "[t]his room reeks of failure" (*Campaign Trail* 185) to convey his fear of writer's block, in a chapter that treats the assassination attempt on George Wallace. Thompson's personal directness extends to the political domain, about which he utters angry comments as opposed to Lowell's polished asides, but the gulf between the two writers' directness is not as wide as it might at first seem.

Both Lowell and Thompson were driven by political convictions, both championed a Democratic presidential nominee, and both took to writing letters to editors, journalists and politicians to express their anger. Lowell's ire was not as directly conveyed in the *Notebook 1967–68* sonnets, but published letters from the period show us a writer who did not acquiesce. In a 1968 letter to the editors of *Commentary* he referred to right-wing columnists as "mice [...], nerved for blood, but with fingers stretched to their typewriters" (*Letters* 509), and in a 1971 letter to the editors of the *New York Review of Books* he called Nixon "our own Huckleberry Finn who has to shoot everyone else on the raft" (*Letters* 571). It is true that neither comment made it into the sonnets, but both were made publicly, and in print, and can and should be seen as corollaries to *Notebook 1967–68*.

Lowell's and Thompson's books were the end products of witnessing, and to one extent or another being involved in, two decades of political history. A 'silent majority' voted Nixon into office on his own, or on a ticket with Eisenhower, seven times out of nine. Both *Fear and Loathing on the Campaign Trail '72* and *Notebook 1967–68* devolved from living over decades in a country shaped to no small extent by Richard Milhous Nixon. He is not the sole cause for the fear that invests both books, nor is the loathing directed at him alone. He is, however, an arch-representative of an era that drove people like Lowell and Thompson to the brink. Although only one of the two of them was a journalist, both their books were reports from the edge of the abyss.

References

ALVAREZ, A. "Robert Lowell in Conversation." In: Jeffrey Meyers (ed.). *Robert Lowell, Interviews and Memoirs*. Ann Arbor: University of Michigan Press, 1988. 74–78.

AXELROD, Steven Gould. "Baudelaire and the Poetry of Robert Lowell." In: *Twentieth Century Literature* 17,4 (1971): 257–74.

– "Robert Lowell and the Cold War." In: *The New England Quarterly* 72,3 (1999): 339–61.

BEARDSWORTH, Adam. "Learning to Love the Bomb: Robert Lowell's Pathological Poetics." In: *Canadian Review of American Studies/Revue canadienne d'études américaines* 40,1 (2010): 95–116.

BLACK, Conrad. *Richard M. Nixon: A Life in Full*. New York: PublicAffairs, 2007.

BURT, Stephen. "Rebellious Authority: Robert Lowell and Milton at Midcentury." In: *Journal of Modern Literature* 24,2 (2001): 337–47.

CALDER, Alex. "*Notebook 1967–68*: Writing the Process Poem." In: Steven Gould Axelrod and Helen Deese (eds.). *Robert Lowell: Essays on the Poetry*. Cambridge: Cambridge University Press, 1986. 117–38.

CHAPPELL, David L. "The Triumph of Conservatives in a Liberal Age." In: Jean-Christophe Agnew and Roy Rosenzweig (eds.). *A Companion to Post-1945 America*. Oxford: Blackwell, 2007. 303–27.

COOLEY, Peter. "Reaching out, Keeping Position: New Poems by James Wright and Robert Lowell." In: *The North American Review* 254,3 (1969): 67–70.

CRAMER, Richard Ben. *What It Takes: The Way to the White House*. New York: Vintage, 1993.

DUTLI, Ralph. *Meine Zeit, Mein Tier: Ossip Mandelstam, eine Biographie*. Zurich: Amman, 2003.

ELIOT, T.S. *Collected Poems 1909–1962*. London: Faber and Faber, 1989.

FARBER, David. *Chicago '68*. Chicago: University of Chicago Press, 1988.

FLANZBAUM, Hilene. "Surviving the Marketplace: Robert Lowell and the Sixties." In: *The New England Quarterly* 68,1 (1995): 44–57.

GILES, Paul. *American Catholic Arts and Fictions: Culture, Ideology, Aesthetics*. Cambridge: Cambridge University Press, 1992.

HELLMANN, John. *Fables of Fact: The New Journalism as New Fiction*. Urbana: University of Illinois Press, 1981.

HODGSON, Godfrey. *In Our Time: America from World War II to Nixon*. London: Macmillan, 1976.

HOLLOWELL, John. *Fact & Fiction: The New Journalism and the Nonfiction Novel*. Chapel Hill: University of North Carolina Press, 1977.

HOWARD, Richard. "Fuel on the Fire." In: *Poetry* 110,6 (1967): 413–15.

KAIHLA, Paul. "Thirty-Six Manic Hours in Toronto with Dr. Hunter S. Thompson, Guru of Gonzo Journalism." In: Anita Thompson (ed.). *Ancient Gonzo Wisdom: Interviews with Hunter S. Thompson*. Cambridge: Da Capo, 2009. 143–46.

KEARFUL, Frank. "Circling American Poetry." In: *Partial Answers* 1,2 (2003): 125–57.

– "Connecting Rooms: Entering 'Father's Bedroom' in Robert Lowell's *Life Studies*." In: *Partial Answers* 6,1 (2008): 111–33.

LINDSAY, Geoffrey. "Drama and Dramatic Strategies in Robert Lowell's *Notebook 1967–68*." In: *Twentieth Century Literature* 44,1 (1998): 53–81.

LOOMIS, Burdett A. "Book Review." In: *The Wisconsin Magazine of History* 57,4 (1974): 317–19.

LOUNSBERRY, Barbara. *The Art of Fact: Contemporary Artists of Nonfiction.* New York: Greenwood Press, 1990.

LOWELL, Robert. *Notebook 1967–68.* New York: Farrar, Straus and Giroux, 2009 [1969].

– *Notebook.* New York: Farrar, Straus and Giroux, 1970.

– *Collected Prose.* Edited by Robert Giroux. New York: Farrar, Straus and Giroux, 1987.

– *Collected Poems.* Edited by Frank Bidart and David Gewanter. New York: Farrar, Straus and Giroux, 2003.

– *The Letters of Robert Lowell.* Edited by Saskia Hamilton. New York: Farrar, Straus and Giroux, 2007.

LUKAS, J. Anthony. *Nightmare: The Underside of the Nixon Years.* New York: Viking Press, 1976.

MACDONALD, Dwight. "Parajournalism, or Tom Wolfe and his Magic Writing Machine." In: Ronald Weber (ed.). *The Reporter as Artist: A Look at the New Journalism Controversy.* New York: Hastings House, 1974. 223–33.

MACKINNON, Lachlan. *Eliot, Auden, Lowell: Aspects of the Baudelairean Inheritance.* London: Macmillan, 1983.

MAILER, Norman. *The Armies of the Night.* New York: New American Library, 1968.

– *Miami and the Siege of Chicago.* London: Penguin, 1969.

MARIANI, Paul. *Lost Puritan: A Life of Robert Lowell.* New York/London: W.W. Norton, 1994.

MAZZARO, Jerome. *Robert Lowell and America.* Bloomington, IN: Xlibris, 2002.

MILLER, Warren E. and Teresa E. LEVITIN. *Leadership and Change: Presidential Elections from 1952 to 1976.* Cambridge, MA: Winthrop, 1976.

O'ROURKE, P.J. "Interview by P.J. O'Rourke for the 25th Anniversary of *Rolling Stone* Magazine." In: Anita Thompson (ed.). *Ancient Gonzo Wisdom: Interviews with Hunter S. Thompson.* Cambridge: Da Capo, 2009. 153–58.

PATTERSON, James T. *Grand Expectations: The United States, 1945–1974.* New York/Oxford: Oxford University Press, 1996.

PERLOFF, Marjorie. *The Poetic Art of Robert Lowell.* Ithaca: Cornell University Press, 1973.

PERLSTEIN, Rick. *Nixonland: The Rise of a President and the Fracturing of America.* New York: Scribner, 2008.

RAFFEL, Burton. *Robert Lowell.* New York: Frederick Ungar, 1981.

RUBIN, Martin. "'Make Love Make War': Cultural Confusion and the Biker Film Cycle." In: *Film History* 6,3 (1994): 355–81.

RUDMAN, Mark. *Robert Lowell: An Introduction to the Poetry.* New York: Columbia University Press, 1983.

SHAW, Daron R. and Bartholomew H. SPARROW. "From the Inner Ring Out: News Congruence, Cue-Taking, and Campaign Coverage." In: *Political Research Quarterly* 52,2 (1999): 323–51.

SMITH, Ernest J. "'Approaching Our Maturity': The Dialectic of Engagement and Withdrawal in the Political Poetry of Berryman and Lowell." In: Suzanne Ferguson (ed.).

Jarrell, Bishop, Lowell, & Co.: Middle-Generation Poets in Context. Knoxville: University of Tennessee Press, 2003. 287 – 302.

STAUB, Michael E. "Black Panthers, New Journalism, and the Rewriting of the Sixties." In: *Representations* 57 (1997): 52 – 72.

SULLIVAN, James. "Investing the Cultural Capital of Robert Lowell." In: *Twentieth Century Literature* 38,2 (1992): 194 – 213.

TAMONY, Peter. "On Gonzo." In: *American Speech* 58,1 (1983): 73 – 75.

THOMPSON, Hunter S. *Hell's Angels: A Strange and Terrible Saga.* New York: Ballantine Books, 1996.

– *Fear and Loathing: On the Campaign Trail '72.* New York: Warner Books, 1983.

– *Fear and Loathing in America: The Brutal Odyssey of an Outlaw Journalist, 1968 – 1976.* Edited by Douglas Brinkley. New York: Simon & Schuster, 2000.

VEITCH, Jonathan. "'Moondust in the Prowling Eye': The 'History' Poems of Robert Lowell." In: *Contemporary Literature* 33,3 (1992): 458 – 79.

VETTER, Craig. "Playboy Interview: Hunter Thompson." In: Anita Thompson (ed.). *Ancient Gonzo Wisdom: Interviews with Hunter S. Thompson.* Cambridge: Da Capo, 2009. 31 – 56.

WALLINGFORD, Katharine T. "Robert Lowell's Poetry of Repetition." In: *American Literature* 57,3 (1985): 424 – 33.

WHITFIELD, Stephen J. "Richard Nixon as a Comic Figure." In: *American Quarterly* 37,1 (1985): 114 – 32.

WILLIAMSON, Alan. *Pity the Monsters: The Political Vision of Robert Lowell.* New Haven/ London: Yale University Press, 1974.

WOLFE, Tom. "The New Journalism." In: Tom Wolfe and E.W. Johnson (eds.). *The New Journalism: with an Anthology.* New York et al.: Harper and Row, 1973. 3 – 52.

YENSER, Stephen. *Circle to Circle: The Poetry of Robert Lowell.* Berkeley/London: University of California Press, 1975.

Klaus Scheunemann

Fight or Flight – Fear in War Movies

I.   Introduction

The survival instinct is beyond doubt one of the most powerful mechanisms at work in all creatures. Humans are no exception to this – despite their mental faculties, which allow them to identify such fundamental behavioural patterns and reflect on them. Moreover, humans are more adept at securing their survival than most other species because of their ability to influence their environment and to quickly develop new strategies to achieve their goals. When human beings are confronted with a life-threatening situation the normal reaction is to either fight or flee. Walter Cannon was the first scholar to describe the physiological activities of nerves and glands in animals and humans when these are faced with external danger. Cannon referred to this basic dual stress reaction as "fight-or-flight syndrome".[1]

War is certainly one of the most life-threatening situations a human being can be exposed to. The normal reaction to the large-scale destruction typical of most wars in the modern age would be to flee. Yet the primary active participant in a war, the soldier, who is part of a strict hierarchy, is almost never allowed to act in accordance with his survival instinct. Instead of preserving his life and health by getting away from danger, the soldier is supposed (and ordered, of course) to stand and fight for something beyond his own person. Fear, therefore, is perhaps the emotion most intimately connected to war.

It is surprising, then, that the depiction of fear has not been among the most prominent features of war movies. Instead, concepts like duty, glory, camaraderie and heroism have been reiterated in classic war movies. Of course one has to keep in mind in this context that war movies are not necessarily produced to provide the audience with an accurate picture of what a real war is like.[2] They are

---

1 Cf. ZIMBARDO, Philip G. and Richard J. GERRIG. *Psychologie*. Translated by Siegfried Hoppe-Graff and Irma Engel. Berlin et al.: Springer, 1999 [1996]. 370.
2 Some filmmakers may try to achieve a mimetic impression of war, of course, for instance

meant to garner support, to commemorate important historical battles – or simply to make a quick buck at the box office.[3] The fact that classic war movies do not dwell on the soldiers' emotions is at least partially due to the predominant concepts of masculinity. Traditionally, fear has not been an emotion compatible with notions of masculinity. Moreover, fear and cowardice may appear to be too closely connected to take the risk of blemishing the memory of war heroes by depicting them as being frightened in the face of danger. This has changed in recent years, however.[4] Many recent movies and TV productions aim at giving war (and especially battle scenes) a more convincing, more authentic look,[5] and this includes the convincing depiction of the emotional state of the main participants.[6] In the following I will try to illustrate this change regarding the

---

Steven Spielberg in *Saving Private Ryan:* "By depicting the horror and brutality of war as truthfully as possible, Spielberg wanted to make a film that veterans could recognise and be moved by. In conversations with veterans, Spielberg was struck by the fact that they universally dismissed the cinematic recreation of war: 'They all said, there were two wars fought, there was our war and there was Hollywood's war'." (HAGGITH, Toby. "D-Day Filming: For Real. A Comparison of 'Truth' and 'Reality' in *Saving Private Ryan* and Combat Film by the British Army's Film and Photography Unit." In: *Film History* 14,3/4 War and Militarism (2002): 332–53, 333.) Spielberg seems to have been successful in this venture for HAGGITH states: "Significantly, and what must have been most gratifying for Spielberg, was the fact that the film was widely endorsed by US veterans. Even servicemen of the current generation were struck by the realism and even truth of the battle scenes in the film" (ibid.). Consequently, the "release of *Saving Private Ryan* is regarded as a landmark in the history of war films, because of the visceral power and brutal realism of its treatment of combat, particularly in the opening 26 minutes which covers the landing of US soldiers on the 'Omaha' sector of the Normandy beachhead." (ibid. 332)

3 More often than not, the making of a war movie is motivated by more than one reason: *The Longest Day,* for example, "was intended to commemorate the approaching twentieth anniversary of the invasion. But the real explanation for Zanuck's interest is evident from a glimpse of Twentieth Century Fox's financial difficulties, particularly the colossal losses associated with *Cleopatra* (U.S., 1960)." (AMBROSE, Stephen E. "*The Longest Day* (U.S., 1962): Blockbuster History." In: John Whiteclay Chambers (ed.). *World War II, Film and History.* New York et al.: Oxford University Press, 1996. 97–106, 99.)

4 One of the questions Robert Brent TOPLIN raises in his paper "Hollywood's D-Day From the Perspective of the 1960s and the 1990s: *The Longest Day* and *Saving Private Ryan*" (*Film & History* 36,2 (2006): 25–29) is "in which way do [the critics' different reactions to the two movies] throw some light on changing attitudes toward war?" (ibid. 25) He states that *Saving Private Ryan* and *The Longest Day* "communicated very different impressions of war and warfare" (ibid. 25).

5 McCOSKER states that "[s]cholarly accounts of the combat film genre often refer to its consistent attempt to present, in ever more detail and traumatic self-identity, the actions and suffering of soldiers in battle as a way of presenting a sense of the experience itself." (McCOSKER, Anthony. "Suffering with Honour: The Visual Brutality of Realism in the Combat Film." In: *Scope* 2 (2005): online, 14 pages. 3)

6 One has to distinguish between what the characters feel and what the viewers are supposed to feel: In war movies, the viewers will not fear for their own lives, no matter how close to reality the chaos of battle is depicted. The utmost a war movie can hope to achieve is to make the audience fear for a character and empathize with the soldiers' emotional state. The horror

representation of fear in war movies drawing upon three different films: *The Longest Day* (1962), *Saving Private Ryan* (1998), and, finally, the German movie *Die Brücke* (1959).

II.   Days of Heroes – *The Longest Day*

The Longest Day, based on the eponymous book by Cornelius Ryan, depicts the landing of the Allied forces in Normandy on the 6th of June, 1944. The movie was meant to be a memorial of this turning point in World War II and boasts an abundance of military hardware, a cast of several dozen international movie stars and the support of dozens of military consultants – most of them actual participants in this battle.[7] Despite its re-writing of historically confirmed incidents for dramatic reasons, the movie tries to convey a more or less accurate picture of the events on this day from a multitude of different perspectives.[8] The soundtrack is one of the features that contribute to the realistic effect produced by *The Longest Day*. In contrast to conventional war movies – for instance *The Horse Soldiers* (1959) and *The Green Berets* (1968), to name just two examples – *The Longest Day* features music only very sparingly. The fighting generally takes place without heroic tunes or dramatic musical themes, which is a departure from earlier movies, in which the heroic character of a battle was usually re-

---

movie, in contrast, aims to induce fear the characters feel in the viewers as well. Fear is the primary emotion in horror movies – to induce a thrill (through fear) is their goal. War movies aim at other things. Individual reactions can, of course, vary a lot, as Simon McBURNEY states in his article "Touching History: Private Ryan and the Filming of War" (*Brick: A Literary Journal* 62 (1999): 24 – 32, 25): "The experience of a film is singular; one is alone. So it was I who was on Omaha beach and it was I who was terrified. This is Mr. Spielberg's intention. As I glanced briefly around the theatre at the faces that surrounded me, they were all flinching at the same moments."

7 Cf. AMBROSE. "*The Longest Day* (U.S., 1962): Blockbuster History." 99 – 100.

8 This attempt at realism succeeded only partially, however: "Darryl Zanuck spent a lot of money trying to obtain authentic-looking airplanes, ships, and tanks for his film, but, with regard to another aspect of authenticity, many critics blasted him for failing to deliver. They noted that *The Longest Day* depicted combat death as rather painless. The sensibilities of critics and audiences in 1962 called for more realistic portrayal of the idea that war is hell and men suffer terribly from it." (TOPLIN. "Hollywood's D-Day from the Perspective of the 1960s and the 1990s: *The Longest Day* and *Saving Private Ryan*." 26) The depiction of death as quick and not particularly bloody is not really Zanuck's fault, however. If the Production Code Administration (the Hollywood film industry's self-censorship office) had had its way, there would have been even fewer dead in *The Longest Day*: "[…] Code administrator Geoffrey Shurlock was concerned about 'what seems to us to be an excessive amount of slaughter in this story.' Shurlock asked that Zanuck and Fox try to avoid the "'blood bath' effect'. […] However, the filmmakers seem to have ignored the comment about excessive slaughter." (LEV, Peter. "Filming *The Longest Day*: Conflicting Interests." In: *Literature – Film Quarterly* 33,4 (2005): 263 – 69, 268)

inforced by means of the soundtrack. In general, music and the soundtrack as a whole are an important tool for creating fear, for instance in horror movies. In war movies, in contrast, the musical score is rarely used to convey fear. Here, the music mainly emphasizes the triumph, drama, tragedy or the sublime nature of a moment.

No matter how realistic *The Longest Day* may appear in comparison to other war movies from that time, the topic of fear is not elaborated on. The soldiers' fear of death or injury is only occasionally alluded to and is in many cases even implemented primarily for the sake of a comic effect, rather than a realistic one. A case in point is a scene in which we see Gert Fröbe as a German soldier who is bringing breakfast in clanking tin cans to the troops defending the coast: when he is slowly becoming aware of the massive Allied invasion fleet, his eyes are getting bigger and bigger. A Frenchman, whose house the soldier passes every morning and who despises Fröbe's character for being a representative of the enemy, is equally surprised by the fleet he sees upon opening the shutters of his bedchamber. Perplexed, the German starts fumbling with his rifle when the Allied bombardment by the battle fleet's main cannons is beginning. With shells exploding right and left, the German is running around confusedly, while the Frenchman is laughing and shouting, heedless of the explosions and the danger to himself.[9] The reaction and look of the bumbling German soldier is clearly meant to make the audience laugh (just like the mad glee displayed by the Frenchman), but viewers will certainly not empathize with the character embodied by Fröbe despite his fear. In this scene, the expression of fear by means of body language and facial expression is clearly used to ridicule a character (as well as the 'shock and awe' German soldiers might have felt when beholding the gigantic Allied fleet). There is another scene later in the movie which also uses fear (or frightened behaviour) as a source of amusement. Here, an agitated American soldier first throws a grenade into a bunker; immediately after this he comes across a troop of German soldiers and gleefully shoots them after springing from cover like a jack-in-the-box. All this is done in fearful excitement, making the US soldier come across as a mischievous boy – again, the effect is primarily comic and aimed at ridiculing the enemy. But, in all fairness, one has to admit that, all in all, the Germans (especially the officers) are portrayed as comparatively competent and sometimes even congenial in *The Longest Day*.[10]

---

9 *The Longest Day*. 1:39,58 – 1:41,12.
10 That German officers are portrayed in a rather impartial way is due to the changed political landscape after the war, as AMBROSE suggests: "By 1962, the war had been over for nearly two decades; West Germany had been rearmed and brought into the NATO alliance to block a possible invasion by the Soviet Union. A larger purpose of the film, thus, was to show reconciliation among the Germans, British, French, and Americans, now acting together

Most of the military characters in this movie behave in a highly professional and courageous way, thus conforming to the ideals reiterated in many older war films. Nearly none of the soldiers displays any obvious signs of fear. Consequently, occasions in which the fear of soldiers is depicted in a serious manner are rare in *The Longest Day* – there are only three instances of this in the entire movie. One of these shows British troops aboard gliders who are approaching a bridge held by Germans, which they are supposed to secure. Only one of the troopers is shown to be trembling with fear so badly that he cannot fasten his helmet-strap. The rest of the troop appears to be indifferent to the danger they are in, which is characteristic of nearly all of the military personnel in *The Longest Day*. All in all, the viewer is left with the impression that the Allied soldiers in this movie do not have to choose between the two options offered by Cannon's 'fight-or-flight syndrome'. They fight without showing any hesitation, and they certainly never flee. There is only one occasion where a soldier is deprived of both of these options – a paratrooper, embodied by comedian Red Buttons, whose parachute gets caught on the church steeple of St. Mère Église. When he is discovered by a German soldier, we are confronted with one of the few really frightened faces in the movie that is not used for a comic effect. One can conclude that fear is not prominent in *The Longest Day*: If a character is shown to be afraid, this is done either for the sake of a comic effect or due to the fact that this character is obviously inexperienced. The average soldier in this movie, to all appearances, does not know fear.[11]

III.   War as a Psychological Challenge – *Saving Private Ryan*

More recent productions, such as *Saving Private Ryan*, present a markedly different picture of the emotional effect war may have on soldiers. Here, fear of death and injury is omnipresent, and the audience is confronted with frightened faces and cowering bodies time and again. This is already apparent as soon as *Saving Private Ryan* shifts from an introductory scene to D-Day; the sequence showing the battle for Omaha Beach has attracted much attention, as Toplin states:

---

against a Communist threat from the east." (AMBROSE. "*The Longest Day* (U.S., 1962): Blockbuster History." 105)

11 This connects to TOPLIN's statement that "*The Longest Day* is essentially information-driven" while, as will be seen below, "*Saving Private Ryan* is more emotion-driven" (TOPLIN. "Hollywood's D-Day from the Perspective of the 1960s and the 1990s: *The Longest Day* and *Saving Private Ryan*." 29).

More than any other aspect of the movie, critics and audiences focused on the emotional impact of watching the first half-hour of *Ryan*. They sensed the soldiers' fear in
the midst of danger, chaos, and confusion on the beaches. Through abundant use of the
shaky handheld camera, numerous loud and distinct noises, occasional silences, and
shocking imagery, Spielberg gave his movie the appearance of a documentary film shot
at the scene of military action by combat cameramen. The story lacked the heroics in
these opening sequences that might be expected from figures such as John Wayne or
Robert Mitchum in earlier war movies. Men travelling on the Higgins boats vomited
from seasickness and fright; many were cut to ribbons when they charged the beaches.
Others fell quickly in horrible deaths that left mangled torsos and spilled intestines.
Some cried in fear.[12]

In contrast to *The Longest Day*, *Saving Private Ryan* shows nearly every participant in combat to be full of fear – not just the newcomers, but also the
veterans, who mostly fight on bravely but sometimes break down emotionally
once the fighting is done.[13] This is epitomised in Captain Miller (played by Tom
Hanks). The first thing the viewers see of him is his shaking hand – a theme that
is revisited throughout the movie. Despite his constantly trembling hand Captain Miller is portrayed as a highly competent and unflinching officer, and his
men never doubt his courage, although they are concerned when they notice
Miller's hand.[14] This display of constant underlying fear in war throughout

---

12 TOPLIN. "Hollywood's D-Day from the Perspective of the 1960s and the 1990s: *The Longest
    Day* and *Saving Private Ryan*." 27. One can certainly argue that the visual style of war movies
    has changed along with their depiction of the soldiers' psyche – a development of which
    Saving Private Ryan was not the starting point but arguably the culmination, as Sarah
    HAGELIN observes: "At the time of the film's release, film critic Neal Gabler pointed out that
    Platoon, Apocalypse Now, and *The Deer Hunter* are each as violent and uncompromising as
    Ryan" (103); consequently, "Vietnam war films made during the decades between Vietnam
    and the end of the Cold War – such as *The Deer Hunter* (Cimino 1978), *Apocalypse Now*
    (Coppola 1979), *Platoon* (Stone 1986), and *Full Metal Jacket* (Kubrick 1986) [already] pro-
    vide audiences with an image of combat as dehumanizing and a new iconography of the
    American soldier as a psychological casualty of war." (HAGELIN, Sarah. "Bleeding Bodies and
    Post-Cold War Politics: *Saving Private Ryan* and the Gender of Vulnerability." In: Karen
    Randell and Sean Redmond (eds.). *The War Body on Screen*. New York: Continuum, 2008.
    102–19, 102.)
13 Especially the opening battle – the storming of Omaha Beach by US-troops – has been
    commented on for its visceral, brutal, unflinching depiction of violence, affecting the audi-
    ence by its hyper-realism. Michael HAMMOND states that this realistic depiction of battle "is
    an attempt to create an affect that literally approximates shell shock in order to memorialise
    'what those kids did for us' but also to make manifest those experiences for the audience so
    that the catharsis of the experience is not only the soldiers' but also theirs. This intent was
    successfully conveyed to the press on the film's release, mobilising popular conceptions of
    shell shock or the more contemporary term post-traumatic stress disorder." (HAMMOND,
    Michael. "*Saving Private Ryan*'s 'Special Affect'." In: Yvonne Tasker (ed.). *Action and Ad-
    venture Cinema*. London/New York: Routledge, 2004. 153–66, 158.)
14 Peter BÜRGER, for instance, argues: "Die vorzügliche Identifikationsfigur Captain Miller
    (Tom Hanks) fühlt sich im Krieg nicht am richtigen Ort und wird durchgehend von einem

Saving Private Ryan is indicative of a change regarding notions of masculinity: In many earlier war movies, the heroes apparently simply felt no fear (or at least they never showed it); in more recent productions, the soldiers are allowed to be afraid. One can even argue that overcoming this fear in order to accomplish one's mission is the new mark of heroism and masculinity.[15] That fear is taken seriously in *Saving Private Ryan* can be inferred from the fact that this emotional state is never used for comic effects. Even when a German soldier, in deadly fear, makes a fool of himself by jabbering everything American he can think of, this is definitely not funny. In this respect, Spielberg's movie clearly departs from productions such as *The Longest Day*.

The convincing depiction of fear in war films depends mainly on the actors' performance. In contrast to a novel, in which a narrator may describe the fact that a character is frightened, audiovisual media mostly have to convey fear without explicit descriptions. Moreover, in contrast to other filmic genres, such as horror movies, war films hardly ever make use of the soundtrack (including music) to externalise the characters' emotional state. Thus, the actors' facial expressions, their body language as well as the pitch of their voice are the main vehicles for letting the viewers know that the characters are afraid. This works for individuals as well as for groups, as the following scene from *Saving Private Ryan* illustrates: a group of American soldiers are on their way through an embattled French town; suddenly, a wall, which has been weakened by the fighting, collapses, revealing a squad of German troopers, obviously taking a break from the fighting. Both groups are totally surprised by being all of a sudden eye to eye with the enemy without any cover. They quickly train their weapons on each other but refrain from shooting. In this life-threatening situation, everybody is under enormous stress, veterans and rookies alike. Flight is not really an option in this instance; thus, Americans and Germans resort to

---

unerklärlichen Angstzittern der rechten Hand geplagt: 'Jeder Mann, den ich töte, bringt mich weiter von Zuhause weg!'" (BÜRGER, Peter. *Kino der Angst: Terror, Krieg und Staatskunst aus Hollywood*. Stuttgart: Schmetterling, 2007 [2005]. 203) According to BÜRGER, Miller is not the only veteran character that shows signs of fear: "Der 'begnadete' Scharfschütze des US-Sondertrupps leitet jeden Schuss mit präzis gewählten Psalmversen ein. Doch sonst dienen Gebet, Rosenkranz und Kreuz-Talisman im Film nirgends der Überhöhung. Sie sind Ausdruck purer Angst." (ibid.)

15 HAGELIN detects at least a partial shift in the depiction of masculinity in *Saving Private Ryan*: "The instability [created] around the gendered meaning of vulnerability threatens dominant cultural ideas about gender and war because it challenges an important assumption that even most antiwar films maintain: that society sends the strong (able-bodied men) to war in order to protect the weak or vulnerable (women, children, and nonmasculine men). [...] If we admit that men are just as vulnerable as women to the gunshot wounds and bomb attacks that constitute much of modern warfare, we undermine this sacrificial logic." (HAGELIN. "Bleeding Bodies and Post-Cold War Politics: *Saving Private Ryan* and the Gender of Vulnerability." 103–04.)

threatening each other, while clearly being afraid of shooting first because the retaliation is bound to be lethal.[16]

Although *Saving Private Ryan* stresses the fact that everybody participating in the war is bound to feel fear, the distinction between combat veterans and rookies is still paid attention to – namely in the person of Corporal Upham. Upham, a clerk without any combat experience, is recruited by Captain Miller as a translator. In the course of the movie it is made quite clear that Miller and his men have by now steeled themselves psychologically against the emotional stress of war at least to a certain degree by means of their war experience. Upham, in contrast, has no 'armour' of this sort and is visibly shaken by much of what he sees. At the end of the movie, Upham is forced to participate in the desperate defence of a bridge against superior German forces. This battle is his baptism of fire, and at first he seems to fail, freezing in terror while his comrades are fighting for their lives and losing. Thanks to the performance of actor Jeremy Davies, Upham's fear is portrayed in a very convincing way in this scene – and is certainly far from being understood as despicable 'cowardice'. In the end, Upham manages to overcome his fear and challenges the enemy, thereby taking his place as a 'real' soldier and reiterating a standard pattern one can identify in many war movies. In the character of Corporal Upham *Saving Private Ryan* provides the viewers with an identification figure whose actions, reactions and fears are likely to be very accessible because he is new to war.

While one would presumably search in vain for a character like Upham portrayed in a convincing fashion in earlier war movies, the topic of fear in battle is certainly not an invention of modern audiovisual depictions of war. Traditionally, fear as a motif can be found in anti-war movies and novels at least as far back as Stephen Crane's novel *The Red Badge of Courage* (1895), which focuses on a young soldier who runs away in his first battle but later on finds the courage to rejoin the fight. Many war films have an inherent potential to convey messages critical of war in general or at least of certain elements of warfare. Neither *The Longest Day* nor *Saving Private Ryan* were meant to be anti-war films: the former was meant to commemorate the heroic Allied soldiers at this turning point of World War II; the latter admittedly throws a critical light on what war does to the soldiers and raises several ethical questions, but never seriously challenges the idea that war (or, at least, the Allied invasion that is depicted) is ethically justified. In contrast to these two movies, the German production *Die Brücke* is definitely meant to be an anti-war film. This as well as the fact that the topic of war tends to be approached differently in Germany for well-known historical reasons is crucial for understanding the prominence of fear in this particular

---

16 *Saving Private Ryan*. 55,20 – 56,15.

movie – despite its having been produced in 1959 and, thus, long before today's widespread acceptance of depicting soldiers experiencing fear.

IV.   War's Ugly Face – *Die Brücke*

Die Brücke focuses on a group of young German boys who are drafted right before the end of World War II. Indoctrinated by party propaganda and endowed with strict notions of masculinity, most of them are eager to fight.[17] Their attitude towards fear is demonstrated in a scene early in the movie in which two of the boys talk about this topic:

> 'Sag mal, Hans. Damals bei den Bombenangriffen…'
> 'Ja, was denn?'
> 'Hast du da Angst gehabt?'
> 'Na, und wie!'
> 'Was, du warst richtig feige?'
> 'Na klar.'
> 'Und das gibst du einfach so zu?'
> 'Warum denn nicht?'
> 'Das find ich toll!'[18]

As can be seen in this dialogue, fear is regarded as an expression of cowardice, and therefore unmanliness – a notion that was ubiquitous in the nineteenth century as well as in the first half of the twentieth. One day before American forces reach their town, the boys are drafted and begin their basic training. Because of several unlucky coincidences, they are left to defend a bridge in their hometown without any supervision. This defence is totally pointless, as the bridge is supposed to be blown up anyway. Yet the boys do not know about this, and the majority of them impatiently wait for the arrival of the enemy to prove themselves as men and soldiers.[19] When the Americans arrive, however, flam-

---

17 Reinhold T. SCHÖFFEL states: "Wickis Film folgt dem Roman von Manfred Gregor, der als 30jähriger Autor seine eigenen Erlebnisse niedergeschrieben hat. Gregors Roman und Wickis Film halten nicht nur die Atmosphäre der letzten Kriegstage überzeugend fest, sondern zeichnen auch das Porträt einer Generation, die in ihrem Denken Opfer der Nazi-Ideologie wurde." (SCHÖFFEL, Reinhold T. "*Die Brücke.*" In: Alfred Holighaus (ed.). *Der Filmkanon: 35 Filme, die Sie kennen müssen.* Bonn: Bundeszentrale für Politische Bildung, 2005. 120–25, 123). Klaus KANZOG interprets the movie as "psychologische Studie [...], als Psychogramm, das den Wahn der Jungen, sich als Männer und Helden zu bewähren, zu der Zeit in Beziehung setzt, in der sie aufgewachsen sind." (KANZOG, Klaus. "'Warten auf das entscheidende Wort': Pubertät und Heldenwahn in Bernhard Wickis *Die Brücke* (1959)." In: Klaus Kanzog (ed.). *Der erotische Diskurs: Filmische Zeichen und Argumente.* München: Schaudig, Bauer, Ledig, 1989. 127–55, 127.)
18 *Die Brücke.* 21,43–22,08.
19 The fact that the viewers know that the bridge is about to be demolished while the boys are

boyant behaviour quickly gives way to mortal fear. Again, as in *Saving Private Ryan*, the fear the characters experience is exclusively conveyed by means of acting, and the young actors evidently are up to the challenge. The boys' initial willingness to fight is quickly diminished once the danger to their lives has become apparent to them and the first of them have died. But their urge to flee is checked, partly by their comrades, partly by outdated notions of masculinity – which is one of the issues the film criticises.[20] It can safely be said that the intense fear and the emotional breakdown these boys are put through by society are the main argument against war provided in *Die Brücke*.

V.   Conclusion

In general, one can observe that soldiers' fears were far less prominent in older movies than in more recent ones, but this is true only with regard to conventional war films – in anti-war movies the depiction of fear has always been an integral part. At least since the 1980s, however, it has become a staple of war movies, too, to depict fear among soldiers as a common and serious issue. No recent war

---

not aware of this is one of the elements employed by Wicki to bring home the futility and madness of the battle ahead (cf. SCHÜTTE, Oliver. *Die Kunst des Drehbuchlesens*. Konstanz: UVK Verlagsgesellschaft, 2009 [1999]. 172).

20 While *Die Brücke* was generally highly praised for its political admonition as well as for the way the indoctrination of the German youth is condemned, Rolf SCHÖRKEN criticises the message and validity of the film. He marks the depicted naiveté and zeal of the boys, just a week before the end of the war, as highly improbable (SCHÖRKEN, Rolf. *Die Niederlage als Generationenerfahrung. Jugendliche nach dem Zusammenbruch der NS-Herrschaft*. Weinheim and München: Juventa, 2004. 73). He states that too much dramatic leeway has been exerted by the creators just to hammer their message home (ibid. 75). SCHÖRKEN states: "Der chancenlose Kampf schlecht bewaffneter Jugendlicher gegen eine erdrückende Übermacht wird aus der Charakteristik der Jungen heraus entwickelt und nicht aus dem blinden und brutalen Zwang der Militärmaschinerie und des politischen Systems, aus dem es kein Entrinnen gab. So wird den Jungen eine Art Mitschuld an ihrem eigenen Untergang aufgeladen, denn wenn sie nicht so wider alle Vernunft gehandelt hätten und wenn nicht noch ein paar Zufälle dazu gekommen wären [...], dann wäre das alles nicht geschehen. Genau das ist die falsche Botschaft, wenn man mißbrauchte und verratene Jugend darstellen will. [...] Gerade weil der Tod der Jungen aus ihren verschiedenen Wesenszügen entwickelt wird, werden die Zwänge, denen sie unterschiedslos unterworfen sind, unwichtig. [...] Die *politische* Aussage hätte lauten müssen: Der Tod der Jugendlichen war weder eine Sache ihrer eigenen psychischen Verfassung noch eine Sache des Zufalls. Vielmehr hat das Regime selbst, d. h. die nationalsozialistische ebenso wie die militärische Führung, diesen Einsatz der Halbwüchsigen in aussichtsloser Situation gewollt [...]." (ibid. 76–77). He concludes: "Indem die Aufmerksamkeit auf individuelle Unterschiede und gruppendynamische Prozesse gerichtet wird, verlagert man die Frage nach der Verantwortung auf einen Nebenschauplatz. Man entlastet in letzter Konsequenz die politische und militärische Führung, die man eigentlich anklagen wollte." (ibid. 78) SCHÖRKEN's reasoning is convincing, but does not invalidate the impact of the way in which the youths' fear is depicted in the movie.

movie or TV series that wants to be taken seriously can do without references to fear, as countless examples prove: The TV series *Band of Brothers* (2001) and *The Pacific* (2010) as well as the movies *Flags of Our Fathers* (2006) and *Letters from Iwo Jima* (2006) are obvious cases in point. This shift concerning the attitude towards fear among soldiers is partially due to changed notions of masculinity. Apparently the existence of fear in life-threatening situations (such as war) is now taken for granted in Western societies, and men are no longer expected to be more or less immune to fear.[21] Fear is not denied in modern war movies any-more; instead, overcoming fear and fighting despite being frightened seems to be the new distinction of soldiers and the new definition of heroism. To this end, many recent productions provide at least one young and inexperienced char-acter who has to conquer his fear before he can become a 'real' soldier. This can be seen as a kind of 'coming-of-age ritual', which ultimately reiterates an ancient idea: since the beginning of written history and probably long before then war was considered the primary proving ground for men. Perhaps it might be a good idea to keep an eye on upcoming war movies in order to be alerted to future changes of notions of masculinity.

References

AMBROSE, Stephen E. "*The Longest Day* (U.S., 1962): Blockbuster History." In: John Whiteclay Chambers (ed.). *World War II, Film and History.* New York et al.: Oxford University Press, 1996. 97–106.

ANNAKIN, Ken, Andrew MARTON, Bernhard WICKI, Darryl F. ZANUCK, dirs. *The Longest Day.* 20th Century Fox, 1962.

BÜRGER, Peter. *Kino der Angst: Terror, Krieg und Staatskunst aus Hollywood.* Stuttgart: Schmetterling, 2007 [2005].

HAGELIN, Sarah. "Bleeding Bodies and Post-Cold War Politics: *Saving Private Ryan* and the Gender of Vulnerability." In: Karen Randell and Sean Redmond (eds.). *The War Body on Screen.* New York: Continuum, 2008. 102–19.

HAGGITH, Toby. "D-Day Filming: For Real. A Comparison of 'Truth' and 'Reality' in *Saving Private Ryan* and Combat Film by the British Army's Film and Photography Unit." In: *Film History* 14, 3/4 War and Militarism (2002): 332–53.

HAMMOND, Michael. "*Saving Private Ryan*'s 'Special Affect'." In: Yvonne Tasker (ed.). *Action and Adventure Cinema.* London/New York: Routledge, 2004. 153–66.

---

21 Movies generally are a fairly good indicator of changes in attitude. Catherine KODAT gets at least this right in her paper "Saving Private Property: Steven Spielberg's American Dream Works" (*Representations* 71 (2000): 77–105): "The work of the Frankfurt School particularly, and contemporary cultural studies more generally, has helped to establish the commonplace in analyses of historical representations – be they literary, cinematic, pictorial, or histor-iographic – that all such representations are more about the moments of their production than about the period they purportedly represent." (ibid. 79)

KANZOG, Klaus. "'Warten auf das entscheidende Wort': Pubertät und Heldenwahn in Bernhard Wickis *Die Brücke* (1959)." In: Klaus Kanzog (ed.). *Der erotische Diskurs: Filmische Zeichen und Argumente.* München: Schaudig, Bauer, Ledig, 1989. 127–55.

KODAT, Catherine. "Saving Private Property: Steven Spielberg's American Dream Works." In: *Representations* 71 (2000): 77–105.

LEV, Peter. "Filming *The Longest Day:* Conflicting Interests." In: *Literature-Film Quarterly* 33,4 (2005): 263–69.

MCBURNEY, Simon. "Touching History: Private Ryan and the Filming of War." In: *Brick: A Literary Journal* 62 (1999): 24–32.

MCCOSKER, Anthony. "Suffering with Honour: The Visual Brutality of Realism in the Combat Film." In: *Scope* 2 (2005): online, 14 pages.

SCHÖFFEL, Reinhold T. "*Die Brücke.*" In: Alfred Holighaus (ed.). *Der Filmkanon: 35 Filme, die Sie kennen müssen.* Bonn: Bundeszentrale für Politische Bildung, 2005. 120–25.

SCHÖRKEN, Rolf. *Die Niederlage als Generationenerfahrung. Jugendliche nach dem Zusammenbruch der NS-Herrschaft.* Weinheim/München: Juventa, 2004.

SCHÜTTE, Oliver. *Die Kunst des Drehbuchlesens.* Konstanz: UVK Verlagsgesellschaft, 2009 [1999].

SPIELBERG, Steven, dir. *Saving Private Ryan.* Dreamworks, 1998.

TOPLIN, Robert Brent. "Hollywood's D-Day from the Perspective of the 1960s and the 1990s: *The Longest Day* and *Saving Private Ryan.*" In: *Film & History* 36,2 (2006): 25–29.

WICKI, Bernhard, dir. *Die Brücke.* Fono Film, 1959.

ZIMBARDO, Philip G. and Richard J. GERRIG. *Psychologie.* Translated by Siegfried Hoppe-Graff and Irma Engel. Berlin et al.: Springer, 1999 [1996].

Christian Knöppler

Remaking Fear: The Cultural Function of Horror Film Remakes

Fear is what drives the horror genre. As Noël Carroll argued in his *Philosophy of Horror*, "[t]he cross-art, cross-media genre of horror takes its title from the emotion it characteristically or rather ideally promotes; this emotion constitutes the identifying mark of horror."[1] Horror narratives, whether fiction or films, are designed to evoke this affect of intense fear in their audience, using a variety of techniques, and direct it towards monsters, whether human or inhuman, natural or supernatural. These monsters are not simply dangerous, they are impure and unnatural, they disturb the order of things, and they go beyond categories of understanding, which distinguishes them from the threats in other suspense genres.[2] This quality of disturbance is the key, as the simple presence of monsters doesn't create horror on its own.[3]

The audience of horror, in what seems like a paradox, wants to be scared, or at least to experience from a safe distance the thrill of danger. The question why there is pleasure to be found in the normally deeply unpleasant experience of fear has been the subject of much discussion among scholars.[4] Given the production habits of the horror film industry, however, another question arises: why do we seem to revisit the same fears and the same monsters again and again? In the following article, I will argue that constant remaking of horror film classics is not merely a nuisance and a money-making strategy (which it also is), but integral to the cultural function of the horror genre. By updating and reframing their monstrous threats, horror films maintain venues of negotiating cultural fears.

---

1 CARROLL, Noël. *The Philosophy of Horror. Or: Paradoxes of the Heart.* New York: Routledge, 1990. 14.
2 CARROLL. *The Philosophy of Horror.* 23; 34.
3 CARROLL. *The Philosophy of Horror.* 16; 50.
4 See, for instance, TUDOR, Andrew. "Why Horror? The Peculiar Pleasures of a Popular Genre." In: Mark Jancovich (ed.). *Horror. The Film Reader.* London: Routledge, 2002. 47–55.

I.   Scare Me Again

Horror film, and specifically the American, Hollywood-produced horror movie, is infamous as a genre characterized by repetitions, whether in the shape of sequels or remakes. A successful film is likely to be followed by sequels, and current horror franchises like the *Saw* series reliably present a new installment each year. When a chain of sequels runs out of steam, the film may be remade instead, with a new version of the same title. John Carpenter's *Halloween* (1978) was followed by seven sequels between 1981 and 2002, then there was a remake in 2007, then a sequel to that remake for a total of ten films, and the next one is in production as of this writing. The similar *Friday 13ᵗʰ* series followed the same pattern, with ten sequels from 1981 to 2003[5] and a remake in 2009. Another example that shaped its genre and still enjoys attention in academic circles is George Romero's cycle of zombie films and their legacy. Romero not only made six zombie films in his ". . . of the Dead" series, but his first three films – *Night of the Living Dead* (1968), *Dawn of the Dead* (1978) and *Day of the Dead* (1985) – also got individual remakes in 1990, 2004 and 2008, respectively.[6] Those remakes are not connected to each other at all, as they were made by entirely different directors and companies.

Frankly, there remains hardly a classic horror film that has not been continued or remade at some point, and even small, independently produced features like *The Blair Witch Project* or *Paranormal Activity* are snatched up for sequels if they attract enough attention. At the same time, foreign horror films (that is, those not produced in the USA) are remade quickly and frequently enough to form their own genre, most notably the wave of remakes of Asian films that came and passed after *The Ring* (2002).

While sequels and remakes form two sides of the same process of re-production, the remake may be the more interesting case for analysis. A remake, in a nutshell, is a newly produced version of a previously realized film. As such, it walks a line between honoring its predecessor and replacing or even erasing it from cultural memory, an ambiguous relationship that Leitch calls a dynamic of acknowledgement and disavowal. As Leitch explains,

> [...] remakes by definition establish their value by invoking earlier texts whose potency they simultaneously valorize and deny through a series of rhetorical maneuvers de-

---

5 The count includes the crossover with the equally prolific *Nightmare on Elm Street* series, *Freddy vs. Jason* (2003).

6 In fact, *Night of the Living Dead* was remade again (in 3D) in 2006, but had a very limited release and gained little attention. "Night of the Living Dead 3D." *boxofficemojo.com* <http://www.boxofficemojo.com/movies/?id=nightofthelivingdead3d.htm> (accessed June 30, 2011).

signed at once to reflect their intimacy with these earlier texts and to distance themselves from their flaws.[7]

Furthermore, as they are produced either decades after or in a different country
than their predecessors, remakes aim for new audiences in an entirely different
socio-political situation. The seemingly simple act of repetition therefore requires the complex negotiation of multiple texts and audiences. While some of
the challenges and opportunities involved in remaking may apply to sequels as
well, the mere expansion of a given narrative in the shape of a sequel is a less
drastic step than its rewriting in the shape of a remake.

Even though remakes, also labeled 'reboots' or 'reimaginings' by film studios,
are well established as a type of film, they are commonly met with a distinct lack
of appreciation. Film critics generally do not hold the practice in high regard,
instead criticizing it as a result of Hollywood's commercial rather than artistic
interest and as evidence of a terminal lack of ideas.[8] Similarly, dedicated fans
regard most remakes as an affront to film classics, even reducing the value of the
original films by merit of their very existence.[9] Of course, there are exceptions,
especially when well-regarded directors are involved, or a relatively unknown or
flawed film is remade. Martin Scorcese, for instance, received positive reviews
for his 1991 remake of *Cape Fear*, and several Oscar awards for *The Departed*, a
remake of the Hong Kong drama *Infernal Affairs*. Despite these exceptions,
remakes are still seen as lesser fare or "comfort food" for a less demanding
audience.[10]

The above criticism is based on an aesthetic that values perceived innovation
over the repetition of familiar patterns, and views art and industry as dichot-
omies.[11] Academic studies dealing with different questions and approaches,
however, have discovered remakes as subjects for study whose obviously and
consciously repetitive quality sheds light on various cultural processes, whether

---

7 LEITCH, Thomas. "Twice-Told Tales: Disavowal and the Rhetoric of the Remake." In: Jennifer
   Forrest and Leonard R. Koos (eds.). *Dead Ringers: The Remake in Theory and Practice.*
   Albany: State University of New York Press, 2002. 53.
8 FORREST, Jennifer and Leonard R. Koos. "Reviewing Remakes: An Introduction." In: Jen-
   nifer Forrest and Leonard R. Koos (eds.). *Dead Ringers: The Remake in Theory and Practice.*
   Albany: State University of New York Press, 2002. 2; VEREVIS, Constantine. *Film Remakes.*
   Edinburgh: Edinburgh University Press, 2006. 4.
9 As a striking example of this attitude, see Dave WHITE's article "I Spit on Your Horror Movie
   Remakes, Sequels: A Horror Fan Laments the State of One of His Favorite Genres." The title
   of the article quotes the title of the 1978 film *I Spit on Your Grave*, thus underlining the
   author's fan credibility and outrage. (WHITE, Dave. "I Spit on Your Horror Movie Remakes,
   Sequels: A Horror Fan Laments the State of One of His Favorite Genres." MSNBC.com. Oct
   25, 2005. <http://www.msnbc.msn.com/id/9805698/> (accessed March 22, 2010).)
10 WHITE. "I Spit on Your Horror Movie Remakes, Sequels."
11 ECO, Umberto. "Innovation and Repetition: Between Modern and Post-Modern Aesthetics."
   In: *Daedalus* 114,4. The Moving Image (1985): 161–84, 161.

by revealing the workings of commercial film production or documenting social changes between iterations.[12] Divorced from concerns of artistic value, the remake thus becomes intriguing as a meditation on the continuing historical relevance of a particular narrative, concerned with "unfinished cultural business, unrefinable and perhaps finally unassimilable material that remains part of the cultural dialogue."[13]

Judging by the number of publications over the last decade, the academic study of remakes has only recently gained popularity, and still remains insufficient considering the overwhelming number of remakes produced every year. English language studies usually refer back to Druxman's *Make It Again, Sam* (1975), which laid some groundwork for the discussion of remakes, but admittedly catered more to film buffs than scholars.[14] More recently, the amount and quality of research picked up with anthologies like *Play It Again Sam: Retakes on Remakes* (1998) and *Dead Ringers* (2002), and with Constantine Verevis publishing the most comprehensive treatment of the phenomenon to date in his monograph *Film Remakes* (2006).[15] Nevertheless, the film remake is by no means an easily defined subject.

II.   Defining the Film Remake

Although, or rather because the term 'remake' enjoys widespread use in popular, academic and industrial contexts, there are serious disagreements about its boundaries. The initial definition of "a newly produced version of a previously realized film" still leaves the question of what exactly makes a film a new version of another. The narrowest definition requires a completely new production, consciously drawing on an earlier film, which is also legally sanctioned by the use of the same title.[16] The producers need to have obtained the rights to the previous film and announce that fact in the credits.

---

12 VEREVIS. *Film Remakes*. 3; FORREST and KOOS. "Reviewing Remakes: An Introduction." 4–5; HORTON, Andrew and Stuart Y. MCDOUGAL. "Introduction." In: Andrew Horton and Stuart Y. McDougal (eds.). *Play It Again, Sam. Retakes on Remakes*. Berkeley: University of California Press, 1998. 1–11, 6.

13 BRAUDY, Leo. "Afterword: Rethinking Remakes." In: Andrew Horton and Stuart Y. McDougal (eds.). *Play It Again, Sam. Retakes on Remakes*. Berkeley: University of California Press, 1998. 327–34, 331.

14 DRUXMAN, Michael B. *Make It Again, Sam. A Survey of Movie Remakes*. South Brunswick: A.S. Barnes, 1975. 10.

15 HORTON, Andrew and Stuart Y. MCDOUGAL (eds.). *Play It Again, Sam. Retakes on Remakes*. Berkeley: University of California Press, 1998; FORREST, Jennifer and Leonard R. KOOS (eds.). *Dead Ringers: The Remake in Theory and Practice*. Albany: State University of New York Press, 2002; VEREVIS. *Film Remakes*.

16 LEITCH. "Twice-Told Tales: Disavowal and the Rhetoric of the Remake." 38.

However, this requirement excludes a number of films that are commonly considered to be remakes due to their significant similarities to other films, but fail to acknowledge any sources. Allegations of plagiarism, or 'rip-off' in more colloquial terms, are not uncommon in film criticism and fandom.[17] At the same time, the narrow definition still includes Druxman's category of "non-remakes", which covers films of the same title whose content has no relation to the previous film whatsoever.[18] This opens up a key problem in the discussion of remakes: If titles are insufficient as a marker, how do we measure the number of elements that have to be repeated for a film to count as a remake?

Druxman understood remakes simply as recycled scripts, which means that a script from the studio archives is altered and rewritten for a new production.[19] Therefore, a remake should be the same story (sequence of events) packaged in a new narrative discourse (presentation of events). Yet, determining whether or not the same sequence of events is present is highly subjective and cannot work as an absolute measure,[20] especially considering Hollywood's use of standardized genre stories.[21] The distinction between a story that repeats genre conventions and one that repeats a specific film is by no means clear.

Furthermore, several studies use broader definitions of 'remaking'. For instance, a remake could precisely reproduce the style and mood of the previous film, making it recognizable as a derivation without notable parallels in terms of story.[22] Horton and McDougal go further by suggesting an extension of the term remake to cover other intertextual forms. Their definition calls the remake a "special pattern which re-represents and explains at a different time and through varying perceptions, previous narratives and experiences".[23] Given the vagueness of "narratives and experiences", the number of potential remakes would multiply under this definition.

Others view adaptations simply as remakes that occur in a different medium, as Lukas does in his discussion of films based on videogames.[24] Likewise, Perkins

---

17 As a prominent example, Sergio Leone's western *For a Fistful of Dollars* (1964) was accused of plagiarizing Akira Kurosawa's *Yojimbo* (1961), leading to a lawsuit and settlement. Today, DVD versions of *Yojimbo* point out the relation to Leone's more famous film on the box for advertising purposes (cf. VEREVIS. *Film Remakes*. 89).

18 DRUXMAN. *Make It Again, Sam*. 15.

19 DRUXMAN. *Make It Again, Sam*. 13.

20 VEREVIS. *Film Remakes*. 29.

21 FORREST and KOOS. "Reviewing Remakes: An Introduction." 17.

22 VEREVIS. *Film Remakes*. 28.

23 HORTON and McDOUGAL. "Introduction." 2.

24 LUKAS, Scott A. "Horror Video Game Remakes and the Question of Medium: Remaking *Doom*, *Silent Hill*, and *Resident Evil*." In: Scott A. Lukas and John Marmysz (eds.). *Fear, Cultural Anxiety and Transformation: Horror, Science Fiction and Fantasy Films Remade.* Lanham: Lexington, 2009. 221–42, 222. In contrast, Leitch distinguishes 'readaptations' from 'true remakes'. While still counted under the broad category of remakes, a readaptation

concludes that sequels, too, can be a type of remake.[25] While neither of these claims is without merit, they also stretch the meaning of the term 'remake'. Summing up too many phenomena under the label 'remake' runs the risk of it becoming an unnecessary synonym for larger processes and concepts. Maes' (purposefully vague) definition – "In order to be called a remake, a movie must in some relevant way be comparable to a previous movie"[26] – demonstrates this dilemma by turning remake into an expression of general intertextuality.[27] Therefore, in order for the term to serve a useful purpose in analysis, we need to differentiate the film remake and remaking as wider processes of repetition and reproduction.

Some of the issues with the term 'remake' derive from its origin. As Braudy explains, "'[r]emake' is a term imported to academia from movie journalism and the movie business".[28] Therefore, any attempts to theorize the remake redefine a term from the discourse of industrial film production, which has also gained new meanings in popular discourses. This does not make the term ineligible for academic uses; on the contrary, but we need to keep the industry that coined it, and that keeps using it, in mind.

In the end, the exact limits of the remake are drawn arbitrarily. "Identification of exactly which elements shall count as fundamental units of narrative [...] becomes [...] a theoretical construct", as Verevis points out.[29] The construction of intertextual relations is thus an act of interpretation, "limited and relative" to one's "interpretive grid".[30]

The outer limits of the remake may be blurry, but there is no disagreement about the center: the conscious, official, legally sanctioned remake that reproduces a previous film without being a sequel. Therefore, this type of film promises to be a solid starting point for the discussion of remakes.

---

actually ignores the previous film and goes back to the common literary source. (LEITCH. "Twice-Told Tales: Disavowal and the Rhetoric of the Remake." 45.)

25 PERKINS, Claire. "Remaking and the Film Trilogy: Whit Stillman's Authorial Triptych." In: *Velvet Light Trap* 61 (2008): 14–25, 15.

26 MAES, Hans. "A Celestial Taxonomy of Remakes?" In: *Cinemascope* 2 (2005): 7. <http://www.madadayo.it/Cinemascope_archive/cinema-scope.net/Numero%20due/articolo05.html> (accessed April 14, 2010).

27 For an extended discussion of remaking and intertextuality, and an overview of research on the topic, see KNÖPPLER, Christian. "Intertextualität und das Filmremake." In: Marion Grein, Miguel Souza and Svenja Völkel (eds.). *Polyphonie, Intertextualität, Intermedialität: Ein Interdisziplinäres Forschungsfeld.* Aachen: Shaker, 2010. 113–46.

28 BRAUDY. "Afterword: Rethinking Remakes." 327.

29 VEREVIS. *Film Remakes.* 29.

30 Frow, quoted from: VEREVIS. *Film Remakes.* 29. Braudy makes a similar point: "The remake – like its close kin, the adaptation and the sequel – is a species of interpretation." BRAUDY. "Afterword: Rethinking Remakes." 327.

III.   Horror and Remakes: A Match Made in Hell?

Like remakes in general, horror remakes enjoy a rather bad reputation among film fans and critics alike. Yet, much to the frustration of both groups, these films keep getting made and surprisingly enough, they keep finding an audience. Even though some may dispute this claim on the basis of numbers, the perception that horror produces most remakes, along with most sequels, remains widespread.[31] So why is it that horror stands out?

The obvious response to any discussion of the remake phenomenon is to point to the commercial reasons behind remaking, and horror remakes are no exception. Film studios and the corporations that own them aim to make money, and from a business perspective, remakes (like sequels) make perfect sense. Much of the costly development work is already done with the first film, since a script and characters are already developed, and there is a recognizable brand in place, which cuts down the need for promotion and, hopefully, leaves film studios with a readymade core audience. This all adds up to a fairly safe investment, and there is no denying that film production depends on these concerns. Still, as these factors apply to remake production in all genres, they do not explain why horror films in particular are so prone to repetition.

It may seem odd that a genre that depends on shock and disturbance, which in turn rely to some extent on surprise and novelty, would lend itself to such frequent repetitions. It stands to reason that, through experiencing the same scares over and over again, the audience of horror would get a sense of familiarity and even comfort in seeing a tale of terror unfold roughly as expected, perhaps lessening its effect. At the same time, the delivery of particular tropes within a narrow generic frame is a necessary prerequisite for most commercial genre works, and plenty of horror scare tactics work whether the audience sees them coming or not.

The abundance of horror remakes suggests that there is a demand, perhaps a need for them. These films are made because they are profitable, and they are profitable because there are enough people who want to see the same horror films again and again. Therefore, I suggest that these films keep working because they do something for us (that is, their audience). They accomplish something that does not require innovation, but on the contrary, works within a narrow

---

31 AREND, Wolfgang. *Auf der Jagd nach Hexen und Zuschauern. Mediensoziologische Bausteine zu einer Theorie des Remakes am Beispiel von Hexenfilmen.* Mainz: Bender, 2002. 44. Arend's survey rates horror remakes below the wider category of drama remakes. However, non-academic sources like the box office tracking website *boxofficemojo.com* rate horror remakes as the most prolific remake genre. 'Horror Remake' yields 53 results, ahead of 43 for 'Comedy Remake'. "Genres." *boxofficemojo.com* <http://www.boxofficemojo.com/genres/> (accessed June 15, 2011).

frame of repeated tropes. Their continued proliferation suggests that the functions of remaking, as a practice of production, and horror, as a genre, complement each other.

The connection between fear and remaking also occurred to the editors of the anthology *Fear, Cultural Anxiety and Transformation: Horror, Science Fiction and Fantasy Films Remade*. Even though the essays cover more genres, the focus on fear and anxiety is a natural fit for horror. In the introduction, the editors speculate on the repetition of fears, drawing on Aristotle and Kierkegaard: "The desire repeatedly to engage in encounters with fanciful and dreadful characters within the illusory realm of cinema attests to our need to experiment safely with our own reactions to fear and anxiety."[32] Engaging with horror remakes would thus represent an attempt at mastering genuine fear.

Many scholars in the field have taken the approach that the scenarios and monsters of horror films express the fears of their time, that they tap into cultural anxieties that might otherwise not find expression. In his influential study of subversive potential in 1970s horror film, "American Nightmare", Robin Wood called this feature of horror the "return of the repressed".[33] The term is drawn from Freudian psychoanalysis, which forms the main framework for Wood's theory. According to Wood, "one might say that the true subject of the horror genre is the struggle for recognition of all that our civilization represses or oppresses, its reemergence dramatized, as in our nightmares, as an object of horror".[34] Wood thus sees the root of fear in the Self, defining the monster as a projection of what is repressed in the Self onto the Other[35] and a "dramatization of the dual concept of the repressed/the Other".[36] In other words, we make up monsters to stand in for all the things we do not want to accept in ourselves.

At the same time, the psychoanalytic approach also offers a possible explanation for the close ties between horror and repetition. Wood's model already mentions Freud's repetition compulsion (*Wiederholungszwang*), which means that if you fail to master a repressed traumatic experience, a compulsion may force you to relive it as current experience instead of recalling it as memory.[37]

32 LUKAS, Scott A. and John MARMYSZ. "Horror, Science Fiction and Fantasy Films Remade." In: Scott A. Lukas and John Marmysz (eds.). *Fear, Cultural Anxiety and Transformation: Horror, Science Fiction and Fantasy Films Remade*. Lanham: Lexington, 2009. 1–20, 15.
33 WOOD, Robin. "The American Nightmare: Horror in the 70s." In: Robin Wood. *Hollywood from Vietnam to Reagan*. New York: Columbia University Press, 1986. 70–94, 77.
34 WOOD. "The American Nightmare." 75.
35 WOOD. "The American Nightmare." 73.
36 WOOD. "The American Nightmare." 75.
37 FREUD, Sigmund. *Beyond the Pleasure Principle*. Trans. C.J.M. Hubback. London/Vienna: International Psycho-Analytical, 1922; Bartleby.com, 2010. <www.bartleby.com/276/> (accessed June 28, 2011).

Thus, with a bit of a stretch, culture, unable to finally deal with the fears around which horror films revolve, may be forced to relive them in a never-ending chain of remakes, or, as Zanger puts it: "Through endless repetitions, the cinematic institution is relentlessly trying to reframe the non-frameable."[38]

Even without these psychoanalytic underpinnings, horror can be read as a dramatization of current cultural concerns. Tudor, for example, takes issue with psychoanalytic models, as they make universal assumptions about the minds of the audience and see the effects of horror as an unconscious release. Instead, Tudor advocates models that have the audience actively correlate horror with their particular social experience, conceding them more agency and allowing for more diverse ways of viewing and using horror.[39] His argument touches upon one of the issues with attempts to discern the workings of horror: the fact that audience reactions span a wide range "from repulsion through ambivalent fascination and on to self-conscious, knowing humor".[40] However, this does not render any of the approaches discussed so far useless, but rather opens up more potential.

Regardless of these concerns, cultural interpretations of horror films and of American horror in particular abound. Maddrey, for instance, takes the familiar approach in claiming that certain horror stories "tap into our most primal fears", and, drawing on Kracauer, he asserts that "popular films also often seem to reflect the desires and anxieties of the time and place in which they are made."[41] Both quotes require collective, widespread fears for horror narratives to work with. Notably, Maddrey includes "re-imagining" and repetition as essential features of the genre, as monsters "shape-shift from decade to decade as the fears of the popular audience change".[42]

Phillips works with the same category of shared fears, yet argues for a slightly more limited and nuanced effect, in that only a few films successfully touch collective fears, becoming "cultural moments".[43] Furthermore, these films do not create or reflect fears (as fixed allegories), but "resonate – connect in some sympathetic manner – to trends within the broader culture."[44] Their success requires a "combination of familiarity and shock" that Phillips terms "resonant

---

38 ZANGER, Anat. *Film Remakes as Ritual and Disguise: From Carmen to Ripley.* Amsterdam: Amsterdam University Press, 2006. 23.
39 TUDOR. "Why Horror?" 52.
40 TUDOR. "Why Horror?" 50.
41 MADDREY, Joseph. *Nightmares in Red, White and Blue: The Evolution of the American Horror Film.* Jefferson: McFarland, 2004. 1.
42 MADDREY. *Nightmares in Red, White and Blue.* 2.
43 PHILLIPS, Kendall. *Projected Fears. Horror Films and American Culture.* Westport: Praeger, 2005. 3.
44 PHILLIPS. *Projected Fears.* 6.

violation".[45] Its purpose, and thereby the cultural importance of horror, lies in basically shocking people into new ways of coping with their fears.[46] Phillips' focus on a handful of groundbreaking films would exclude remakes, which are by definition not original. However, the combination of familiar and unexpected that Phillips posits as essential to the function of horror is found just as much in remakes, which take familiar narratives and update them with new, if often minor, twists.

In summary, as a well-established genre, horror narratives offer a standardized access to issues or fears that may be difficult to confront otherwise. Through constant repetition and refiguration, they are adapted to current times or different cultural situations. That process underlies all production of genre texts, but becomes especially visible in remakes. A sequel is usually shot within a few years of its predecessors, perhaps with part of the same crew, which leads to only moderate deviation. A remake, however, appears often decades after the previous film. It poses the challenge to adapt it to the times and current audience tastes, and looking at the results closely gives us an interesting comparison as to what fears might have worked at different historical moments.[47] The process is similar in the case of international remakes, which translate to a different cultural (as opposed to historical) background.

Simply put, if evoking a sense of fear is the goal of the horror film, then a remake must assure that the objects of fear still work, or update them to current and local sensibilities to remain effective. This is not limited to capturing sweeping changes and insecurities in society through metaphor, but also includes implementing current styles of filmmaking and technology. More sophisticated special effects aim to convince a more demanding audience and increasingly graphic depiction of violence likewise aims to disturb more jaded viewers.

These technical or cosmetic updates serve to assure part of a remake's effectiveness, but the disturbing qualities of a monster do not simply boil down to how credible its appearance or acts look. Rather, they are located on a discursive level. If we intend to look into broader cultural concerns, we need to scrutinize this discourse, and by comparing how monstrosity is established, we can draw conclusions about the cultural fears they resonate with.

---

45 PHILLIPS. *Projected Fears.* 8.
46 PHILLIPS. *Projected Fears.* 8 – 9.
47 LUKAS and MARMYSZ propose interpreting remakes as "a sort of barometer of society, indicating not just technical or stylistic changes in the various genres of film, but also indicating changes within the mythos of society itself." LUKAS and MARMYSZ. "Horror, Science Fiction and Fantasy Films Remade." 16.

IV.   Case Study: *Invasion of the Body Snatchers* and its Three Remakes

In order to demonstrate this approach, I will draw on an example that is already well known in academic circles. *Invasion of the Body Snatchers* is one of the usual suspects for the study of the genre, and certainly the most respected 1950s monster B-movie. It is a fairly popular text in American Studies, for the paranoid scenario which is read in the context of McCarthy's anti-communist frenzy in the 1950s. The film's ambiguous political stance and its checkered production history offer plenty of material for such readings, but these approaches usually focus on the 1956 film only.[48]

However, the film also makes an excellent example for the updating and adaptation of fears, since it has proven to be a highly popular subject for re-making. Based on the novel *Body Snatchers* by Jack Finney, it was initially adapted to film as *Invasion of the Body Snatchers* by Don Siegel in 1956. That film was remade in 1978, with Philip Kaufman directing and Donald Sutherland in the lead. It was remade again as *Body Snatchers* in 1993, with Abel Ferrara directing, and yet again as *The Invasion* in 2007 with Oliver Hirschbiegel directing and Nicole Kidman and Daniel Craig in the lead roles. Even by Hollywood standards, three remakes in just over five decades are remarkable.

Each remake is set in the respective contemporary period. The first version of 1956 is set in a small town in California and follows the physician Miles Bennell and his idle love interest Becky Driscoll. The 1978 version moves the action to San Francisco and revolves around health inspector Matthew Bennell and lab assistant Elizabeth Driscoll. The 1993 version again shifts to a different type of community, focusing on the Malones, a troubled civilian family arriving at a military base in the American South. Finally, the 2007 version, set in Baltimore, invokes its earlier predecessors by naming its protagonist Carol Bennell, a psychiatrist and mother aided by her colleague Ben Driscoll.

The basic story remains the same throughout all versions. Alien life forms, grown from seeds or microbes, land in an American town or city and start to take over the inhabitants' bodies or replace them with duplicates while the humans are sleeping. These duplicates, often referred to as 'pods', are indistinguishable from their human models, except for a complete lack of emotion and a drive to secretly further their takeover. The protagonists figure this out and attempt to alarm authorities, only to find that the alien infiltration has spread too far

---

48 As a starting point for further analysis, LAVALLEY's volume collects both the script and a choice of secondary materials on the 1956 film. LAVALLEY, Al (ed.). *Invasion of the Body Snatchers.* New Brunswick/London: Rutgers University Press, 1989.

already. As the last humans left, the protagonists have no choice but attempt a desperate escape, whose conclusion differs from film to film.

Regardless of the outcome, there is always one key scene in which the human protagonists confront and debate the aliens. This scene is crucial for any reading of the pods' metaphorical role or ideological stance, simply because the monsters do us the favor of articulating their position. The source of fear is always based on the same concept – the loss of individuality and humanity in a collective – yet in each version, it is reframed and connected to cultural concerns of the time.[49]

In the 1956 version, the town psychiatrist Kaufman acts as spokesperson for the pods, proclaiming the advantages of their emotionless state: "Love, desire, ambition, faith – without them, life is so simple." Transformation into a pod is called a rebirth "into an untroubled world", in which "everyone is the same". To the heroic protagonist Miles Bennell, though, this promise is one of horror, especially since he would no longer feel love towards Becky. Throughout the film, this personal dread of the pod-state is coupled with Cold War rhetoric, which links the pods' conspiracy and their vision of a world without faith, where everyone is the same, with fears of communist subversion.[50] While the discourse of individuality and group pressure allows for more ambiguous ideological readings, from anti-communist screed to a critique of more general 1950s trends towards social conformity, these are nevertheless tied to the specific historical moment of the film's production.[51]

The concerns of the 1950s and the Cold War are distant to the 1978 remake. Instead, the focus shifts to property and personal anxieties. The pod spokesperson Kibner is still a psychiatrist, but publishes self-help books, and the pod state and materialism complement each other in this iteration. As one of the pods explains, the transformation makes little difference for consumers: "Nothing changes; you can have the same life, the same clothes, the same car." Again, the pods offer the promise of rebirth into an "untroubled world", now "free of

---

49 Huygens extensively describes a number of tropes in the Body Snatchers films, including dehumanization, fear of engulfment, fear of others, uncanny doubles, invading forces, hysterical bodies and castrating and monstrous females. HUYGENS, Ils. "Invasions of Fear: The Body Snatchers Theme." In: Scott A. Lukas and John Marmysz (eds.). Fear, Cultural Anxiety and Transformation: Horror, Science Fiction and Fantasy Films Remade. Lanham: Lexington, 2009. 45–59.

50 SAYRE, Nora. "Watch the Skies." In: Al LaValley (ed.). Invasion of the Body Snatchers. New Brunswick/London: Rutgers University Press, 1989. 184.

51 Cf. LAVALLEY. Invasion of the Body Snatchers. 4. On the subject of social conformity, see JANCOVICH, Mark. Rational Fears. American Horror in the 1950s. Manchester: Manchester University Press, 1996 and SAMUELS, Stuart. "The Age of Conspiracy and Conformity: Invasion of the Body Snatchers." In: John O'Connor and Martin Jackson (eds.). American History – American Film. New York: Ungar, 1980. 203–17.

anxiety, fear, hate". This change has been interpreted as commentary on a sense of rising egotism in late 1970s America, while the pods' creeping subversion is read as echoing post-Watergate paranoia, the dissolution of 1960s counter-culture, which was swallowed up by mainstream society just as the film's characters are absorbed into the pod collective.[52] The fear of dehumanization and collectivity persists, only now it is connected to a numbing consumerism and relationship anxiety.

The 1993 remake takes some radical departures from its predecessors by choosing a subculture in which group conformity is already stronger and more visible by default – the military. Following the existent hierarchies, the base commander now serves as the pods' spokesperson and promotes the pod state as a solution to all conflicts, military and otherwise: "When all things are con-formed, there'll be no disputes, no conflicts, no problems any longer." His fellow pods chime in to assert that "it's the race that's important, not the individual" and that "the human race left to its own devices is doomed". Casting the mili-tary's strict conformity as a monstrous trait and having the soldiers who are trained to fight wars reject them after the subtle alien takeover, the film ends on the note that conflict and violence are only human, while complete peace and unity are alien, even monstrous. The Malones' nuclear family falls apart under the pressure,[53] amidst a discourse on infection and chemical contamination that again touches on contemporary fears.[54]

The 2007 version takes a similar stance on conflict; only now the focus is global, taking a media-saturated post-9/11 world into account. Even though the aliens in this version no longer grow from pods, their approach and their case for transformation remain the same. Their spokesperson Ben offers an alternative to the world that appears on the television news: "A world without war, without poverty, without murder, without rape, a world without suffering, because in our world, no one can hurt each other, or exploit each other, or try to destroy each other, because in our world, there is no other." These lines not only spell out the persistent draw and horror of the pods' annihilation of individuality, but also demonstrate the remakers' awareness of the Other as a theoretical concept and its relevance to *Invasion of the Body Snatchers'* place in the genre canon. Throughout the film, the context of post-9/11 politics and terror fears is clearly established through prominent news footage that features George W. Bush shaking hands with leaders of so-called rogue states, and lists all the con-

---

52 MUIR, John Kenneth. *Horror Films of the 1970s.* Jefferson: McFarland, 2002. 547–50. On the cultural contexts of the late 1970s, see: HOBERMAN, J. "Paranoia and the Pods." In: *Sight and Sound* 45,2 (1994): 29–31, 30.
53 HOBERMAN. "Paranoia and the Pods." 31.
54 HUYGENS. "Invasions of Fear: The Body Snatchers Theme." 58.

temporary hotspots, from Iraq and Afghanistan to Darfur.[55] The 2007 version makes every effort to appear as up-to-date, and in unambiguous terms presents conflict and insecurity as a more natural human state, for better or worse.

While a more detailed analysis of the four films would reveal more complex insights, even the brief comparison of this one scene already shows how motives are updated from one version of the *Body Snatchers* story to the next. Overall, the fear of dehumanization in an emotionless collective remains a constant, even though it is projected onto various historically specific contexts.

V.   A Horror Remake Complex

As the previous section shows, a comparison of films and their remakes can yield intriguing results about the individual films and their time. If we are to investigate the functions and developments of the horror genre as a larger phenomenon, we need to stop focusing on individual films alone, take a step back and view the entire chain of production and reproduction as an ongoing dialogue or discourse. Each version picks up on the discussion, reframes it, adds to it, and returns the narrative to the wider generic discourse. Therefore, attempts to find one definite or 'best' version of a film and dismiss the others as worthless may please film critics, but ignore the ongoing process that these films form a part of. As Jancovich remarks on the horror films of the 1950s, there are many ways "in which earlier periods are constantly available for reworking and reinterpretation, and are not simply dispensed with, or rendered redundant."[56] Horror, like any genre, is always repetitive, and the remake makes this fact clearly visible.

I suggest that horror and remaking are such a prevalent, successful combination because they supplement each other. They both work for a particular purpose and the reliability of remakes supports the expected fears of the horror film. A number of factors, from the film industry's commercial motivations to changing audience tastes, media technologies and socio-political situations, add up to result in a constant stream of remaking. We could sum that all up into a complex, a machine of cultural production that produces and recycles horror narratives. It is a system with two components: horror negotiates fears, and remaking keeps it functional. A recent change in Hollywood nomenclature may serve to underline this idea: remakes such as *Halloween* (2007) that are designed

---

55 ROBINSON, Juneko J. "Immanent Attack: An Existential Take on *The Invasion of the Body Snatchers* Films." In: Scott A. Lukas and John Marmysz (eds.). *Fear, Cultural Anxiety and Transformation: Horror, Science Fiction and Fantasy Films Remade*. Lanham: Lexington, 2009. 23–44, 39.

56 JANCOVICH. *Rational Fears*. 303.

as the starting point of a new cycle of sequels and spin-off products are now commonly labeled 'reboot'. That term is a recent addition to everyday language and comes from computers. You do not reboot an individual piece of art, you reboot a system.

Some will object to reading all versions of a film as essentially one functional unit, contributing to one monster discourse. After all, how many viewers are actually familiar with all the iterations of one film? That seems to apply only to a handful of hardcore fans. However, we should not underestimate the remake 'literacy' of audiences, as Verevis calls it.[57] At the previous high point of Hollywood remaking in the 1930s and 40s,[58] availability of older versions of films was very limited, as audiences depended on the movie theaters' schedules. With the spread of television, and after that, Video, DVD and the Internet, films have become more easily available. In addition, the intertextual links in a chain of film remakes can be found easily online. Now, any viewer can by accident stumble across various versions of the same film on TV, or be alerted to it by online stores, DVD rental or video streaming services. Looking back over film history, knowing various versions of the same film and being able to use them has never been more likely. And even if a viewer decides on one definite version of a horror film, the awareness of related films means that the monstrous threats and the fears they resonate with are likely to overlap, rendering exclusive distinctions obsolete.

Ultimately, every sequence of reproduction, every couple of film and remake offers an angle for comparative analysis regarding cultural fears at different times and places and their continuing development. Since remakes are not going to go away anytime soon, we might as well attempt to gain new insights from them.

References

AREND, Wolfgang. *Auf der Jagd nach Hexen und Zuschauern. Mediensoziologische Bausteine zu einer Theorie des Remakes am Beispiel von Hexenfilmen.* Mainz: Bender, 2002.

Boxofficemojo.com <http://www.boxofficemojo.com/> (accessed June 30, 2011).

BRAUDY, Leo. "Afterword: Rethinking Remakes." In: Andrew Horton and Stuart Y. McDougal (eds.). *Play It Again, Sam. Retakes on Remakes.* Berkeley: University of California Press, 1998. 327–34.

CARROLL, Noël. *The Philosophy of Horror. Or: Paradoxes of the Heart.* New York: Routledge, 1990.

---

57 VEREVIS. *Film Remakes.* 17.
58 DRUXMAN. *Make It Again, Sam.* 13.

Druxman, Michael B. *Make It Again, Sam. A Survey of Movie Remakes.* South Brunswick: A.S. Barnes, 1975.

Eco, Umberto. "Innovation and Repetition: Between Modern and Post-Modern Aesthetics." In: *Daedalus* 114,4. The Moving Image (1985): 161–84.

Ferrara, Abel, dir. *Body Snatchers.* Warner, 1993. DVD: Warner, 2009.

Forrest, Jennifer and Leonard R. Koos. "Reviewing Remakes: An Introduction." In: Jennifer Forrest and Leonard R. Koos (eds.). *Dead Ringers: The Remake in Theory and Practice.* Albany: State University of New York Press, 2002. 1–36.

Freud, Sigmund. *Beyond the Pleasure Principle.* Trans. C.J.M. Hubback. London/Vienna: International Psycho-Analytical, 1922; Bartleby.com, 2010. <www.bartleby.com/276/> (accessed June 28, 2011).

Hirschbiegel, Oliver, dir. *The Invasion.* Warner, 2007. DVD: Warner, 2008.

Hoberman, J. "Paranoia and the Pods." In: *Sight and Sound* 45,2 (1994): 29–31.

Horton, Andrew and Stuart Y. McDougal. "Introduction." In: Andrew Horton and Stuart Y. McDougal (eds.). *Play It Again, Sam. Retakes on Remakes.* Berkeley: University of California Press, 1998. 1–11.

Huygens, Ils. "Invasions of Fear: The Body Snatchers Theme." In: Scott A. Lukas and John Marmysz (eds.). *Fear, Cultural Anxiety and Transformation: Horror, Science Fiction and Fantasy Films Remade.* Lanham: Lexington, 2009. 45–59.

Jancovich, Mark. *Rational Fears. American Horror in the 1950s.* Manchester: Manchester University Press, 1996.

Kaufman, Philip, dir. *Invasion of the Body Snatchers.* MGM, 1978. DVD: MGM, 2003.

Knöppler, Christian. "Intertextualität und das Filmremake." In: Marion Grein, Miguel Souza and Svenja Völkel (eds.). *Polyphonie, Intertextualität, Intermedialität: Ein Interdisziplinäres Forschungsfeld.* Aachen: Shaker, 2010. 113–46.

LaValley, Al (ed.). *Invasion of the Body Snatchers.* New Brunswick/London: Rutgers University Press, 1989.

Leitch, Thomas. "Twice-Told Tales: Disavowal and the Rhetoric of the Remake." In: Jennifer Forrest and Leonard R. Koos (eds.). *Dead Ringers: The Remake in Theory and Practice.* Albany: State University of New York Press, 2002. 37–62.

Lukas, Scott A. "Horror Video Game Remakes and the Question of Medium: Remaking *Doom, Silent Hill,* and *Resident Evil.*" In: Scott A. Lukas and John Marmysz (eds.). *Fear, Cultural Anxiety and Transformation: Horror, Science Fiction and Fantasy Films Remade.* Lanham: Lexington, 2009. 221–42.

Lukas, Scott A. and John Marmysz. "Horror, Science Fiction and Fantasy Films Remade." In: Scott A. Lukas and John Marmysz (eds.). *Fear, Cultural Anxiety and Transformation: Horror, Science Fiction and Fantasy Films Remade.* Lanham: Lexington, 2009. 1–20.

Maddrey, Joseph. *Nightmares in Red, White and Blue: The Evolution of the American Horror Film.* Jefferson: McFarland, 2004.

Maes, Hans. "A Celestial Taxonomy of Remakes?" In: *Cinemascope* 2 (2005) <http://www.madadayo.it/Cinemascope_archive/cinema-scope.net/Numero%20due/articolo05.html> (accessed April 14, 2010).

Muir, John Kenneth. *Horror Films of the 1970s.* Jefferson: McFarland, 2002.

Perkins, Claire. "Remaking and the Film Trilogy: Whit Stillman's Authorial Triptych." In: *Velvet Light Trap* 61 (2008): 14–25.

PHILLIPS, Kendall. *Projected Fears. Horror Films and American Culture.* Westport: Praeger, 2005.

ROBINSON, Juneko J. "Immanent Attack: An Existential Take on *The Invasion of the Body Snatchers* Films." In: Scott A. Lukas and John Marmysz (eds.). *Fear, Cultural Anxiety and Transformation: Horror, Science Fiction and Fantasy Films Remade.* Lanham: Lexington, 2009. 23 – 44.

SAMUELS, Stuart. "The Age of Conspiracy and Conformity: *Invasion of the Body Snatchers.*" In: John O'Connor and Martin Jackson (eds.). *American History – American Film.* New York: Ungar, 1980. 203 – 17.

SAYRE, Nora. "Watch the Skies." In: Al LaValley (ed.). *Invasion of the Body Snatchers.* New Brunswick/London: Rutgers University Press, 1989. 184.

SIEGEL, Don, dir. *Invasion of the Body Snatchers.* Republic, 1956. DVD: Artisan, 1998.

TUDOR, Andrew. "Why Horror? The Peculiar Pleasures of a Popular Genre." In: Mark Jancovich (ed.). *Horror. The Film Reader.* London: Routledge, 2002. 47 – 55.

VEREVIS, Constantine. *Film Remakes.* Edinburgh: Edinburgh University Press, 2006.

WHITE, Dave. "I Spit on Your Horror Movie Remakes, Sequels: A Horror Fan Laments the State of One of His Favorite Genres." *MSNBC.com.* Oct 25, 2005. <http://www.msnbc.msn.com/id/9805698/> (accessed March 22, 2010).

WOOD, Robin. "The American Nightmare: Horror in the 70s." In: Robin Wood. *Hollywood from Vietnam to Reagan.* New York: Columbia University Press, 1986. 70 – 94.

ZANGER, Anat. *Film Remakes as Ritual and Disguise: From Carmen to Ripley.* Amsterdam: Amsterdam University Press, 2006.

Elena Baeva

'A Little Gasp Went Around [...] Like a Scream' – The Use of Time-Tried Motifs of Fear in Shirley Jackson's *We Have Always Lived in the Castle* and Quentin Tarantino's *Inglourious Basterds*

I.   Introduction

Most debates about fear acknowledge that there are two types: psychologists and psychoanalysts differentiate between extreme temporary shocks and a chronic, long-lasting state of fear.[1] Similarly, already since the rise of the Gothic and the sensational novel, authors and literary critics alike have discussed the merits and effects of horrific scenes described in gruesome, shocking detail on the one hand, and a less explicit, prolonged, suspense-based terror on the other[2] – Anne Radcliffe's essay "On the Super-Natural in Poetry" (1816) being one of the most widely known examples. Both approaches have developed over the centuries and are still distinguishable in today's fiction, perhaps most easily if one compares a gory 'splatter' or horror film with a slow-paced psychological thriller. However, they have also found their way into texts which do not belong to any of these genres, into novels and films whose main goal is not to scare or continuously thrill their audience but which instead depict fear itself and discuss the state of constant tension – by many considered to be the defining feature of the Gothic genre[3] (or its German counterpart of the 'Schauerroman'[4]) – as part of a wider context. Two such texts form the basis for this paper.

Shirley Jackson's *We Have Always Lived in the Castle* is a comparatively unknown novel, written as far back as the 1960s, addressing the secluded life of two young sisters (eighteen-year-old Merricat Blackwood and the slightly older Constance) in a small US town. By contrast, Quentin Tarantino's *Inglourious Basterds* (2009) is a recent, multi-plot, multi-perspective blockbuster. Mainly a mix of old-school spaghetti western and contemporary action film, it also in-

---

1 Cf. BERNSEN, Michael. *Angst und Schrecken in der Frühliteratur des französischen und englischen 18. Jahrhunderts.* München: Fink, 1996. 21.
2 Cf. KILGOUR, Maggie. *The Rise of the Gothic Novel.* London/New York: Routledge, 1997. 189.
3 Cf. SCHNEIDER, Gerd. *Transformationen des Gothic.* Frankfurt M.: Peter Lang, 2002. 65.
4 Cf. CONRAD, Horst. *Das Schreckliche in Schauerromantik und Detektivgeschichte.* Düsseldorf: Bertelsmann, 1974. 13.

corporates elements from historical drama and meta-cinema to depict an alternate ending to World War II.[5] At first glance, these two works of fiction might easily appear to have nothing in common. Yet what film and novel *do* share is their way of depicting fear. In *We Have Always Lived in the Castle* a sense of extreme anxiety is omnipresent, subtly creeping into every conversation, every action of the protagonists. In *Inglourious Basterds*, the same thing happens as soon as SS Col. Hans Landa, a former Austrian detective turned "Jew Hunter" for the Nazis, enters the frame.[6] The emotional state depicted in both works is very similar, and what is even more so are the means author and director have chosen to invoke it – means which have their origins in the sensational and Gothic novels of the eighteenth and nineteenth centuries.

II.   *We Have Always Lived in the Castle*

The acknowledgement of the Gothic tradition is unmistakeable in *We Have Always Lived in the Castle*. (Seemingly) helpless, orphaned young women who, due to a mysterious crime in the family,[7] find themselves virtually locked up in a mansion, explicitly referred to as a 'castle' in the title – all these features are typical elements of the eighteenth- and nineteenth-century Gothic novel.[8] The same applies to the motif of a dying and decaying aristocracy (in Jackson's text mainly represented by the girls' family) which, however, still longs for its former glory. Walking through town on one of the unavoidable grocery shopping days, Merricat makes the following observation on the state of the formerly noble local buildings: "Perhaps the fine houses had been captured – perhaps as punishment

---

5 As a result of the achievements of a group of Jewish American soldiers known as the Basterds, who fight a bloody guerrilla war against the German occupation in France, as well as of the efforts of young Jewish fugitive Shosanna and traitorous SS Col. Landa, Tarantino's World War II ends when all heads of the German national socialist party are killed in an explosion at a cinema where the premiere of Goebbels' latest and last film is held.

6 Since Tarantino's film is too complex to be discussed here in its entirety, I restrict my analysis to scenes featuring Landa, given the fact that the atmosphere of fear is most pertinent in these. For the reason of conciseness I shall refrain from discussing the film's soundtrack, since Tarantino's use of music is a vast topic in itself and its contribution to the scenes I will focus on is comparatively minor.

7 Many years ago, most of the girls' rather aristocratic family was poisoned during dinner (except for an uncle who survived but is in a mentally as well as physically rather invalid state). The readers, eventually, learn that Merricat herself murdered her parents and aunt as an act of revenge for having been sent to bed without supper. For the villagers, however, the crime has remained a mystery once Constance was acquitted in court, and they have used it ever since as an excuse to ostracise the last two remaining members of a family they had always disliked on account of their money and airs.

8 Cf. CONRAD. *Das Schreckliche*. 20.

for the Rochesters and the Blackwoods and their secret bad hearts? – and were held prisoner in the village" (*Castle* 6). The implied mood of captivity, the identification of homes with families and of course the family names themselves – Gothic references are everywhere. Scholars have often shown how in eighteenth- and nineteenth-century Gothic texts, such as Horace Walpole's *The Castle of Otranto* (1764) or Edgar Allan Poe's "The Fall of the House of Usher" (1839), buildings themselves become protagonists.[9] Jackson clearly picks up this idea and makes it culminate in the villagers' final attack on the Blackwood house, which feels more like the murder and disembowelment of a person than the mere destruction of property (cf. *Castle* 102 ff).

Jackson employs an equally traditional Gothic plot element when she has an impoverished cousin enter the girls' lives with the intention of marrying the older sister to get his hands on her money. Incestuous desires and greed are amongst the oldest literary motifs, and once more even the wording of the respective passages is an allusion to eighteenth- and nineteenth-century writing. For example, Merricat's description of the young man's intrusion reads as follows: "I still could not see him clearly, perhaps because he was a ghost, perhaps because he was so very big" (*Castle* 63). "Even the garden had become a strange landscape with Charles' figure in it" (*Castle* 79). Through characters with spectre-like appearances and the highly symbolic landscape, whose perception is closely interlinked with the heroine's emotional state, novels like Charlotte Brontë's *Jane Eyre* (1847) are constantly brought to mind.

What is striking is that none of these scenes, none of these descriptions, are the ones which actively invoke a feeling of fear. Simply reiterated in their traditional form, these motifs no longer seem to have a thrilling effect. When they are subverted, however, the novel immediately starts building up a sense of tension and anxiety. Let us go back to the mansion the girls live in: for most parts of the novel it is as far from being 'in ruins' as it can possibly be. It is clean, light-coloured and elegant, all rooms are full of sunshine. From the way the sisters behave one may get the impression that they are perfectly happy there. Even though they are confined to it, they do not appear to experience any of the gloomy claustrophobia one might expect as a reader. Just as in classic texts such as Charlotte Perkins Gilman's "The Yellow Wallpaper" (1899), this discrepancy causes discomfort: the reader is disconcerted and he or she immediately starts to doubt the reliability and mental state of the narrative voice. The incongruity between expectations and actual description is particularly strong at the end of the novel, when, after the fire and the villagers' pillaging, the sisters are confined to an even smaller space, consisting of only their kitchen (in which all windows are barred), pantry and a very limited patch of ash-covered garden. Still, the girls

---

9 Cf. CONRAD. *Das Schreckliche*. 21 ff.

seem perfectly content with the situation and the novel ends with the following unsettlingly joyful lines:

> 'Poor strangers,' I said. 'They have so much to be afraid of.'
> 'Well,' Constance said, 'I'm afraid of spiders.'
> 'Jonas[10] and I will see to it that no spider ever comes near you. Oh, Constance,' I said, 'we are so happy.' (*Castle* 146)

The banality of the dialogue and the suggested happy ending are the exact opposite of what one would associate with the sisters' increasingly prison-like state of utter isolation.

What makes the discrepancy even stronger is the fact that the feeling of claustrophobia *does* exist in the text and *is* considered to be something terrible. It sets in every time Merricat experiences strong fear – but then it is associated with something threatening the existence of the supposed idyll, in particular with any mention of Constance considering going back out into the world. "I was held tight, wound round with wire, I couldn't breathe" (*Castle* 57) and "I could not breathe, I was tied around tight, everything was cold" (*Castle* 61) is how her younger sister describes her feelings in these situations. In other words, within the girls' emotional world, being locked up means being cosy and happy, while being free is soul crushing. This rather agoraphobic attitude constitutes a complete inversion of values, which the rest of the novel suggests is the result of living in constant fear.

When Merricat describes her daily life and thoughts, she regularly mentions her unlocking and, more importantly, locking of doors; her perceiving herself as vulnerable and exposed; her deciding not to run away from social interaction. She compares her walk into town with board games in which players "lose a turn" if they step onto a wrong field (cf. *Castle* 4 ff.). All these descriptions, while conveying a subtext of terror, are given by the girl completely in passing, presented in the same tone as information about a particular route she takes or on the order in which she and her sister do their chores. Merricat seems incapable of differentiating between everyday things and those that would be considered terrible by most people. This inability of hers is already apparent in the opening lines of the novel, when the girl introduces herself: "My name is Mary Katherine Blackwood. [...] I dislike washing myself, and dogs, and noise. [...] I like my sister Constance. [...] Everyone else in my family is dead." (*Castle* 1) Following the traditional approach of defining oneself through likes and dislikes, the last revelation is simply out of place. Naturally, this passage could be read as nothing more than proof of the narrator's unreliability. Yet, combined with the descriptions of her life referred to earlier, it can also be seen as an example of how

---

10 Merricat's cat.

horrors have ceased to be shocking for the girls after fear itself has become part of their everyday routines, has become something 'normal'.

This state of affairs is not only shown to have made some tension-filled habits necessary – such as the aforementioned focus on the locking of doors – but also to have perverted perfectly innocent ones, like that of cleaning a home. Merricat describes the process as follows:

> We *always* put things back *where they belonged*. We dusted and swept under tables and chairs and beds and pictures and rugs and lamps, but we *left them where they were*; the tortoise-shell toilet set on our mother's dressing table was *never off place by so much as a fraction of an inch*. Blackwoods had always lived in our house, and kept their things *in order*; as soon as a new Blackwood wife moved in, a place was found for her belongings, and so our house was built up with layers of Blackwood property weighting it, and *keeping it steady against the world*. (*Castle* 1, my emphasis)

The girls' neatness borders on an obsessive-compulsive disorder – a widely acknowledged mechanism for coping with anxiety.[11] Some psychologists explain this reaction by saying that, for many children, one of the first conscious fears is that of punishment for lack of orderliness. This link, then, gets drilled into the children's minds so forcefully that even as adults they start cleaning every time they feel frightened so as to avoid the 'punishment'.[12] Considering the strict ways in which Jackson's protagonists are said to have been brought up, this certainly sounds plausible. Yet the last sentence suggests something more: it describes creating order as an act which gives you steadiness, and, derived from that, control. With this association, cleaning becomes just another part of Merricat's arsenal of mystical rituals which are supposed to keep evil influences at bay. Just like the offerings of gratitude (cf. *Castle* 5), the burial of certain objects (cf. *Castle* 41), or the nailing of items to trees (cf. *Castle* 53), the girl invests the cleaning of their house with near-magical power. From a psychological point of view, this behaviour invokes a variety of theories on how anxiety- and OCD-patients bend reality so that their defence mechanisms can keep working: they invest otherwise meaningless actions with meaning, thus creating duties that simply *have to* be done.[13] It furthermore corresponds with many studies which argue that this type of patients are particularly prone to seeing patterns, to seeing 'uncanny' coincidences, and hence to believing in superstitions such as it being possible to kill somebody simply by wishing it.[14] From a literary perspective, however, these passages are also once again references to the tradition of the

---

11 Cf. LEVITT. *Die Psychologie der Angst*. 48 – 49.
12 Cf. LEVITT. *Die Psychologie der Angst*. 50 ff.
13 Cf. LEVITT. *Die Psychologie der Angst*. 50 ff.
14 Cf. FREUD, Sigmund. *Das Unheimliche. Aufsätze zur Literatur*. Frankfurt M.: Fischer, 1963. 68 – 69.

sensational novels – to their supernatural elements and the question of how these fit into our otherwise rational world, as well as to the general motif of control and lack thereof which is central to the relationship between all Gothic villains and their victims.[15]

Still, what needs to be pointed out about Merricat's narration of her mystical practices is that it does not suggest any actual terror being felt consciously by the girl. Once more, all actions are presented as something ordinary – after you have eaten you do the dishes, after a good day you make an offering of jewellery. Experiencing fear is something as everyday as sitting down for a meal in the girls' world. It is so normal that it is beyond eliciting an 'appropriate' emotional response. The sisters, in fact, are even playing with it. Merricat as well as the otherwise quiet and loving Constance are shown to enjoy frightening the few villagers they still come into contact with. During her shopping trips, for example, Merricat loves to stress those ingredients she is buying which were used in the lethal family dinner:

> 'A small leg of lamb,' I said, 'my Uncle Julian always fancies a roasted lamb in the first spring days.' I should not have said it, I knew, and a little gasp went around the store like a scream. I could make them run like rabbits, I thought, if I said to them what I really wanted to, but they would only gather again outside and watch for me there. (*Castle* 8)

Especially the middle sentence, the one I have used as the title of this paper, in addition to being in and of itself a nod to the fainting and gasping Gothic heroines, shows perfectly just how high-strung the tension is – and yet the whole scene implies that Merricat is rather enjoying this state and the power it gives her. The rest of those games are described in what on the surface appears to be an even more playful tone. The visit by Helen Clarke and Mrs. Wright, for example, approaches situational comedy:

> I went back to Constance and took up the plate of rum cakes and brought them to Mrs. Wright. [...] 'My sister made these this morning,' I said.
> 'Thank you,' she said. Her hand hesitated over the plate and then she took a rum cake and set it carefully on the edge of her saucer. I thought that Mrs. Wright was being almost hysterically polite, and I said, 'Do take two. Everything my sister cooks is delicious.'
> 'No,' she said. 'Oh, no. Thank you.' (*Castle* 28)

Similarly, when Uncle Julian describes to the two visiting ladies the feeling of being poisoned with the lines "I assure you the pangs were fearful; you say you have never tasted arsenic? It is not agreeable." (*Castle* 37), the situation is undeniably comic. All Blackwoods are in the best of spirits during the visit, delighted to be able to frighten their guests (cf. *Castle* 39). The way they achieve this

---

15 Cf. CONRAD. *Das Schreckliche*. 38.

is striking. There are never any explicit threats but instead what could have been ordinary acts of politeness and friendly talkativeness are invested with unspoken terrors. The same approach is used by the villagers when they in turn try to scare Merricat when she is on *their* turf, for example at the central coffee shop. Suddenly, compliments on the Blackwoods and their land, as well as offerings of assistance with packing and moving away, are full of ominous subtext (cf. *Castle* 12 ff.). In both these situations the fear-inducing party, be it the sisters or their neighbours, need do nothing more than drop a hint and watch their victims squirm.

Psychoanalyst Johanna Vennemann has argued, in accordance with Lacan, that one of the most prototypically frightening concepts is that of the 'Evil Eye': it exposes the object to the desires of others, is highly judgemental to the point where it makes the object freeze – in other words, lose control – and, most importantly, it gains its power mainly from the fact that the desire is never verbalised.[16] This concept, once again highly Gothic in nature, might not be exactly the one Jackson works with but it certainly lies at the core of the interaction between the villagers and the girls, since said interaction is based entirely on watching from afar, judging and wishing for things to happen while never, actually, communicating any of these thoughts. Instead, everything is suppressed under a mask of civility and humorous remarks.

It is exactly this clash between the lightness of the tone and the 'objective' painfulness of the situation that makes the novel so very discomforting. And while the supposedly light mood and simplicity of the descriptions might prevent direct associations with the Gothic or the sensational, the basic concept behind this approach is clearly derived from those early novels of terror. Ultimately, it is a concept of subversion, the 'uncanny' taken one step further.

It is well established that the principle of showing the unfamiliar, the strange and the dangerous in something familiar lies at the heart especially of Victorian Gothic. The perversion of ideals such as that of domesticity is a typical motif of the time[17] – and one that Jackson uses, too, as for instance the depiction of the lethal family dinner illustrates:

> 'A family gathering for the evening meal,' Uncle Julian said caressing his words. 'Never supposing it was to be our last. [...] My brother, as head of the family, sat naturally at the head of table [...] with the windows at his back and the decanter before him. John Blackwood took pride in his table, his family, his position in the world.' (*Castle* 31 – 33)

---

16 Cf. VENNEMANN, Johanna. "Der böse Blick." In: André Michels et al. (eds). *Angst.* Tübingen: Edition Diskord, 2001. 166 – 72, 168.
17 Cf. KILGOUR. *The Rise of the Gothic Novel.* 9 ff. and PUNTER, David and Glenn BYRON. *The Gothic.* Malden, MA/Oxford: Blackwell, 2004. 38.

The passage is full of references to traditional family values, but what should be an ideal soon turns into a crime scene, and the poison is distributed through one of the most homely of ingredients: the sugar for the blackberries, served in a heavy silver bowl, which is a valued family heirloom.

The Victorians probably would have presented this scene full of gloomy terrors, hence showing the dangers lurking beneath a rational surface. In fact, they used this initially subversive motif so often that by the end of the period it had itself become a norm – defying its own purpose in the process, as many critics have argued. Maggie Kilgour, for example, describes the development as follows: "The defamiliarisation of conventions, which, according to the Romantics, enables us to see the world anew, becomes itself a new convention. Created as an alternative to the mechanistic order, the gothic itself became stale and mechanical."[18] This, however, is where Jackson takes the Gothic concept of subversion one step further using a motif which itself has been around for centuries, namely that of the grotesque.

David Punter, in reference to William Beckford's *Vathek* (1786) and several grotesque paintings, defines the term as follows: "The grotesque, in a general sense, violates the laws of nature; visually, it is a world, where classifications break down, resulting in an inherent tension between the ludicrous and the fearful."[19] And it is exactly this type of tension that lies at the heart of Jackson's novel as well. In a slightly different approach, Manfred Schumacher describes the grotesque as a game which brings up ancient joys and desires (supposedly inherent in every human being) to turn norms and conventions upside down, yet which can quickly turn into something serious when it brings up abysses[20] – something which is equally exemplified in *We Have Always Lived in the Castle* when Merricat's playfulness, as well as the villagers' teasing, turn into highly destructive violence. Critics have voiced different opinions as to the cultural categorisation of the term. Maggie Kilgour, starting off from describing the grotesque as transgressive, defines it as being prototypically Gothic.[21] Rudolf Fritsch, by contrast, classifies it as being prototypically modern. The whole point of the grotesque, he argues, is that it goes beyond a dualistic view of the world, in which good and evil are clearly defined categories; it is, therefore, the perfect mode of depiction for a Modernity which has accepted perversion as an inherent part of itself.[22] What Jackson does with her novel is to combine those two

---

18 Cf. KILGOUR. *The Rise of the Gothic Novel.* 189.
19 Cf. PUNTER. *The Gothic.* 183.
20 Cf. SCHUMACHER, Manfred. *Das Groteske und seine Gestaltung in der Gothic Novel.* Frankfurt M.: Peter Lang, 1990. 123.
21 Cf. KILGOUR. *The Rise of the Gothic Novel.* 9.
22 Cf. FRITSCH, Rudolf. *Absurd oder grotesk? Über literarische Darstellung von Entfremdung bei Beckett und Heller.* Frankfurt M.: Peter Lang, 1950. 24 ff.

approaches: she employs the grotesque, an inherently Gothic mode of writing, so that she can use its transgressive properties to make seemingly stale Gothic writing itself transgressive again, updating it for the modern readers and times of the twentieth and twenty-first centuries.

By choosing a lighter tone for her writing, the author, rather than showing the dark side of what is considered 'normal' as the Victorians used to do, points out the normality of what is considered to be dark. Essentially, she depicts a world in which things are even worse than the eighteenth- and nineteenth-century writers suggested: Gothic novels criticise, to put it in a highly simplified manner, the difference between the 'good' surface and the 'evil' beneath it[23] – but Jackson's text suggests that there is no such distinction at all. Since the atmosphere of fear is routine and omnipresent, up to the point where it is not really recognised and felt by the protagonists as such, the distinction between the frightening and the non-frightening disappears. As a consequence the one between dangerous and safe, between evil and good, likewise dissolves. The reader is left with no values to hold onto; hence all that remains is uncertainty, the unknown – a state which is not uncommon in classic Gothic novels dealing with the supernatural, and which is argued by many psychologists to be the basis of all fear.[24]

III. *Inglourious Basterds*

The sense of terror emanating from SS Col. Hans Landa in *Inglourious Basterds* functions very similarly to that in Jackson's text. While plot and setting are not as clearly (or maybe at least not as consciously) inspired by eighteenth- and nineteenth-century traditions as they are in the novel discussed above, Landa is undeniably a modernised version of the typical Gothic villain: 'evil' and fascinating at the same time, he is arguably the most complex among the film's characters. David Punter has described Landa's literary predecessors as

> awe-inspiring, endlessly resourceful in pursuit of [their] often opaquely evil ends, and yet possessed of a mysterious attractiveness, [they] stalk[] from the pages of one Gothic novel to another, manipulating the doom of others, while the knowledge of [their] own eventual fate surrounds [them] like the monastic habit and cowl which [they] so often wore.[25]

Tarantino's 'Jew Hunter' lives up to all of these expectations. He is certainly a very resourceful investigator, pursuing his assignment relentlessly, bringing

---

23 Cf. PUNTER. *The Gothic.* 26–27.
24 Cf. LEVITT. *Die Psychologie der Angst.* 9 ff.
25 PUNTER, David. *The Literature of Terror: A History of Gothic Fictions from 1765 to the Present Day.* London: Longman, 1980. 11.

death and destruction to others. While he is no aristocrat or monk, he still shares their central sombre characteristic: absolutist, seemingly unlimited power and the capacity for utter tyrannical control.[26] Scholars such as Maria Purves have correctly pointed out that to say that the villains of Gothic texts represent a class or a religion as a whole is to generalise too much. Instead, if one looks closely, the critique is mainly aimed at their restrictive and oppressive properties.[27] Similarly, Landa is not shown as a simple personification of NS tyranny. His monologue on the parallels between rats and Jews (Basterds 0:13:52 – 16:08), his deprecating reference to Goebbels' premiere as an "illustre soirée" (Basterds 0:56:53), and of course his final involvement in the execution of all party heads make it quite clear that he, in fact, does not believe in the NS cause at all. As he puts it himself, he is just "a detective, a damn good detective. Finding people is [his] specialty so, naturally, [he] work[s] for the Nazis finding people and, yes, some of them [a]re Jews" (Basterds 1:59:36 – 43). This quote, incidentally, fits very well with another motif of eighteenth- and nineteenth-century writing. Many scholars have argued that Gothic texts were written as a form of rebellion against the cold rationalism of the Victorian Age[28] and the 'Jew Hunter's' statement is a perfect example of the attitude which said novels and stories aimed to criticise. While his approach is certainly highly rational, it also comes with a problematic lack of concern for other people – a quality which constitutes one of the most frightening traits of villains, Gothic and modern alike.[29]

Landa might not believe in NS ideology but there is one thing he does believe in, and does enjoy: power. The exertion of control is a constant in each of his scenes. He never literally threatens or forces somebody to subdue to his will but subtle hints and manipulations are more than enough with this character. Yes, there is the SS uniform, which in itself demands obedience, but he achieves just as much with what he says and does.

The most prominent means of control he employs is a physical one: his perpetual intrusion into people's personal space. It is enough to take a look at his first appearance at the LaPadite farm and the way Tarantino has framed most of those shots. When Landa walks onto the property, his hand outstretched, Perrier LaPadite remains stationary in the far right corner (Basterds 0:03:55). When they shake hands, it is again Landa's arm which is extended and takes up two thirds of the frame while LaPadite barely raises his hand (Basterds 0:04:00). When invited to lead the way, Landa gently pushes LaPadite ahead by taking

---

26 Cf. CONRAD. Das Schreckliche. 38.
27 Cf. PURVES, Maria. The Gothic and Catholicism. Religion, Cultural Exchange and the Popular Novel 1785 – 1829. Cardiff: University of Wales Press, 2009. 55.
28 Cf. KILGOUR. The Rise of the Gothic Novel. 17.
29 Cf. PALMER, Jerry. Thrillers. Genesis and Structure of a Popular Genre. London: Edward Arnold, 1978. 16.

hold of the latter's upper arm (*Basterds* 0:04:14). After carefully selecting the youngest daughter for a hand-kiss (*Basterds* 0:04:35), he keeps holding on to her for just a little bit longer than necessary (*Basterds* 0:04:41). He stops the second daughter from going to get wine by gripping her hand gently whilst, with both arms outstretched, once again taking up two thirds of the frame (*Basterds* 0:05:05). And when he, eventually, starts the 'interview' of Perrier LaPadite (in his exaggerated politeness Landa would never call it an interrogation), he does so by leaning over the table (*Basterds* 0:06:15), taking off his gloves and throwing them far across it (*Basterds* 0:06:56). This motif of intrusion into another character's side of the frame, as well as the use of seemingly innocent and friendly gestures to direct and in consequence oppress people, is picked up again and again throughout the whole film and culminates in Landa's demonstrative touching of the cuffed and hooded Aldo Raine (*Basterds* 1:57:37). The leader of the Basterds is already completely under the control of the SS and still Landa can't help but, literally, point it out.

His speech patterns function in a very similar way: he barely ever raises his voice or bellows orders – he has second-in-commands to do this for him (*Basterds* 1:40:49) – but he still always remains the one in control of the conversation. Once more, while the motif can be traced throughout the whole film, the scene at the LaPadite farm is a perfect example. Landa is the one to speak first and to immediately take the lead. His complimentary references to the daughters' beauty sound like a threat used to establish his position and affirm his knowledge of the family's life (*Basterds* 0:04:40). He frequently requests permission, e. g. to switch languages (*Basterds* 0:07:12), but they always come across as orders. Finally, he repeatedly asks seemingly innocent questions which, however, just like his use of physical contact, are clearly aimed at manoeuvring opponents into a corner, where they will be completely helpless.

Tarantino puts further non-diegetic stress on control by constantly focusing the camera on the 'Jew Hunter's' precisely executed manual actions and by imbuing isolated movements with increased significance by placing them centre frame. Again, one only needs to look at the farm scene: in addition to the inquiring gesture of Landa stepping onto the LaPadite grounds, the handshake (framed in a close-up), and the removal of the gloves, there are the long pause while he is drinking his milk (*Basterds* 0:05:40 – 56) and the emphasis on him lighting his bigger pipe (*Basterds* 0:16:24). The arguably most striking ones of this type of shots are those during the scene in which he arranges his writing utensils before interrogating Perrier LaPadite (*Basterds* 0:08:00 – 51), and then continuing to meticulously check off names and take down ages. Just like Merricat in Jackson's novel, Landa displays an OCD-like tendency during this procedure which, in other films, might function as a comic element but here only serves to make him appear more frightening – an embodiment of control which renders everyone else powerless: a self-providing head of a family suddenly feels the need to ask for permission to smoke in his own house (while Landa sits at the head of the table) (*Basterds* 0:09:20); later on an independent woman eats, drinks and smokes whatever he orders for her, in exactly the way he tells her to (*Basterds* 0:54:24); and another does whatever he says even if it means going beyond the normal limits of decency, like putting her foot in his lap (*Basterds* 1:53:57). All the while, the world around these characters starts to blur and dissolve – quite literally, if one looks at the backgrounds in these shots (e.g. *Basterds* 0:17:12 or even more clearly at 0:55:46). Eventually, all that is left is an oppressive empty darkness and the powerful figure sitting opposite them (e.g. *Basterds* 0:17:30).

The atmosphere created in the manner described above is highly claus-trophobic, seemingly exercising such pressure on Landa's victims that they do not even think of running, fighting, screaming, or even gasping, but can only hold their breaths (e.g. *Basterds* 0:58:18). In other words, they find themselves in a position distinctly reminiscent of the Gothic fainting damsels in distress. This is, of course, a 'realistic' depiction of the physical reactions to fear scientists have observed over the years: quicker breathing, sweating, shaking, a racing heart, involuntary emptying of the bladder, etc.[30] Yet if one looks closely, all these symptoms are also nothing else than signs of a total loss of control, in particular over one's body. From there the concept can be developed even further. In "A Philosophical Enquiry into the Sublime and the Beautiful" (1757), Robert Burke writes that

> [w]hatever is fitted in any sort to excite the ideas of pain, and danger, that is to say, whatever is in any sort terrible, or is conversant about terrible objects, or operates in a manner analogous to terror, is a source of the sublime; that is, it is productive of the strongest emotion which the mind is capable of feeling. [… As a result] the mind is so entirely filled with its object, that it cannot entertain any other, nor by consequence reason on that which employs it.[31]

In other words, it is not only the body but also the mind that becomes powerless during the experience of fear – and it is exactly this concept that Tarantino works with in his depiction of the 'Jew Hunter's' victims.

Landa's presence not only has an effect on the people in his vicinity; he seems to affect rooms and objects as well. In perfect accordance with the Gothic trad-ition, he subverts everything around him that is idyllic and homely and turns it into something frightening: a country farm becomes a gloomy prison-like cell (*Basterds* 0:19:38); a glass of milk, while he is drinking it, turns into a symbol of a

---

30 Cf. RACHMANN, Stanley. *Angst: Formen, Ursachen und Therapie.* München: Urban und Schwarzenberg, 1975. 57.
31 WRIGHT, Angela. *Gothic Fiction.* New York: Palgrave Macmillan, 2007. 39.

family's entire existence under scrutiny; afterwards, when the glass just stands on the table during the interrogation, always more or less centre-frame, it acts as a constant reminder of Landa's intrusion and of the fact that his demands are not to be denied; the ashtray, closely associated with Perrier LaPadite's wish to steady his nerves by smoking, is deprived of any calming effect by the looming skull on the SS officer's hat lying next to it (*Basterds* 0:10:38); and later on in the film, strudel with cream is transformed from being one of the most homely dishes in popular culture (in both the Austrian/German and the American context of 'apple pie') into a form of torture – for Shosanna, who has to force herself to swallow it, but also for the viewer, who has to witness Landa stuff himself with it in between highly inquisitive questions, picking up single raisins with his fork in an obsessive-compulsive manner, before he, finally, abuses what is left of the dessert as an ashtray (*Basterds* 0:55:07 – 58:07).

As with Jackson's novel, what makes Landa even more terrifying is the fact that all this oppression and destructiveness is delivered in the lightest of tones. Just as with the sisters and villagers in *We Have Always Lived in the Castle*, causing fear has become a game for the 'Jew Hunter', who, at least initially, finds every aspect of it highly entertaining, including the nicknames the SS officers receive from the pursued (*Basterds* 0:12:30 – 13:20). The way his soldiers know precisely what to do at the end of the interrogation scene (*Basterds* 0:18:53 – 19:12) is indicative of routine, and the manner in which Landa lets Shosanna go (*Basterds* 0:19:53 – 20:20) proves just how much he enjoys the hunt. If one takes into account that he purposefully uses English to prevent the hiding Dreyfuses from understanding him (*Basterds* 0:18:20) but at the same time makes a point of mentioning them all by name during the interrogation, it becomes obvious that he enjoys causing fear. Add to that his constant joking and sing-song rhyming (e. g. *Basterds* 0:09:54 or 2:02:06), his radiant smile, his strong Austrian accent, his at times nearly child-like, 'dorky' behaviour (*Basterds* 1:39:37, 1:47:20, 2:03:39) – once again all boundaries between danger and harmlessness, between the homely and the uncanny start to blur.

Many scholars have written about the fact that humour, while it can decrease fear, can also increase the sense of danger by estranging the object[32] and how it is exactly this incongruity in grotesque writing which results in a highly emotional response, involving revulsion as well as fascination.[33] Such observations on the function of this particular narrative tone, together with many of those discussed in the context of Jackson's novel, make it quite clear why its supposedly light-hearted quality is a perfect choice for a modern villain of Gothic origin. First and

---

32 Cf. FRITSCH. *Absurd oder grotesk?* 30.
33 Cf. CLAYBOROUGH, Arthur. *The Grotesque in English Literature.* Oxford: Clarendon, 1965. 70 ff.

foremost, the combination of 'revulsion' and 'fascination' has always been a defining feature of this type of character. Furthermore, the simultaneous increase and decrease of potential danger forms a perfect link to all other motifs of the 'uncanny'. Once more everything is about constant subversion, about creating tension through discrepancy on the one hand, and about reviving an old character by making it unpredictable again on the other.

Landa, in fact, quickly becomes and remains so ungraspable that during many of his scenes, when he is not actively seen to be doing anything 'evil', one might start to wonder whether he really is that dangerous – whether he, truly, will perform any terrible action – or whether one, as a viewer, is not simply being paranoid. For it should be kept in mind that he does let Shosanna go at the LePadite farm; and the way he orders milk for her with her strudel (*Basterds* 0:53:38) and begins to say that there was one more thing he wanted to ask her (*Basterds* 0:58:00) suggests that he maybe recognises her and again decides to let her go (either because he enjoys the hunt too much, or because he does not enjoy being the 'Jew Hunter' enough, anymore, the novelty of it being gone). In addition, as he himself observes, he wins the war for the Allies virtually single-handedly (*Basterds* 02:03:03) and seems to be honestly distraught when Aldo Raine kills a German radio operator (*Basterds* 2:21:20). So perhaps not everyone needs to be afraid of Landa all the time?

A closer look at the situations presented throughout the film soon reveals that the question as to whether one as a viewer is being paranoid or not is, ultimately, insignificant. For the most terrifying aspect of the worlds depicted in both *Inglourious Basterds* and *We Have Always Lived in the Castle* is exactly the fact that the entire concept of paranoia is fundamentally negated: it is one of the main characteristics of paranoia, after all, that there might not be a 'real' reason to be afraid[34] – but when fear is omnipresent and normal, this speculative quality is not possible.

Landa inevitably ends up causing pain and/or death, just like the villagers and Merricat do in Jackson's novel, yet these temporary flashes of actual physical terror make him appear insane and hysterical rather than terrifying (e. g. *Basterds* 1:55:54). They are harmless in comparison to the continuous fear of not knowing for certain what he will do before, after, or maybe even whilst he is smiling. As Jerry Palmer observes, thrill and tension result from "potentiality of situation", not its realisation[35] – an observation which, once more, already played an important role in eighteenth-century writing, causing Robert Burke to argue in his essay that "[t]o make anything very terrible, obscurity seems in

---

34 Cf. NAZIRI, Gérard. *Paranoia im amerikanischen Kino. Die 70er Jahre und die Folgen.* Sankt Augustin: Gardez! Verlag, 2003. 28.
35 PALMER. *Thrillers.* 59.

general to be necessary. When we know the full extent of any danger, when we can accustom our eyes to it, a great deal of apprehension vanishes".[36] In Tarantino's film, Landa seems to be constantly and consciously exercising this concept. He never lets his victims, or the audience for that matter, "know the full extent" of his character, and by withholding information he withholds any possibility from his opponents to break out from the near-paralysis of apprehension and regain control.

IV.   Conclusion and Implications for our Concept of Fear

Looking at these two (comparatively) contemporary works of fiction, it becomes clear that the approaches to what fear is and to what it is triggered by have not changed much over the last few centuries. Psychologists have always debated whether there are such things as inherent fears[37] – whether fear, in fact, exists outside of time and culture.[38] After discovering so many devices and motifs employed in traditional Gothic novels as well as in twentieth- and twenty-first-century texts, this theory certainly seems to be substantive. While the different times and cultures unquestionably do have an influence on how terrifying things are depicted (how gory or how subtle, how gloomy and dramatic or supposedly light-hearted), the actual basic terrors themselves seem to be unchanging: the unknown, the loss of straightforward values and familiar things which offer a sense of security and function as an anchor, and through the loss of those the loss of basic control over one's whole life. These literary findings are also very similar to those made by some of the aforementioned psychologists based on patient studies: Stanley Rachman, for example, referring to Gray, has suggested strangeness as one of the basic triggers of fear,[39] and Ernest R. Hilgard and Eugene E. Levitt have argued that fear results from lost roots and a change of values.[40]

This correspondence automatically raises the question, exceedingly time-tried itself, of what came first: do people fear many of those things and situations listed above exactly *because* culture and specifically fiction have taught them to do so by repeatedly showing how frightening and dangerous they are over the centuries – or does, maybe, as some scholars have suggested, fear in fiction only work when readers (or viewers, respectively) associate it with something they

---

36 WRIGHT. *Gothic Fiction.* 40.
37 Cf. RACHMANN. *Angst.* 42.
38 Cf. LEVITT. *Die Psychologie der Angst.* 9 ff.
39 Cf. RACHMANN. *Angst.* 44–45.
40 Cf. HILGARD, Ernest R. "Vorwort." In: Eugene E. Levitt. *Die Psychologie der Angst.* Stuttgart: Kohlhammer, 1976. 7.

have previously experienced themselves.[41] Already Freud himself pointed out that the uncanny comes into existence when suppressed, archaic beliefs start breaking through[42] and that, subsequently, it only has an effect in literature when the latter seems to depict a world very close to our own. Otherwise, he argues, the surfacing ancient beliefs would be accepted as merely a part of a foreign fantasy universe and would lose their potential for the uncanny.[43] Yet this idea of the importance of previous real-life experiences would mean that there are some fears we all, or at least most of us, share since not only a few people react to the terrors depicted in fictional works such as those discussed above. The logical conclusion of this would be to say that in our world, those particular fears are 'normal' – a fact which, in turn, would imply that the worlds portrayed in *We Have Always Lived in the Castle* and *Inglourious Basterds* are not as dystopian and 'other' as we might suppose or want or indeed even need them to be. This shows just how uncanny our own reality is and suggests one possible explanation for why the century-old Gothic ideas and motifs are still relevant, functional and omnipresent today, albeit in an adapted and modified form.

References

BERNSEN, Michael. *Angst und Schrecken in der Frühliteratur des französischen und englischen 18. Jahrhunderts.* München: Fink, 1996.
CLAYBOROUGH, Arthur. *The Grotesque in English Literature.* Oxford: Clarendon, 1965.
CONRAD, Horst. *Das Schreckliche in Schauerromantik und Detektivgeschichte.* Düsseldorf: Bertelsmann Universitätsverlag, 1974.
FREUD, Sigmund. *Das Unheimliche. Aufsätze zur Literatur.* Frankfurt M.: Fischer, 1963.
FRITSCH, Rudolf. *Absurd oder grotesk? Über literarische Darstellung von Entfremdung bei Beckett und Heller.* Frankfurt M.: Peter Lang, 1950.
HILGARD, Ernest R. "Vorwort." In: Eugene E. Levitt. *Die Psychologie der Angst.* Stuttgart: Kohlhammer, 1976. 7.
JACKSON, Shirley. *We Have Always Lived in the Castle.* London/New York: Penguin, 2006.
KILGOUR, Maggie. *The Rise of the Gothic Novel.* London/New York: Routledge, 1997.
LEVITT, Eugene E. *Die Psychologie der Angst.* Stuttgart: Kohlhammer, 1976.
NAZIRI, Gérard. *Paranoia im amerikanischen Kino. Die 70er Jahre und die Folgen.* Sankt Augustin: Gardez! Verlag, 2003.
PALMER, Jerry. *Thrillers. Genesis and Structure of a Popular Genre.* London: Edward Arnold, 1978.
PUNTER, David. *The Literature of Terror: A History of Gothic Fictions from 1765 to the Present Day.* London: Longman, 1980.

---

41 Cf. CONRAD. *Das Schreckliche in Schauerromantik und Detektivgeschichte.* 19.
42 Cf. FREUD. *Das Unheimliche.* 70 ff.
43 Cf. FREUD. *Das Unheimliche.* 81 – 82.

PUNTER, David and Glenn BYRON. *The Gothic.* Malden, MA/Oxford: Blackwell, 2004.

PURVES, Maria. *The Gothic and Catholicism. Religion, Cultural Exchange and the Popular Novel 1785 – 1829.* Cardiff: University of Wales Press, 2009.

RACHMAN, Stanley. *Angst: Formen, Ursachen und Therapie.* München: Urban und Schwarzenberg, 1975.

SCHNEIDER, Gerd. *Transformationen des Gothic.* Frankfurt M.: Peter Lang, 2002.

SCHUMACHER, Manfred. *Das Groteske und seine Gestaltung in der Gothic Novel.* Frankfurt M.: Peter Lang, 1990.

TARANTINO, Quentin, dir. *Inglourious Basterds.* Universal Pictures, 2009.

VENNEMANN, Johanna. "Der böse Blick." In: André Michels et al. (eds). *Angst.* Tübingen: Edition Diskord, 2001. 166 – 72.

WRIGHT, Angela. *Gothic Fiction.* New York: Palgrave Macmillan, 2007.

Barbara Puschmann-Nalenz

Nothing to be Frightened of? The Expulsion of Fear in Kazuo Ishiguro's Novel *Never Let Me Go*

The essay proposes to examine different aspects of fear and their representation in a novel which at first sight seems to proclaim that there is nothing to fear, as the above title of Julian Barnes' recently published essay also suggests. I added the question mark.

I.   The Explicit Expression of Fear by Characters of the Novel

An initial observation seems to marginalize the topic of fear in *Never Let Me Go*: hardly anybody in this novel is afraid, and my opening statements are dedicated to this discovery. Only two instances of an explicit manifestation of fear can be found. The first occurs in one of the minor characters who is represented as fearful; it is the person anonymously called "Madame", one of the outside visitors at Hailsham, the co-ed boarding school which the first-person narrator attended and received her education from. "She's scared of us" (*Never Let Me Go* 30) Ruth, the quickest child among the narrator's friends, states repeatedly, and Kathy H., the protagonist and first-person narrator, agrees: "Ruth had been right. Madame *was* afraid of us." (*Never* 32, emphasis in original) The pupils wonder why; like the reader they are still far from the detection of the secret shrouding their existence. "Madame" regularly visits them to collect the outstanding sample of the students' "works of art" for her "gallery", about which there is no precise knowledge, but much speculation. The central significance of the artefacts will be discussed further down.

Later in the novel – and this can be identified as the second instance of fear – the protagonist, now a young adult, visits Madame and the former head of Hailsham together with her closest friends to learn more about the secrets of their own destiny and their former boarding school. It is through the explanations of the two elderly women, who confess that they all were afraid of their charges (*Never* 246), that they get to know why experiments like Hailsham, where the pupils were well treated and respected, were given up and their

teachers and guardians resigned. The reason is that another experimental institution called Morningdale had aroused deep-rooted anxieties, not because
members of society shrank from crossing borders and trespassing ethical laws,
but because they were afraid of the superior beings created there. Regular citizens experienced fear towards the project of designer babies planned for the
future, because they would mean a threat to the mainstream society and its
individuals and easily win any competition, being healthier, more intelligent,
more attractive, stronger etc., in short, the optimised human breed. This fear of
members of society to become losers in the competitive race of life is given as the
reason why experiments like a privileged education for the clones at Hailsham
were equally terminated, because

> [i]t reminded people, reminded them of a fear they'd always had. It's one thing to create
> students, such as yourselves, for the donation programme. But a generation of created
> children who'd take their place in society? Children demonstrably *superior* to the rest of
> us? Oh no. That frightened people. They recoiled from that. (*Never* 241, emphasis in
> original)

These are the only passages in the narrative where fear is explicitly addressed. In
the case of Madame who flinches in xenophobia from the children, we observe
through Kathy her unaccountable body language: "[...] she just froze [...] I can
still see it now, the shudder she seemed to be suppressing, the real dread that one
of us would accidentally brush against her." (*Never* 32)

The fright of the majority of mainstream society is merely verbally reported
by a guardian in the second example quoted above.

II.   Absence of Fear

Thus fear seems to be extremely rare and obviously not felt at all by the young
protagonists in this novel, least of all by the narrator who in the present of the
story is perpetually confronted with mortality and whose own death is imminent, for readers are from the very beginning made to feel the sense of an
ending (*Never* 4). The setting of her childhood and education was shaped by a
boarding school's bleakness, isolation and lack of emotional ties. These pupils
are also 'orphans' who later try to find their 'parents' – their originals – called
"possibles" by them.[1] The adulthood of the protagonist and her friends, how-

---

1 Ishiguro's novels *Never Let Me Go* and *When We Were Orphans* are by no means the only
   contemporary narratives in which the *topos* of the orphaned child is central; a surprising
   number of protagonists in current fiction prove to be without parents, from John Fowles' *The
   French Lieutenant's Woman* to *Waterland* and *Last Orders* by Graham Swift, to Peter Ack-
   royd's *The Clerkenwell Tales*, J.M. Coetzee's *The Life and Times of Michael K.*, Margaret

ever, can only be described as a desolate life, a "life [that] must run the course that's been set for it" (*Never* 243). Neither this other-directed total predestination nor loss and loneliness, nor death can cause fear in this narrator, whose peculiarity is step by step made known to the reader almost in the same pace as it is disclosed to the protagonist herself; the first crucial revelation is accomplished by Miss Lucy, one of the guardians at Hailsham, when they are school-age children (*Never* 73).[2] The communication of "schemes and plans" (*Never* 233) invented by members of the main world, including the rare 'benevolent' ones, is leaked half-heartedly to the children by governesses or the occasional visitor. This leads to the nebulous atmosphere which envelops the inner and outer landscape of the fictional universe: only a glimpse "through the misted-up windows" (*Never* 120) into the outer world is possible for the students.

Instead of fear the teenage Ruth expresses anger about their presumed origin, when she shouts at her friends that clones are modeled on "trash", on the basest and meanest specimens of society; she is immediately silenced by her peers (*Never* 152 – 53). Tommy is the only one who eventually rages at their destiny and throws a fit after their aging former teachers have revealed the meaninglessness of all efforts to them (*Never* 250 – 51).[3] His screams are to Kathy expressions of a maniac, and to calm him down remains the only goal she can think of. She is the model carer for whom the welfare of her protégés lies in his/her quiet submission and acceptance of his/her fate. Whenever therefore 'agitatedness' is diagnosed in one of the donors, who expect being murdered for the harvesting of their vital organs, it is the task of carers like Kathy H. to sedate them, and she fully embraces her present role prescribed to her from elsewhere.

Tommy's raving madness for which he even apologizes to Kathy, calling himself an "idiot" (*Never* 252), remains incomprehensible to Kathy, just like his earlier tantrums in the boarding school were inexplicable for all of them. Even to the other boys his conduct was blamable and inappropriate – he was 'the odd one out', and occasionally considered 'beyond the pale' in their community.

Atwood's *The Blind Assassin*, and *The Pregnant Widow* by Martin Amis, apart from the most popular of all orphans, Harry Potter. Derived from the Greek word for 'bereaved' the symbolic signifier points at the dislocation fundamental to the postmodern condition.

2 These informative lessons, which are officially forbidden at Hailsham, are the equivalent of the explicatory 'guided tours' of the utopian/dystopian world, as we find it in classic novels like Aldous Huxley's *Brave New World*.

3 About anger and its wider context cf. ROBBINS, Bruce. "Cruelty is Bad: Banality and Proximity in *Never Let Me Go*." In: *Novel. A Forum on Fiction* 40 (2007): 289 – 302, 297 – 98. His reading is mainly based on a sociological approach to an understanding of late twentieth-century British society.

III.   Gender, Fear and the State of the Nation

The above-mentioned temporary exception can prompt the conclusion that
Never Let Me Go exemplifies gendered behaviour in Tommy the rebel versus
Kathy the perfect carer and model of compliance. The following quotation from
a critical comment that avoids a closer examination of clichés illustrates this:

> Kathy's ability to understand the emotions of those around her and to make things
> right between them, leaving her own needs and desires out of play, has been one of her
> genuine attractions both as a character and as a narrator. It certainly makes her as
> convincing as she is.[4]

These traits indeed characterize her, I will argue, as a convincing model of
femininity, as does her trusting humility in regard to the larger system in which
she lives. Whether the praise quoted above obtains common consent from the
readers can be doubted; Robbins himself at least admits that the protagonist's
indifference towards the clones' fate is not pleasant but shocking.[5]
   Their universe is a strikingly feminized world, governed and internally
shaped by female characters, focalized by a female protagonist and at any time
filled with occupations and concerns generally associated with girls and women,
culminating in the self-sacrifice for the relief of others.[6] The tutors are women,
whether gentle and likeable or severe; the only male adult is the old caretaker
Keffers at the Cottages. They are all subdued by a cold and cruel, if shady, outside
world, where resistance and scruples are crushed and benevolence is dis-
approved of or unknown. The top-down dominance imposed from outside upon
those living in the parallel world of the clones opposes their communal reality in
which Tommy has to ask forgiveness for his rebellion and even a 'bossy' girl like
Ruth can be converted to team-spirit and resilience by the gentleness of her
peers.[7]

---

4 Robbins. "Cruelty is Bad." 300.
5 Robbins. "Cruelty is Bad." 300. Fluet, Lisa. "Immaterial Labors: Ishiguro, Class, and Affect."
   In: *Novel, A Forum on Fiction* 40 (2007): 265 – 88, 283 considers Kathy H. a typical Ishiguro
   hero(ine), regardless of her sex: "Like the butler Stevens, she will put up with practically
   anything" and simply describes her "as a little too tolerant" (ibid.). Her submissiveness,
   however, is not the same as that which 'the gentleman's gentleman' Stevens embodies, who in
   his own way is limited and to a degree comical, while Kathy emerges as an increasingly tragic
   figure without her being fully conscious of it.
6 Similar to Robbins. "Cruelty is Bad." 294, Lisa Fluet sees the service professional class of our
   time represented in this universe (Fluet. "Immaterial Labors." 268), regardless of gender
   concepts.
7 Chertoff calls her "a typical power-mongering 'queen of the classroom,' [...] whose primary purpose is to shape conditions for excluding others." Chertoff, D. and L. Toker.
   "Reader Response and the Recycling of Topoi in Ishiguro's 'Never Let Me Go'." In: *Partial
   Answers: Journal of Literature and the History of Ideas* 6,1 (2008): 163 – 80, 172.

Lisa Fluet's statements about social service culture are worth considering in the context of a feminization of this novel. She marginally mentions the discussion "concerning the mobilization of maternality and domesticity within the genealogy of welfare state provisions in twentieth-century Britain" and the ensuing consequences for feminism as a political philosophy without further involvement.[8] To Fluet 'feminine values' like caring and homemaking determined the laws essential for the creation of the Welfare State, where men took the political decisions. After all, this would prove restrictive for the opportunities of girls and women and largely delegate the work of the welfare system to the female members of society. On this historical background several questions emerge from the narrative with renewed acuteness: Do humanitarian, philanthropic ideals correspond to models of femininity? Is the social gendered, and are there cultural reasons for it?

If a philosophical or 'natural' affinity between social affairs, the welfare system and gender is presupposed Ishiguro's novel contributes to the public discussion in an unusual way. Caring and unselfishness as the protagonists' main endeavour and the official purpose assigned to them even as their only *raison d'etre* are not restricted to the *female* clones, so that here the concept of "gender and the social" is extended compared to much of our empirical reality and would not necessarily collide with feminism. Maternality and the social, however, are associated in a new manner in *Never Let Me Go*, as exemplified in the character of Kathy: she interpreted the song "Baby, Baby, never let me go" quite literally (*Never* 64) and believed that it referred to the relation of mother and small child, something she as a teenager intensely wished for. In her longing, however, she curiously reverses positions: the child is asked by the speaker to hold on to the mother forever.

Her performance of a mother/child symbiosis in a rare moment of privacy while listening to the music is observed by Madame without Kathy noticing this. It leads to an emotional outburst in the visitor, who knows that Kathy will never be a mother (*Never* 65). The scene as a key experience for both is later remembered in the conversation between Kathy, Tommy, Miss Emily and Madame (*Never* 247–48). Regarding motherhood and motherly feelings, biology and the social are disconnected in Kathy, as are gender-concepts and biological sex, because young men among the clones are made to be aides as well and share the same fate as women. Selflessness and helpfulness are the duties of all clones, regardless of their – infringed – biological sex. Unable to reproduce and physically as psychologically constrained they perform the functions of altruistic and virtually idealistic individuals for the greater part of society. To the narrative's dystopian world they become indispensable.

---

8 FLUET. "Immaterial Labors." 284, n 17.

The feminist statement that 'The Future is Female' has been enhanced by contemporary scientists, psychologists and politicians alike.[9] Whereas it aims – with the exception of the geneticists – at an optimistic assessment of the importance of women in all spheres of public life Ishiguro's novel stimulates a different interpretation of the above slogan. He represents the 'future of the recent past' as in one part governed by the presence of the feminine, in the other, major part ruled according to principles commonly regarded as masculine. The narrative's guideline is that of division and separation, of drawing borderlines between one part of Britain's population and the other, between gender and sex, between humane and inhuman or post-human, between art and genetic engineering, body and soul, love and sexuality, while challenging one borderline in particular: that of ethical issues, which have been and will be controversially discussed, whether we think of in-vitro-fertilization or PID. Ishiguro's fiction is again political.

IV. The Implicit Distribution of Fear in the Novel

That aggressiveness just like fear is eliminated in the clones points to the fundamental truths ruling the world of those by whom these children were created. They result from the contradictory, even paradoxical emotions arising from the awareness of death in human life: universal certainty that each of us must die is opposed to universal anxiety of death; the accepted universal necessity of dying contradicts the universally necessary will to live.[10] The inevitable incongruity of attitudes towards death has been partly 'resolved' or at least made bearable in Ishiguro's novel by separating the inherent contraries and dismissing the insupportable into a parallel world. Henceforth the clones carry the gene of death-acceptance as an inescapable certainty. Anxiety and the will to live, on the other hand, are the motor driving the ingenuity of the main world. This division, of course, makes them imperfect clones.

The 'hidden fears' which underlie the plot of Never Let Me Go remain alien to the protagonist and therefore absent from the text. The implied reader disguised as a listener to this life-story, as shown for example in "I don't know how it was

---

9 Die Zukunft ist weiblich is a study by Margarete Mitscherlich first released in the 1980s, which redefines women's role in society; Angela Merkel published her book Deutschlands Zukunft ist weiblich in 2005, and recently British geneticists Steve Jones and Bryan Sykes from Oxford University seriously claimed the same for the biological future of mankind in general.

10 This 'death paradox' is explored by Heinrich VERSTEEGEN in his article "Dying with Laughter: The Inherent Joke Structure of Death and Bereavement." In: Journal for the Study of British Cultures (2012).

where *you* were, but at Hailsham" (*Never* 12, 62, emphasis added) has at his/her disposal a frame of reference which in a prefatory note the author claims to be "England, late 1990s".[11] The undisclosed recipient of her monologue could be another fatalistic clone with a less privileged upbringing, but the reader may well shudder, because it soon becomes clear that Kathy is a carer for young people her own age whose death is obviously meticulously planned. The contemporary reader's fear would be based on the recognition that neither ethics nor empathy reign in a dystopian society which brings about the parallel universe of the clones. They are created for the sole purpose of serving as living material for repeated organ transplants which will inevitably lead to their early death. The end of the receivers' lives in the mainstream society can thus be deferred, and the reader is aware that the normal people's fear of disability, suffering or an untimely death is thereby suppressed and diminished in an exorcism achieved through violence and unscrupulous exploitation of scientifically feasible acts.

The homodiegetic narrative perspective precludes this insight which can only be the conclusion of our empirical extradiegetic knowledge. Since the fear of mortality, though vital for the contrivance of the plot, is never made thematic on account of the strictly limited narrative perspective it can only be brought about by the reader's complementary imagination during the reading process.[12] The complementary effort adds to the recipient's role as detective who has to draw his conclusions from the recognition of the obvious euphemisms used from the beginning of the novel, e. g. 'completion' instead of willful murder, 'donor' instead of 'victim' and 'donation' for life-threatening operations, 'student' for 'captivated child', 'special' – an attribute for the children – as a description of their origin and their end. The fact that this vernacular is "the middle class's own optimistic, system-trusting language"[13] and not 'Newspeak' as in George Orwell's *1984* – there are donors as well as carers in the world every Briton knows – denounces the relation this dystopian world bears to contemporary reality and adds to the normality of the intradiegetic world.[14]

---

11 McDonald, Keith. "Days of Past Futures: Kazuo Ishiguro's *Never Let Me Go* as 'Speculative Memoir'." In: *Biography* 30 (2007): 74 – 83, 79 defines the meaning of an interjection such as the one above as both authenticity-enhancing and author-distancing, since the "governing intelligence" behind the fictional autobiography withdraws a further step from the internal focus.

12 This aspect is permanently neglected by critics who, like Myra Seaman, treat the narrative as if it were the full description of a future society. Seaman, Myra J. "Becoming More (than) Human: Affective Posthumanisms, Past and Future." In: *Journal of Narrative Theory* 37,2 (2007): 246 – 75, 265 – 66 (abstract via MUSE 2010).

13 Robbins. "Cruelty is Bad." 294.

14 Thematically, Huxley's dystopia is the closest to Ishiguro's. – The conceit that the future is remembered as the narrator's past and differs from the reader's experience is explored in McDonald's ("Days of Past Futures") and Currie's articles (Currie, Mark. "Controlling Time: *Never Let Me Go*." In: Sean Matthews and Sebastian Groes (eds.). *Kazuo Ishiguro.*

As opposed to the powerful fear of mortality that governs the main world, a lack of fear of unethical behaviour has become natural there and is taken for granted by Kathy and her peers. It epitomizes the lack of emotion generally originating from the main society of which we can barely catch a glimpse, since by the projected "poverty of experience"[15] of the clones and Kathy's mono-perspectival narrative it is largely banned from explicit representation.[16] The poverty of experience includes lack of educational instruction normally provided by parents and adult role model function, so that many of the notions the clones grow up with border on the grotesque, for example in regard to the process of donation (*Never* 79) and their "possibles" (*Never* 126 – 33, 145 – 46).

V.   Relation between Fear and Value-System

The exploration of the value-system represented in the narrative reveals an intricate relation to fear, exposing its social as well as its psychological side. The abolition of fear in the parallel world of the clones demonstratively annihilates fear's natural function as an instinct warning humans of dangers or menacing situations which reduce the quality of life or life-expectancy or threaten life itself. Whereas the clones, whose controversial definition as humans causes a violent debate inside and outside the narrative, are resigned without fear, the outside majority society which makes this possible has eliminated empathy and an ethics committee concerned with genetic engineering and its purposes. The horror felt is that of the reader only, and he is most alarmed by the unquestioned acceptance of these standards by the narrator. Yet to the reader a compelling inversion of humane or ethical values also emerges. The students are raised to help strangers selflessly by donating their organs, moreover to excel in their assignments of taking care of the sick and the dying among themselves, in short to sacrifice their health, happiness and life for others and to understand this "as a bizarrely well-intentioned, skilled service to those who will later benefit from

---

London: Continuum 2009. 91 – 103); cf. also the comment on the novel's "looping narrative movement" where "proleptic touches" alternate with "informational gaps" by CHERTOFF and TOKER. "Reader-Response." 169.

15 McDONALD. "Days of Past Futures." 78.

16 The trip to Norfolk to search for the clones' models and find a copy of the tape with the song as their key experience of the mainstream world is interpreted in MILDORF, Jarmila. "Kazuo Ishiguro, *Never Let Me Go.*" In: Susanne Peters (ed.). *Novels*, Part 2. Trier: WVT, 2008. 279 – 96, 289 – 94. Even when as adults they go out and venture into the surrounding world the clones still inhabit their 'invisible prison' which they share only with their peers: "the likes of us" are perceived as divided from "everyone else" (*Never* 249).

their deaths".[17] 'Bizarre' is the distinctive word in the critic's comment, while for the narrator her function is a source of pride.

Thus the protagonists embody in an extreme way altruistic values acknowledged as humaneness and propagated by the Enlightenment as well as religion, and whose universally embraced form, according to the sociologist among literary scholars, is the ideology of the Welfare State.[18] The values of humanitarianism and charity have been so to speak exported or removed into the parallel universe of the clones, while they were discarded in the majority society of regular people to be there replaced by brutal selfishness. A dividing line separates the humanitarian from human nature, only to ask again for a redefinition of the human in the world of "traditional Enlightenment and post-Enlightenment humanism", a humanism which conceived of the human as an independent subject "generally assumed male" and of "utterly rational intelligence".[19] Myra Seaman refers to Michel Foucault and Claude Levi-Strauss who both claim that 'the human' was not 'discovered', but constructed by the Enlightenment. Ishiguro deconstructs it quite literally by inventing the human clone living apart from the human race as the carrier of humaneness. The question arises: Is the clone thereby made human, and is the society of regular individuals still human?[20] Or do both clones and 'regulars' lack one or more characteristics which are traditionally considered part of human nature?

Here lie some of the crucial paradoxes essential for the whole plot of the novel and even more for its intellectual substance as well as the disturbing impact on the reader. I agree with Jonathan Yardley's statement that one realizes, provoked by the novel, that a new definition of humanity is necessary in a new world.[21]

Not only is the reader solicited to torment himself with the above-mentioned philosophical and ethical questions, but the narrative – in the ironical manner of postmodern self-reflexivity – focuses on still another element as proof of humanity: art. Especially the estimation of the clones' creativity by well-meaning guardians circles around the significance of their little achievements. The students' handicrafts and writings are collected by some exceptional individuals like Madame who want to find out whether these "poor creatures", as she

---

17 FLUET. "Immaterial Labors." 269.
18 ROBBINS. "Cruelty is Bad." 294; his article, which is obviously rooted in the social sciences, scrutinizes the collusion of the ideology of the Welfare State with that of upward social mobility in Ishiguro's novel.
19 SEAMAN. "Becoming More (than) Human." abstract.
20 To SEAMAN this does not seem to be a question any longer: according to her the clones "confirm their humanity – the 'regulars' are revealed to be lacking in the humanity expressed in so many ways by their scientific offspring." (SEAMAN. "More Human." 266.)
21 YARDLEY, Jonathan. "'Review of Never Let Me Go." In: The Washington Post, 17 April, 2005.

eventually comes to call them (*Never* 249), have souls – art would serve as their infallible expression.

It is impossible to discuss this evaluation of art here in all its aspects.[22] However, the question whether the students have souls – that would make them definitely simulacra of humanity – seems to me to be answered by yet another symptom, namely the autobiographical narrative itself, which testifies to cognitive as well as to emotional capacities in giving retrospectively structure to Kathy's life. By her depiction of love, friendship, curiosity, sorrow and grief, by narrating the kindness she and her friends, especially Ruth and Tommy, show towards each other in their desolate lives, her gift is further enhanced.[23] "To represent the process of giving meaning to and by the narration" ["den Prozess der narrativen Sinnstiftung darzustellen"], a special characteristic of the first-person narrative according to Dorothee Birke, is even achieved by *this* narrator, whose limitations result from her existence and nevertheless show all the features of memorizing and narrating the past and one's own life.[24] Thus the clone is not, after all, an alien, but a near-perfect simulation, since she definitely possesses what is traditionally called a soul, last but not least evidenced by precisely this achievement of telling her story.[25] I wish to argue that the clone has become a monument of humanity, or of the myth of humanity.

That the novel presents an attempt to define human existence results in a split and trans-lation in the attribution of human traits. Biological characteristics – shared with man by other mammals – like fear and survival instinct, or fertility and the ability to reproduce are not to be found in the protagonist, who abounds in sensitivity, pity, softness and reconciliation, whereas we can see and conclude that none of these qualities has survived in the majority society. In addition, only

22 BLACK, Shameen. "Ishiguro's Inhuman Aesthetics." In: *Modern Fiction Studies* 55,4 (2009): 785–807, displays great sophistication in dealing with this theme (798–801), though this approach and the conclusions are quite different from mine. To BLACK and several reviewers quoted Kathy is a mechanical clock (801), and this metaphor, the critic claims, exposes the readers' lack of 'souls', their submissiveness and indifference. In this construction of meaning, by which the levels of 'tenor' and 'vehicle' of a metaphor are exchanged, one has to recognize Kathy as human, because she shares the shortcomings of civilized man.
23 The question whether the dismal layout of the clones' lives is a metaphor pointing out the failed and dejected quality lives can have is discussed as one of Ishiguro's strategies by ROBBINS. "Cruelty is Bad."; cf. CHERTOFF and TOKER "Reader Response." 178, who are of the opinion that "the artificially created and controlled life of the Hailsham students is a condensed version of the normal human experience". Ishiguro himself supports this view, stating "I wanted rather to write a story in which every reader might find an echo of his or her own life" (ANON. *bookbrowse* interview).
24 BIRKE, Dorothee. "Fictions of Memory: Kazuo Ishiguro." In: Vera Nünning (ed.). *Der zeitgenössische englische Roman. Genres – Entwicklungen – Modellinterpretationen.* Trier: WVT, 2007. 101–16, 104, my translation.
25 BLACK. "Inhuman Aesthetics." 801, only concedes that the clones evoke the reader's empathy merely through pity with their mechanical artificiality; they are, to him, "soul-less".

man is known to have had art almost from his earliest beginnings. If Joseph Beuys said that every man is an artist this creed is reversed in Ishiguro's dystopia where the most idealistic guardians believe that if the students can produce art they have human souls.[26]

The intradiegetic uncertainty of teachers and guardians in regard to their charges contrasts with the reader's conviction of the narrator's 'soul'. Unaware of their guardians' dilemma the teenagers attached still another, romantic meaning to their creative achievements: they had concluded that their works might show whether they were capable of a deeper feeling of true love. If they could prove this *they* might attain a 'deferral' of death! This is disclosed as a myth and self-delusion by their former head-mistress and the mysterious Madame before the end.[27] Therefore also Kathy and her longtime friend Tommy are doomed. Neither their love nor their art, both lifted out of the ordinary by the Romantic poets, can save them.[28]

VI.   Fear and Lack of Fear as Agents

The creation of human clones and the parallel dystopian world, which the sociological approach simply calls "an immense moral obscenity",[29] are the result of mankind's common fear of mortality. That only the reader is able to state this and not either the first-person narrator, another internal focalizer or a heterodiegetic narrator distinguishes this novel from several dystopian classics. Kathy's lack of fear is replaced by a mood of sadness and bleakness which pervades the whole text, even when telling about the little adventures, the quarrels or emotionally upsetting conflicts, whose significance seems unduly magnified by the narrator. The closed, claustrophobic universe in which the clones move

---

26 Whether there is self-defeating irony in the intradiegetic appraisal of creativity and art as proof of humanity has been explored by BLACK. "Inhuman Aesthetics." 800, who shares the view that created memories and the narrative as a verbal construct are also clones with CHERTOFF and TOKER. "Reader Response." 176. The latter convincingly argue that literary characters are "not quite whole", being "imitations of possible persons". Literary characters are therefore clones, their fictional realities simulacra.

27 CHERTOFF and TOKER. "Reader Response." 174, point to the signifying intertextual reading of *One Thousand and One Nights* by Kathy while caring for Tommy, where the narrator's lifetime is extended and ultimately saved by narrating.

28 BLACK. "Inhuman Aesthetics." states that Wordsworth as well as Shelley ascribes "empathetic imaginative projection" (787) to the poet in particular. – SCHABERT, Ina. *In Quest of the Other Person. Fiction as Biography.* Tübingen: Francke, 1990. 19 equally emphasizes that since the Romantic age the poetic capacity has declared participation of and insight into the mysteries of another person possible.

29 ROBBINS. "Cruelty is Bad." 291.

makes trivial events appear out of proportion: the essential is marginal and the petty everyday occurrence important.[30]

Sadness, unlike fear, is shared by narrator, guardians and readers alike, the horror at the absence of a dread of this world is entirely the reader's. The circumstance that Kathy is not afraid of illness and death – old age they will never reach – makes this secondary world possible; it eliminates despair and terror. The Gothic element of the 'unreal reality' of this novel, I claim, is a paradoxical effect of the absence of fear, which does not equal stoicism. The anxious uncertainty about the meaning of life or the question of what will happen experienced by an 'ordinary' individual is replaced by quiet submission in the clone, here without use of drugs or violence. The protagonist takes for granted what 'human beings' would be afraid of: to be cannibalized and have one's life destroyed. By human standards she would have to be regarded as an unreliable and elliptic narrator, while inside her universe her narrative must be considered subjective, but coherent and reliable.

When the author said that he had wanted to write "a story that was simple, but very fundamental, about the sadness of the human condition",[31] he left it to our interpretation whether by this he means character traits exposed by the majority *and* the clones taken together or the menacing ethical transgressions to which our attention is drawn in this nightmarish alternate history – or perhaps whether he meant both.

VII.   The Fear of the Readers

Intradiegetically, there are no indications that the addressee of the narrative can be horrified or scared by the state of the nation in the late 1990s as represented here. Yet the opinions evident in reader response are as manifold as there are critical voices. They express fear of scientific progress rushing ahead uncontrolled, fear of human hybris as in the romantic novel *Frankenstein*, where the 'being' is also given a human voice to narrate his life-story, fear of class struggle and the extremes of the British class system[32] or of the stranger or the Other, of post-humanism or, ultimately, of the failing ethics of art at the turn to the twenty-first century, as the following quotation shows: "While the novel attracts attention for its theme of genetic engineering, its *deepest anxieties* arguably

---

30 The episode of the beached boat (*Never* 204 – 05) can be seen as signifying a stifled attempt to escape. Like other debris and like its visitors, it is "washed up" (*Never* 263); cf. the footnote on the "abandoned transportation devices" in CHERTOFF and TOKER. "Reader Response." 175.

31 ANON. Interview in *BookBrowse*, n.d.

32 BLACK. "Inhuman Aesthetics." 796, ROBBINS. "Cruelty is Bad." 292.

concern the ethics of artistic production and consumption in an age of multi-
culturalism and globalization."[33]

This critic's statement that art is intradiegetically abused to mask the clones'
non-human nature and indirectly the regular world's inhuman ethics can, like
his analogies with underprivileged migrants in a globalized economy, not remain undisputed. Another, more optimistic comment calls the novel an example
of "aestheticized inhumanity" which is apt to awaken the reader's awareness of
inhuman practices in our times; thereby it contradicts the accusation of
"abusing" art since, extradiegetically, art is put to the use of didactic purposes in
revealing dreadful realities.[34] Alexander Bain sees in Ishiguro's approach even
"the contours of an emerging genre that I will call 'humanitarian crisis fiction'".[35] While the scientific achievements represented here – cloning, genetic
engineering, organ transplants, prolongation of life – deserve attention and
supply the plot it is the stand taken towards philanthropy, art and the reflexivity
of memoir that is innovative and most thought-provoking for literary analysis.

The fact that experienced and less experienced readers alike call the novel a
"very weird book"[36] or "strange"[37] points towards the troubling deconstruction
of traditional liberal humanism as well as to the narrative's self-reflexivity with
its time-loops and logical somersaults and, last but not least, the fact that it
subversively discloses the inescapable perspectivization of human experience of
reality, as the best examples of dystopian and science-fictional texts always do.
Yet another, more momentous function of literature in our contemporary culture
emerges when we discuss this novel, a role which has been defined and challenged in recent reflections on the purpose of the humanities:

> Thus literature functions for example as a 're-integrative inter-discourse' which con-
> veys different discourses and the forms of life-science they produce into a dialogue
> (often controversial) in the media of art. Literature may equally well assume the role of a
> 'culture-critical meta-discourse', which disputes with socially prevailing forms of life
> and dominant concepts of life-science.[38]

---

33 BLACK. "Inhuman Aesthetics." 785, emphasis added; ibid. 790 and 803.

34 CHERTOFF and TOKER. "Reader Response." 177.

35 BAIN, Alexander M. "International Settlements: Ishiguro, Shanghai, Humanitarianism." In:
   Novel, A Forum on Fiction 40 (2007): 240–63, 243.

36 DYER, Geoff. "Even in Arcadia there are Big White Vans: '*Never Let Me Go*', by Kazuo
   Ishiguro." In: *The Independent*, February 27, 2005.

37 YARDLEY, Jonathan and John MULLAN. "Afterword: On First Reading *Never Let Me Go*." In:
   Sean Matthews and Sebastian Groes (eds.). *Kazuo Ishiguro.* London: Continuum, 2009. 104–
   13, 113.

38 NÜNNING, Ansgar. "Lebensexperiment und Weisen literarischer Welterzeugung: Thesen zu
   den Aufgaben und Perspektiven einer lebenswissenschaftlich orientierten Literaturwissenschaft." In: Wolfgang Asholt and Ottmar Ette (eds.). *Literatur als Lebenswissenschaft. Programm – Projekte – Perspektiven.* Tübingen: Narr, 2010. 45–63, 56–57 (my translation).

Ishiguro's novel, like several of Ian McEwan's,[39] surprises its readers by fulfilling this purpose, as shown by the controversy above: diverse critics, such as sociologists, philosophers, biologists, and politicians recognize 'their' concerns in the narrative.

If storytelling is supposed to contribute to contemporary "humanitarian and human rights discourses"[40] then the worried vexation of the readership at this novel, whose ambiguous title *Never Let Me Go* expresses a longing for permanent relations and a yearning for the acknowledgment of individual personhood is certainly justified. Like another much-discussed writer of our time, Martin Amis, Ishiguro in *Never Let Me Go* adapts a "post-human theme" on the background of a "neo-humanist branch of criticism" and the ongoing critical debate about ethics in postmodern fiction.[41] Among the "current fantasies about science producing a posthuman world"[42] Ishiguro's novel is one of the most frightening and also one of the most effective narratives concerning the renegotiation of humanistic ideas for critics and scholars in the age *After Theory*[43] or, if we are inclined to believe in it, at *The End of Postmodernism*.[44]

References

ANON. "Interview. A Conversation with Kazuo Ishiguro about *Never Let Me Go*." http://www.bookbrowse.com/author_interviews/full/index.cfm?author_ number=477, (accessed November 23, 2010).

BAIN, Alexander M. "International Settlements: Ishiguro, Shanghai, Humanitarianism." In: *Novel, A Forum on Fiction* 40 (2007): 240–63.

BARNES, Julian. *Nothing to Be Frightened of.* London: Vintage, 2009 [2008].

BIRKE, Dorothee. "Fictions of Memory: Kazuo Ishiguro." In: Vera Nünning (ed.). *Der zeitgenössische englische Roman. Genres – Entwicklungen – Modellinterpretationen.* Trier: WVT, 2007. 101–16.

BLACK, Shameen. "Ishiguro's Inhuman Aesthetics." In: *Modern Fiction Studies* 55,4 (2009): 785–807.

CHERTOFF, D. and L. TOKER. "Reader Response and the Recycling of Topoi in Ishiguro's

---

39 Vera NÜNNING takes one of McEwan's novels, *Enduring Love*, as an example of literature as life-science in the same volume (145–67).
40 BAIN. "International Settlements." 240.
41 Reviews of Martin Amis' *Night Train* by John Updike and Anita Brookner, quoted from MARTINEZ-ALFARO, María Jesús. "Experimental Fiction and the Ethics of a Vérité: The Encounter with the Other in Martin Amis' *Night Train*." In: Jean-Michel Ganteau and Susana Onega (eds.). *The Ethical Component in Experimental British Fiction Since the 1960's.* Newcastle: Cambridge Scholars Publishing, 2007. 131–49, 144.
42 SEAMAN. "More Human." 267.
43 Cf. EAGLETON, Terence. *After Theory.* London: Penguin, 2004.
44 Cf. ZIEGLER, Heide. *The End of Postmodernism: New Directions.* Stuttgart: Metzler, 1993.

'Never Let Me Go'." In: *Partial Answers: Journal of Literature and the History of Ideas* 6,1 (2008): 163–80.

CURRIE, Mark. "Controlling Time: *Never Let Me Go.*" In: Sean Matthews and Sebastian Groes (eds.). *Kazuo Ishiguro.* London: Continuum, 2009. 91–103.

DESAI, Anita. "A Shadow World." In: *The New York Review of Books*, September 22, 2005, http://www.nybooks.com/articles/archives/2005/sep/22/a-shadow-world/ (accessed October 13, 2010).

DYER, Geoff. "Even in Arcadia there are Big White Vans: 'Never Let Me Go', by Kazuo Ishiguro." In: *The Independent*, February 27, 2005. http://license.icopyright.net/user/viewFreeUse.act?fuid=MTAzMTM4NTY (accessed October 13, 2010).

EAGLETON, Terence. *After Theory.* London: Penguin, 2004.

FLUET, Lisa. "Immaterial Labors: Ishiguro, Class, and Affect." In: *Novel, A Forum on Fiction* 40 (2077): 265–88.

ISHIGURO, Kazuo. *Never Let Me Go.* London: Faber and Faber, 2005.

KEMP, Peter. Review in *The Sunday Times*, February 20, 2005. http://entertainment.timesonline.co.uk/tol/arts_and_entertainment/books/article514753.ece, (accessed September 12, 2010).

MARTINEZ-ALFARO, María Jesús. "Experimental Fiction and the Ethics of a Vérité: The Encounter with the Other in Martin Amis' *Night Train.*" In: Jean-Michel Ganteau and Susana Onega (eds.). *The Ethical Component in Experimental British Fiction since the 1960's.* Newcastle: Cambridge Scholars Publishing, 2007. 131–49.

MATTHEWS, Sean and Sebastian GROES (eds.). *Kazuo Ishiguro.* London: Continuum, 2009.

MCDONALD, Keith. "Days of Past Futures: Kazuo Ishiguro's *Never Let Me Go* as 'Speculative Memoir'." In: *Biography* 30 (2007): 74–83.

MILDORF, Jarmila. "Kazuo Ishiguro, *Never Let Me Go.*" In: Susanne Peters (ed.). *Novels*, Part 2. Trier: WVT, 2008. 279–96.

MULLAN, John. "Afterword: On First Reading *Never Let Me Go.*" In: Sean Matthews and Sebastian Groes (eds.). *Kazuo Ishiguro.* London: Continuum, 2009. 104–13.

NÜNNING, Ansgar. "Lebensexperimente und Weisen literarischer Welterzeugung: Thesen zu den Aufgaben und Perspektiven einer lebenswissenschaftlich orientierten Literaturwissenschaft." In: Wolfgang Asholt and Ottmar Ette (eds.). *Literaturwissenschaft als Lebenswissenschaft. Programm – Projekte – Perspektiven.* Tübingen: Narr, 2010. 45–63.

NÜNNING, Vera. "Literatur als Lebenswissen. Die Bedeutung von Literatur für menschliches Verstehen und Zusammenleben am Beispiel von Ian McEwans Roman *Enduring Love* (1998)." In: Wolfgang Asholt and Ottmar Ette (eds.). *Literaturwissenschaft als Lebenswissenschaft. Programm – Projekte – Perspektiven.* Tübingen: Narr, 2010. 145–68.

ROBBINS, Bruce. "Cruelty is Bad: Banality and Proximity in *Never Let Me Go.*" In: *Novel. A Forum on Fiction* 40 (2007): 289–302.

SCHABERT, Ina. *In Quest of the Other Person. Fiction as Biography.* Tübingen: Francke, 1990.

SEAMAN, Myra J. "Becoming More (than) Human: Affective Posthumanisms, Past and Future." In: *Journal of Narrative Theory* 37,2 (2007): 246–75 (abstract via MUSE 2010).

VERSTEEGEN, Heinrich. "Dying with Laughter: The Inherent Joke Structure of Death and Bereavement." In: *Journal for the Study of British Cultures* (2012).

YARDLEY, Jonathan. "Review of *Never Let Me Go.*" In: *The Washington Post*, 17 April, 2005. www.washingtonpost.com/ac2/wp-dyn/A54996 – 2005Apr14? language=printer (accessed November 23, 2010).

ZIEGLER, Heide. *The End of Postmodernism: New Directions.* Stuttgart: Metzler, 1993.

Nina Liewald

'Do not be frightened by my beard. I am a lover of America' – Fear and Nostalgia in Mohsin Hamid's *The Reluctant Fundamentalist*

Excuse me, sir, but may I be of assistance? Ah, I see I have alarmed you. Do not be frightened by my beard: I am a lover of America. I noticed that you were looking for something; more than looking, in fact you seemed to be on a *mission*, and since I am both a native of this city and a speaker of your language, I thought I might offer you my services. (*The Reluctant Fundamentalist* 1)

Those are the first sentences of Mohsin Hamid's novel *The Reluctant Fundamentalist*, published in 2007. The title of the novel, the Pakistani origin of the author's name, and the fact that more than one reviewer called the book a post-9/11 novel that mirrors an "infatuation and disenchantment with America"[1] might rouse specific expectations on buying such a book. According to the *Encyclopedia Britannica* definition, 'fundamentalism' denotes a "militantly conservative religious movement characterized by the advocacy of strict conformity to sacred texts."[2] Thus, we are led to expect a novel about religious issues. With the hint at American policies, moreover, Islamist movements come into play. As Axel Stähler and Klaus Stierstorfer elaborate in their anthology *Writing Fundamentalism*, the term fundamentalism "has become an issue in political, cultural and social debates both globally and locally" that is "fraught with misconceptions and generalizations" and laden with fear:

Originating in fear (of loss of faith), fundamentalism generates fear and intolerance, thus creating a vicious circle of insecurity and deep angst. Not only does it widen the rift between those considered to be fundamentalists and those who are not, but it extends to and polarizes other groups 'tainted' by association.[3]

---

1 Lasdun, James. "The Empire Strikes Back." In: *The Guardian* 3 March, 2007. http://www.guardian.co.uk/books/2007/mar/03/featuresreviews.guardianreview20 (accessed 17 April, 2011).

2 Munson, Henry et al. "Fundamentalism." In: *Encyclopedia Britannica*, http://www.britannica.com/EBchecked/topic/1191955/fundamentalism (accessed 16 April, 2011).

3 Stähler, Axel and Klaus Stierstorfer. "Introduction." In: Ibid. (eds.). *Writing Fundamentalism*. Newcastle: Cambridge Scholars Publishing, 2009. vii-xvii, vii.

In an interview, Hamid explained that his story wasn't about a clash of religions or racism, but about people's pragmatic struggles and political differences. This provokes the question about the interrelationship between title and content.

The Reluctant Fundamentalist is a story about falling in and out of love with America, about dreams and loss, fear and nostalgia. The condensed plot, narrated by the protagonist to an ominous and enigmatic American he happens to meet in Lahore, presents the reader with Changez' world: Coming from a Pakistani family, he makes his way through America's most prestigious institutions. A scholarship enables him to study at Princeton, where he shows so much outstanding achievement that he is hired by the prominent valuation company Underwood Samson. Falling in love with a fellow student, Erica, and enjoying the rewards of his hard work, he seems to blend perfectly into American society and especially New York with its multicultural environment. However, the turning point of the plot – the terrorist attacks of 9/11 and the following war on Afghanistan as well as the deteriorating situation in the Middle East as a whole – disturb Changez. Political events make him question American values and lead to a reinforcement of loyalty towards his country of origin. Disillusioned with his relationship with the Western world, he returns to Pakistan, where he becomes more involved in politics as a university lecturer and increasingly fervent critic of America.

What is so interesting and striking about The Reluctant Fundamentalist is that the novel deals with different facets of fear and simultaneously manages to instill fear in the reader by its quite extraordinary narrative structure. First, rational anxieties are presented very vividly through Changez' experience as a non-white and comparatively poor immigrant in a society of privileged young Americans. Second, irrational anxieties move into the focus of the novel as the plot develops. They are embodied in silent hostilities against Changez after the terrorist attacks, as well as in the suffering and nervous breakdowns of his love Erica, who fears letting go of the past and moving on. On a third level, I argue that the author skilfully plays with the fear of the reader, which he achieves by an ambiguity effected by the narrative structure. As a fourth point of analysis, a short discussion of traditional gothic features is worthwhile to see how they inform The Reluctant Fundamentalist and in which ways they contribute to the significance of anxiety or fear in the novel.

Anxieties related to cultural differences, the challenges of multicultural societies and the discrimination against migrants are widespread, and have attracted much attention as a central topic of fiction over the last decades. Post-9/11 novels often either point to the domestic realm and the problems of trauma resolution, or turn – even more than before – towards fictions of migration that deal with matters of immigration, otherness and strangeness, thereby reacting to the political developments in the US that have brought about a re-racialization of citizenship, the blocking of borders and the curtailment of civil liberties.[4] But Hamid's protagonist is neither a victim of violence or abuse, nor is the fear of social marginalization a major concern of the novel. Initially, the reader is led to suspect that political events might have set in motion a dynamic for the protagonist that will finally deliver an explanation for the title of the novel. A case in point is Changez' reaction to the terrorist attacks of September 11:

> I stared as one – and then the other – of the twin towers of New York's World Trade Center collapsed. And then I *smiled*. Yes, despicable as it may sound, my initial reaction was to be remarkably pleased. Your disgust is evident; indeed, your large hand has, perhaps without your noticing, clenched into a fist. But please believe me when I tell you that I am no sociopath. [...] So when I tell you I was pleased at the slaughter of thousands of innocents, I do so with a profound sense of perplexity. [...] I was caught up in the *symbolism* of it all, the fact that someone had so visibly brought America to her knees. (*The Reluctant Fundamentalist* 72 – 73)

Even though this scene exemplifies a subliminal aggression directed towards America, the author plays with our preconceptions to undermine them in the end. Changez does not seem to be religious. Apart from the fact that he utters a relieved 'Thank God' after getting a job, he does not engage in any religious actions. His final attitude rather seems to be the result of an amplified loyalty towards his culture and an increasing reluctance to serve the ideals of the American economy. At the end of the novel the reader realizes that the real fundamentalism at issue is that of US capitalism, presented as an all-encompassing and potentially threatening and destructive system. This fundamentalism is embodied in Changez' employer Underwood Samson (a company with the initials U.S.), whose guiding principle is: "Focus on the fundamentals" (*The Reluctant Fundamentalist* 98). According to Hamid, it stands for a "remorselessly forward-looking meritocratic, transformative, outward-looking, future-oriented America."[5] This surprising turn artfully calls our attention to the fact that the term 'fundamentalism' originally was an invention of American ideology, coined for a very strict current of evangelical Protestantism. In this context, fundamentalism embodied a reaction against many elements of modernity such as secularization or the rise of science.[6] Hamid's representation of American 'fundamentalism' today ironically contradicts this traditional understanding in

---

4 Cf. Rothberg, Michael. "A Failure of the Imagination: Diagnosing the Post-9/11 Novel: A Response to Richard Gray." In: *American Literary History* (2008): 152 – 58, 155.

5 Hamid, Mohsin. "Slaying Dragons: Mohsin Hamid discusses *The Reluctant Fundamentalist*." In: *Psychoanalysis and History* 11,2 (2009): 225 – 38, 235.

6 For interesting background information about the relationship between literature and recent political negotiations of the term 'fundamentalism', cf. Stierstorfer, Klaus. "Tariq Ali and Recent Negotiations of Fundamentalism." In: Catherine Pesso-Miquel and Klaus Stierstorfer (eds.). *Fundamentalism and Literature.* Basingstoke et al.: Palgrave Macmillan, 2007. 143 – 60.

that his version only seems to serve the values of profit and power, disregarding religious or humanist values. The capitalist system – even though it is seen as one of the trademarks of modernity, and modernity is said to be founded on the 'institutionalisation of doubt' – demands compliant behaviour. As Ruthven outlines, fundamentalists reject choice and often have an "obsession with the drawing of boundaries that will set the group apart from the wider society by deliberately choosing beliefs or modes of behaviour which proclaim who they are and how they would like to be seen."[7] This is in a way what also happens in Changez' Princeton and Underwood Samson circle. The clothes you wear, the university you graduated from, the places you go to for holidays, the money you spend and the people you know determine who you are and if you belong to that group or not.

Changez has been trying hard to obey these rules of the game. Nevertheless, this life triggers feelings in him which bring the above-mentioned cultural anxieties to the fore. What the protagonist comes to fear most is stabbing his countrymen in the back if he continues to stay loyal to the laws of a system that poses an elemental threat to his country of origin. He realizes:

> I was a modern-day janissary, a servant of the American empire at a time when it was invading a country with a kinship to mine and was perhaps even colluding to ensure that my own country faced the threat of war. Of course I was struggling! Of course I felt torn! (*The Reluctant Fundamentalist* 152)

The Janissaries, Christian boys captured by the Ottoman Empire to be soldiers in a Muslim army, were utterly loyal and ferociously fought against their own people. On this level, the novel deals with fear in connection to questions of cultural identity and the problems of America as a multicultural society. It is about an immigrant's fear of serving the wrong ideals and betraying his roots. Before this turning point Changez suffered from a lot of insecurity about where he really wanted to belong. Ironically, it is his attempt to assimilate and please, of all things, which brings about his failure on many levels.

> I lacked a stable *core*. I was not certain where I belonged – in New York, in Lahore, in both, in neither – and for this reason, when she reached out to me for help, I had nothing of substance to give her. Probably this was why I had been willing to try to take on the persona of Chris, because my own identity was so fragile. But in so doing – and by being unable to offer her an alternative to the chronic nostalgia inside her – I might have pushed Erica deeper into her confusion (*The Reluctant Fundamentalist* 148).

Playing completely according to the rules of Erica – or America – Changez not only loses his self-respect but also causes suspicion and fear because he seems to

---

7 Ruthven, Malise. *Fundamentalism. The Search for Meaning.* Oxford: Oxford University Press, 2004. 201.

have no substance: People do not know who he really is and wants to be. This decision may be so difficult to make, due to the fact that he starts looking at his country of origin with Americanized eyes: He now sees the poverty and affliction of many people in Pakistan with the eyes of a Princeton graduate and Underwood Samson employee and does not know if he is to cherish his country or to feel ashamed of the current political and economic misery and the declining status of his own family.

> I recall the Americanness of my own gaze when I returned to Lahore that winter when war was in the offing. I was struck at first by how shabby our house appeared [...] I was saddened to find it in such a state – no, more than saddened, I was shamed. *This* was where I came from, this was my provenance, and it smacked of lowliness. [...] it occurred to me that the house had not changed in my absence, *I* had changed; I was looking about me with the eyes of a foreigner. (*The Reluctant Fundamentalist* 124)

On a higher level, the novel also deals with the fears of a country that is scared of changes, that wants to look into the future but is paralyzed and unable to move on because of an idealized past it cannot let go of. Erica, the woman Changez falls in love with, is an emblem of this deep-rooted fear, standing for a very different notion of America than Underwood Samson. She counters the company's ruthless activism with an introspective passivity. This hints at the inner conflict America has to face in a time of changes and great political insecurities – a conflict between a traditional belief in progress and an increasing inability to cope with a changing world. Many books in recent years have been concerned with growing anxieties about multiculturalism and the disillusionment with an assumed American ascendency in all disciplines. As Rubin states, the cataclysmic events of 9/11 – which is also the turning point of Hamid's novel – caused fundamental fears and paralysis since it has brought about an increasing rift between "a heightened concern about national security and a long-standing commitment to civil liberties."[8]

Paralleling these developments, Changez' lover is not able to come to terms with the death of her first boyfriend Chris and sinks more and more into absent-mindedness and psychosis. Changez perceives that Erica really likes him: She is interested in his culture, fascinated by his strangeness and impressed by the values he was brought up with. Notwithstanding, he has to admit that "she was struggling against a current that pulled her within herself, and [that her...] smile contained the fear that she might slip into her own depths, where she would be trapped, unable to breathe" (*The Reluctant Fundamentalist* 86). The protagonist's name can be read as a synonym for 'changes', and the fact that the name

---

8 RUBIN, Derek and Jaap VERHEUL. "Introduction." In: Ibid. (eds.). *American Multiculturalism after 9/11: Transatlantic Perspectives.* Amsterdam: Amsterdam University Press, 2009. 7–20, 10.

'Erica' is contained in the word 'America' may not be an accident. Hamid has frequently been criticized for an assumed lack of subtlety.[9] But no matter how blunt it may appear, the comparison offers some valuable starting points for an interpretation. As Gray outlines in an essay about 'American Prose Writing at a Time of Crisis',

> American culture may have become internationally dominant but the US itself has been internationalized; America may be the sole remaining superpower, but it is a superpower that seems haunted by fear – fear, among other things, of its own possible impotence and potential decline. [...It] has witnessed the disappearance of the boundary between the 'center' and the 'margins' [...losing] any claim it may have tried to make once to a Eurocentric character and an exclusive destiny.[10]

At this point nostalgia comes to play a major role. On the one hand, Erica longs to embrace Changez and to let him enrich her life. On the other hand, she fears to accept 'changes', since her idea of life is inextricably interwoven with her longing for an idealized past with Chris. Ultimately, the protagonist's relationship with Erica fails just like his initial bond with the United States. Their unusual love story is a story about the impossibility of competing with an ideal that only exists in someone's imagination: something that can neither be retrieved nor pushed aside to open up a space for new ideas and values. Changez might earn temporary sympathy in this country, but no real acceptance, love and integration. This is also what he experiences after 9/11 in New York. His social status and assimilated life-style do not save him from stares and whispers, even from his own colleagues, when he starts growing a beard:

> [...] it seemed to me that America, too, was increasingly giving itself over to a dangerous nostalgia that time. There was something undeniably retro about the flags and uniforms, about generals addressing cameras in war rooms and newspaper headlines featuring such words as *duty* and *honor*. I had always thought of America as a nation that looked forward; for the first time I was struck by this determination to look *back*. [...] What your fellow countrymen longed for was unclear to me – a time of unquestioned dominance? Of safety? Of moral certainty? I did not know – but that they were scrambling to don the costumes of another era was apparent. I felt treacherous for wondering whether that era was fictitious, and whether – if it could indeed be animated – it contained a part written for someone like me (*The Reluctant Fundamentalist* 114 – 15).

As Mizruchi observes, risk is not only connected to real sources of danger but also to its perception and is thus culturally constructed. She sees the search "for

---

9 Cf. for example LASDUN, n.p.
10 GRAY, Richard. "Open Doors, Closed Minds: American Prose Writing at a Time of Crisis." In: *American Literary History* (2008): 128 – 51, 128 – 29.

boundaries and differences, between ourselves, the victims, and the culprits"[11] as a common cultural response to catastrophe and fear of risks. Beck even speaks of a tendency of risk societies to become "scapegoat societies".[12] Yet the novel shows that there is fear and nostalgia on both sides: Changez, as an immigrant with a different religion and culture, brings change to the United States but similarly finds himself unable to accept the changes happening in his own country. He feels a deep nostalgia for the past grandeur of Pakistan that seems to clash so painfully with the current economic and political misery.

> Often, during my stay in your country, such comparisons troubled me. In fact, they did more than trouble me: they made me resentful. Four thousand years ago, we, the people of the Indus River basin, had cities that were laid out on grids and boasted underground sewers, while the ancestors of those who would invade and colonize America were illiterate barbarians. Now our cities were largely unplanned, unsanitary affairs, and America had universities with individual endowments greater than our national budget for education. To be reminded of this vast disparity was, for me, to be ashamed. (*The Reluctant Fundamentalist* 34)

As a result, there are limits to mutual understanding that none of the parties in this novel is able to overcome. Changez resents the stereotypes, rejection and dominance in all fields that he comes to hate about the country he once admired, but sees no other solution to this problem than a complete shift in attitude and lifestyle. Increasingly angry and emotional he confesses to the stranger:

> As a society, you were unwilling to reflect upon the shared pain that united you with those who attacked you. You retreated into myths of your own difference, assumptions of your own superiority. And you acted out these beliefs on the stage of the world, so that the entire planet was rocked by the repercussions of your tantrums, not least my family, now facing war thousands of miles away. Such an America had to be stopped in the interests not only of the rest of humanity, but also in your own (*The Reluctant Fundamentalist* 168).

The quote exemplifies the tendency of the protagonist's remarks to be of an increasingly aggressive, reproachful and threatening quality, which creates an ever more oppressive atmosphere. Regarding the title, Hamid undermines our preconceptions, as already mentioned. No spectacular events take place and religion or violence does not play a large role in the plot.

However, apart from dealing with fear with regards to content, *The Reluctant Fundamentalist* also manages to *instill* fear in the reader, by means of its narrative structure. The reader is put into the shoes of the American listener since the latter remains silent throughout the novel and thus opens a space for the

---

11 Mizruchi, Susan. "Risk Theory and the Contemporary American Novel." In: *American Literary History* 22,1 (2009): 109–35, 128.

12 Beck, Ulrich. *Risk Society: Towards a New Modernity.* London: Sage, 1986. 75.

reader to fill with his own potential reactions. The story is narrated in a directly confrontational mode, which can be understood as a provocation, because its cultural critique is directly addressing an implied white audience. The narrator is overt and never fades into the background. He directly addresses his inter-locutor, explains circumstances, intrudes into the story to pass metanarrative comments, uses emotive expressions and has a distinctive voice. He dominates the novel, which is also an autodiegetic narration, with Changez as the 'experi-encing I' and protagonist of his story. There is no exposition-oriented prologue. For an introduction of the two interlocutors, we are thrown into the action immediately. This beginning *in medias res* gives us a first unmediated insight into the thoughts and perceptions of the main character and sets the frame for Changez' narration which evolves as a dramatic monologue – or skaz narrative[13] – with a silent conversational partner.

The two stories are set on different time levels. During the evening in the café nothing special happens. Nonetheless, it is this frame that builds up an enor-mous amount of tension as it constantly interrupts the flashbacks, comments on them and picks up the implicit reactions of the listener. The stranger is very tense, seems to carry a gun and is extremely cautious, as if he was lying in wait for something. But this is only visible through Changez' hints and comments, which gives the scene in the café a large significance for the story as a whole. Listening to the protagonist's voice it is clear to the reader that the narrator is very well-educated, polite and sophisticated. Nevertheless, we expect some violent cul-mination of the scene because this over-politeness increasingly clashes with the content of the story. The narrative structure gives the novel a surreal quality and at the same time deprives it of subtlety and causes a feeling of unease. The following example from the frame story is only one of many to illustrate this claim:

> [...] you, sir, continue to appear ill at ease. I hope you will not mind my saying so, but the frequency and purposefulness with which you glance about – a steady tick-tick-tick seeming to beat in your head as you move your gaze from one point to the next – brings to mind the behavior of an animal that has ventured too far from its lair and is now, in unfamiliar surroundings, uncertain whether it is predator or prey! (*The Reluctant Fundamentalist* 31)

---

13 The name is derived from the Russian word 'skaz' signifying 'speech'. According to Jahn, it is "a literary form that represents an oral (or 'conversational') story-telling situation in which a speaker tells a story to a present audience. Apart from having a distinctly oral diction and syntax, a skaz-narrator's discourse is also characterized by a high incidence of phatic and appellative elements, signaling the presence of the listening audience. Skaz is closely related (and usefully compared to) the poetic genre of the 'dramatic monologue'." JAHN, Manfred. *Narratology: A Guide to the Theory of Narrative.* English Department, University of Cologne, 2005. In: http://www.uni-koeln.de/~ame02/pppn.htm , N3.3. (accessed 16 April, 2011).

Comments like this simultaneously play with the possible stereotypes of an imagined Western audience, draw attention to biases, and hint at the possible dangerousness of the American. The bluntness of this style is beyond argument, but it is just this over-accentuation that makes us suspicious of the purpose of this strategy. It confuses the reader, because we do not know whom we can trust: Is Changez just naïve and does not see the danger he is in? Or does he follow a completely different agenda, and constantly reassures the American to entice him into a trap? Or maybe he has just gone mad, having a conversation with himself?

Reading this monologue does not give the reader any clue with respect to the narrator's voice and intonation: The tone of Changez' speech might be luring, provocative, angry, patronising, accusing or sarcastic – it might as well be just calm, polite and matter of fact. The whole story seems to be built towards an important confession, but the one-sidedness of the conversation leaves the reader in doubt about its intention and outcome. Since the interlocutor is only present as an echo, it is up to us to fill this gap, to associate any kind of atmosphere with the conversation and to imagine our reaction to Changez' story and the way he tells it. Moreover, the novel offers nearly no information about the American. What is the purpose of his travels and why does he mainly remain silent? Is he just shy and prejudiced or a CIA agent, waiting for the right moment to execute his bloody order? Similarly, we neither know Changez' reasons for telling his story to a complete stranger, nor can we comprehend the real extent of his hatred for America. Is he making a lifetime confession to the man, feeling the inevitability of his imminent assassination, or does he want to take revenge for all the crimes America committed in his eyes? Hamid plays with those insecurities: The most important questions are never answered and the end is relatively open and thus provokes a debate about our own possible assumptions and stereotypes.

Adding to this ambiguity, certain gothic elements found their way into the novel. A quite obvious element to rouse fear in the reader is the peculiar setting – a common feature of gothic novels since their emergence in the late eighteenth century. The increasingly tense and claustrophobic atmosphere is intensified by a gothic setting, characterized by growing darkness, flying bats, uncanny people lingering around a confusing web of dark alleyways, a waiter with an intense gaze and a brooding manner, strange noises, disfigured beggars, and power cuts that suddenly plunge the whole scene into darkness.

> It is odd how the character of a public space changes when it is empty; the abandoned amusement park, the shuttered opera house, the vacant hotel: in films these often feature as backdrops for events intended to frighten. So it is with this market. [...] Perhaps it has to do with the cloudy sky above, through which one occasionally glimpses a gash of moon, or perhaps it is the darkening shadows in the warren of

alleyways slipping away from here in all directions, but I would suggest that it is instead our *solitude* that most disturbs us, the fact that we are all but alone despite being in the heart of a city. (*The Reluctant Fundamentalist* 155 – 56)

However, this is one of the rare descriptions of gloomy places in the novel. Whereas classical gothic novels often feature repetition and exaggeration, describing excesses of villainy in typical claustrophobic settings,[14] Hamid abstains from this strategy and does the opposite to create tension. Gloomy surroundings and coincidences are casually mentioned along the way in a matter-of-fact tone and thus let the reader imagine the details – a strategy that does not cause fear but excites the fear of being afraid. This feeling is called 'Angst' or anxiety as the condition of mind prior to being afraid, oscillating somewhere between pleasure and pain. It is this randomness and apparent indifference that makes the reader suspicious. Even though the narrative form, structure and tone of the novel seem to have nothing in common with traditional gothic works, I argue that the creation of fear in *The Reluctant Fundamentalist* is achieved by the use of some elements of the gothic tradition.

A first case in point is ambivalence. Gothic novels often put their readers off the scent and combine "convincing realism with a nightmarish quality"[15], to rouse feelings of confusion and insecurity. This also holds true for Hamid's work. We are suspicious and alarmed, because we know about the one-sidedness and bias of Changez' account and cannot be sure who is hunter and who is prey. Until the end we never get to know whom we can trust and which agenda the two conversational partners have in mind. This is also linked to misconceptions. Plots in gothic novels are often generated by misunderstandings. Such misunderstandings also occur between Changez and the ominous American. Additionally, the central misconception that determines our reaction to the novel is our own initial failure to understand the title. The mystery is solved only later when Changez reveals the secret of his disillusionment with what he perceives as American 'economic fundamentalism'. The revelation of a secret needed as the key to a story is a well-known gothic element used in many classical works from Walpole's *The Castle of Otranto* and Radcliffe's *The Italian* to Lewis' *The Monk*, to mention but a few. Moreover, much suspense in gothic fiction is created by a plot structure which leads towards a revelation, culmination or turning point. This effect is increased by means of disguise or masking – a prominent motif which also informs *The Reluctant Fundamentalist*. Obviously, none of the

---

14 Cf. WRIGHT, Angela. *Gothic Fiction*. Basingstoke et al.: Palgrave Macmillan, 2007. 52. WRIGHT here refers to Walpole's *Castle of Otranto* as a typical example, showing these features.

15 STEVENS, David. *The Gothic Tradition*. Cambridge et al.: Cambridge University Press, 2005. 54.

characters in Hamid's novel explicitly adopts a false identity. All the same, we get the uneasy feeling, as outlined before, that both Changez and the ominous American have a lot to hide. We cannot see behind the curtain and we learn that even education does not prevent people from blindness. Just as Victor in Mary Shelley's famous novel *Frankenstein* is led into despair and an irresolvable inner conflict through the impact of his education and his adherence to science, Changez is led into a serious personal crisis through his Western education, when he realises the incompatibility of his way of life with his cultural roots.

The most striking commonality is perhaps the simple fact that gothic fiction originally used to be politically subversive and mocking in that it criticised real-life circumstances and grievances in a symbolical, imaginative way. The period in which the gothic tradition emerged was a time of accelerated change in all walks of life. The literature of this time reflects those "uncertainties about the nature of power, law, society, family and sexuality".[16] Fear and nostalgia are never far where fundamental new developments and cataclysms change people's lives. While the first gothic novels were written at a time of spiritual transition away from religion to science and economics, *The Reluctant Fundamentalist* was written at a time that is characterised (in many regions of this world) by a return to religion and non-economic values. As David Stevens outlines,

> there is a striking resemblance between the final years of the 20th century and the 1790s [...]: uncertainty about how to visualize the future, veering from excited optimism to profound despair. Revolutionary politicization, reactionary nostalgia, and deliberate escapism are all possible reactions, and all are represented in different ways in the gothic.[17]

It is worth pointing out that *The Reluctant Fundamentalist* can be seen in this context: It deals with the increasing insecurities of the twenty-first century, which is troubled by terrorism, the problems of multiculturalist societies and a growing rift between rich and poor. The book provokes us, directs our attention to our own stereotypes and arrogance, and directly addresses us without giving us the chance to answer. Interestingly, Hamid explained in an interview that American readers reacted most strongly to his book, perceived the tone of the novel as very hostile and felt attacked by its content and style. This reaction confirms the potential of the novel to question established power relations.

Objections might be raised here to a simple categorization. I do not argue that *The Reluctant Fundamentalist* can be seen as a gothic novel. Its tone is rational rather than emotional, it neither features supernatural elements and multiple narrators, nor stock characters. Nonetheless, the parallels mentioned above

---

16 BOTTING, Fred. *Gothic*. London/New York: Routledge, 1996. 5.
17 STEVENS. *The Gothic Tradition*. 16.

serve to illuminate why it rouses anxiety in the reader. On the whole, the novel is manipulative – but it manipulates openly. Apart from creating tension and subverting expectations through his skillful narrative strategy, the author also forces us to reconsider our preconceptions about terms – such as fundamentalism – in times when the media seem to talk about issues such as terrorism and Islam with great certainty, pinning down many foreign people by negative generalizations. We have to realize that there are always two sides to a coin and that there are no clear-cut concepts. This is also indicated by Changez' name: it might stand for the changes America cannot cope with; it might stand for the changes going on inside of him, as he may or may not follow a call towards terrorism. Thirdly, Changez is also the Urdu name for Genghis – the famous invader and destroyer of the Caliphate, one of the largest and most successful Muslim empires of his time. Thus, his appearance may signify a turn towards a distinctive Muslim nationalism, but his name supposes the opposite. Asked in an interview why he chose to write a one-person narrative, Hamid refers to exactly this possibility of different interpretations as his major instrument to create tension:

> I like that frame, because it parallels the way the world looks at each other. Pakistan, or the Muslim world, looks at America and the West, and wonders exactly that: Are you out to get us? Are you a bunch of completely aggressive maniacs or are you people we see on *Seinfeld* and *Friends*? Similarly, America wonders that about the Muslim world: Are you a bunch of terrorists, or just regular people with families and kids? That sense of ambiguity, or not knowing, I think, is what the frame allows me to capture.[18]

In conclusion, *The Reluctant Fundamentalist* is a very topical book. It gives interesting insights into the contemporary American psyche that is, on the one hand, moulded by successful and forward-looking but also ruthless economic ideals, and at the same time tortured by a backward-looking fear and nostalgia. But the novel shows us that this phenomenon is a symptom of our times and exists on both sides. In this context, the US is presented as a cultural contact zone, where oppositions are challenged and inverted. During this process a mutual transformation takes place. As Salman Rushdie once wrote: "To migrate is certainly to lose language and home, to be defined by others, to become invisible, or, even worse, a target, it is to experience deep changes and wrenches in the soul. But the migrant is not simply transformed by his act; he transforms

18 BHANDARI, Aparita. "Changed Man. Mohsin Hamid's *The Reluctant Fundamentalist* Explores Post 9/11 Tension. (Interview)." 16 May, 2007. In: http://www.cbc.ca/arts/books/hamid.html (accessed 5 June, 2011)

his new world."[19] Or, as Changez puts it with considerable nostalgia for his initial relationship to America,

> [...] it is not always possible to restore one's boundaries after they have been blurred and made permeable by a relationship: try as we might, we cannot reconstitute our-selves as the autonomous beings we previously imagined ourselves to be. Something of us is now outside, and something of the outside is now within us. (*The Reluctant Fundamentalist* 173–74)

References

BECK, Ulrich. *Risk Society: Towards a New Modernity.* London: Sage, 1986.

BHANDARI, Aparita. "Changed Man. Mohsin Hamid's *The Reluctant Fundamentalist* Explores Post 9/11 Tension. (Interview)." 16 May, 2007. In: http://www.cbc.ca/arts/ books/hamid.html (accessed 5 June, 2011).

BOTTING, Fred. *Gothic.* London/New York: Routledge, 1996.

GRAY, Richard. "Open Doors, Closed Minds: American Prose Writing at a Time of Crisis." In: *American Literary History* 21,1 (2009): 128–48.

HAMID, Mohsin. "Slaying Dragons: Mohsin Hamid Discusses *The Reluctant Fundamen-talist.*" In: *Psychoanalysis and History* 11,2 (2009): 225–38.

JAHN, Manfred. *Narratology: A Guide to the Theory of Narrative.* English Department, University of Cologne, 2005. In: http://www.uni-koeln.de/~ame02/pppn.htm, N3.3. (accessed 16 April, 2011)

LASDUN, James. "The Empire Strikes Back." In: *The Guardian* 3 March, 2007. http:// www.guardian.co.uk/books/2007/mar/03/featuresreviews.guardianreview20 (accessed 17 April, 2011).

MIZRUCHI, Susan. "Risk Theory and the Contemporary American Novel." In: *American Literary History* 22,1 (2009): 109–35.

ROTHBERG, Michael. "A Failure of the Imagination: Diagnosing the Post-9/11 Novel: A Response to Richard Gray." In: *American Literary History* 21,1 (2009): 152–58.

RUBIN, Derek and Jaap VERHEUL. "Introduction." In: Ibid. (eds.). *American Multi-culturalism after 9/11: Transatlantic Perspectives.* Amsterdam: Amsterdam University Press, 2009. 7–20.

RUSHDIE, Salman. *Imaginary Homelands: Essays and Criticism, 1981–1991.* London: Faber, 1991.

RUTHVEN, Malise. *Fundamentalism. The Search for Meaning.* Oxford: Oxford University Press, 2004.

STÄHLER, Axel and Klaus STIERSTORFER. "Introduction." In: Ibid. (eds.). *Writing Fun-damentalism.* Newcastle: Cambridge Scholars Publishing, 2009. vii-xvii.

STEVENS, David. *The Gothic Tradition.* Cambridge et al.: Cambridge University Press, 2005.

---

19 RUSHDIE, Salman. *Imaginary Homelands: Essays and Criticism, 1981–1991.* London: Faber, 1991. 210.

STIERSTORFER, Klaus. "Tariq Ali and Recent Negotiations of Fundamentalism." In: Catherine Pesso-Miquel and Klaus Stierstorfer (eds.). *Fundamentalism and Literature*. Basingstoke et al.: Palgrave Macmillan, 2007. 143 – 60.

WRIGHT, Angela. *Gothic Fiction*. Basingstoke et al.: Palgrave Macmillan, 2007.

Imke Lichterfeld

'Timor mortis conturbat me. Fear of death disturbs me' – Fear and Terror in Frank McGuinness' *Speaking like Magpies*

Words of fear – "Timor mortis conturbat me. [...] Fear of death disturbs me"[1] – are uttered by King James VI of Scotland when ascending the throne of England as James I in Frank McGuinness' historical drama *Speaking like Magpies* (2005). James is afraid of unknown dangers threatening his royal person. A possible reason for this inexorable fear is the execution of his mother Mary, Queen of Scots by the English Queen Elizabeth I, whose successor James becomes at the beginning of the modern historical play. His mother's death and a suspected hostility from England still seem to scare James (*Magpies* 7). Simultaneously, his ascension to the throne of England and his faith and political decision-making pose a threat to the Catholics in England, who were hoping for an end to persecution and the right to free exercise of religion. Due to the disappointment caused by the Protestant-favouring politics of the new monarch, the familiar story of the Gunpowder Plot evolved: a group of frustrated young Catholics conspired and, on 5 November 1605, tried to blow up the royal family in Parliament by means of a gunpowder explosion in the cellar of the building.

On 5/11, which is the British way of abbreviating this date, however, nothing was destroyed, since the event celebrated each 5 November did not take place as planned. What most people still celebrate on this day all over England with huge bonfires and fireworks is the detection of gunpowder, treason and plot, i.e. a release from fear. The story of Guy Fawkes has become a popular myth, which often neglects the role of the leading conspirators associated with the failed explosion and instead puts an emphasis on the gunpowder expert Fawkes.[2] The play *Speaking like Magpies* introduces a fictionalised, staged version of this

---

1　All citations from *Speaking like Magpies* are taken from the following edition: MCGUINNESS, Frank. *Speaking like Magpies*. London: Faber and Faber, 2005. The play is abbreviated as *Magpies* in the quotations.

2　For a general introduction to the history of the Gunpowder Plot, see among others: HAYNES, Alan. *The Gunpowder Plot: Faith in Rebellion*. Stroud: Alan Sutton Publishing, 1994; HOGGE, Alice. *God's Secret Agents: Queen Elizabeth's Forbidden Priests and the Hatching of the Gunpowder Plot*. New York: Harper Collins, 2005.

event,[3] and addresses the private hopes and fears of its protagonists. Fear and self-fashioning are presented as motors to reasonable and unreasonable actions in McGuinness' drama. The question addressed in this paper is how the event of 5/11 is presented on stage in *Speaking like Magpies* and how the plot is charged with the king's fear of his own vulnerability and a politico-religious conspiracy. It seeks to explore the interpretation and staging of the Gunpowder Plot in McGuinness' play specifically with regard to topics such as the presentation of religious motives and political activism, subversive and extremist attitudes towards the English state and its ruling distrustful and vulnerable Scottish monarch and his government, the desires and fears politics cause, and, finally, the abuse of power and terrorist acts, even keeping in mind implications for today's society. It thus seems rewarding to look at the representation of the Gunpowder Plot of the seventeenth century in a modern drama, in particular with respect to the motivation of the conspirators (martyrs, obsessed freedom fighters, or terrorists?[4]) who are prepared to attack and weaken the state. The depiction of the revolutionary ambition of a small group of men who caused fear and terror at the beginning of the seventeenth century on today's stage may illuminate the ambivalence of the historical conspiracy and its relevance today. A further question that arises through the date of its composition in 2005 and that will be briefly discussed at the end of this paper is whether 5/11 can be compared to 9/11 – 11 September 2001 – when depicted on stage in 2005 in a post-9/11 world.[5]

Frank McGuinness wrote *Speaking like Magpies* in 2005 for the 400th anniversary of the 1605 Gunpowder Plot; the play was commissioned by the Royal Shakespeare Company.[6] When performed in the autumn of 2005 during their

---

3 On the differentiation between historical and fictionalised content in modern historical drama, see BERNINGER, Mark. *Neue Formen des Geschichtsdramas in Großbritannien und Irland seit 1970.* Trier: Wissenschaftlicher Verlag Trier, 2006.

4 One question that needs to be raised is whether a person who uses terrorism in the pursuit of political aims can be depicted as sympathetic and his actions as reasonable. As will become clear at the end, this also resembles Brigitte NACOS' comments on the American tragedy in "Mass-Mediated Terrorism in the New World (Dis)Order": "[C]ontroversies over the definition of terrorism are rooted in the disagreements about how to classify the use of force by politically motivated groups or individuals on one hand and by governments on the other." (NACOS, Brigitte L. "Mass-Mediated Terrorism in the New World (Dis)Order." In: J. David Slocum (ed.). *Terrorism, Media, Liberation.* New Brunswick/London: Rutgers University Press, 2005. 185–208, 193.)

5 The play was rehearsed shortly after the London bombings in July 2005, and though these might not have influenced the writing process, they can also be included when interpreting the RSC's staged version from late 2005: the first preview on 29 September took place less than three months after the terrorist attack on the London transport system.

6 *Speaking like Magpies* was first performed on 21 September 2005 by the Royal Shakespeare Company in Stratford-upon-Avon in the Swan Theatre. The season lasted until 5 November, the date of the Gunpowder Plot, and then relocated to the Trafalgar Studios in London after a short tour to Newcastle.

'Gunpowder Season', the play comprised a large cast and featured an impressive stage design with fireworks and colourful performances depicting the gloomy spectacle. *Speaking like Magpies* is a poetic study of power relations and religious fundamentalism. These are ideas that could of course also be addressed in more or less undetermined circumstances, unspecified in place and time. By addressing the 5 November and its celebratory character of the detection and the circumvention of a royal assassination, *Speaking like Magpies* centres around a specific date, but it also evokes thoughts on general, timeless motives of extremist politics and religion, possible fundamentalist aggression and might recall a "presence of the past"[7] in today's theatre in that an audience might associate the dramatic spectacle of the past event, as presented on stage, with recent historical events.[8] However, the drama deals with the Catholic conspiracy to blow up the Stuart monarch King James I and his Parliament at the beginning of the seventeenth century and the conspirators' aim to change the course of history: McGuinness' historical play shows an approach that highlights the preparation of the plot as a theatrical spectacle.[9] There is no true physical impact of the plot, but it is used as a performative display and produced on the twenty-first-century stage to entertain a contemporary audience. The king's life is never in any real danger – though the audience witness his fear. The conspirators die an almost "symbolic and sacrificial death",[10] but their death in the theatrical performance is not functionalised as a weapon that incites further Catholic upheavals. What happens is fatal only to them, but neither to their society nor to the audience of the play today. *Speaking like Magpies* thus depicts the early years of the reign of the former King James VI of Scotland in England, as James I, and follows his struggle on the English throne, which is supported by his personal

---

7 HUEHLS, Mitchum. *Qualified Hope. A Postmodern Politics of Time.* Columbus: Ohio State University Press, 2009. 7. The term is used by HUEHLS for the 9/11 attack. This phrase is applied to the recalling of a historical attempt of terrorism and simultaneously could remind the audience of present terrorist threats that instil fear in today's society: this paper will look at the presentation of 5/11 and whether its interpretation might evoke the audience's memories of 9/11 and remind of present danger through fundamentalism.

8 This aspect will be briefly addressed at the end of this paper.

9 This could be interpreted as a reference to any event presented as a spectacle, not only theatre. In "Simulations and Terrors of Our Time" Robert MERRILL explores images and representations of fear and terror as a spectacle. His "analysis relies upon an understanding of terrorism more as a spectacle or simulacrum than as a real event" (MERRILL, Robert. "Simulations and Terrors of Our Time." In: J. David Slocum (ed.). *Terrorism, Media, Liberation.* New Brunswick/London: Rutgers University Press, 2005. 171–84, 172). This, in turn, could be relied on when interpreting theatrical interpretations of fear and terror on stage.

10 The quote is taken from Jean BAUDRILLARD's essay on terrorism after 9/11. (BAUDRILLARD, Jean. "L'Esprit du Terrorisme." Translated by Michel Valentin. In: Stanley Hauerwas and Frank Lentricchia (eds.). *Dissent from the Homeland. Essays after September 11.* Durham/London: Duke University Press, 2003. 149–61, 154.)

fears that are caused by the awareness of his own mortality,[11] as mentioned above, possibly triggered through the violent death of his mother. The first time James appears on stage, he is woken up by the scream of the dying Queen Elizabeth and is subsequently soothed by the pan-like, meta-dramatical figure of the Equivocator, who pretends to be James' guardian angel.[12] Throughout the play, the king remains vulnerable and is depicted as fearful and insecure. He confesses to his councillor and spymaster Lord Cecil: "Timor mortis conturbat me." – "Fear of death disturbs me." (*Magpies* 35) James seems to be ruled by insecurity, as the whole play is in fact accompanied by the premonition of a possible attack on the monarch and the planned gunpowder explosion obviously on every spectator's mind.

After his ascension as James I, the official wish uttered by the new king of England concerns peace and politico-religious harmony: "Let me hear each voice/ That pleads for justice. May pity reign in my soul,/ So that hatred which divides our country/ Be banished from this realm. [...] Healing the wounds, the bitter wounds,/ Of Protestant and Catholic." (*Magpies* 15) As is made clear right from the beginning, the conflicts in *Speaking like Magpies* are dominated by religious fears and struggles. James feels haunted by the memory of his Catholic mother Mary Stuart and seeks appeasement: "We must not do harm to each other." (*Magpies* 15) He protests that he is his "martyred mother's Protestant son" (*Magpies* 15). Thus, right from the beginning of *Speaking like Magpies*, James seems almost traumatised by his past, by the interpretations of the

---

11 James feels dependent on some kind of guidance. On the idea of fear caused by vulnerability, see among others: KNAPP, Guntram. *Angst und Depression. Grundformen und Pathologie.* Sternenfels: Verlag Wissenschaft & Praxis, 2000. 54. As was pointed out above, it seems likely that James' fear could have arisen from his awareness of his mother having been executed by Queen Elizabeth – yet this link is never made explicit in the play.

12 The Equivocator is a "furry-legged, half-naked creature with little devil's horns and a gloatingly subversive manner, he undermines both sides and represents the ambiguities that are rife in a kingdom of dual allegiances." LATHAN, Peter. Review *Speaking like Magpies* <www.britishtheatreguide.info/reviews/RSCspeakmag-rev.htm> (accessed 14 May, 2011). He is defined as speaking with a different tongue, as being a liar who addresses the audience but cannot be fully understood because he is creating a fake reality. His choice of words is ambiguous and plurivalent in order to conceal the truth and feign support. The Equivocator "*resembles the satyr in Piero di Cosimo's painting* Satyr Weeping Over A Nymph" (*Magpies* 1) and is pan-like with goat's hooves and horns, evoking a devilish figure. He seems to step out of the smoke of an infernal fire after an explosion at the beginning of the play, but at the same time he appears to have some kind of divine power. In an entertaining and attractive manner, almost courting the audience, the equivocator leads the audience just as he guides the characters in the plot; he plays with the knowledge of the spectator, communicates above the level of the historical plot and plays the spectators' guide through history, of which only short impressions are conveyed in the course of the drama.

"narratives" of his life, as Aimee Pozorski puts it in "Trauma's Time".[13] Yet he seems determined to fight his fear and to appear strong and confident. When publicly and officially arriving in England, James is apprehensively received by a Puritan demanding free worship. This is contrasted by the following, mocking threat from stout Catholics: A *"burst of music. A figure dressed as a Pope mock-terrifies the crowd. He is on short stilts, covered by his cassock. On his head there is a large mitre. He is attended by two minions dressed as terrifying dogs. The dogs can breathe fire"* (*Magpies* 20). This excessive interpretation of the threat associated with Catholicism simultaneously emphasises the threatening quality of fire, which is frequently referred to throughout the play. Fire is a recurring image, obviously anticipating the planned explosion. The Pope on stilts explicitly threatens English Protestantism: "I want your souls" (*Magpies* 20), thereby offending the court. When James arises, he flatly accuses the mock-pope: "Do you have two faces, two mouths,/ One that kisses me,/ and another,/ Another conspires against me" (*Magpies* 23). With the reference to conspiracy, the idea of a plot against the ruling monarch seems to be present from the very beginning of *Speaking like Magpies*. Even though the threat is only attributed to a parody at first, the spirit of anti-Catholicism continues and grows and, thus, the first scene becomes an emblem of the rift and suspicion between James and the Catholics.

The insecurity which pervades James' private and political decisions makes his court, but even more so his mind rather prone to danger. As far as the dynamics of the play are concerned, this seems to permit not only an excellent dramatic opportunity for the representation of politically explosive material but also one for a psychological exploration of the fear of conspirators' ideals and unknown plots. They pose a direct and immediate threat on stage, even though a modern audience is aware that their plans will fail even before the first scene opens. The threat is stressed, albeit at the same time parodied, by the powerful beginning of the performance. "A burning fuse runs from front to back of the Swan stage and under a blood-red curtain that drops to the sound of a powerful explosion."[14] The action that is – for a brief moment of theatrical history – presented on stage is a successful gunpowder explosion. For a split second, the Gunpowder Plot is apparently enacted as truth. Only after that and an assurance that "no harm is promised" (*Magpies* 1),[15] the audience is presented with the dramatic interpretation of the play's version of the Plot. It is thus confronted with

---

13 Pozorski, Aimee. "Trauma's Time." In: *CTReview/ Connecticut Review* 28,1 (2006): 71–76, 72.
14 Bradley, Kathrine. "*Thomas More*, directed by Robert Delamere for the RSC, The Swan Theatre, Stratford-upon-Avon." Unpublished review. 12 May, 2005. 3.
15 This comment turns out to be an equivocative lie, as will become apparent when innocents are tortured towards the end of the play.

the idea of make-belief, and asked to be critical with respect to the events that are then presented as a true account of history. The spectator is therefore also challenged to question the reliability of this kind of dramatised historiography. Mockingly depicting events that have never taken place, the play sets the scene for a representation of history to an audience that is familiar with the myth of Guy Fawkes. The spectator is thus immediately encouraged to see the events from an interpretative metahistorical[16] level and to explore the motives usually hidden behind the historical documents.[17]

When Queen Elizabeth dies in 1603, her political power is reduced to memory, just like that of Mary, Queen of Scots. King James in *Speaking like Magpies* is afraid of exactly this kind of decay and loss of immediate control. In the RSC production, the frightened king is born from Elizabeth's deathbed and is confronted by the Equivocator, whom he accepts as his 'guardian angel' and who proves to be a supernatural plot-shaping figure. Feelings of fear, which James repeatedly utters in the presence of others, are overcome when he can rely on the Equivocator.[18] Assured of control through the support of the Equivocator, James is even convinced of being able to "cheat death" (*Magpies* 16). The power that transcends James' fear seems almost grotesque and provides an absurd theatrical opportunity: the formerly frightened king uses a meta-dramatical and a-historical figure to crush his fears. While this would obviously be impossible in any realistic depiction of the course of events, the theatre may present situations that inspire or even battle feelings of terror in unusual ways. Instead of simply using a monologue or a soliloquy, McGuinness presents a scene that shows James having a dialogue with this supernatural character in order to explore the king's fear. As Peter Brook points out, "the theatre is a vehicle, a means for self-study, self-exploration, a possibility of salvation. The actor has himself as his field of work. [...]. So that the act of performance is an act of sacrifice, of sacrificing

---

16 At the same time, the Equivocator presents a level of awareness of this metahistorical quality which makes him metadramatic. See fn 12.

17 This essay does not address the issue of whether *Speaking like Magpies* should be classified as historiographic metafiction or metadramatic historiography. The implications of the awareness of historical facts on the part of the audience could be interpreted along the lines suggested for different types of historical novels by NÜNNING, Ansgar. *Von historischer Fiktion zu historiographischer Metafiktion.* Trier: Wissenschaftlicher Verlag Trier, 1995. As far as drama is concerned, the following study is also relevant: BERNINGER. *Neue Formen des Geschichtsdramas in Großbritannien und Irland seit 1970.*

18 The Equivocator's function for the different characters is dependent on the characters themselves and their specific needs. For James, he is a wise helper and a servant to the powerful, and though his name suggests an unreliability of his accounts, his behaviour allows no intervention apart from his concessions. McGuinness wrote on 13 September, 2005 that "[t]he Equivocator [is] the spirit of the times personified, an extraordinary character who would act as the storyteller." <www.bbc.co.uk/coventry/content/articles/2005/09/13/speaking_like_magpies_prev_feature.shtml> (accessed 14 May, 2011).

what most men prefer to hide – this sacrifice is his gift to the spectator."[19] This quote stresses the double character of metadramatic performance that is supported by the character of the Equivocator: through the dialogue between king and intimate confidant, the actor (Will Houston) of King James is allowed to utter self-pity, fear, and a childish wish for mere security, a thought that every spectator needs to read from the performance and understand. The play thus toys with conveying fictionalised facts and historiography but a scene like the one described above between the historical king and a metadramatic character also demonstrates that it incorporates psychological approaches to the matter of politics and fear.

Apart from the supernatural figure of the Equivocator, the king is supported by various characters in his fear of the unknown, e. g. by his loving but unloved queen. James also trusts his loyal servant Robert Cecil and confides in him: "What have you learned about me?/ Shall I tell you in a whisper?/ Timor mortis conturbat me./ [...] Then, remove my fear of death,/ Remove the threat to me." (*Magpies* 35) The king's naivety seems ridiculous at first. How should it be possible to remove an unspecified fear of death? However, Cecil has indeed found out that there is a Catholic conspiracy. Cecil is furthermore made aware of the king's fear by the Equivocator, who stresses James' fear concerning an unknown threat: "I, too, serve his majesty. [...] In different capacities./ Sometimes I protect him./ Sometimes I question him./ Times he tells me what I am – / What he wants me to be./ I have heard him whisper,/ Timor mortis conturbat me – / Fear of death, fear of life." (*Magpies* 36–37) Fear thus not only guides the monarch's psyche, but also his politics.

Robert Cecil is the most trusted minister at court, and he plays a crucial role in the detection of the Gunpowder Plot. He is shown to be a powerful and almost Machiavellian figure. He is devout, self-loathing and a loyal servant to his king in *Speaking like Magpies*; yet he resembles a scheming politician who knows about the conspiracy against his king before anybody else does: "Who conspires to create terror?' 'Catholics –/ They would kill the king –/ I will save him." (*Magpies* 40) Often watching the stage from the corners in the 2005 RSC production, Cecil (in this production portrayed by Nigel Cooke) is apparently controlling politics. He becomes James' pragmatic tactician and knows who is dangerous and who is a threat to the monarchy. For James, he embodies the qualities of a surveyor and a spymaster, because he has found out that frustration over religious politics starts to surface among disappointed Catholic noblemen. As the king's councillor, Cecil has a powerful political position, and as spymaster he can direct and control politics; he knows that "[t]here is a conspiracy –/ Against our beloved sovereign" (*Magpies* 39). The conspiracy in fact seems to be very real and

---

19 BROOK, Peter. *The Empty Space.* Harmondsworth: Penguin, 1979 [1968]. 66–67.

dangerous. Yet the Gunpowder Plot will fail, and, as the audience knows, the king will be saved and the assassins will be executed. Nevertheless, the atmosphere in *Speaking like Magpies* is dominated by the threat of death.

This threat is impersonated by two of the historically documented group of Catholic conspirators: Robert Catesby and Thomas Wintour. Their beliefs are introduced as fatal, or rather lethal to faith, as will become clear. Even before they appear on stage for the first time, they are associated with the notion of 'terror'. They are described by Cecil as speaking in "lying tongues […] [I]n evil languages of the world. […] They mean to kill God" (*Magpies* 40). Cecil is aware of the dangers that this kind of stout Catholicism and its practitioners embody, especially because they are acting secretly: "This realm is rotten with them./ They are wearing masks." (*Magpies* 41) Though the Catholic conspirators are described as acting in disguise, their conspiracy is unmasked by Cecil. He observes Robert Catesby and Thomas Wintour from a distance and can confirm his impression of them as religious extremists. Being feared for his outspokenness and his egotism, Catesby is described with the following attributes even by the Jesuit Father Henry Garnet: "His is a frantic faith. […] He'd die for our faith. […] And he would kill for it." (*Magpies* 51 – 52) This provides a further distinction of religion. The King and his councillor generalise the Catholic threat. Here, though, it surfaces that even the stout Jesuit Father Garnet calls the faith of the conspirators frantic.

The priest seems reasonable in this; Henry Garnet is, in reality, a central character in the Catholic plot; in the play he is depicted in largely positive terms in contrast to Cecil. He is a Jesuit priest, living secretly in England, and represents the strength of the Catholic faith and supports its believers. However, in comparison to Catesby, Father Garnet appears as a kind but rather quiescent and not very tangible Catholic force. He is introduced to the audience as a peace-seeking and very human character, but also a fallible person. In his role as a Jesuit, he nevertheless seems to embody an inspiration to the younger Catholics who eventually become conspirators in the Gunpowder Plot. This is why Garnet is later on also branded as a traitor (*Magpies* 43 and 45).

Nevertheless it is difficult to simply categorise the conspirators in this drama as evil, because, in many ways, they appear to be appealing figures. Catesby and Wintour are presented as "*handsome men, magnificently attired*" (*Magpies* 54); they are charismatic and manage to convey that they are utterly convinced of their calling. They provide a poetic explanation of their motives to Henry Garnet: They speak in unison in their confession of the plot and argue for the necessity of what they are doing, in this way appealing to the empathy of the audience: "We sing to you in confession/ What we believe the Lord desires./ […] And you shall see a burst of fire." (*Magpies* 60 – 61) Especially Robert Catesby is shown as an enigmatic and prophetic figure. He is inspired by destructive ideas and by a trust in an eternal glory overruling earthly hopelessness. The audience is left in awe of the dramaturgical presentation of the conspiracy and is likely to feel admiration and sympathy for the young Catholics who are intriguing characters and initially do not evoke fear, but fascination. Clothed in robes of a blood-red colour, they seem excessive in their determination to achieve their goal. Even Father Garnet is too weak to reason with them when they confess gunpowder, treason and plot: "We each have had a dream. [...] In it we killed the king." (*Magpies* 58) Catesby's and Wintour's fundamentalist trust in having the right to destroy king and parliament and their violent religious stance are even called blasphemy by Garnet. Nevertheless, Catesby insists that he is guided by a "noble, Catholic faith" (*Magpies* 62).

Though they appear to be arrogant and proud young men, they are likely to seduce the spectator into neglecting the danger they embody: not only do they look attractive, but they also evoke sympathy by means of their intelligence, which is revealed when they trick Father Garnet into hearing their confession of the Gunpowder Plot. Catesby and Wintour complete each other's sentences, adhere to their religious conviction, confess to their priest, and reveal their need to act. This shows a psychological mutuality that enforces their common determination to carry out this act of assassination, which they consider a sanctified strife for freedom. They express their belief in a divine sanction via their poetry; for them, the plot is not a political struggle, but a plan based on hope, trust and determination. Firm in their belief, they show neither signs of frustration nor of fear. Right from the start they are resolute in their plan to commit the deed. Being utterly convinced of his motives, Catesby challenges sacrosanct royalty and monarchical rights in order to destroy oppressing forces; he undermines Garnet's insistence on law, authority and the protection of innocent people via confession.

The play thus introduces the thin line between sacrificial killings and the murder of innocent people under extreme circumstances. It addresses the question of the legitimacy of performing extreme acts in the name of faith and justice. The timelessness of human sacrifice and collateral damage underlines the topicality of the play. Catesby and Wintour are willing to sacrifice themselves and they accept collateral damage. Because innocent people are tortured to reveal the names of the plotters and thus have to suffer as well,[20] the audience is provided with harsh criticism clearly directed against the reasoning of the frantic, if not fundamentalist conspirators. This allows the spectator to judge the conspirators and see their flaws, despite the generally positive way they are presented. The power of the dramatic fiction in *Speaking like Magpies* is likely to

---

20 Henry Garnet's maid May is tortured by Cecil to confess the Catholic's part in the Gunpowder Plot in "Scene Thirteen: Appetite" (*Magpies* 91–102).

capture the attention of the audience, inviting them to see unanswered questions raised in the play.

Nevertheless, given the fact that both sides are presented in a way that may encourage the audience to feel empathy with them, the spectators are not left with simple value judgments. The conspirators' firm conviction as well as the fear and insecurity experienced by the monarch may be appealing. James demands loyalty from the Protestant and Catholic religious leaders: "Are you loyal to me –/ Above all loyalties?" (*Magpies* 82) Yet the answers he receives disappoint him, causing him to feel devastated and frightened, which evokes compassion: "Save me from death./ I am frightened of death." (*Magpies* 82) Being frightened by the inevitability of death, he repeats the same request to Protestant as well as Catholic courtiers and even to his queen: "Can you save me from death?" (*Magpies* 82, 83 and 84) Cecil's answer, promising self-sacrificing service, does not appease him, neither does the one by the Equivocator – "I will save you from death" (*Magpies* 84) – fully satisfy him. The detection of the Gunpowder Plot and a release from fear in McGuinness' play is only made possible by supernatural, divine intervention. Even Cecil's qualities as a spy seem insufficient in comparison.

The Equivocator, James' 'guardian angel' shows the king the conspirators' fraternisation in a mask play, set in darkness: "Darkness that will reveal all." (*Magpies* 84) Only his supernatural powers seem to be able to save James. He is lifted up into the air above the stage and thus he can defeat his fear and prevail against danger, which is obvious in the Catholic plot. Suspended on strings over the stage in the 2005 production, James watches the conspirators presenting their gathering as a 'Masque of Darkness',[21] a ritual choric ensemble piece. In this scene the whole group of the conspirators are masked and cannot be identified; their names, as indicated in the stage direction, however, flash "*electronically onto a back wall. They come with such speed, clashing, in colours, they should be impossible to decipher individually.*" (*Magpies* 87) Thus, their individuality seems to be lost in the flashes of lightning. They address James in a purely dramatical and unrealistic scene: "You affront the King of Heaven,/ You make our blessed Lady cry./ Your faith is like an infidel's,/ You will burn in brightest hell" (*Magpies* 87). They are calling their own frantic Catholicism the only true belief, and the king's Christian faith that of an infidel. Dressed in purple robes, they sing, invoke the authority of the Holy Virgin, and profess their fearlessness with regard to the consequences of their acts: "We do not fear divine justice" (*Magpies* 86). On the contrary, they clearly expect divine appreciation and claim divine authority for their conviction and extremist action.

With this claim of righteousness the thin line between true religious faith and

---

21 "Scene Twelve: The Masque of Darkness" (*Magpies* 85 – 91).

a fundamentalist terrorist faith is addressed: there are two possibilities of interpreting their action: either Catesby and his men are motivated by an intensity
of faith that is often not understood by non-believers or they prove to be vain,
obsessed and violent seekers of martyrdom. The conspirators threaten James
with fire: "Our gift, great king, is gunpowder" (*Magpies* 88). The king is to burn
like a heretic at a stake or like a disbeliever in hell. However, the Gunpowder Plot
is wonderfully circumvented: In the 2005 RSC production, James descends like
an eagle from his position above the stage precisely at the moment when Fawkes
wants to light the taper for the explosion. He snatches the taper from him and
extinguishes the flame (*Magpies* 88). Not only metaphorically but also literally
James, like an incarnation of divine majesty, prevents the Gunpowder Plot from
being successful, remains the head of state, and even, finally, loses his fear.

The conspirators are executed, and their dead bodies are displayed on stage.
The political circumstances are investigated, and all those associated with the
Catholic conspiracy are interrogated. Father Garnet, who scolded the young
conspirators for their treacherous plan, is tortured, and – instead of the king – it
is now the stout Jesuit priest who admits: "I am frightened of death, [...]/
Frightened of falling into hell. [...] I will fall into hell./ I am frightened of death."
(*Magpies* 112, 114) Even his faith apparently cannot conquer fear; it seems as if
this was indeed only possible for those as frantic and extreme in their faith as the
conspirators, who are neither afraid of risking their own life nor that of innocent
bystanders. Garnet's innocent maid May is also tortured. She is force-fed with
raw beef by Cecil in a disgusting mock-communion and threatened with a knife
and fork, which Cecil holds close to her body. Her suicide is a consequence of the
conspiracy and thus can be seen as collateral damage, as "the death of so many
innocent victims of religious intolerance".[22]

Fear is present on both sides; everybody is affected by the plot of a small
group of Catholic conspirators. Although the attack and planned assassination
could be prevented, the plot still causes pain and suffering. Torture serves as the
traditional method of gathering secret information, but it is exhibited as being
inhuman and barbarous. Torture is a means and display of political power. Its
main executioner is Robert Cecil, a pragmatic power politician. Fear of the
unknown – terror in its true sense – and terrorism clearly engender further
terror. Robert Merrill observes that "[b]oth crime and the punishment of crime
are public spectacles with quasi-religious implications"[23] – an idea that is clearly
picked up in *Speaking like Magpies*. The plotters stage themselves and are up-

---

22 BRADLEY. "*Thomas More*". 3.
23 MERRILL. "Simulations and Terrors of Our Time." 182.

staged by the court.[24] They are executed as the government celebrates its success; their death is thus instrumentalised by the monarchy, politics, and politicians.

This spectacle indeed is reminiscent of the use of the media in current politics and in particular of the impact pictures have on the minds of people in today's media-oriented world. The spectacle does not mean that fear has been eliminated from the nation. On the contrary: fear seems to provide the basis for further political action. The idea of being haunted by a constant threat is apparent in *Speaking like Magpies*, too. The play ends with a sceptical view of politics and religion. It closes with a premonition of further dispute. In the last scene of the play, James' wife Queen Anne meets the Catholic Lady Anne Vaux, who previously gave shelter to Henry Garnet: Lady Anne addresses an implied conversion towards Catholicism by the queen as a "danger never dreamt of" (*Magpies* 118). She assessess that this might pose a future threat to the politico-religious state of the nation: "A fuse has been lit./ There is no peace./ We must wait and watch./ Wait and pray" (*Magpies* 118). Religious struggles continue at the end of *Speaking like Magpies* but not in the open. Thus the note that the play ends on refers to political quarrel, danger and a society that is potentially under a continuous threat. This discussion has proved that the 2005 play's interpretation highlights politico-religious action and determines the analysis of the 1605 Catholic conspiracy as a fictionalised historical, but also current political matter that addresses the fear of a society, here represented by its head.

A question that needs to be raised in this context of threatening political activism is whether the conspirators are presented as terrorists or as freedom fighters in McGuinness' play. This is a decisive issue for any analysis of their characterisation and motivation. For King James and his family they certainly embody a dangerous force, endangering the royal family's lives. In the play, the conspirators use politically motivated violence to communicate a powerful message. However, the question of whether their acts should be seen as terrorism or as a fight for religious freedom ultimately is not answered in a satisfactory way and even appears to remain unresolved. In McGuinness' play the assessment of the conspirators is partially left to the audience, but it is of course influenced by factors such as the casting, the director's decisions, and the performance of the actors: In *Speaking like Magpies* both sides are presented in a manner that invites empathy on the part of the audience. In particular the characters' scepticism as well as their personal fears and convictions make them appear 'human' and accessible for a modern audience. King James and his court evoke the

---

24 Compare the idea of a 'cynical nationalism' in FOSTER, Thomas. "Cynical Nationalism." In:
    Dana Heller (ed.). *The Selling of 9/11. How a National Tragedy Became a Commodity.* New
    York/Houndsmills: Palgrave Macmillan, 2005. 254 – 87. See especially the introductory notes
    to this essay.

audience's compassion in this staging of events, but not only they do: the Catholics, too, even the conspirators demand empathy, and even sympathy, from the spectator. They are presented as self-defined martyrs, ready to "exchange their deaths against a place in paradise",[25] yet this terminology used by Baudrillard for extremist terrorists does not fully capture their spirit. Here, they are also vain young men, absorbed in their conviction. Their fearlessness conveys awe and even appeals to the audience's sympathy, but the spectator is still aware of the cruel nature of the conspirators' goals: the play presents the unfulfilled hopes of a small extremist group of young fundamentalist Catholics willing to commit murder.

Kath Bradley states that *"Speaking like Magpies* overtly addresses the religious divisions still present in the England of Elizabeth's successor and these are no more dramatically staged than in the prevention of planned terrorist action, and in the torture of an innocent servant in its aftermath",[26] including terrorist negligence towards human collateral damage. This, too, is an aspect that will bring emotional attention to the collateral damage of today's acts of terrorism.

These putative parallels demand a comparison between the impact of 5 November 1605, 5/11 and that of 9/11, 11 September 2001, which Baudrillard has referred to as 'mother event', a terrorist plot that destroyed the Twin Towers in New York and that has created suspicion and fear within a global society. 9/11 caused a cultural trauma and a "national rupture",[27] leaving a fearful society with a "[p]sychic wound"[28] and affecting not only the American nation but the world. It might also be of interest to compare 5/11 not only to 9/11, but also to 7/7, a further terrorist attack: the London underground bombings on 7 July 2005.

Speaking like Magpies was written and rehearsed at a time when both events were deeply shocking the world, and the English(-speaking) nations in particular. Frank McGuinness' historical play *Speaking like Magpies* opened on 29 September 2005. It becomes clear that the play must have been finished before the London bombings took place but at a time when 9/11 was shaping global

---

25 This, in the heat of 9/11 events, was presented by Baudrillard as a possible explanation for the action of suspected modern fundamentalist *jihadi* (BAUDRILLARD. "L'Esprit du Terrorisme." 157). On these ideas, see also the introduction to Edward Kemp's *5/11*, especially his interest in the "unreasonableness of faith". In: KEMP, Edward. *5/11*. London: Nick Hern Books, 2005. iii-iv. The issue of the Gunpowder Plot as a terrorist religious conspiracy is also the topic of Edward Kemp's historical play. This play can be interpreted as a dialogue between 1605 and 2001, too.

26 BRADLEY. *"Thomas More."* 3.

27 ROTHBERG, Michael. "Seeing Terror, Feeling Art. Public and Private in Post-9/11 Literature." In: Ann Keniston and Jeanne Follansbee Quinn (eds.). *Literature after 9/11.* London/New York: Routledge, 2008. 123–42, 123.

28 BRUSTEIN, Robert. "Theater after 9/11." In: Ann Keniston and Jeanne Follansbee Quinn (eds.). *Literature after 9/11.* London/New York: Routledge, 2008. 242–45, 244.

politics, and the RSC rehearsal process must in turn have been influenced by the
recent London attack as well the destruction of the Twin Towers. With these
recent terrorist attacks in mind, the production team as well as the audience
might realise and could draw parallels between the constant possibility of destruction and shock then and now. A few years after 9/11, the feeling of fear
might not be as imminent anymore as it was in 2001 directly after the event, yet
terrorist acts can always inspire fear because they can affect anybody. In the early
twenty-first century it seems virtually inevitable to assume that the play
Speaking like Magpies must consciously reflect the post-9/11 atmosphere. After
all, it is a representation, or, to be more precise, a literary and dramaturgical
interpretation of the preparation for and the aftermath of a planned terrorist
(-like) attack. Michael Rothberg in "Seeing Terror, Feeling Art" addresses the
idea that "literature and other forms of art are important sites of response to
terrorism".[29] In this respect, *Speaking like Magpies* not only draws upon the
Renaissance, which provides its historical setting, but it also proves to be a
modern history play and therefore embodies qualities of a chronicle of events at
the beginning of the twenty-first century, having been written for today's audience even though it addresses a story that took place 400 years ago. Especially
after 9/11, the experience of history – even in the theatre – might often be
influenced by an unspecified fear of terrorist acts; it is a similar atmosphere of
dread that controls King James in *Speaking like Magpies*. Fear rules the monarch
as it rules a society potentially threatened by terror. The Gunpowder Plot, no
matter how 'glorious' its outcome may seem in its portrayal on stage, therefore
can – in this representation – have some connections to a "watershed moment"[30]
like 9/11: There is no promise of an end to political, religious struggle. *Speaking
like Magpies* presents "the tragic consequences of a faith which admits no
other".[31] The reference to a "[d]anger never dreamt of" (*Magpies* 118) sounds
ominously like the threats associated with what has been called an 'axis of evil'.

However, at the same time, it seems as if the play addresses very different
questions that do not seem to have a global but rather a personal impact. The
state of shock that a nation like the United States was confronted with in the
aftermath of 9/11 is here applied to one personal version of 5 November. The
Gunpowder Plot in *Speaking like Magpies* does not reflect the trauma of a nation;
it only speaks to the nation to a certain extent in that the audience is familiar with
the Fawkes myth, but this knowledge is not much more than a folk custom today:
a celebration of fireworks. Instead of global politics and fundamentalist ex-

---

29 ROTHBERG. "Seeing Terror, Feeling Art." 123–24.
30 GRAY, Jeffrey. "Precious Testimony." In: Ann Keniston and Jeanne Follansbee Quinn (eds.).
    Literature after 9/11. London/New York: Routledge, 2008. 261–84, 261.
31 BRADLEY. "*Thomas More.*" 3.

tremism, the play draws upon the personalities of a few protagonists and their individual fortunes. Foremost, the monarch and the conspirators are portrayed as individuals: their aims, hopes and fears come to the fore in the play. A parallel cannot be drawn between every feature that is attributed to the conspirators in this fictionally dramatised seventeenth-century plot and those ascribed to the executors of the twenty-first century attacks.

In *Speaking like Magpies*, 5/11 is charged with the king's fear of his own vulnerability in the face of a conspiracy that has its reasons in vain and frantic Catholicism; it is neither a global nor a national fear that pervades James, but a private and very personal fear: "Timor mortis conturbat me. [...] Fear of death disturbs me". As such, *Speaking like Magpies* is a drama that is not generally concerned with constant feelings of terror, but very individual and private fears that can determine the politics of an individual monarch in a timeless story that interprets the quadricentenary anniversary of the Gunpowder Plot.

References

BAUDRILLARD, Jean. "L'Esprit du Terrorisme." Translated by Michel Valentin. In: Stanley Hauerwas and Frank Lentricchia (eds.). *Dissent from the Homeland. Essays after September 11.* Durham/London: Duke University Press, 2003. 149–61.

BERNINGER, Mark. *Neue Formen des Geschichtsdramas in Großbritannien und Irland seit 1970.* Trier: Wissenschaftlicher Verlag Trier, 2006.

BRADLEY, Kathrine. "*Thomas More*, directed by Robert Delamere for the RSC, The Swan Theatre, Stratford-upon-Avon." Unpublished review. 12 May, 2005.

BROOK, Peter. *The Empty Space.* Harmondsworth: Penguin, 1979 [1968].

BRUSTEIN, Robert. "Theater after 9/11." In: Ann Keniston and Jeanne Follansbee Quinn (eds.). *Literature after 9/11.* London/New York: Routledge, 2008. 242–45.

DER DERIAN, James. "9/11: Before, After, and In Between." In: J. David Slocum (ed.). *Terrorism, Media, Liberation.* New Brunswick/London: Rutgers University Press, 2005. 321–35.

FOSTER, Thomas. "Cynical Nationalism." In: Dana Heller (ed.). *The Selling of 9/11. How a National Tragedy Became a Commodity.* New York/Houndsmills: Palgrave Macmillan, 2005. 254–87.

GRAY, Jeffrey. "Precious Testimony." In: Ann Keniston and Jeanne Follansbee Quinn (eds.). *Literature after 9/11.* London/New York: Routledge, 2008. 261–84.

HAYNES, Alan. *The Gunpowder Plot: Faith in Rebellion.* Stroud: Alan Sutton Publishing, 1994.

HOGGE, Alice. *God's Secret Agents: Queen Elizabeth's Forbidden Priests and the Hatching of the Gunpowder Plot.* New York: Harper Collins, 2005.

HUEHLS, Mitchum. *Qualified Hope. A Postmodern Politics of Time.* Columbus: Ohio State University Press, 2009.

KAPLAN, E. Ann. *Trauma Culture. The Politics of Terror and Loss in Media and Literature.* New Brunswick/London: Rutgers University Press, 2005.

KEMP, Edward. *5/11.* London: Nick Hern Books, 2005.

KNAPP, Guntram. *Angst und Depression. Grundformen und Pathologie.* Sternenfels: Verlag Wissenschaft & Praxis, 2000.

LATHAN, Peter. Review of *Speaking like Magpies:* <www.britishtheatreguide.info/reviews/ RSCspeakmag-rev.htm> (accessed 14 May, 2011).

MCGUINNESS, Frank. *Speaking like Magpies.* London: Faber and Faber, 2005.

– Interview: <www.bbc.co.uk/coventry/content/articles/2005/09/13/speaking_like_ magpies_prev_feature.shtml> (accessed 14 May, 2011).

MERRILL, Robert. "Simulations and Terrors of Our Time." In: J. David Slocum (ed.). *Terrorism, Media, Liberation.* New Brunswick/London: Rutgers University Press, 2005. 171–84.

NACOS, Brigitte L. "Mass-Mediated Terrorism in the New World (Dis)Order." In: J. David Slocum (ed.). *Terrorism, Media, Liberation.* New Brunswick/London: Rutgers University Press, 2005. 185–208.

NÜNNING, Ansgar. *Von historischer Fiktion zu historiographischer Metafiktion.* Trier: Wissenschaftlicher Verlag Trier, 1995.

POZORSKI, Aimee. "Trauma's Time." In: *CTReview/ Connecticut Review* 28,1 (2006): 71– 76.

ROTHBERG, Michael. "Seeing Terror, Feeling Art. Public and Private in Post-9/11 Literature." In: Ann Keniston and Jeanne Follansbee Quinn (eds.). *Literature after 9/11.* London/New York: Routledge, 2008. 123–42.

SIMPSON, J.A. and E.S.C. WEINER (eds.). *The Oxford English Dictionary.* Oxford/New York: Clarendon Press, 1989.

SMELSER, Neil J. "Psychological Trauma and Cultural Trauma." In: Jeffrey C. Alexander et al. (eds.). *Cultural Trauma and Collective Identity.* Berkeley/Los Angeles/London: University of California Press, 2004. 31–59.

– "September 11, 2001, as Cultural Trauma." In: Jeffrey C. Alexander et al. (eds.). *Cultural Trauma and Collective Identity.* Berkeley/Los Angeles/London: University of California Press, 2004. 264–82.

Antonio Wojahn

Fear of Death in J.G. Ballard's *Crash*

I.   Accessways

In 1973, the orbital motorway M25 had not been built yet, so that James Graham Ballard's *Crash* (1973) takes place in a central location, the intersection at the Western Avenue flyover (*Crash* 11). Locations play a paradoxical role in both the novel and the film,[1] as the narrative projects itself onto the automobile's possibilities. More to the point, the displacement of the narrative into a mobile perspective informs the surreal effect of the text, where an imaginary world that looks unsettlingly real is created. For example, minutely precise locations of the London area are referred to; they are all familiarly accessible by car. Hence, what drives the narrative is the transposition of virtually every aspect of life onto the car. The conceit lies in the double vision of the car as an object that offers intimacy, protection, mobility, and the horrible dangers it creates. Remarkably, the idea of safety is shattered in the course of the narrative, turned inside out by Ballard's surreal treatment of the intimidating aspects of the car-crash, which this paper aims to demonstrate through seeking the traces of fear of death. The key aim of this paper is the idea that the narrative is driven by the transformation of fear into a repetitive, traumatic narrative.

Crash offers a variety of angles to its readers, which is reflected in its treatment by critics such as Jeanette Baxter, focusing on Ballard's surrealism,[2] or Heinrich Keim in his exploration of Ballard's fascination with 'concrete' matters.[3] These polar extremes demonstrate the need to focus attention on a specific aspect of the novel. The notion of fear is, however, suppressed in *Crash*. Rarely, the characters refer to fear or exhibit fearful behaviour, e. g. when the *protagonist*

---

1 CRONENBERG, David, Dir. *Crash*. Perf. Holly Hunter, James Spader, Elias Koteas and Deborah Kara Unger. Fine Line Features, 1996.
2 BAXTER, Jeanette. *J.G. Ballard's Surrealist Imagination: Spectacular Authorship*. Farnham: Ashgate, 2009.
3 KEIM, Heinrich. *New Wave: Die Avantgarde der modernen anglo-amerikanischen Science Fiction?* Meitingen: Corian, 1983. 271–314.

James Ballard (called 'James' for the purposes of this paper; the author will be referred to as 'Ballard') angrily says "Vaughan, you're not on a bloody stunt track now." (*Crash* 91) he expresses his *anger* about fearing for his partner Catherine, who was the object of Vaughan's aggressive near-accident drive. One must not forget that attitudes towards machinery and technology change over time – even the wearing of seat belts was not mandatory in 1975.[4] From this point of view, the characters are fearless in their casual treatment of driving and safety regulations. The seatbelt is only a minor detail to them as to the narrative, but it matters as a mark of the changeable attitude towards fear.

In reading *Crash*, critics face a variety of challenges. Among them is the looming question of the text's defining moment(s). The issue of fear is arguably under the surface of the text's central concerns, but it also represents a gaping hole in the fabric of Ballard's claim that "the role of *Crash* is cautionary, a warning against that brutal, erotic and overlit realm that beckons more and more persuasively to us from the margins of the technological landscape" (*Crash* iii). The conceit lies in the fact that Ballard's fearless characters seem to accept this beckoning without caution. Caution, then, is a missing link between the element of fear and the text's preoccupation with danger and sexuality. Authorial comments such as Ballard's have to be treated with caution themselves, but regardless of the tension such comments create for a reading, the question remains how the imaginary world of *Crash* can be read if there is nothing to be cautious of inside of the text.

The 'fear of death' is a construct which needs to be treated with even greater caution, for it is muddled at best and certainly larger than life in terms of its potential impact on readings of *Crash*. To proclaim that the novel inverts the fear of death into a displaced sexuality would miss the point of investigating how Ballard turns James' fear into a repetitive-traumatic narrative. Hence, this paper expressly aims at transforming the text of *Crash* by developing a tailor-made reading of the fear of death between the lines of *Crash*. The surreal suppression of fear in the text amounts to an inversion of the roles of fearful victim and sexualized spectator. Thus, Ballard manages to highlight the role of the car-crash as a cautionary tale about the attitude towards deathly technology in the twentieth century. As a starting point for exploring the notion 'fear of death', several ways of entering the aesthetics of *Crash* will be explored.

---

4 *RoSPA- Our History.* The Royal Society for the Prevention of Accidents. <http://www.rospa.com/about/history/default.aspx> (accessed: 29 July, 2011). Hence the comments by James (*Crash* 11 – 12) on himself and Helen Remington wearing seatbelts by pure luck.

II.   Gateways to *Crash*

To argue – for a moment – with Freud,[5] 'fear' is too broad a term, since it refers to
a wide range of behaviour. A brief excursion into Freud's discussion of the death
drive (*Todestrieb*) is beneficial to illustrate the role that fear and specifically the
'fear of death' could then have in this paper. Although Freud never consistently
abided by the following differentiation he proposed in a highly speculative
piece,[6] it is a helpful starting point for creating assessment criteria of the
characters of *Crash*'s reaction to the automobile accident:

> Angst bezeichnet einen gewissen Zustand der Erwartung der Gefahr und Vorbereitung
> auf dieselbe, mag sie auch eine unbekannte sein; Furcht verlangt ein bestimmtes Ob-
> jekt, vor dem man sich fürchtet; Schreck benennt aber den Zustand, in den man gerät,
> wenn man in Gefahr kommt, ohne auf sie vorbereitet zu sein, betont das Moment der
> Überraschung.[7]

Of course, there are equally many terms related to fear in English, but, unfortunately, borrowed terms such as 'angst' confuse the translation effortlessly.
The case in point is that the vague term 'fear' has to be related to something to
make sense at all. In the case of *Crash*, it should relate to the car-crash, of course.
'Angst' (anxiety), which Freud refers to above, lends a neat metaphor to readers
of *Crash* for the anticipation of the accident by its characters. 'Furcht' (fear) at
best relates to the injuries that can be expected of a car-crash without seatbelts
worn (bear in mind, this is 1973). And finally, the best term of all is 'Schreck'
(shock), because it drives home the very nature of experiencing an accident as a
sudden interruption of normal, 'safe' life. If, for a moment, the characters of the
novel are treated as real patients, the conflict of the nicely differentiated terms
above becomes apparent. Not only are all of these terms applicable at once, but
they also overlap and lose their significance as tools of analysis. Thus, *Angst* can
result from the shock of an accident, and then turn into fear as its object is not a
'danger', such as 'the risk of an accident', but intimately connected to an object,
i. e. the car. Their use becomes relevant again when the tension between these
terms is utilized as a motivating force for character development in *Crash*.

From the very outset, the novel is a retrospective narrative which distances its
reader from immediate action, while simultaneously shocking with gruesome
detail (e. g. *Crash* 3, describing Vaughan as he is covered with blood and semen).
The violent nature of the car-crash is set up carefully, in order to create a

---

5 FREUD, Sigmund. "Jenseits des Lustprinzips." In: *Freud Studienausgabe: Psychologie des
   Unbewußten.* Edited by Alexander Mitscherlich, Angela Richards and James Strachey. Vol. 3.
   Frankfurt M.: Fischer, 1975. 213 – 72.
6 FREUD. "Jenseits des Lustprinzips." 223.
7 FREUD. "Jenseits des Lustprinzips." 222 – 23.

mesmerizing effect in between shock and awe at the surreal treatment of factual detail that is provided in the minute descriptions: "Once we were the first to reach the crashed car of an injured woman driver. [...] she sat unsteadily in the crushed compartment, fragments of the tinted windshield set in her forehead like jewels." (*Crash* 4) To add to the confusion, Freud's neat triptych of fear is preceded by his inspiring observation that "[n]ach schweren mechanischen Erschütterungen, Eisenbahnzusammenstößen und anderen, mit Lebensgefahr verbundenen Unfällen ist seit langem ein Zustand beschrieben worden, dem dann der Name 'traumatische Neurose' geblieben ist".[8] Freud claims at the same time that the true reason of this neurosis is *not* mechanical, but psychological.[9] The 'mechanical' impact during an accident may not prescribe the psychological reaction to it, but it definitely presents an opportunity to make it instrumental in reading *Crash*.

The notion of safety, as alluded to above in the detail of wearing a seatbelt, becomes a chafing point for the narrative. Hence (compare Cronenberg[10]), James states: "After being bombarded endlessly by road-safety propaganda it was almost a relief to find myself in an actual accident." (*Crash* 28) One might call this a case of wishful thinking, but in a retrospective narrative this statement reads like a coded reference to a suppressed death wish. Clearly, calling the cautioning road-safety advertisements 'propaganda' is a value judgement which masks James' wish to enter the detached spectacle by which he feels 'bombarded' so much. In a complicated twist, the traumatic potential of James' accident is turned by his wish for the 'real thing' and becomes a fulfilment of his desire. This then enables a complete inversion of the reactions to the violent aspects of accidents, of which James is not afraid but seems rather intrigued by. Bear in mind, this is a character whose emotional need is evaluated by statements such as the following: "There were times when I felt that these affairs [Catherine and I had] took place merely to provide the raw material for our sexual games." (*Crash* 21) Fulfilment, then, is a key source for Ballard's narrative transformation of 'normal' reactions to violence and danger. The case in point is that – surreal as it may seem – there is the possibility of an explanation for the behaviour of the character James. Whatever the motivating force of James' character may be, one step ahead lies the conscious erasure of fear by the narrative.

Freud's examination of 'mechanical violence' as a motivating factor furthers the idea that emotional reactions are determined by libidinal forces which channel, direct and strive for a balance, but which also may enter a spiralling

---

8 FREUD. "Jenseits des Lustprinzips." 222.
9 FREUD. "Jenseits des Lustprinzips." 222.
10 CRONENBERG. *Crash*, 8 m50.

escalation of forces. The next quotation almost reads as if it were a recipe for *Crash*:

> So würde also die mechanische Gewalt des Traumas das Quantum Sexualenergie frei machen, welches infolge der mangelnden Angstvorbereitung traumatisch wirkt, die gleichzeitige Körperverletzung würde aber durch die Anspruchnahme einer narziß-tischen Überbesetzung des leidenden Organs den Überschuß an Erregung binden.[11]

Allegedly, by experiencing pain, the repetition of the accident becomes sexually attractive, which then is a way to work through the psychological trauma of this near-death situation. It is specifically mentioned that an *injury* would enable a narcissist reaction which binds the 'excess of arousal' that is caused by the mechanical violence experienced. Yet for James, his traumatic experience is a fulfilment of his existential doubt: "Long before Vaughan died I had begun to think of my own death. With whom would I die, and in what role – psychopath, neurasthenic, absconding criminal?" (*Crash* 8) Vaughan's role as the frame for the narrative provides a neat externalization of James' fascination with death, precisely because James does *not* die telling the story. The tantalizing proximity of death is displaced onto Vaughan, whose death prompts James to tell the story. Arguably, this is a transformed re-imagining by James which reminds of a conscious effort by him to channel the violent experience of Vaughan's death.

The backdrop for these experiences in James' fictional life is provided by Ballard's (again, retrospectively written) foreword to the novel: "*Crash*, of course, is not concerned with an imaginary disaster, however imminent, but with a pandemic cataclysm that kills hundreds of thousands of people each year and injures millions." (*Crash* ii) So, allegedly, there are 'real' deaths which motivate Ballard's writing of the story. It is the gap between Ballard's toying with factual reality and his surreal treatment of the car-crash as a sexual climax which prompts critics such as Elena Lamberti to search for "a different order"[12] of reality in *Crash*. The foreword by Ballard simply plays with this attempt at deciphering the code of the novel's surreal world, yet it also hints at the possibility of overreading the novel for its surrealism.

Hence, Ballard provocatively claims a political role for the novel. In fact, he creates an allegorical dimension in which the novel should be read, thus confusing its 'political' status even further: "Throughout *Crash* I have used the metaphor of the car not only as a sexual image, but as a total metaphor for man's life in today's society. As such the novel has a political role quite apart from its sexual content." (*Crash* iii) The role of the novel is, of course, defined by its appropriation through a given reader. As such, the novel can have a political role,

---

11 FREUD. "Jenseits des Lustprinzips." 243.
12 LAMBERTI, Elena. "*Crash* by J.G. Ballard and D. Cronenberg." In: *Textus* XIII (2000): 173–94. 176.

but the question has to be put into reverse. The characters of the novel offer vaguely 'political' views, which are immediately subverted through their connection to the overdrawn reactions that follow: "Like everyone else bludgeoned by these billboard harangues and television films of imaginary accidents, I had felt a vague sense of unease that the gruesome climax of my life was being rehearsed years in advance" (*Crash* 28). The metaphor of the rehearsal of life is evidently a further case of suppressed fear, since the billboards are obviously cautionary in nature, but perceived as a simulated future by the narrator.

Surprisingly, few commentators focus on the specific role of the car-crash in the novel, although it has a central place and connects all other branches of narrative to each other (such as discourses of sexuality, death, the body, drug abuse). The ambiguous nature of its narrative voice may add to the dismissal of specific statements such as the following: "At times I had even speculated on the kind of traffic accident in which I would die." (*Crash* 28) James implicitly states that he is driven by his fear of the automobile, which is emphasized by the obsessive focus on the menacing aspects of the automobile accident. The role of road safety advertising is turned inside out, precisely because it is a reality in waiting. Hence, the added detail that James was reading while driving towards his accident with Helen Remington (cf. Cronenberg[13]) underlines that road safety advertisements offer to James' perspective only possibilities of injuries and accidents. The narrative perspective is inverted on an authorial level before the impact of this accident can become a cause for character development. What is more, the book emphasizes this inversion additionally by foregrounding James' obsessing about his own, yet to come death. Curiously, the anticipation of death becomes a driving force of *suppressing* fear in the novel, rather than unleashing it.

The explosion of James' sexuality effectively rehearses the life-cycle of the accident in a displaced metaphor of sexual violence. He always yearns for, but never achieves the 'ultimate' accident, i. e. the deadly accident. In this vein, James can faithfully assert that "[d]uring our friendship [Vaughan] had rehearsed his death in many crashes, but this was his only true accident" (*Crash* 1). The conceit lies in the fact that Vaughan does not achieve his aim to collide with Elizabeth Taylor's car, but crashes into an airline bus and dies killing faceless "passengers" (1). Therefore, the narrative puts failure first and then moves on to rehearse this anticipated death over and over again throughout the text, closely resembling the pornographic distance between voyeuristic spectator and the only watched, detached performer. This adds the element of continuous deferral to the narrative, which enables the infinite postponement of James' death. Of course, the narrative would just as easily be capable of including a dead narrator, but the

---

13 CRONENBERG. *Crash*, 6 m24–25.

decision to keep James alive underlines Ballard's attempt to 'realize' his text as a surreal alternative present.

The deferral of death also provides a vehicle to enjoy the pleasures of anticipation. As Freud puts it, in his speculation on the causes of the 'death drive', it is a tension between reproduction and dying that channels and discharges the energies of life:

> Wir haben alle erfahren, daß die größte uns erreichbare Lust, die des Sexualaktes, mit dem momentanen Erlöschen einer hochgesteigerten Erregung verbunden ist. Die Bindung der Triebregung wäre aber eine vorbereitende Funktion, welche die Erregung für ihre endgültige Erledigung in der Abfuhrlust zurichten soll.[14]

Although the generalizing and rhetorically questionable appeal to 'everybody's experience' undermines Freud's point, it is nevertheless enlightening to read *Crash* as a metaphor of postponed consumption. If violent death is the sexually tantalizing threat offered by fearing the automobile, then the fetishistic rehearsal and re-enactment of violent death has to at least come close to its target. Hence James' fascination with his future death – he cannot afford to die rehearsing his own death. However, Freud's highly speculative theory of the death drive may not be at the root of Ballard's fascination with automobile death. Rather, since Ballard claims that "Freud's classic distinction between the latent and manifest content of the dream, between the apparent and the real, now needs to be applied to the external world of so-called reality" (*Crash* ii) it is evident that the repression of the fear of death in *Crash* is arguably a literalization of what Ballard perceives to be suppressed in the 'fiction' of reality. Put simply, the characters act out an overdrawn, larger than life version of suppressed fear, instead of 'becoming' perverse through the accident. Otherwise, James would not welcome the possibilities of the accident as a foreseeable fulfilment of his own latent death wish.

III.   The Imaginary World of *Crash*

In this segment, the imaginary world of Ballard's narrative will be examined for its potential in creating an extension of the suppression of the fear of death, which has been argued for on the preceding pages. Here, the nature of technology becomes apparent as an arbiter between imaginary and suppressed aspects of reality. The notion of road safety as a chafing point for the narrator James is one of the background textures of the narrative which make it relevant as a re-evaluation of the 'real' danger of automobile disaster. The ultimate ac-

---

14 FREUD. "Jenseits des Lustprinzips." 270.

cident is the deadly accident which Vaughan's "true accident" (*Crash* 1) represents. This harsh reality is underpinned by the material aspects of injuries,
deformed cars and fragments of accidents on the road. However, James is depicted as being estranged from naturalizing perspectives, which provides his
narrative voice with a claim to an enlightened perspective. From this vantage
point, James provides a commentary on the 'story' he narrates which is at once
highly imaginary and horribly graphic. Jeanette Baxter is right in calling for
reading *Crash* as a performance text,[15] since James' authority relies on narrating
his experience from a heightened perspective, almost as if from a stage set by his
accident.

The reversal of the power to define the world is transferred from the readers
onto James' eye-witness account, at the expense of James' own sense of be-
longing. "[A]ll the hopes and fancies of this placid suburban enclave [...] fal-
tered before the solid reality of the motorway embankments, with their constant
and unswerving geometry, and before the finite areas of the car-park aprons."
(*Crash* 36) In a way, then, James is already one of the dead, since his world has
collapsed into the concrete landscape of the motorway which defines human
existence and the possibilities of death. By breaking through the boundaries of
the motorway, the accident victim transgresses and leaves the coded safety of the
motorway barriers. These barriers are "[...] the confused [dimensions] of
technology and of sex (united in a work of death that is never a work of
mourning)".[16] The notion of mourning, from the perspective of a somehow dead
narrator, is obviously irrelevant. But the reversal of what defines the flow of life
(traffic routes) is forced by Ballard, since it is *James* who creates the atmosphere
of impending doom. He might just be a little too shaken to be relied upon in his
role as a prophetic (but unreliable) narrator.

Hence, the proclamation of an impending apocalypse has to be treated with
caution: "The passengers in the airliners lifting away from the airport were
fleeing the disaster area, escaping from this coming autogeddon." (*Crash* 37)
Instead of subscribing to the prophecy of a coming "autogeddon", readers of the
novel may be tempted to look for a reason why James is so obsessed with a
catastrophe that, after all, never arrives in the course of the narrative (barring the
'personal' catastrophe of Vaughan's death). The impact of James' accident is
curiously restricted to the psychological realm, heightening the impression that
James is just 'misbehaving' because of his severe shock: "The firemen [...]
assumed that I was bleeding to death from a massive open-heart wound. I was
barely injured." (*Crash* 11) However, James is also "severely bruised", weirdly

---

15 BAXTER. *Surrealist Imagination*. 99.
16 BAUDRILLARD, Jean. *Simulacra and Simulation*. Translated by Sheila Faria Glaser. Ann
   Arbor, MI: The University of Michigan Press, 1994 [1981]. 116–17.

claiming that "my only serious injury was a severed nerve in my scalp" (*Crash* 12). The confusion of the narrative voice here becomes understandable when the accident is related to fear. Rather than dealing with the displacement of fear into an awakened sexuality, James' reaction is readable as an *almost* complete and violent suppression of his fear of death which was awakened by the accident. Freud's observation that mechanical shocks can cause psychological shocks[17] comes to mind again. The displacement of the defining qualities of reality by James reminds one of an attempted re-writing of his reality. Ballard's text achieves this by James' naturalizing tendencies as a narrator, which displaces the values and expectations of a post-crash victim's traumatic experience. This suggestion, however, works from unattainable premises. As Jean Baudrillard puts it:

> The death drive is irritating, because it does not allow of any dialectical recovery. This is where its radicalism lies. But the panic it provokes does not confer the status of truth on it: we must wonder if, in the final instance, it is not itself a rationalisation of death.[18]

In other words, James' traumatic experience results not in a heightened awareness of his mortality, but in a sexual displacement thereof. His defiant stance is confused from the outset, when he marginalises his injuries and excludes psychological injury completely. The "severed nerve in [his] scalp" (*Crash* 12) provides a neat metaphor for this unacknowledged impact upon his psyche. This also becomes evident in his recovery process, where his immediate reaction is not to try and recover, but to challenge his relationship to the automobile.

In this challenge, the narrative reveals glimpses of 'normality', e.g. when James tries to confront his traumatic experience by re-enacting its elements. Surprisingly, his decision to drive again immediately connects himself to the suppressed notion of his own death.

> What began as an ironic gesture intended to provoke Catherine and Renata – both women wanted me never to drive again – soon took on a different role. My first brief journey to the accident site had raised the spectre of the dead man and, more important, the notion of my own death (*Crash* 44).

In following a logical sequence, Ballard creates a sense of normality which actually is not there at all. James is trying to recover from his accident by confronting his potential fear of driving, but, instead, he enters into a complex negotiation of dealing with the death of Helen Remington's husband and his own potential death. Rather than affirming the normality of driving again, James

---

17 FREUD. "Jenseits des Lustprinzips." 222.
18 BAUDRILLARD, Jean. *Symbolic Exchange and Death.* Translated by Iain H. Grant. London/ New York: Sage, 2007 [1993]. 151.

develops an obsessive compulsion to re-visit the location of his accident, almost
as if he cannot find closure for this incident. He even goes to the length of hiring
a variety of different cars in which he tries the route, negating the possibility that
his trauma might be related to the car as such: "In each of these cars I drove along
the accident route, visualizing the possibility of a different death and victim, a
different profile of wounds." (*Crash* 44) Quite to the contrary, James cannot let go
of the 'notion of death', of which, in turn, little is offered by way of an explication.

At this key junction of the text, the readers' perspective becomes focused on
James' surreal obsession with accidents. The constant tension of the narrative's
preoccupation with the car-crash thus springs from James' own traumatic experience. Since he provides the narrative voice, his own trauma rarely surfaces in
an overt description of his struggle with structuring the story. This fuels
speculations about the nature of the text, because James is telling a one-sided
story. Readers may be tempted to read the text as a spectacle, rather than an
obsessive account of re-living trauma. Jeanette Baxter proposes that this theatricality is intentional, for the text does not escape this obsessive loop (after all,
James begins and ends with Vaughan's accident). Consider her suggestion,
however, as a description of the text's appeal: "[T]he process of reading is
pushed to its limits and becomes something else – performance. With each (re)
reading, the violent textual encounters are performed once more as the spectator
becomes an interactive and inevitable participant in Ballard's theatre of
cruelty."[19] The dissolution of the text into layers of credibility and normality, on
the other hand, would result in an analysis of the mechanical structure of how
this theatrical performance is enabled. Since the act of reading is necessarily
interactive (cf. Wolfgang Iser's commentary on the appellative structure of
texts[20]), Baxter's point remains valid as one of several possibilities of reading
Crash. The surreal effect of the narrative certainly relies on a theatrical illusion of
credibility, but this illusion may break.

Driving through traffic, James recalls: "[...] I had to force myself to drive
carefully, as I offered my own body to the projecting steering columns and
windshield vizors." (*Crash* 44) The immediate impression is that James is fascinated by the automobile's sexual possibilities, but it also becomes doubtful
why he can 'force' himself to drive safely at all. What makes this remarkable is
that the notion of care is set against the conscious effort to 'offer' his body to the
car's materiality. James seems to be careful for the sake of maintaining his

---

19 BAXTER. *Surrealist Imagination.* 102.
20 Cf. ISER, Wolfgang. *Die Appellstruktur der Texte.* Konstanz: Universitätsverlag Konstanz,
    1970. 21: "Indem [der Kommentar des Autors] die eindeutige Bewertung des Geschehens
    ausspart, schafft er Leerstellen, die eine Reihe von Erfüllungsvariablen zulassen; da er aber
    zugleich Möglichkeiten der Bewertung anbietet, sorgt er dafür, daß diese Leerstellen nicht
    beliebig aufgefüllt werden."

encounter with the car, which creates an absurdly normal fetishistic behaviour – he cannot live his pleasure of deadly injuries without living. The fact that this precedes the cautionary comment by Helen Remington, who asks "[a]fter this sort of thing, how do people manage to look at a car, let alone drive one?" (*Crash* 54), serves to emphasize the abject nature of James' behaviour, but also justifies it. Metaphorically, the surreal landscape of the novel can only be created by these ironical snippets of 'normality', which in turn are the result of a subtext of repression.

This repression need not be a uni-directional metaphor for a dystopian society where the violence of car-crashes is sublimated by road safety 'propaganda'. In fact, the curious balance between James' behaviour throughout and the *careless* behaviour by Catherine[21] at the beginning of the novel underlines the tacit message that nobody is 'normal' per se. The true criticism of the novel might be that 'car culture' ignores its darker sides to create a repression of its own, which James reacts to in his personal denial of death. Jeanette Baxter remarks that "[i]n response to the illusion of transparency, *Crash* posits an alternative, corrupt and stratified world of waste, dirt and excess which threatens to antagonise and rupture the clean and coherent social surface."[22] Since Catherine stands for cleanliness at the beginning of the novel, her participation – always described through James' eyes – in the 'crash culture' clearly mocks the notion of a clean and safe world, free from accidents. The reality of the accident then should be acknowledged, something which James tries to achieve through his twisted sexuality and by participating in the 'rehearsals' of accidents at the Road Research Laboratory.

IV.   Repetition and Rehearsing Death in *Crash*

Repeatedly (*Crash* 57 and 61), James re-drives the route of his accident, once even while he masturbates while driving, inspired by Helen Remington's presence (*Crash* 57). The notion of repetition, of course, is tantamount to obsessively (re-)experiencing the traumatic accident. The loop which is created by the framing of the narrative with the death(s) of Vaughan indicates that the whole story is encapsulated in the circular logic of Vaughan's never-ending accident. Interestingly, the film shows the intention of Cronenberg's adaptation[23] as an

---

21 Later, her behaviour turns into an active participation in James' fantasies, see *Crash* 130 ff.

22 BAXTER. *Surrealist Imagination*. 104.

23 The film enacts a complex doubling of the attempts to kill Catherine by Vaughan (CRONENBERG. *Crash*, 1 h22 m30) and by James (CRONENBERG. *Crash*, 1 h32 m09). The added finale features a chase where James stands in for Vaughan, driving his Lincoln Continental in

open repetition or, more accurately, rehearsal of the 'perfect' crash with a changing cast. Hence, Catherine is a flat character, but her position is important because she never directly experiences a crash (in the book). Her husband tells of many 'near death' scenarios, but one never witnesses them until the final scene. She is a mere prop for Vaughan, someone to practise his car-crashing on. Thus, the lived-out fantasy dehumanizes both characters and makes them actors in a morbid play. The narrative thus questions narrative 'solutions' to fear of death which invariably involve ethical 'stories' which prevent or prohibit living the fantasy.

Death is a final destination which can only be transcended by metaphysical fictions, because its acknowledgement presents unanswerable questions to the human mind. By rehearsing the perfect accident, James either re-lives the trauma of the accident or creates an illusion of control over his own death, something which he most likely came to fear through his accident. The inverted vocabulary of his descriptions is symptomatic for the difficult task of merging conflicting concepts in the attempt to control the uncontrollable. The car be-comes the container for this conflict: "In each sexual act together we [James and Helen Remington] celebrated her husband's death, re-seeding the image of his body [...] within the metal and vinyl compartment of the car." (*Crash* 64) The celebration of death simply makes it easier to push aside any shadow of sur-vivor's guilt and to come to terms with one's own future death. The key scenes for this rehearsal of death are provided through the crashes staged by Vaughan and the crash-tests at the Road Research Laboratory.

If anything, the differences between the book and the film underline the theatricality of rehearsing death. Both include the staging of accidents with an audience, where (in the novel) "Vaughan's present role in the stadium seemed that of a film director" (*Crash* 67). Strangely enough, James is appalled by the realistic result of the show, which highlights the crucial point that the rehearsal of a car-crash should not fulfil the feared conclusion of the crash in death. Put simply, James is afraid of seeing a realistic accident, as much as he seeks to control his own, 'future' deadly accident by endlessly rehearsing, but never concluding it. This is reflected in his description of the morbid show: "The accident re-enactment had been a fiasco – struck by the skidding truck, Sea-grave's [a stunt driver instructed by Vaughan] car had been locked on to the raw fenders like a myopic bullfighter running straight on to the bull's horns." (*Crash* 68) The text does not give a clear impression of what went wrong, but it is sufficiently clear that the rehearsal should not have ended in a real accident with real injuries to the stunt drivers. A further chafing point is the difference between

---

the exact same manner – only the crash is reversed from Vaughan to Catherine hurtling their car over the left hand barrier.

James' and Vaughan's reaction, since "Vaughan alone was unmoved" (*Crash* 68) by the all-too realistic accident. It is almost as if Vaughan represents the consummation of the 'real' accident which ends in death, which James is most afraid of. At this point in the narrative, however, James still clings to his traumatic interpretation of danger and voices his fear clearly: "Vaughan had frightened me. The callous way in which he had exploited Seagrave, playing on the violent fantasies of this punch-drunk stunt-driver, warned me that he would probably go to any lengths to take advantage of the immediate situation around him." (*Crash* 85) The projection of his fears onto Vaughan masks James' anxiety that an actual accident might kill him by chance. The notion of a chance accident is doubly rejected through the rehearsal of accidents and the superficial fear that someone like Vaughan might put oneself in fatal danger.

Interestingly, the film's condensed version of this spectacle adds the notion of safety to the staged crash. The re-enactment of James Dean's fatal crash substitutes for the elaborate Seagrave sub-plot of the novel. Here, Vaughan doubles as the narrative voice and announcer of the show: "You'll notice that we're not wearing helmets or safety padding of any kind. Our cars are not equipped with roll cages or seat belts. We rely solely on the skill of our drivers for our safety, so that we can bring you the ultimate in authenticity."[24] Further on, the scene climaxes in the illusion of a real crash when Vaughan and Seagrave 'play dead' after the collision. The tension is lifted once they finish their acting to take their applause. At the same time, it is unclear what, except for the intention to crash, differentiates the spectacle from the real accident. At this junction in the present paper, it becomes vital to understand that the notions of repression and trauma may derive from Freudian terminology, but are not confined by Freudian definitions thereof.

Bradley Butterfield remarks in his paper on Ballard and Baudrillard that "[t]he death drive in Baudrillard is therefore not a matter of repressed instinct, as in Freud, or even of a universal force within language, as in Lacan, but, rather, the trope for the incipient implosion of all terms valued in opposition, collectively termed the code."[25] Instead of arguing about the short-comings of Freud's (anyway speculative) theory of the death drive, one should notice the meta-critical level on which Butterfield reads the text. *Crash*, as a novel, makes sense to read. It may sound naïve and simplified, but it is unnecessary to complicate the process of reading the novel. On a superficial level, the narrative just traces the traumatic experience of its narrator while being framed by the death of his alter

---

24 CRONENBERG. *Crash*, 26 m13.
25 BUTTERFIELD, Bradley. "Ethical Value and Negative Aesthetics: Reconsidering the Baudrillard-Ballard Connection." In: *PMLA* 114,1 Special Topic: Ethics and Literary Study (1999): 64–77. 68.

ego, the protagonist (of James' narrative!) who experiences the escalation of James' fears. The 'code' of oppositions, such as sex and death, may become blurred, but it is not necessary to argue for its implosion. Nevertheless, Butterfield's argument is valid and highly illuminating, precisely because the narrative displaces fear from the reactions of its characters so radically.

Clearly, when Butterfield reminds his readers that "[t]he accident, a conception borrowed from Octavio Paz, is the site of a postmodern symbolic exchange with death where one signifying system breaks into another and thus ruptures the semiotic wall between self and other, life and death, real and imaginary",[26] the notion of death is disjoined from the fear of death as a motivating factor for James' escalating sexual narrative. The solution to bring together the disrupted code which Butterfield identifies and the novel's remaining readability as a piece of alternative code lies in replacing the term repetition with the concept of the rehearsal. Instead of arguing that "[t]he entire narrative [the reversal of death into sexuality, e.g.] can be conceived of in terms of such a fundamental breakdown in the semiotic process",[27] the disruption of the code should be valued as a coherent narrative of the traumatic experience of near-death by James. Freudian interpretations of the death drive necessarily fall short of the reactions described by Ballard, simply because he is not interested in a realistic portrayal of psychological reactions, but in the perverse suppression of the rather real dangers of car-culture, which are confined to the bombardment with "road-safety propaganda" (Crash 28).

Perhaps it is necessary to re-visit Jean Baudrillard's text, Symbolic Exchange and Death, where the Freudian speculation about the death drive is seen as an opportunity to expand the code of life and death beyond mere oppositions: "The death drive must be understood as acting against the scientific positivity of the psychoanalytic apparatus as developed by Freud. The death drive is not just the limit of psychoanalysis's formulations nor its most radical conclusion, it is its reversal [...]".[28] Rather than exploding the code in a breakdown of the semiotic destabilization, the finality of death acts as a magnetizing force which reverses the polarity of James' inner life. The process of his narrative then traces a traumatic repetition of the high-impact accident, which sets James into perspective with his own death, the only remaining certainty in his emotional world.

The turning point inversion of the role of the victim into that of the spectator is achieved in the climactic scene of the crash-test at the Road Research Laboratory (see Crash 99–104). James recalls this in his narrative as if he was

---

26 BUTTERFIELD. "Baudrillard-Ballard Connection." 70.
27 BUTTERFIELD. "Baudrillard-Ballard Connection." 73.
28 BAUDRILLARD. Symbolic Exchange and Death. 153.

disembodied, underlining the surreal quality of the experience: "As we watched, our own ghostly images stood silently in the background, hands and faces unmoving while this slow-motion collision was re-enacted. The dream-like reversal of roles made us seem less real than the mannequins in the car." (*Crash* 104) The passivity of the audience is, of course, an illusion, since the slow-motion replay of the test-crash is not a real crash in any way. But the description also captures the source of James' fearlessness, because the situation of his own crash is reflected in the passive stance of himself and the audience. Put another way, he cannot actively re-live the role of the unwilling passenger which he experienced during his own crash.

The displacement of fear into sexual energy and of death into a theatrical rehearsal of the accident culminates in Vaughan's fantasies about Elizabeth Taylor's possible death in a car-crash. He ponders that "[w]ith a little forethought she could die in a unique vehicle collision, one that would transform all our dreams and fantasies. The man who dies in that crash with her..." (*Crash* 105; original punctuation). This fantasy is another small part of the fractured reality effect of Ballard's surreal text, since it unites the living actress with the threatening possibility of death which rules the fantasies of James' narrative. It is a touch of class by Ballard to ironically assess this possibility as James rejects Vaughan's accusation that he was "too obsessed with [himself] to realize" the potential of Taylor's death in a car-crash: "Vaughan, the likelihood of her being killed in a car-crash is remote. You'll have to follow her around until doomsday." (*Crash* 120) Following the logic of rehearsing death to control fear, James' refusal of this possible icon marks his refusal of Vaughan's violent fantasies. The flat character of Vaughan acts here as a reflector (or refractor) for James' denial of his own fear. James is caught in the loop of his narrative, so to speak, because he cannot break the code of his fearful trauma.

The ending of the novel clearly reflects this when the police first identifies Vaughan's body with James', only to have James experience the same disembodiment that he felt at the Road Research Laboratory: "When we reached the accident site below the flyover I felt that I was visiting, incognito, the place of my own death. Not far from here, my own accident had taken place in a car identical to the vehicle in which Vaughan had died." (*Crash* 181–82) Unable to accept his own role as a survivor, he repeatedly dies a metaphorical death in a never-ending postponement of his own fear of death. The attempt to control his death drives James' narrative, but it denies a final conclusion, leaving him to end on a note of looming disaster: "Already I knew that I was designing the elements of my own car-crash. Meanwhile, the traffic moves in an unceasing flow along the flyover." (*Crash* 185) James, in a way, has become undead, unable to fear death.

V.   Destinations and Departures

At the heart of Freud's speculation about the death drive lies the fictionalizing act
of interpreting experience. In *Crash*, James narrates the story of his sexual
awakening enveloped in a traumatic loop, represented by Vaughan's double
death. Superficially, the frame of the narrative obsessively repeats the death of
James' alter ego, but by reading the text as being driven by the mechanical shock
to James' perspective, it becomes clear that the constant anticipation and desire
for the ultimate car-crash masks a deep suppression of the fear of death. The
answer to both lies in Ballard's structuring of the narrative as a flashback.
Sexuality is here a counterfeit symbol for our only graspable 'drive' when we face
death: the will to live, quite simply. Modern car culture is symbolical for the
distortion of our sexual desire into a morbid fantasy of dying in the ultimate car-
crash, where the car is the vehicle for transcending life by dehumanizing ourselves. The flashback references voyeurism and the anxiety to lose our lives. This
becomes apparent in James' desire to fertilize his feared grave – the car. Catherine and James live to see Vaughan die, but Vaughan's second death does not
provide closure for James.

   Still further, this curiously open framing device signifies that the internal
logic of the narrative is contained within itself. For Vaughan, the accident is a
failure in that he misses his intended target – his theatrical death in a head-on
collision with Elizabeth Taylor has become a pure fantasy after his real, accidental death. Not only does the deliberate car-crash represent an element of
madness and danger in everyday life, but it also exposes the fear of this as an
imaginary fear which is only barely masked by James' narration. The theatrical
illusion of credibility which the text builds on with the precise naming of locations, medical vocabulary and pseudo-Freudian reactions of the characters (e. g.
Helen Remington's remark, *Crash* 54) is a fractured mask for James' loss of the
sense of safety. The circuitous logic behind Vaughan's demise is that the fear of
death is ever present but also never consummated in life. The absurdity of death
in *Crash* is that the way someone dies matters more than the fact that people die
in numbers through automobile technology.

   The theatrical transformation of death into a rehearsed spectacle utilizes the
open frame of the narrative in order to defer the final destination of death
infinitely. Instead of breaking down the 'code', as Butterfield suggests, *Crash* has
the surreal effect of destabilizing the narrative voice to the point where it only
provides a fractured reality effect, but at the same time weirdly makes sense of
James' behaviour in a perfect inversion of 'the code'. The text, then, could be a
fantasy as a whole: "We had heard nothing of Vaughan since he had taken my car
from the garage. Increasingly I was convinced that Vaughan was a projection of
my own fantasies and obsessions, and that in some way I had let him down."

(*Crash* 181) James might just be the blueprint for Tyler Durden,[29] but at this point, this paper turns into a departures table. The key result of this paper is that the narrative is driven by the transformation of fear, something which often has been ignored in favour of the various tantalizing exits out of the text itself into the vast and surreal landscape of its readings. *Crash* remains a collision of fictional truths whose pieces have not solidified into a concrete image of the novel's "cautionary" message (*Crash* iii).

References

BALLARD, James Graham. *Crash*. London: Harper Perennial, 2008 [1973].

BAUDRILLARD, Jean. *Simulacra and Simulation*. Translated by Sheila Faria Glaser. Michigan: The University of Michigan Press, 1994 [1981].

– *Symbolic Exchange and Death*. Translated by Iain H. Grant. London/New York: Sage, 2007 [1993].

BAXTER, Jeanette. *J.G. Ballard's Surrealist Imagination: Spectacular Authorship*. Farnham: Ashgate, 2009.

BUTTERFIELD, Bradley. "Ethical Value and Negative Aesthetics: Reconsidering the Baudrillard-Ballard Connection." In: *PMLA* 114,1 Special Topic: Ethics and Literary Study (1999): 64–77.

CRONENBERG, David, Dir. *Crash*. Perf. Holly Hunter, James Spader, Elias Koteas and Deborah Kara Unger. Fine Line Features, 1996.

FINCHER, David, Dir. *Fight Club*. Perf. Edward Norton, Brad Pitt, Helena Bonham Carter et al. Twentieth Century Fox Home Entertainment, 1999.

FREUD, Sigmund. "Jenseits des Lustprinzips." *Freud Studienausgabe: Psychologie des Unbewußten*. Edited by Alexander Mitscherlich, Angela Richards and James Strachey. Vol. 3. Frankfurt M.: Fischer, 1975. 213–72.

ISER, Wolfgang. *Die Appellstruktur der Texte*. Konstanz: Universitätsverlag Konstanz, 1970.

KEIM, Heinrich. *New Wave: Die Avantgarde der modernen anglo-amerikanischen Science Fiction?* Meitingen: Corian, 1983.

LAMBERTI, Elena. "*Crash* by J.G. Ballard and D. Cronenberg." In: *Textus* XIII (2000): 173–94.

RoSPA-Our History. The Royal Society for the Prevention of Accidents. <http://www.rospa.com/about/history/default.aspx> (accessed: 29 July, 2011).

---

29 FINCHER, David, Dir. *Fight Club*. Perf. Edward Norton, Brad Pitt, Helena Bonham Carter et al. Twentieth Century Fox Home Entertainment, 1999.

Contributors

Elena Baeva is currently a research assistant at the Department of English, American and Celtic Studies at the University of Bonn.

Uwe Baumann is Full Professor of English and American Literary and Cultural Studies at the Department of English, American and Celtic Studies at the University of Bonn.

Stella Butter teaches English and American Literary and Cultural Studies at the English Department of the University of Mannheim.

Marcel Inhoff is a PhD student at the Department of English, American and Celtic Studies at the University of Bonn.

Marion Gymnich is Full Professor of English and American Literary and Cultural Studies at the Department of English, American and Celtic Studies at the University of Bonn.

Christian Knöppler teaches at the Research Center of Social and Cultural Studies Mainz.

Imke Lichterfeld is currently Studies Coordinator at the Department of English, American and Celtic Studies at the University of Bonn.

Nina Liewald is a PhD student of English and American Literary and Cultural Studies and she is currently an assistant at the Equal Opportunities Office at the University of Bonn.

Barbara Puschmann-Nalenz teaches English Literary and Cultural Studies at the University of Bochum.

Gislind Rohwer-Happe teaches English Literary and Cultural Studies at the English Department of the University of Bonn.

Andrea Rummel teaches English Literature and Cultural Studies at the English Department of the University of Gießen. She is the Department's Study Abroad Coordinator.

Klaus Scheunemann is currently Studies Coordinator at the School of Humanities at the University of Bonn.

Sara Strauß is a PhD student at the University of Paderborn.

Antonio Wojahn is a PhD student at the University of Bonn.